Nationalism
and Progress
in Free Asia

NATIONALISM

and PROGRESS

in FREE ASIA

Edited by PHILIP W. THAYER

with the assistance of
WILLIAM T. PHILLIPS

Introduction by CHESTER BOWLES

THE JOHNS HOPKINS PRESS
Baltimore, 1956

Distributed in Great Britain by Geoffrey Cumberlege,
Oxford University Press, London

Printed in U.S.A. by Reese Press, Baltimore

Library of Congress Catalog Card No. 56–9414

Preface

In the summer of 1952 the School of Advanced International Studies sponsored a conference in Washington on Southeast Asia in the Coming World. Twenty-one papers presented at the conference were published subsequently by The Johns Hopkins Press in a book bearing the same title.

Since that time the areas of South and Southeast Asia have become more and more a focal point of world interest and attention. Born in a world of divided allegiances and growing tensions, beset by internal problems of the utmost difficulty, the newly independent countries of Free Asia have shown rare qualities of courage and determination in their pursuit of the fruits of liberty. Their success or failure is a matter of grave concern to the Western world.

Convinced therefore of the importance of these countries to the future of the world community, the School decided in 1955 to sponsor two conferences on "Nationalism and Progress in Free Asia." The first conference, in August, 1955, was held as before in Washington. The second, in October, was held in Rangoon, where the School, with the co-operation of the University of Rangoon, maintains a study center. It was felt that in this way the knowledge and experience of the leading authorities of both the West and the East could be invoked to the best possible advantage, with resulting value to the published materials. The sessions of the Rangoon conference were opened on behalf of the Prime Minister of Burma by the Honorable U Raschid, Minister of Trade Development.

Although space limitations have compelled some omissions, the present volume contains most of the papers read at the two conferences. It is hoped that they may constitute a much needed and worthwhile contribution to the literature on an area of great significance to the free world.

My grateful thanks are due to the loyal encouragement and support of the faculty and staff of the School, and to the understanding helpfulness of the officers of The Johns Hopkins Press. In particular, I am indebted to William T. Phillips, Professor of International Economics at the School and Co-Director of the Rangoon Study Center, and to Dr. Htin Aung, Rector of the University of Rangoon. Without their devoted labors, the Rangoon conference never could have taken place.

Philip W. Thayer

SCHOOL OF ADVANCED INTERNATIONAL STUDIES
THE JOHNS HOPKINS UNIVERSITY

Washington, D.C., March, 1956

Contents

* Papers marked with an asterisk were presented at the Rangoon conference.

Introduction

CHESTER BOWLES

To a world which has many reasons to despair of man's ability to cope with the crisis of our times this volume of essays should bring a degree of reassurance and even grounds for hope. Within its pages the insights of thirty-seven able minds from East and West are brought to bear on the process of revolution in South and Southeast Asia. These men speak with temperance; but they also speak with candor. Their very differences shed new light on the issues and alternatives which face both East and West.

To say that Asia is in ferment is a commonplace. The primary problem is to isolate the catalytic agents which are producing the ferment, to learn what is a cause and what is a symptom, and to discard outdated premises.

Unhappily, this is precisely what we Americans, in spite of our good intentions, have often failed to do. At the end of World War II our prestige among the colonial peoples of the earth was at its peak. As the Burmese Ambassador reminds us, they looked to us then "as the source of those ideas and moral principles of government which have been the inspiration and hope of Asia for nearly a century." But by our course of action in the ensuing years we have steadily depleted that reservoir until today our prestige has reached its all time low.

This record is tragic. To those who are unacquainted with the insights of this volume, it has also been baffling. This is why such a symposium, held fittingly both in Washington and Rangoon, is of such immense value at this juncture.

In these essays, for instance, we see vividly both the strength and complexity of anticolonialist thought in South and Southeast Asia. To those citizens of the Atlantic nations who proclaim the death of the old Western colonialism, others from the East respond with reminders of the tens of millions in Africa and Asia who still remain under European colonial rule. To those Westerners who argue that these remaining strongholds of traditional colonialism are relatively unimportant in the face of the new menace of Soviet imperialism, there is the response that man fears most intensely that which he has spent a lifetime fighting. In conditioned human minds, a new danger can seldom displace the old enemy as long as the old enemy still shows signs of life.

The recurring stress on anticapitalism will be equally difficult and yet equally important for Americans to understand. The extent to which the Leninist theory of imperialism has been accepted through wide areas of Asia comes into focus only when we consider the economic exploitation which colonial peoples have assumed to be an essential corollary of colonialism. The dynamic system of private ownership characterized by small unit profits, large volume, and vigorous labor leadership—which we have associated with the word "capitalism" in this country—has almost no counterpart in Asia.

The number one objective of all Asian nations with their long tradition of poverty is rapid economic development. In an area which suffers from a lack of indigenous entrepreneurs and capital and where foreign investment faces formidable risks, the government, for better or for worse, must inevitably play the central economic role.

In considering such development problems, it is symptomatic to contrast Mr. Nehru's quoted assertion that "we have suddenly arrived at a stage when we have to run . . . walking is not enough . . . " with Professor Cady's warning that "the need for speedy solutions has been overestimated." Somewhere between the impatience of the East and the caution of the West lies that elusive middle ground of "modest objectives . . . more likely of achievement" which one would long to discover in the course of scholarly analysis.

Yet Mr. Nehru is persuasive when he insists that time is limited and that the battle is on, as our essays almost universally testify. The Ambassador from Ceylon puts it cogently: "The question today in Asia is whether economic development and social progress can be achieved faster by countries following a democratic method or by those following a totalitarian method." The revolution of rising expectations makes demands which will not await the considered answers of men of good will who reason and reflect far beyond the turmoil of the struggle. In its most basic form the choice is indeed between the alternatives advocated by Mao Tse-tung on the one hand and Jawaharlal Nehru on the other.

Yet I would suggest that economic progress measured in statistical terms of steel production, irrigation water, improving health standards and literacy is only one facet in the critical competition. An even more important measure for the long haul may be the sense of participation, of belonging, of community purpose that accompanies the material gains.

Another common theme which runs throughout these essays relates to Asia's fervent desire for peace and her dread of war. Under the circumstances, it is not altogether strange that our often vocal concentration on military alliances, contractual relationships, and nuclear striking power would strike a discordant note in impoverished, insecure nations which desire above all else "the command of their own fortunes."

In the West we are prone to speak conveniently of Southeast Asia as an entity, and it is fortunate that these essays point out the narrowness of this view. The rich diversity within Southeast Asia is a product both of highly variegated native heritages and the even more varying impacts of European colonial occupation.

Common currents such as nationalism and a desire for a greater measure of human dignity, and common problems such as poverty run through the turbulence of the Asian revolution. But the picture varies radically from the Muslim areas recently emerged from Dutch rule to the predominantly Hindu and Buddhist areas recently free of British rule to the Roman Catholics who were once under American rule. Highly diverse religious, cultural, and linguistic traditions give a basis in substance to the patchwork manifestations of nationalism.

A by-product of this diversity is the degree to which the new nations of Southeast Asia are alienated from each other. On this point the essays are insistent. Indeed, the symposium seems to be extraordinarily concerned with intra-regional adjustment. "In many respects," we hear, "they have more to learn from each other than from the West."

It is encouraging to see that Asians are coming to know Asians as never before. While Asians seek to adjust these new relationships, one can expect a period of discovery—the discovery of common ties, side by side, with profound differences. Ultimately, too, they may discover new common purposes beyond the understandable but negative anticolonialism which has heretofore helped to give Asia so much cohesiveness. Eventually the fact that Mao is a Communist may seem to them more important than the fact that he is an Asian.

Asia's friends await the outcome of these next vital years of intra-regional adjustment with as great curiosity and impatience as the Asians themselves. In these new nations a new, promising, creative force is being unleashed upon the world. The obstacles in its development are formidable, and they are outlined in this volume by experts in the field of political and economic analysis. It may be said that Asians themselves must largely see to it that these obstacles are not insuperable. Their obvious determination to see to it as expressed in their papers is significant if only because even economists have come to admit that to some extent at least "development is a state of mind."

Our thirty-seven able scholars and statesmen have given us what amounts to a comprehensive mid-term report. Their judgments are compelling, their dispassionate approach admirable, and their degree of agreement heartening.

What does all this mean to the United States? What lesson can American policy-makers draw from the contents of this volume?

We can begin by taking pride in the leadership of The Johns Hopkins University in organizing such a meeting of minds, and express the hope that the experiment in varying forms will often be repeated. The study of South and Southeast Asia is still a neglected field in our country.

What we need desperately, of course, is many more able minds committed to this field, many more university curricula rapidly amended to give the necessary training. Our people and our policies in this crucial and perhaps decisive part of the world will never be as wise and sound as they should be while our universities lag so far behind in treating Asia's history, economics, politics, cultures, and languages, and our primary and secondary schools ignore Asia almost entirely.

But beyond such an obvious need for further study and training, these essays, it seems to me, contain a message about national behavior and national policy. Throughout them runs an injunction which every American who would understand modern Asia or Africa should take to heart: the need to look closely to our own history and traditions, to recapture our own liberal heritage.

It is ironical that our nation, which was the first in modern times to win its freedom from a colonial power, is now suspect in the eyes of so many former colonial peoples of Asia. It is all the more ironical since we are told time and again that our national example has served as Asia's inspiration and that the words of great American presidents are remembered and revered by new nationalist leaders from Manila to Marrakesh. Asians and Africans see the irony, too. Their version of the story in the years since World War II is often bluntly stated: we have betrayed our heritage.

Perhaps they have expected too much of us, for the heirs of Jefferson, Lincoln, and Wilson have had a weighty tradition to uphold in a period of great and conflicting pressures. Yet few can deny that in recent years our primary concern with the military aspects of international Communist aggression has caused us dangerously to compromise certain of our traditions not only abroad but also at home. Our debut as a great power on the world stage has included some maneuvers of almost grotesque awkwardness and insensitivity.

An Indonesian who writes in this volume points out, "The job of building our own house for the first time generates a sense of exhilaration perhaps long forgotten by older nations which have become settled in their ways." This is a polite way of saying that we Americans have lost our own sense of youthful exhilaration and entered as a nation upon a premature and paunchy middle age.

We can effectively discredit this charge only if we are prepared to put aside negativism, reaffirm our national creativeness, and construct a framework of understanding and common purpose grounded in our memory of a great common experience. And if we wish to influence the minds of our world neighbors, we must buttress this framework with a stricter adherence to our traditional dedication to human rights— economic, political, and social.

We may logically start by shedding our naïve and often angry assumption that "he that is not with us is against us." In South and Southeast Asia "he that is not with us" is more often than not just plain apprehensive of everybody. For the young nations of Asia, the world appears in many shades of grey. We Americans could profit from a similar perspective.

Within such a framework of sympathy and explicit anticolonialism, the conditions of Asia will call for a pragmatic and flexible policy adapted to the changing subtleties of our relationships. We must seek out and cultivate the many areas of mutual self-interest. While main-

taining our military strength, we must place less vocal emphasis on
the strictly military aspects of power.

Our economic assistance should be made available on a substantially
larger scale, on a long term basis, without strings, and with a clear
understanding of what it can and cannot accomplish. It cannot, for
instance, buy the loyalty of allies or the friendship or even the applause
of those to whom it goes. Its aim for the long haul is even more
important: to establish stable and independent Asian nations—proud,
confident, free to command their own destinies, dominated by no foreign
power.

It would also be worth our while to re-examine our government information programs in the harsh light of the world conflict. By this
time everyone in Asia must know that we Americans dislike, disapprove,
and denounce Communism. They must also know that we possess an
awesome array of automobiles, washing machines, and telephones.
What they are curious to know is what we stand for, where we are
headed, how we intend to use our vast power and productivity, and on
what basis we are prepared to work shoulder to shoulder with them
to create a world of individual opportunity, abundance, dignity, and
peace.

I am profoundly convinced that a firm basis exists for understanding
and co-operation between America and Asia. I welcome this volume
as a reassuring proof that many leading thinkers of East and West
are not only grappling with the formidable problems which are involved but are even now in agreement on many of the essentials.

Nationalism
and Progress
in Free Asia

The United States looks
at South and Southeast Asia

WALTER S. ROBERTSON

Assistant Secretary of State for Far Eastern Affairs

The timely subject of this book, "Nationalism and Progress in Asia," is one of great interest to the Department of State. It is of particular interest to me personally inasmuch as many of the problems discussed here fall within my area of responsibility within the State Department.

It is a source of considerable satisfaction to us who work in the governmental sphere of relations between America and Asia to know that there is a group of men and women, distinguished in the scholarly world, who are actively engaged in a private effort to increase understanding between Asians and Americans and to strengthen relations between them.

When the United States surveys this immense area it sees, needless to say, a multitude of problems, aspirations and movements. Some of the most significant of these will be considered in this book: the aftermaths of colonialism; the progress of nationalism; the development of Communism.

What I say here now should be considered in relation to one overriding question, the answer to which it is too soon to determine. That question is: Is the present season of sweetness and light, through which we are passing, a phase only, or have the Soviets and their Communist allies suffered some change of heart as well as of tactic?

There is an old Japanese proverb that, perhaps, has some relevance here. It goes something like this: "The sign in the garden says 'Do not pick the apple blossoms,' but the wind cannot read, and the wind blows the blossoms away."

During the ten years since World War II, the Communist leaders have been like the wind that cannot read the sign and, so, demolishes the apple blossoms. They have ignored the rules and treaties that law-abiding people and nations obey, and they have destroyed the freedom of many nations in the process.

Now the wind suddenly *can* read. What does it mean? Has the wind really lessened its fury and changed its prevailing direction?

The full answer is not yet.

Although in American eyes no problem stands out more prominently in Asia, especially in Southeast Asia, than the threat of Communist aggression and subversion, we realize that to most of the leaders and peoples of this vast region the threat of Communism is of no more than secondary concern and that their interests and emotions are centered on such questions as colonialism, nationalism, and neutralism.

Why is this so? To find the answer we must look to the history of these countries, most of which have so recently emerged from foreign control. The men who now lead the newly independent nations of Asia are in almost all cases the men who led the struggle for independence. Their lives, and those of their countrymen, have been dedicated to gaining freedom from the colonial power. They have been conditioned to regard the colonial power as the one obstacle to their country's liberty and progress, and they have had little time or disposition to worry about dangers from other sources, or threats not directly pertinent to the old, familiar struggle for liberation from colonialism. It is only natural that they should find it hard to realize that the old foe—Western colonialism—is dead, and that they must now turn to face a greater and totally destructive enemy.

One result of the preoccupation of these Asians with their own struggles for independence has been that each country has come to know a great deal about its former occupier and very little about its neighbors. All Asians are opposed in principle to colonialism anywhere, but few have taken any real interest in the development of other Asian nations, and fewer understand the needs and aspirations of their neighbors, with whom they should be working most closely. As a result, there is little feeling of unity, little understanding of the potential collective strength of free Asia, and each country tends to feel isolated and alone.

Many Asians, then, are still preoccupied with colonialism, a term which they use to mean the occupation and control of their countries by foreigners from Europe. What has happened to colonialism? The truth is that Western colonialism entered a period of decline many years ago, a decline which resulted both from the growing resistance of the Asians and from changes in attitude in the colonial powers themselves. The concept that it is right for one people to rule and exploit another came under attack in the West in the last century and lost ground steadily thereafter. By the nineteen-thirties the question in most countries which had colonies was not so much *should* the colonies be given independence, but *when* and *how* should independence be given. World War II, which for the West was a clear-cut struggle for the defense of human freedom, doomed colonialism as a Western concept.

I would like to emphasize at this point that the numerous countries which have gained their freedom in recent years have gained it because it was the will of the people of those countries, and because of changes in the attitudes of the former colonial powers. I know of no instance in which Communism, native or foreign, has played an effective role in the achievement of independence. On the contrary, Communism has destroyed the true independence of several countries in Asia, and threatens all the others with every technique in its arsenal from subversion to armed revolt to external aggression.

The countries of free Asia and the men who lead them are faced with formidable problems. All suffer from various degrees of poverty, from shortage of educational facilities, and from poor public health. Perhaps most important, the great majority suffer from a lack of experience in solving problems of organization. These problems the new colonialism seeks to exploit. The land itself is not poor in most of free Asia, and most of the newly established nations have natural resources which could, if properly used, bring a really new world to several hundred million people. Most of the leaders of Asia are thoroughly aware of the needs of their people and see their task as one of preserving their cherished national freedom while bringing their idle resources into play for the benefit of their countrymen. This is a task of such importance and of such magnitude that the people of Asia want desperately to believe that they will be able to devote all their energies to it, and they are reluctant to face the fact that they and their work are threatened by an implacable enemy dedicated to their destruction by stealth or by force.

How do the Communists fit into this picture? The ultimate goal of world Communism in Asia is easy to detect, as it is identical with the ultimate goal of world Communism anywhere. The Communists seek to create, by subversion or by force, a monolithic structure designed for the benefit of the Communists themselves, which, while preserving the outward appearance of independence for its victim states, suppresses the very human freedoms which that independence was intended to foster and protect. This simple truth is painfully apparent to the people of eastern Europe, of mainland China, of North Korea, and of Ho Chi Minh's Viet-Nam, millions of whom have sought freedom by flight to free territories. To those who are now in bondage, knowledge of the truth about Communism has come tragically late.

In free Asia this knowledge is gained more slowly, partly because the true picture of Communism is not immediate and present, partly because cynical Communist promises about the good things available under Communism appeal to people who are discouraged by the size and complexity of their problems, and partly because old Asian mistrust of the West applies to Western methods of progress by hard work and by trial and error. There is reason to hope that most of the leaders of Asia have learned much in recent years and that Communism has lost its chance for victory by subversion. No free Asia nation today is under major Communist influence, as the Bandung Conference clearly showed.

Free Asia, then, is a vast area of new nations, plagued by shortage of capital and lack of technical skills, striving to solve these problems with inadequate means, still distrustful of the nations which represent old and well understood colonialism, and now, it seems, increasingly distrustful of the Communists. Our relationship with these countries is unique because, in a sense, we are the first modern nation to gain independence by a revolt against a colonial power, a fact recognized by the President of Indonesia when, in his opening address at the Bandung Conference, he cited Longfellow's poem about Paul Revere's ride. We have resisted colonialism since our own Revolution wherever we have been able to do so, from our establishment of the Monroe Doctrine to our heartfelt sponsorship of the Four Freedoms during World War II.

As a result of this history, by 1945 we enjoyed in Asia a position of prestige and respect never approached by any other nation. We have lost ground since 1945, partly because our efforts to help the war-stricken countries of Europe toward recovery were misinterpreted by some Asians as an indication that we supported European colonialism, partly because we failed to prevent the loss to Communism of mainland China, but primarily because the Communists and their allies have waged against us a campaign of hatred based upon total distortion of our motives by attributing to us their own desire to choke out Asian freedom for their own benefit.

The truth is that our hopes for Asia are no different now from what they were after the Boxer Rebellion, when we alone refused territorial or other special privileges from prostrate China, and instead devoted the indemnity owed to us to the education of young Chinese so that they might better serve their own country. What we want in Asia is what we want everywhere—a world made up of independent, responsible, democratic countries whose governmments are devoted to the peaceful development of their own territory and to the welfare and personal freedom of their own people. We want this because it is the only kind of world in which we can lead the kind of life we want. In this picture there is no room for imperialism or colonialism, and we must continue to resist them.

Old colonialism is dead or dying everywhere. Communist colonialism is very much alive and, unless contained, will continue to expand. A simple glance at recent history will prove the point. How many countries have gained their freedom from the West since 1918? India, Pakistan, Burma, Ceylon, Indonesia, the Philippines, Viet-Nam, Laos, and Cambodia, not to mention numerous states in the Near East and Africa.

How many countries have lost their freedom, both national and personal, to Communism in that same time? Estonia, Latvia, Lithuania, Poland, Czechoslovakia, Hungary, Rumania, Albania, East Germany, mainland China including Tibet and Mongolia, North Korea, and North Viet-Nam.

The United States has welcomed the new nations of Asia into the world community and has undertaken various aid programs to assist them in their struggle for well-being. In doing this we have only continued on a governmental scale the work of assistance which

American private citizens have long been carrying on. We have done this, and will continue to do it, because of our conviction that these countries need assistance in order to achieve a level of material welfare and social progress which will permit them to maintain the human freedom and dignity we regard as essential to world security. We are not doing these things because the Communists have frightened us into it. Our attitude toward progress in Asia is positive, not negative.

There is only one reason why we find it necessary to devote so much of our wealth and effort to the defense of these countries. Our aid programs, our bilateral defense treaties, our support of the Manila Pact are not designed, as the Communists allege, to impose our power on Asia, but rather they are intended to help these nations preserve their independence and develop self-sustaining economies. The best efforts of the peoples of Asia toward self-development, massive American economic assistance, would not serve to keep armed Communism across the border if there were no force available to resist. The Communists are interested in the conquest of Asia, not in the welfare of its people.

In summary, free Asia today has completed or is completing its long struggle against the old colonialism. It is now in the early stages of another struggle of equally great importance and greater complexity against age-old poverty, technical underdevelopment and disease, in which it will require and is receiving the moral and material assistance of the Western world and of the United States. This struggle is rendered infinitely more difficult by the aggressive presence of world Communism, which by turns assails Asia with propaganda about nonexistent shortcuts to true freedom and with threats of armed aggression. While recently, as we have seen, the gale-force winds of Communist aggression have become softer and the Communists have professed their wish to live peacefully with their neighbors, it is too soon to tell whether this is a change of heart or a propaganda tactic. In any case, we must continue to help the Asian peoples in their quest for dignity and well-being. We must continue to encourage and assist them in the development of their capacity to defend their independence.

commentary

ROBERT BLUM

President, The Asia Foundation

Secretary Robertson enjoys the immense advantage of speaking from his eminent position in the conduct of our foreign policy. This advantage, however, is at the same time a drawback. Although I cannot emulate his voice of authority, I can perhaps speak with somewhat greater freedom and throw additional light on some of the problems to which he has given an interpretation or an emphasis that may not be shared by everyone.

Both of us have been asked to speak on the same subject: "The United States Looks at South and Southeast Asia." But, whereas he looks at Southeast Asia from a position close to the dizzy heights of what today can only be called the Summit, my observation post is less elevated. For that very reason, however, I do not have to be quite so careful about my footing, and when I look at free Asia from my lower elevation I may be able to see some things that he cannot see.

I am sure that Secretary Robertson would agree with me that it is very deceptive and confusing if we talk about South and Southeast Asia as if there were a large, monolithic undifferentiated region comprising countries all of which have the same outlook and policies. This is certainly not the case and needs to be quite clearly understood by anyone looking at the problems of South and Southeast Asia from an American point of view. The terms "Asia" and "Asian" are simple to use but often misleading, as they conceal as much as they explain. In fact, we have before us a very vast and highly diversified area comprising a large number of countries, each having its own history and culture, and in many cases with different internal problems and systems of government. As a result of these differences and the variety of military, political, and economic problems they face, the countries of Asia often react differently from each other in the present world situation. In their relations with each other, there are varying degrees of understanding, suspicions, and even quarrels, and they are not

7

unanimous in their policies toward the rest of the world. To Americans whose focus is not yet very sharp in looking at Southeast Asia I think that this is a very important consideration to retain. Those who have been friendly to the Asian point of view and those who have been unsympathetic have, in my opinion, been equally guilty in overlooking this point.

There are, however, numerous common problems. Some of those were discussed at the conference of Afro-Asian nations held recently in Bandung, which was a reflection of some degree of unity, although differences were also revealed there. The countries of Asia are concerned primarily with problems of nationalism and national independence, with problems of economic and social development from poor beginnings, and with the great task of establishing political unity. A number of them, newly released from the bonds of colonialism, are particularly concerned lest their independence once again be compromised. Secretary Robertson has expressed his concern lest preoccupation with the issue of colonialism blind the nations of Asia to more formidable issues of greater practical importance today. Perhaps he was somewhat reassured when the Bandung Conference, for example, revealed the different interpretations of the colonial issue by the nations of Asia themselves and showed that some of them fear the new colonialism as much as they do the old.

These countries differ not only among themselves but even more sharply from the United States. In our frequent impatience and our hopeful but naïve expectation that everyone will see things as we do, we often overlook the very great differences in conditions and viewpoint that separate the nations of Asia from ourselves. We forget that they, being located in another part of the world and having other traditions, do not respond to the same arguments that we do. They are very young in the independence that they have acquired. Except for Thailand, the oldest independent country among them is not yet ten years old. They are, moreover, economically weak, and in many cases politically unstable. They do not have the social development that a modern community needs. Unlike ourselves, they are geographically vulnerable to pressures from the Soviet Union and Communist China. All of these conditions mean that they are going to take a very careful look at any insistence that they should take sides in the quarrels and arguments of the present troubled world. Only those nations that have special ties with us or that want our assistance for other reasons will behave differently.

Secretary Robertson has rightly spoken of the opposition of the United States to colonialism, but I think we all know that this opposition has been sometimes tempered by other considerations which he has passed over rather lightly. The result, as in the case of Indochina, has not been a happy one. We cannot remind ourselves too often that a number of these nations were born out of the fight against colonialism, and the last thing they want to see is the persistence or return of any form of colonialism. They are particularly sensitive regarding colonialism that seems to come from the West, from their former white masters, or from ourselves, who are the allies of those former masters. They were born out of the struggle against colonialism, and I think it is somewhat unreasonable for Secretary Robertson to expect the scars of that experience to heal quickly and for them to follow us in all respects in substituting the image of one threat for another.

It is not surprising that many Asians are fond of referring to America's tradition of independence and anticolonialism and to our early history right after our successful revolution against the British. In fact, sometimes they speak rather presumptuously as if they, and not we, were the inheritors and standard-bearers of that tradition. A statistical study might show that there has been a great reversal in the past generation and that today the Asians quote more often than we do from George Washington's Farewell Address. Some of the phrases of that address seem very applicable to the situation faced by the countries in Asia. "With me," said our first President on leaving office in 1797, "a predominant motive has been to endeavor to gain time to our country to settle and mature its yet recent institutions and to progress without interruption to that degree of strengh and consistency which is necessary to give it, humanly speaking, the command of its own fortunes."

Yes, that is what many of the nations of Asia want—command of their own fortunes. If possible, they want to exercise that command independently. If that is not possible, they will request and accept outside support—even from the Communists—if they think they can do it without compromising their independence or if they fear that the pressure from us is too great. One of the reasons, in my opinion, why Communist China seems to have so much fascination for the countries of Asia and why, in some respects, they look to Communist China as an example for themselves is that Communist China seems to them to have this "command of its own fortunes." They see in China an immense Asian country, a yellow race, a nation torn until recently by civil disorder, whose destinies were until now at the mercy of the private plans and agreements among foreign powers which had developed for a hundred years a relentless pattern of interference in the affairs of China. Today, with Communist China having apparently established order and unity at home and talking importantly on the world scene, it is not surprising that the other countries should feel that here is an example deserving their attention. I should add, however, that not one country of Asia seems prepared to emulate voluntarily the totalitarian Communism of China.

We must not expect, therefore, that the nations of Southeast Asia will look only to us for inspiration, leadership or guidance. They want to consider how best they can achieve their domestic objectives and at the same time maintain their security from foreign threats and interventions. Surprising and shocking as it may seem to some Americans, at least some of these nations feel that they have reason to question our motives, and they are not prepared simply to follow our leadership. One of their principal concerns is lest we subordinate their interests to our conceptions of how to fight Communism. In spite of assurances such as Secretary Robertson has given, they see a danger of being made tools of what they regard as a new form of American imperialism which they do not want any more than they want to yield to Communistic imperialism. American military aid programs in Southeast Asia, which we have developed as a means of strengthening the security of the area, have not been interpreted that way by all of the nations there. Also, unfortunately, there have been times when our social and technical aid programs seem to have been inspired by military considerations.

As for communist theory, they being poor nations without well-established political and social theories of their own, have much less reason than we have to reject automatically communist theory as evil and inapplicable. I did not think Secretary Robertson gave this difference enough weight.

Thus, the Asian nations question sometimes whether we are genuinely interested in their welfare or, instead, whether we want to use them for our own purposes; and those are purposes with which they do not always agree. I am not now saying that they are right, but merely pointing out that this is one of the things I see when I look at Southeast Asia. The attitude of most of the countries of Southeast Asia toward our policy in Indochina until a year ago and the attitude of some of them toward the Southeast Asia Treaty Organization is evidence of the relevance of what I am saying.

Each of these nations is subject to many different kinds of outside pressures and feels in its own way that it has to go about balancing those pressures in a manner best suited to its own national purposes. The pressures come, of course, from the Communists. They come from us. But there are also pressures from among the countries of Asia themselves. And then there are the pressures and policies of the British. There are the policies and actions of the French, for example in Indochina. Any American claim for influence or leadership, therefore, has to take its place alongside all of these other claims to be weighed and assessed by each country as part of its appraisal of how to achieve its own national objectives.

I want to emphasize that not everything I am saying can be applied to all of the countries of Asia in an equal way. There are, for example, the so-called neutralist or uncommitted countries, usually defined as including India, Indonesia, and Burma. Now Cambodia seems to be following their example, and there are active or potential neutralist forces in most of the other countries as well. The uncommitted countries exemplify most clearly what I said above when I described the anticolonialist attitude of the countries of Asia, their sensitivity to foreign interference and their desire not to be involved in what they consider to be other people's quarrels. They and their sympathizers are the strongest partisans of the policy of coexistence with the Communist world, and they are the ones who argue most fervently for a friendly attitude toward Communist China and for a policy that avoids the use of provocation or provocative words. Sometimes they seem to point an accusing and admonitory finger at us more than at Communist China, but perhaps this is a tribute to our free society which is more capable of acting on friendly advice and from which more is expected.

In two of the uncommitted countries, India and Burma, strong action is taken against Communist subversion internally, although they do not publicly consider Communism to be an international threat. Thus these nations make a sharp distinction between their fight against domestic communism or subversion and their desire to establish friendly relations with foreign Communist countries. For this reason, there is considerable opposition to following the American lead in anything that would apparently push them into a position of more aggressive opposition to international Communism.

The neutralist or uncommitted elements emphasize that their nations have many domestic problems that need to be settled—problems of social reform, economic progress, political unity. They argue that the strongest defense against Communism, subversion, and any form of totalitarian domination is the creation of strong, unified, and independent nations on a solid foundation of economic welfare and social justice. Some of these elements chide the United States for its fear of communist ideology and they are inclined to exaggerate the stresses and strains that accompany our democratic society. They give only grudging credit, if any, to the enormous contribution that American strength and generosity have made to the protection of free institutions throughout the world.

Strategically, also, the outlook of these countries is not the same as that of the United States, which is located many thousands of miles across the Pacific Ocean and which enjoys tremendous military strength. In a material sense these nations feel that they are weak and vulnerable. In large part, therefore, I think their attitude has its origin less in ideological or moral considerations than in a fear for their own security and a practical recognition that they must nurture their young institutions and avoid major foreign complications with powers stronger than themselves. Perhaps they understand the nature of international Communism better than they are prepared to admit. But even if that is the case there is also something deeper than that. They look upon all of the developments going on in Asia today, whether in Communist China or outside, as being part of the rebirth of modern Asia. They argue that China's regime and internal system of government and society are China's own business provided they see no evidence of China's intention to interfere with them or provided they can ignore such evidence with impunity.

There is another group of countries which have been consistently friendly to the United States in recent years but which are difficult to categorize in any simple way. I am thinking of Thailand, the

Philippines, and Pakistan, which are the three Asian members of the Southeast Asia Treaty Organization. The geopoliticians, who are somewhat out of fashion nowadays, would have a difficult time giving neat explanations why these nations have oriented their foreign policies one way while others see things differently. Each one of the countries I have just mentioned has, for different reasons, chosen to align its own policies with those of the West. Nonetheless, these countries have in common with the other countries in the region the same kinds of domestic problems that I have already referred to.

In my opinion, moreover, the national strength and defensive capabilities of all of the nations in this area—whether allied with us or not—depend much more on their national leadership, moral fiber, and inherent qualities of unity than they do on any foreign aid, whether military or economic. I hope therefore that Secretary Robertson who writes of American aid to help build internal strength in these countries agrees with me that such aid must strengthen and not weaken their determination to maintain their freedom and independence in ways of their own choosing.

I was glad to see Secretary Robertson remind us that the nations of Southeast Asia do not know each other well. The importance of this fact is often overlooked. In spite of the great historical waves, both cultural and military, that have swept over the area, the more recent colonial period imposed a condition of isolation on each of the countries. Their foreign contacts were largely limited to the colonial power thousands of miles away in Europe or America. Thus, the educational and legal systems, the government structure and some of the social and economic patterns have been introduced, if not imposed, by distant alien cultures. Now, the problems of adaptation and readjustment under conditions of independence are tremendous. The understandable tendency for these nations to reject lessons and influences imported from abroad is counterbalanced by their obvious and recognized need to accept outside help. It is important under these conditions that they should avoid any sense of isolation or frustration, for this would only play into the hands of demagogues and weaken the ability of these countries to resist outside pressures. A greater knowledge of each other and a fruitful exchange of ideas among them can help considerably to reinforce the ability of each to deal with its own problems. In many respects they have more to learn from each other than from the West.

All of these considerations have a bearing on what the United States sees in looking at South and Southeast Asia. In addition, when we look at Asia, the image we see is shaped by our relations, commitments, and friendships in other parts of the world. The French, for example, have had a different view than we of how to deal with the situation in Indochina; and in our attempt to meet the French views, and to maintain the friendship of France we have contributed toward alienating some of those whose friendship we sought in Asia. We have had to think of the British as well, and when we look at the problems that face us in Asia we consider at the same time the ways in which those problems can be approached in a manner consistent with the views of our British allies. Some critics of the department to which Secretary Robertson belongs have said, in fact, that United States policy in Asia has been so overshadowed by European considerations that our image of Asia has been completely blurred.

The countries of Asia are primarily concerned with their own problems, their outlook on the outside world, and their unwillingness to be subordinated to outside interests. They do not look upon the United States as their savior from Communism, or if they do they are not prepared to admit it. Military considerations aside, this opinion is largely correct. These countries are not going to be saved from Communism, and they are not going to develop their own economic and social and political strength unless they do it themselves in their own way. They will not do it under dictation from us or from the Communists, willingly at least. Outside assistance can be helpful and even important, but alone it cannot do the job that needs to be done. If badly handled, such aid can be a hindrance rather than a help. I hope that Secretary Robertson and his colleagues bear this in mind as they dedicate their efforts to the task he described of helping to build internal strength as the best guarantee against Communism.

In presenting these considerations to you, I have avoided devoting my comments to a cataloguing of the reasons why Southeast Asia is important to the United States. Whether measured in terms of population, economic resources, strategic location or the Communist danger, the area is, of course, enormously important. But these measurements tell only part of the story. They establish the case for American interest in Southeast Asia, but there is a vital missing ingredient unless we ask ourselves what the countries themselves think of all this. Therefore, rather than describe Southeast Asia as an object for the United States to look at and plan for, I have preferred to emphasize what lies behind the appearances. We must surely realize that our military bases and arms programs will be of little use if genuine understanding is lacking or if political stability is absent. American economic assistance will fall on barren soil unless there is local leadership, will, and sacrifice. American exhortations will fall on deaf ears unless what America says is acceptable to Asians and applicable to their problems. Our alliances and friendships and plans will be meaningless unless the countries of Asia themselves have unity, with faith in their freedom.

If one accepts this analysis of the Asian situation today, there are in turn certain consequences as far as American policy is concerned and I hope that Secretary Robertson will not disagree with me. It seems to me clear that we cannot presume to assert a kind of masterful leadership over that part of the world. What is needed is a formula of partnership, consultation and understanding. Such a policy needs to be protected by the shield of our strength as long as the threats to the peace and freedom of the area are as dangerous as they are today. In such a complicated situation, however, there is little room, in my opinion, for dazzling and spectacular results. This is not a setting in which we can simply play the tune to which others will dance. In fact, I believe that in international politics a Pied Piper holding spellbound his followers swarming behind him would be very dangerous indeed. What we need instead, is to combine our strength with a policy of conciliation and match confidence in our purpose with respect for the view of others.

South and Southeast Asia look at the United States

R. S. S. GUNEWARDENE

Ambassador from Ceylon to the United States

The invitation I received to present the viewpoint of South and Southeast Asia with reference to the United States is a compliment to Ceylon, the smallest independent country in the Commonwealth of Nations. In this respect Ceylon is in a peculiar position to be the interpreter of the East to the West and the West to the East by reason of her 2,500-year-old civilization, her ancient culture, and the impact of three Western civilizations during the last four centuries, namely, the Portuguese, Dutch and English. Added to this, Buddhism, the religion of the majority of the people of Ceylon, has made the Ceylonese a tolerant and understanding people who have never suffered from xenophobia.

Ceylon is also qualified to view Asian relations vis-à-vis the United States in a dispassionate light because of her nonalignment with any power blocs in the world. This policy has made it possible for her to avoid the extremes of both subservience and hostility in her relations with the great powers. This background will be useful to illustrate the dispassionate spirit with which we in Ceylon approach international affairs.

At the very outset I would like to emphasize the fact that there is in the Asian region which I am now surveying a tremendous amount of good will for America. Some of you, I know, will be pleasantly surprised to hear this. Too often, unfortunately, the impression has been conveyed to this country that Americans have encountered, more often than not, hostility and resentment from Asians. I do not deny that there have been some isolated instances. Like you, we in Asia also have our irresponsible politicians and political groups which are only too ready to lay the blame on someone—preferably a foreigner— for their domestic difficulties. As I have said, however, such criticism, if it is of a destructive and malicious kind, has occurred only in isolated instances. The general feeling has been one of friendship and admiration for this great country.

You will be glad to know that Americans have, not only in the present generation but also for several generations past, made a signal contribution to the life, thought, and action of many Asian countries, particularly to those countries which fall within my present survey. In fact, when one assesses the results of their labors, one is amazed by the fact that those pioneers who worked quietly and selflessly without expectation of material gain, achieved such far-reaching results.

Take for instance the labors of the American missionaries and educationalists in Ceylon. Our association with the United States of America began as early as 1816, the very next year after the British gained complete mastery over the island of Ceylon. In 1816 an American mission offered its services in the sphere of education and social services. American missionaries established themselves in the north of the island, lived the life of the people, shared their misery, and did magnificent work in educating them and ministering to the suffering. As a result of the example set by them and the benefactions sent by the men and women of this country, before very long the north of the island became the most literate part of the country, and people from the north made a vital contribution to the administration of Ceylon.

Within a few decades a great American, Colonel H. S. Olcott, arrived in Ceylon, attracted by the teachings of the Buddha. He established the Buddhist Theosophical Society. He laid the foundation for a great Buddhist movement which gave an impetus to the national movement to begin a few years later. The great national leaders consisted mostly of men who came under the influence of the movement started by Colonel Olcott.

Just before World War I another great American known as "Pussyfoot" Johnson rallied the country for a mass temperance movement. Whatever the results of the temperance movement may have been, for the first time the people of Ceylon knew the meaning of massed strength. The leaders of the temperance movement emerged as national leaders. A strong democratic movement for political reform followed which culminated in the grant of independence in 1948.

The national leaders in my country drew inspiration for their struggle for independence from the struggle that your leaders at one time successfully waged. The principles of freedom embodied in your Bill of Rights also served as an incentive to leaders of other national movements in other Asian countries who were then under colonial bondage. The brilliant writings of your political philosophers and the ideals embodied in your magnificent Constitution were a clarion call for the liberty of oppressed people everywhere. "Life, liberty and the pursuit of happiness" is as much a principle of our country as it is of yours. Our leaders too echoed the words of Lincoln for "a Government of the people, by the people and for the people." We also drew inspiration from President Woodrow Wilson's theory of self-determination. No oppressed colonial country could have had a better friend than the United States of America. The principles of liberty on which your charter was based influenced us all in our agitation for freedom from foreign rule. As one who has been connected with the independence movement in my country from its inception until the full attainment of national freedom, I desire to pay my humble respects to the architects of your Constitution.

India's national movement also derived great strength from the American men and women who worked at the headquarters of the Theosophical Society in Adyar. Colonel Olcott rallied around him here a large circle of people from this great continent who provided funds and gave personal service in India. The Theosophical movement in India made the Indians proud of their culture and their civilization. They made a determined effort to revive the arts and music, the paintings, and their indigenous culture. Mrs. Annie Besant, then known as the world's greatest speaker, headed the Theosophical movement some time after Colonel Olcott, and her band of workers, were in the forefront of the political agitation in India. In fact she was for a period head of the Indian National Congress.

The United States took more than a sympathetic interest in the aspirations of India. The India Freedom League, which was established

in New York, received encouragement, and assistance from your people
and was welcomed by Indian philosophers and thinkers.

India thus derived to a substantial degree her inspiration from the
teachings and the actions of your great leaders. The rapid attainment of independence by India was also, to some extent, due to the
moral pressure your country brought to bear upon Great Britain.
Pakistan was then a part of India and so was Burma at one time.
The impact of the Indian national movement naturally had its effect
on what are now countries independent of India—Burma and Pakistan.

In Indonesia, too, the American people and the government brought
moral pressure to bear on the Dutch to free Indonesia. Thus it will
be seen that the whole region of South and Southeast Asia has been
inspired by the idealism of America and by the message of liberty
given by this great country, to achieve freedom from colonial rule.

I have dwelt at length on this aspect of Asia's relations with the
United States because I think it requires emphasis today. There has
been a tendency in this country to feel that Asians look upon America
with suspicion and even fear. What I have said above will help to
correct the wrong impression. Every thinking Asian is fully cognizant
of the fine contribution which the United States has made for the
betterment of the way of life in Asia.

It would be true to say that we in Asia and you in the United States
have, in spite of our differences in habits, customs and, often, thought
and action, a very large area of common ground. We all have reason
to be happy and grateful that there should be such a wide range of
agreement on mutual objectives and ideals.

First of all we are all agreed on the need for world peace. Your
great leader, President Eisenhower, is known the world over as a
"man of peace." No one in Asia doubts his sincerity and his eagerness to prevent a third world war, which can only result in the destruction of our civilization. You have leaders in both political parties
whose vision and foresight are equal to their great responsibilities.
Of course, in any free country there are bound to be all shades of
opinion, and we in Asia do not get unduly alarmed when people in this
country who should know better sometimes indulge in indiscreet loud
thinking which, though good political propaganda for a limited section
of opinion here, can create some degree of misunderstanding abroad.
We have learned to recognize the degree of attention which should be

paid to such hasty statements. In an earlier phase of our relations it is true that they did create some misunderstanding and even some irritation, but I think I can safely say that, happily for America and for Asia, there is now better understanding and a better sense of proportion on either side.

I need hardly stress the point that the Asian countries too, like America, are dedicated to peace. The countries that lie in the South and Southeast Asian region are those which have just emerged from colonialism. They have no interest in war. Some of them suffered so severely from the horrors of World War II that even now, in spite of postwar economic progress, the effects of such damage have not been entirely wiped out. As you know, practically all the countries in this region have a standard of living which is shamefully low. Millions of people are on the verge of starvation. Poverty, want, ignorance, and misery are their lot. It is, as you will agree, a most unfortunate state of affairs.

The peoples of these countries are today more than ever conscious of their rights and their requirements for a decent standard of living. They want to have, and quite naturally so, some of the good things of life which people in your country are so fortunate to enjoy today. The major task of each of the governments of this region, therefore, is to launch rapid schemes of development and progress that will, in as short a time as possible, raise the living standards of their peoples to a level well above their present margin of subsistence. This is indeed a gigantic task, but it is one of immediate necessity. If a government does not make economic progress rapidly enough it meets with impatience and a sense of frustration on the part of its people. There can be no future for such a government in Asia.

No economic progress can be made to any satisfactory extent unless there is perfect stability, both internal and external. Peace in Asia is the very essence of economic progress. You will thus see that in your desire for peace you have in the countries of Asia people who have a similar outlook and a common meeting ground.

On this plane of ideas and principles, the United States and the countries of South and Southeast Asia have a further community of interests. That is in the pursuit of the principles of democracy. I have already spoken of the inspiration which your magnificent Constitution and the speeches and writings of your great leaders gave the countries of Asia in their struggle for freedom. They helped to strengthen the foundations of democracy in that region. Democracy is not something new in Asia, and is not Western-imposed as many people in the West seem to think.

Speaking for Ceylon I can say that our way of life has been democratic since the very inception of our civilization over two thousand years ago. Democracy is inherent in the very principles of Buddhism which is the major religion of the people of Ceylon. Tolerance, individual freedom and responsibility, the spirit of understanding, the value of individual and collective service, all these constitute a part of the Buddhist philosophy of life. Buddhism has been one of the dominant forces influencing the way of life of people not only in Ceylon but also in many of the countries in the region.

Speaking again for Ceylon, and I know this is also true for the vast majority of the other countries in the area, I can say that our people have as much freedom—and perhaps more—than those of any other democracy in the world. We believe in freedom of expression and public meeting. A man can denounce the government in the most violent terms. Political parties can carry on propaganda for any philosophy they believe in, Marxist, capitalist, or anarchist. No man is punished for the views he holds, whether on religion or on government. Nor is anyone penalized for the views he held several years ago.

We believe in the law and the due process of law just as much as you do. Our judiciary is independent, and we have taken care not to relegate any of the functions of the judiciary to any other body of people. Our elections are completely free. We have the secret ballot. Any political party with any kind of program can campaign for election. It is, in short, a remarkably successful example— one of many in South and Southeast Asia—of the maintenance and continuance of healthy democratic traditions in their highest form.

I hope I have made clear the wide sphere of common interest which we in South and Southeast Asia share with you in the United States. Whatever differences we may have are therefore essentially not differences in objectives, because the ends we have in view are practically the same. Such differences as exist, I am convinced, are only differences in our approach towards our objectives. Take, for instance, our attitude to Communism. I have found that Americans are somewhat surprised and perhaps even bewildered by the calmness we display towards the question of the danger of Communism. There is no alarm or hysteria in most of the South and Southeast Asian countries about this problem. This calmness, in spite of the fact that practically all these countries have fairly substantial dissident political minorities wedded to the Marxist creed, seem to some Westerners not only surprising but even naïve. The explanation for this must certainly be of interest to you. It is primarily because the Asian countries have faith in their own people. Their peoples have had civilizations which date back over two thousand years. They have spiritual values gained both from religion and ancient culture. These, to a large extent, give them strength to resist the tide of materialistic totalitarianism. An appeal to the spiritual values of the people has been an approach which has been eminently successful in combating Communism in the Asian area. As I mentioned earlier, Buddhism is a powerful pervading force in South and Southeast Asia. Its doctrine of nonviolence and its belief in "soul force" are powerful influences in combating the materialist values which underlie Communism. The doctrine of nonviolence of Gandhi is a modern manifestation of this selfsame spiritual force. We believe that Communism cannot be suppressed by force. Communism is an ideology and has to be met by a superior ideology. We believe this superior ideology is contained in the democratic way of life and in the spiritual values of religion. We are convinced that these two forces combined can pose an almost insuperable obstacle to Communism as an ideology. It is this confidence that gives us strength to view the problem of Communism calmly, patiently and without excitement, and we believe that this approach is the most desirable one.

This does not of course mean that the Asian countries will not at any time exert their full efforts to ward off Communism. They are just as much opposed to Communism as you are. In fact I think it would be difficult to find, even in the Western hemisphere, a man so diametrically opposed to Communism as my Prime Minister, Sir John Kotelawala. His shattering indictment of Communism at the Bandung Conference and his challenge to the Reds were proof of his genuine sincerity. Among the leaders of other countries of this region there is a similar uncompromising opposition towards Communism. And in the struggle against the inroads of world Communism America can find no better friends and stalwart allies than the leaders of the South and Southeast Asian countries.

There is yet another aspect of this matter in which there is a substantial difference of approach as between the United States and several of the countries of the region under survey. The attitude of the United States has tended to emphasize the importance of military defense as a means of resisting Communism. Most Asian countries agree that a certain degree of preparedness against external aggression is desirable merely for purposes of defense. An entirely defenseless country creates a power vacuum and can be a temptation to an aggressor. While no Asian country will dispute the elementary need for self-defense, there are in this region several countries which feel that it would be both unnecessary and detrimental to the best interests of the area to overemphasize the military aspect. Military pacts and groupings increase rather than decrease international tension by arousing fear and suspicion and can only be a temptation to the opposing camp to find justification for an increase in its own military strength. For this reason we are inclined to feel that the organization of some Asian countries into military blocs is unfortunate and will defeat its own purpose. It becomes particularly objectionable when the initiative for such organization appears to come from the West. Nothing can be more damaging to the prestige of an Asian, or any other government for that matter, than the impression that there has been an imposition on it by a foreign government.

In fairness to the West, I must say that we realize that the arrangement is a defensive one entered upon in all good faith for the benefit of the Asian countries. Nobody suspects the motives of the West, but we feel that the peoples of South and Southeast Asia should be left to their own initiative in these matters. Whatever solution is arrived at, it must be one that has been thought, planned, and executed by the Asians themselves. In these Asian countries which have recently regained freedom and the right to control their own destinies, it is not surprising that there should be suspicions on the part of the people of the motives of any foreign power which appears to dictate to them. Any government which is not sensitive to this public attitude runs the risk of being overthrown. The last thing an Asian wants today is to have any semblance of colonialism or even a suspicion of external interference in domestic or foreign affairs. Western attempts to organize collective military groupings can be misconstrued as acts designed to limit the freedom of these small nations by the great powers in a subtle way.

I have spoken already of the Asian emphasis on the value of religion and belief in democracy as barriers against Communism. On the material plane we believe that the answer to Communism can be found through the improvement of the standards of life of the people. As you know, the masses of the populations of these Asian countries live in dire want and misery. A great task has to be done. It has to be done quickly, too. It poses the greatest challenge to the young governments of Asia. In the outcome of this issue will lie the means not only of staving off Communism, but also of demonstrating that the democratic method is both a faster, less painful, and more desirable method of economic progress than the totalitarian one. We Asians believe that the economic approach is far more important than the military approach in suppressing Communism and should be given absolute priority.

If you will allow me, I would like to take the liberty of using Ceylon as an example of a country where economic and social progress has been highly successful as a weapon in the fight against Communism. Since the achievement of independence the island has seen some of the most spectacular progress in its modern history. In agriculture the government launched a vigorous campaign for the reclamation of land which though cultivated in the time of the Sinhalese kings had later been abandoned, through neglect, to the ravages of the jungle and malaria. Through the restoration of irrigation reservoirs, the construction of canals, the clearing of forest, the preparation of the land, the construction of roads and settlements for the peasants, and the provision of other amenities, the government has opened up each year an extent of about 20,000 acres for cultivation. The once desolate land is now giving way to fertile rice fields, and thriving colonies of settlers are gradually being established over wide areas of this pioneer land. Peasants who were landless or who owned holdings which were insufficient for a decent living in the overcrowded sections of the island now have a carefree, comfortable existence in these new colonization schemes. The entire expense of the schemes is borne by the government. We are well on the way to establishing a sturdy, independent peasantry, happy and contented and unresponsive to the blandishments of Communist agitators.

In social services tremendous results have been achieved. Education is completely free, from the kindergarten to the end of the University course—eighty percent of the population are literate. Free mid-day meals and school books are provided for needy children. Ample scholarships are available. There is equality of opportunity in education to a degree that is seldom found even in Western countries. In the matter of health, malaria which was a scourge a few years ago, is today practically nonexistent. The conquest of this disease is truly a saga in the history of modern preventive medicine. Through an intensive campaign of D.D.T. spraying and drainage control, we have achieved the conquest of this once deadly and widely prevalent disease. Hospitals have been built in practically every sizable town, and dispensaries in practically every village. These health measures have so improved health conditions that the mortality rates in Ceylon are lower than those in Great Britain. In this remarkably short period of time, we have been able to raise the standards of health of our people to very near Western levels. In all of these fields I have touched upon rapid progress is being maintained and Ceylon can look forward to a dynamic period of economic and social progress.

What effects have these measures had in the political field? I can say with conviction born of happy experience, that they have had a shattering effect on the strength of the Marxist groups. In the first election after independence there were twenty left wing members out of one hundred and one members in the House of Representatives. By the time the second election was held, however, the dynamic economic and social progress made by the United National party had so discredited the Marxist groups that they barely managed to retain thirteen seats in the House. The present indications are that these parties have lost further ground. We have no fear at all of these dissident revolutionary elements. Our policy of encouraging spiritual values and adherence to the principles of democracy, and the solid progress we have made in economic and social welfare have been resoundingly successful in defeating Communism. It has more than vindicated our view that the best defense against Communism is not force but the peaceful demonstration of freedom and progress under democracy.

The emphasis on economic development over military preparations as a weapon against Communism will therefore be appreciated. The example of Ceylon is not unique. It has been demonstrated in India, Burma, Indonesia and several other countries too. I think it will be easy for Americans to appreciate it as well because the very rapid development and progress made by America in the early phase of her political history was to a considerable extent due to the fact that she kept aloof from military entanglements. The Asian countries today are in a similar position. They have, like America of the nineteenth century, their untapped natural resources awaiting development. They have yet to go a long way to achieve a comfortable standard of living which will give their peoples the basic necessities of life. All they want is an era of peace and stability, free from foreign entanglements and military preparations. I am sure that students of American history who realize that their own country passed through a similar phase a century ago, will readily grant the validity of the argument in its applicability to the young and independent countries of Asia today.

These minor differences in the approaches to our common objectives make it very necessary that Asians and Americans should try to understand each other better. The East welcomes the friendly co-operation and assistance of the West. In fact the East is heavily dependent on the United States for economic aid and technical know-how. But in this relationship it is always essential for the Western countries to respect Asian sensibilities. Asia is always willing to have friends and partners but it will, quite rightly, resent anything bordering on paternalism. I am happy that your great President and your nation have endorsed the idea of a free and equal partnership of America with her friends abroad. I think this attitude will help to bring America closer to Asia. It will require, however, a little tolerance, understanding, and patience on the part of Americans. I have found that there are voices in this country which are too easily inclined to adopt the attitude that "he that is not with us is against us." I would like Americans to appreciate the fact that in the free world there are bound to be areas of disagreement. These differences, however, do not imply disunity. They merely arise because each country has a different history, pattern of life, and national psychology, and different religious beliefs and cultural traditions. I believe that this concept has now been largely realized in this country and the Asian countries are happy that this is so.

I would like to touch on a subject which has given rise to a great deal of misunderstanding. I refer to the attitude of the South and Southeast Asian countries toward China, which has been somewhat different from the attitude of the United States. I want to make it quite clear to you that none of the democratic governments in the South and Southeast Asian region are happy about the fact that China has gone Communist, but they accept the fact that the Communist government is the *de facto* government. It is the government which is in full control of the territory comprised by the mainland of China. As such, most of us in the Asian region believe that it is time that China was admitted into the United Nations. It would, we feel, be unfair to exclude almost a quarter of the world's population from representation at the United Nations. The United Nations is an international organization in which the members have diverse forms of government and we feel that the question whether a government is good or bad should not be taken into consideration in regard to its admission into the organization.

Several countries in South and Southeast Asia too have not yet been admitted to the United Nations, although they are fully qualified for admission. The Bandung Conference recognized this issue, and in its final communiqué called on the Security Council to support the admission of all those states which are qualified for membership in terms of the Charter. The failure of these states to secure admission has been due to considerations of world power politics, quite unrelated to the question of their eligibility for membership. Their admission would not only help relieve international tensions, but also make the United Nations a more representative organization. These countries look to the United States and to the other great powers to help solve this issue.

The question of Formosa is also a pressing one. India holds the view that Formosa is an integral part of China and should go to China. We in Ceylon hold the view that Formosa should be under trusteeship for a period and that the Formosans should be allowed to decide their own future. We are all agreed that whatever solution is adopted, it should be a peaceful one, avoiding the use of force. We feel that the tension in the Far East should not be allowed to continue because it presents a threat to world peace. Ways and means must be found whereby the United States and China can get together to discuss the situation directly and in this connection we feel that the Asian nations can play a useful role through their good offices in creating a better atmosphere for such a meeting.

I come now to a less controversial point, but one which has, however, not been devoid of misunderstanding. It is the question of American aid to Asia. Asian countries today need a vast amount of foreign capital in order to sustain their programs of economic development, designed to raise the standard of living of their populations. By their own efforts the Asian countries can achieve substantial results, but the tempo of their progress can be increased to spectacular levels largely through assistance from external sources. The vast scheme of foreign aid from the United States comes, therefore, as a source of hope and expectation for the alleviation of misery, want, and disease in stricken Asian countries. There are two aspects of the foreign aid program which I would like to comment upon here. The first is that there has been a tendency for aid to be distributed only to the countries which are in the throes of difficulty and which are practically fighting a losing battle against Communism. A country must be helped in time, and the appropriate time for this is when it is manifesting a sound and healthy democratic tradition and a stable economy. It is of no avail to wait until a country is on the doorstep of disaster to come to its aid. I cannot help contrasting, in this connection, the comparative quantities of aid directed to Indochina on the one hand and India on the other. In the last two years the United States has lavished many more millions of dollars on Indochina than it has spent since the end of the war on the vital task of assisting India.

It must be realized that aid should be given at the right time, in the right quantities, and in the right manner if it is to be of adequate use. Furthermore, if aid is not given in time it often happens that the aid received is not so much in the shape of consumer goods which can alleviate poverty and misery, but in the shape of military weapons.

I respectfully submit that the test for giving aid should not be whether the recipient countries agree with you in all aspects of policy, but whether they are countries dedicated to the cause of democracy; not whether they trade with China or Russia for their own existence, but whether such trade has affected their ways of thinking. Judged by these standards every country in South and Southeast Asia is deserving of the fullest assistance.

The question today in Asia is whether economic development and social progress can be achieved faster by countries following a democratic method or by those following a totalitarian method. It is of crucial importance to the free world that in this field of "competitive coexistence" the democratic method should be more successful. For this method to succeed in South and Southeast Asia, it is vital that adequate aid be provided by the United States. It is for this reason that America should, in her foreign aid policy, use as a criteria for dispensing aid the existence of healthy and democratic traditions and economic stability in the countries of South and Southeast Asia. This is much more important than a rigid technical and legal test. It is also in conformity with the idealism of America. My appeal, then, in the final analysis is that America should return to the idealism which inspired her through her illustrious history.

commentary

JAMES BARRINGTON

Ambassador from the Union of Burma to the United States

South and Southeast Asia cover a vast geographical area and contain between a quarter and a third of the world's population. Many distinct racial strains are to be found in the region. Three of the world's major religions, Buddhism, Hinduism, and Islam, have millions of followers in South and Southeast Asia, and the number who profess Christianity cannot be ignored.

The countries of the region vary greatly in size and population. At one extreme there is India with a population approaching 400 million, and at the other there is Laos with a population of less than two million. Some are on the Asian mainland bordering Russia and China, while others are islands along the fringe of the continent.

Some of the countries recognize the government of the People's Republic of China as the legitimate government of China, while others continue to recognize the Chinese Nationalist government as the *de jure* government of China. Some of them have adopted a policy of nonalignment with either of the world's major power blocs, while others have aligned themselves with the Western powers.

My purpose in setting out these facts is to point up the very great diversities which exist in the region known as South and Southeast Asia. On the surface, it might appear that the existence of these great diversities would preclude any possibility of writing a general essay under the title "South and Southeast Asia Look at the United States" and that the only way to do justice to the subject might be to write a separate chapter on each component country's view of the United States. But as my friend and colleague, Ambassador Gunewardene, has shown, this is not the case. Despite their diversities, the countries of South and Southeast Asia share certain common objectives. Indeed, I do not think it is too forceful to say that the things which are common to them are in fact the things which are most important to each of them individually. It is this which enables them to share a common broad outlook in relation to the United States.

Ambassador Gunewardene is right in stressing at the very outset of his essay, that there is throughout South and Southeast Asia a tremendous amount of good will for the United States. I do not think this can be stressed often enough. The reason for this is not difficult to find. As I see it, the three main broad preoccupations common to all the countries of South and Southeast Asia are:

1. Love of freedom and the determination to gain or retain their independence at all costs;
2. Prevention of war;
3. Anxiety, bordering on impatience, to improve the living conditions of their people.

These preoccupations need little or no explanation or amplification to an American audience, since they are very much part of the American experience and tradition.

Having been for so long under colonial rule, and most of them having only recently emerged from colonial status, it is only natural that Asian countries should rate independence above everything else. And for the independence which they have achieved, these countries feel that they owe a special debt of gratitude to the United States. It could hardly be otherwise. After all, the United States was the source of those ideas and moral principles of government which have been the inspiration and hope of Asia for nearly a century, among them being the following:

1. All men are created equal and must be equal before the law;
2. All men are endowed with certain inalienable rights which it is wrong and immoral of any government to deny or abridge;
3. A right and moral government is a government of the people, by the people, for the people, devoted to the greatest good of the greatest number;
4. A right and moral government is a government of laws, not of men, which derives its just powers from the consent of the governed.

These powerful ideas, more explosive than all the bombs to be found in all the arsenals of the world, had the most profound impact on South and Southeast Asia in which there was under colonial rule no recognition of the equality of man, where fundamental rights were ignored at will, and where governments were imposed from above and usually from without. It would be no exaggeration to say that they played a leading part in the region's struggle for independence; and when it also became apparent that the United States, as its power and influence grew, was bringing moral pressure to bear on the colonial powers to relinquish their hold on their colonies, the admiration and gratitude of the people of South and Southeast Asia knew no bounds. Here, then, was forged an extremely strong tie with America.

All the countries of the region share a common dread of war because they know that another war, even a conventional war, would deprive them of the opportunity which independence has given them to make nations out of their peoples. Their peoples have to be redeemed from the state of physical and moral degradation into which they had been forced and kept by decades and even centuries of foreign domination. The United States has shown by her past actions that she also abhors and dreads war. Not only has she never started a war, but she has stayed out of wars despite the severest provocations and until she was left with no alternative. When, having been forced into war, she emerged victorious, the United States has displayed rare magnanimity toward her enemies; and finally, after having secured victory in the biggest war yet known, the United States took the lead in establishing the United Nations, whose primary purpose was to save mankind from the scourge of war. Here then was another close link between the United States and the countries of South and Southeast Asia.

The third common preoccupation, that of improving the living conditions of the people of South and Southeast Asia, arises partly from humanitarian considerations and partly from the realization that there can be no real stability in this world unless something is done quickly to close the gap between the highest and the lowest standards of living. In this rapidly shrinking globe of ours it is no longer feasible for the peoples of the world to continue to live on a double standard. The peoples of South and Southeast Asia have already waited very long, and they are impatient. They want results, and although this cannot be done overnight, it nevertheless has to be done in a hurry. Governments which fail to meet this test have, as Ambassador Gunewardene says, no future in Asia.

Now Asian governments know that they cannot, unaided, make the kind of quick progress which is required and that they need large amounts of foreign capital and technical assistance if they are to meet the challenge. And it is here that the United States, as the largest source of foreign capital and technical assistance, has an important role to play. The Marshall Plan, designed to rehabilitate the war-torn economies of Europe, captured the imagination of the underdeveloped countries of the world, and they saw in it great hope for the future of South and Southeast Asia. Here was a third tie.

As a result, the prestige of the United States in South and Southeast Asia was never higher than in the five years immediately following the end of World War II. The countries of this region remembered with gratitude that it was the United States which played the major role in the defeat of Japan and thereby brought about the liberation of many of them from Japanese militarist tyranny. They saw the United States keep its ten-year-old promise to give independence to the Philippines, even though the intervention of the Pacific war and the Japanese occupation could have been used as an excuse in delaying it. They saw the emergence of India, Pakistan, Ceylon, Burma, and

Indonesia as free and independent countries, with the strong moral and other support of the United States. In the whole region, only Indochina and Malaya were left under colonial rule, and there seemed little doubt that their emergence as independent states could not be much longer delayed. Further, during the same period, the countries of South and Southeast Asia saw the United States disarm and turn to a program of assistance first to Europe and then to Asia.

I have gone into this at length in order to support Ambassador Gunewardene's contention that there is in South and Southeast Asia a tremendous amount of good will toward the United States. With the United States in active sympathy with each of the major objectives common to all the countries of South and Southeast Asia, there could have been no other result. The reservoir of good will which was built up to the year 1950 still exists. We should never lose sight of this fact. But having said this, I feel compelled to fill what I consider to be an important gap in Ambassador Gunewardene's presentation. In order to complete the picture, I have to say in all honesty that the reservoir is today not as full as it was. America's standing in South and Southeast Asia has, I believe, suffered in recent years.

Now, what are the causes of this decline? As I see it, the decline stems from what many Asians regard as America's undue preoccupation with Communism. It seems to many in South and Southeast Asia that this preoccupation with Communism has resulted in some of the actions and attitudes of the United States in recent years being out of character with traditional American idealism and practice. And ironically enough, it seems to have had greatest impact in the very three fields in which the United States and the countries of South and Southeast Asia had found themselves to be in complete sympathy.

Let us look at each of these fields. The first is colonialism. The somewhat equivocal position taken recently by the United States on some colonial issues has come as a great shock and disappointment to South and Southeast Asia. With the exception of Thailand, there is not a single country in the area which has been independent for more than ten years. Having emerged so recently from colonial rule, it is only natural that we are—all of us without exception—extremely anxious to see all the remaining colonies get their freedom as soon as possible, regardless of where they might happen to be. This is not a matter of interference within the internal affairs of other nations.

It is a matter of principle, of morality, and of conscience. The principle is of course not disputed. But we have been told that we must be
patient, that colonialism is dying anyway, and that another and even
greater evil now stalks the earth. This argument has, I fear, left all
of South and Southeast Asia cold, because one evil, even if it be the
greater, does not cancel out or even mitigate another. They wonder
what sort of appeal this same argument would have had on the America
of 1786. When therefore, the people of South and Southeast Asia see
the United States compromising on this matter of principle, they can
scarcely be blamed if they begin to wonder whether she is losing some
of the idealism which made for her greatness. It certainly makes it
difficult for her friends to come to her defense.

The second field is a common abhorrence and dread of war and
love of peace. In discussing this, I would not wish to be misunder-
stood. I believe, with Ambassador Gunewardene, that America is
dedicated to peace. I do not believe that there is a single responsible
American who wants war. America's moral sense alone would preclude such a possibility. In addition, there is the fact that the United
States has a great deal to lose through war, perhaps more than most
of the countries of the world. But having said that, I am not prepared
to dismiss as lightly as Ambassador Gunewardene has done the impact
on South and Southeast Asia of the statements and utterances of some
Americans high in public life and of a part of America's press. Their
bellicose utterances and statements have undoubtedly been responsible
for creating the impression in certain circles in South and Southeast
Asia that the United States is contemplating a preventive war. As
Ambassador Gunewardene has said, those of us who are familiar with
the American scene know how much importance to attach to these
statements and utterances. But the sad fact of the matter is that the
vast majority of those who read the newspapers in South and Southeast
Asia are not familiar with the American scene and therefore tend to
take what they read at its face value. I realize, of course, that steps
are being taken to check such irresponsibility, and for the sake
of America's relations not only with us but with the rest of the world
I pray that they may succeed. But meanwhile there can be no denying
that some harm has already been done.

Another reason for the decline of United States prestige in recent
years in South and Southeast Asia has been the tendency among large

numbers of American people to see things in terms of black or white, whereas in fact there is very little in this world which is completely black or completely white. This tendency seems to have grown as the cold war became hotter. Out of this has developed the attitude, to which Ambassador Gunewardene has also drawn attention, that "he who is not with us is against us." It is a formula which is often applied, or misapplied, to the so-called neutrals, of whom there are several in South and Southeast Asia. Those who condemn neutrality overlook the fact that the United States followed a policy of neutrality for more than the first hundred years of her existence as an independent state.

The fact of the matter is that all the countries of South and Southeast Asia have ancient civilizations and cultures, from which they have derived a way of life which is particular to themselves. They are not prepared to give up this way of life for any other, be it the Communist way, the American way, the western European way, or any other way. They are all prepared to fight if need be to defend that way of life. Some of the countries of South and Southeast Asia feel that the best way of defending their way of life is to join in a military grouping which includes some of the major Western powers. Others, including Ceylon and Burma, feel that their independence and way of life is best protected by keeping out of any of these military alliances and placing their reliance on the overall security provided for in the Charter of the United Nations. To the peoples of these countries independence is more important than anything else, and any moves made by their governments which seem to surrender even a small measure of independence would lose them the confidence of their peoples. To people who still have vivid recollections of colonialism the entry of their country into an alliance with one or more of the great powers would appear, whatever the facts may be, as the loss of some degree of independence. The loss of confidence would open wide the doors to subversion. This policy of avoiding involvement in any power bloc is therefore dictated by the facts of life in these countries. However some Americans may view it today, I feel sure that George Washington would have both understood and approved it.

I turn now to the question of raising the living standards of the people of South and Southeast Asia. As I said earlier, the implementation of the Marshall Plan in Europe filled Asia with hope. The needs of Asia are very great, and time is pressing. Unless the governments of South and Southeast Asia can do something quickly to improve the living standards of their peoples, the mounting discontents and frustrations are likely to create an extremely serious problem not only for themselves but also for the whole world. This is a problem which stands by itself. It has nothing to do with Communism. Even if Marx had never been born, and Communism had never seen the light of day, the problem would still be facing us in all its stark reality. The peoples and governments of South and Southeast Asia do not ask for charity. They are putting all their available resources into the struggle, but it has long been clear that they cannot make the kind of progress which alone will prevent disaster without substantial assistance from outside. It is in America's own enlightened interest to help solve this problem.

We know, of course, that those in responsible positions in this country are aware of the seriousness of this problem. And a start was made to meet it. But after some years' experience, it has become clear, I think, that it is little more than a start. What has been accomplished so far has been little more than to scratch the surface. Indeed, a recent United Nations survey revealed the alarming fact that there has been a widening rather than a closing of the gap between the highest and lowest living standards in the world. This ought to serve as a grim warning.

We also know the circumstances in which it was decided that it was impossible to embark on the kind of program which the situation called for. We have no wish to criticize this decision. But I would like to endorse here Ambassador Gunewardene's thesis that too much emphasis on military defense measures at the expense of economic and social progress has its drawbacks—and, may I add, its dangers.

This brings me to the end of my commentary. In presenting it, I have tried to be fair and frank. I would like to reiterate here my belief that there is still in South and Southeast Asia a great fund of good will toward the United States. I am also convinced that it can be enlarged and that all that is required to enlarge it is for this great country just to be herself at all times and in all circumstances.

The European impact
on Southeast Asia

D. G. E. HALL

School of Oriental and African Studies, University of London

The impact of the West upon Southeast Asia only begins with Albuquerque's conquest of Malacca in 1511. Stray visitors from the West such as the Polo's, who passed through in 1292, Franciscan friars traveling to and from China during the short period of Mongol dominance, or Italian trading prospectors such as Nicolo di Conti and his successors made no impression whatever upon a world whose geographical knowledge extended hardly at all beyond China and India.

From Malacca the Portuguese controlled the trade between the Indian Ocean and the Far East and thrust their way into the spice trade of the Moluccas and Bandas, the pepper trade of Sumatra, and the tin trade of the western ports of Malaya. In India they achieved some measure of control also over the long-established textile trade of Gujerat and the Coromandel coast with Southeast Asia.

They came also as missionaries, the enemies of Islam. But though Islam was a recent import into Malaya and the archipelago, and Malacca its chief diffusion center, it was always one move ahead of the Portuguese, as they stretched out their tentacles. Moreover, where commerce and religion clashed, they failed to support their missionaries, so that St. Francis Xavier's efforts in the "Islands of Divine Hope" were ruined by the massacres of native Christians carried out by their ally Sultan Hairun of Ternate. St. Francis blamed this setback on their spirit of brigandage, and the theme of Fernão Mendes

Pinto's *Peregrinaçam* is that they were ineffectual missionaries because they were pirates and despoilers. A more significant fact, however, is that Christian missions have never achieved any success against either Islam or Hinayana Buddhism, the two dominant religions in Southeast Asia.

The well-established kingdoms of the mainland made it impossible for the Portuguese to play there so important a role as they assumed in the islands. They served as mercenaries in the armies and navies of Arakan, Burma and Siam, and colorful rogues such as Philip de Brito and Gonsalves Tibão played at seizing control over kingdoms. But at the beginning of the seventeenth century, Portuguese power was in rapid decline, and the Dutch and English had already broken through the ring fence of secrecy maintained by the Portuguese around their Eastern empire.

The newcomers appeared almost simultaneously seeking cargoes of the precious spices. The Dutch East India Company, the V.O.C., represented a great national effort bent on establishing a monopoly and ousting the Portuguese. The English East India Company, with only one-tenth of the initial capital of its rival and a precarious position at home, could make no headway against Dutch hostility. The Dutch, like the Portuguese, relied on powerful fleets and forts with garrisons; the English could afford neither. Their factories depended upon the good will of local potentates. When this failed, as at Macassar in 1667 and Bantam in 1682—in both cases through Dutch pressure—they had to clear out.

In building up and enforcing a monopoly of trade, the Dutch company found itself willy-nilly involved in a policy of territorial expansion, with consequences of fundamental importance to the archipelago. Thus Batavia became by the end of the seventeenth century the capital of an empire, which included much of Java, the Moluccas and Bandas, and the sultanate of Macassar in Celebes, and was in the course of the next two centuries to expand over the greater part of the island world. The methods used to control spice production and prevent smuggling reduced the prosperous Moluccas and Bandas to abject poverty. This and the destruction of native trade among the islands caused piracy to increase to an uncontrollable extent. When, with the decline in the relative importance of the spice trade, the Dutch began to concentrate upon the development of new marketable cultures such as sugar and coffee in Java, they reduced the position of the native producer to serfdom. For the policy was carried out through the medium of the local rulers and by the method of "forced deliveries and contingencies." Moreover, their "buy cheap, sell dear" policy reduced the ability of the native to buy their imports, and the mounting expenses of their military, naval, and administrative commitments more than swallowed up the profits of the V.O.C. Throughout the eighteenth century its debt accumulated relentlessly until, in 1799, it could no longer pay its way and had to be taken over by the state.

In Siam the Dutch attempt to monopolize that country's valuable trade with China and Japan caused King Narai, who came to the throne in 1662, to call in the French as a counterpoise. Louis XIV, who under the influence of Madame de Maintenon had begun to cherish the ambition to convert the whole of the Far East to Christianity, made the Siamese capital of Ayuthia the advanced base for his missionaries. The Greek adventurer Constant Phaulkon, who in 1682 became the dominant personality at the Siamese court, propounded to Louis' Jesuit confessor a scheme to give France control over Siam; and Louis sent an expeditionary force which occupied strategic points such as Bangkok and Mergui. There was a plan to develop Mergui as a French naval base, which caused Britain some alarm. But the mortal illness of Narai in 1688 enabled the antiforeign party to seize control. Phaulkon was put to death, and the French in face of growing national resistance had to evacuate Siam. The experience aroused so much xenophobia in Siam that for more than a century and a half she practically closed the door to European enterprise.

The Anglo-French struggle for dominance in India had momentous effects upon Southeast Asia. The brilliant Dupleix, acutely aware of the strategic factors involved in securing the upper hand in the Bay of Bengal, looked to the Burmese port of Syriam as a naval depot and, after becoming Governor of Pondicherry, propounded to the authorities at home a plan to gain control over Lower Burma by helping the rebellious Mons against the Burmese. It was vetoed, but the British at Madras, who smelt a rat, seized the island of Negrais at the mouth of the western arm of the Irrawaddy; and Dupleix had gone too far to draw back. That was in 1753. But before the onslaught of the new Burmese champion Alaungpaya the Mons failed. For with the recall of Dupleix and the onset of the Seven Years' War, French assistance was inadequate. In 1756 he captured Syriam and liquidated the French there. Three years later he massacred the English at Negrais.

The experiences of the Seven Years' War made the English all the more convinced of the need for a naval station on the eastern side of the Bay of Bengal, but farther south than Burma; for the China trade was becoming very important, and the V.O.C.'s ability to maintain its monopoly of Indonesian trade was visibly weakening. The fourth Anglo-Dutch war of 1780-84 demonstrated the alarming weakness of the Dutch in the Eastern seas and thereby paved the way for the occupation of Penang by the East India Company. Moreover, to safeguard the new British-Indian empire during the struggles with Revolutionary France and Napoleon, Britain assumed control over the Dutch possessions in the East to prevent them from falling into French hands.

Young Thomas Stamford Raffles, who became Lieutenant-Governor of Java in 1811, wanted to substitute British rule for Dutch permanently in Indonesia. He hated the Dutch monopoly system and believed that the object of European rule should be the betterment of the native peoples. But he failed to make Java pay its way. Moreover, at the Congress of Vienna, Castlereagh's policy was to strengthen France's neighbors so as to restrain her from ever threatening Europe again. So the Netherlands Indies were restored to the Dutch. And with the return of peace the doctrine of nonintervention, laid down in Pitt's India Act, became once more the basic precept of British policy, and there was strong opposition to extensions of territory. How difficult it was under the circumstances to honor the precept in practice is shown by Raffles's seizure of Singapore in 1819. In those days of slow communications it was possible for a man on the spot to gamble on achieving his object by presenting the home government with a *fait accompli*. To his clear perception it was vital for Britain to control the Straits of Malacca, and Penang was unsuitable for that purpose. Thus, when the respective spheres of interest of the British and the Dutch were defined by the Anglo-Dutch treaty of 1824, whereby Britain acquired Malacca, she was in a position to interfere decisively in the affairs of the Malay Peninsula. For the empire of Johore, founded after the Portuguese conquest of Malacca, had collapsed; and the Malay states were in a state of chronic unrest. That for half a century every attempt to exploit this situation was frustrated by the home authorities was due largely to their preoccupation with affairs in India.

In Burma's case, on the other hand, the East India Company's reluctance to assume new responsibilities broke down before the expansionist moves of the Alaungpaya dynasty. Its conquest first of Arakan and next of Assam tempted the weak Bagyidaw's brilliant general Maha Bandula to essay the invasion of Bengal by a pincer movement. Hence, when Burma was defeated in 1826 Britain sought to ensure the safety of India's northeast frontier by annexing Assam, Arakan, and Tenasserim. So with one foot inside Burma, very much as in the case of Malaya, the great problem was how to avoid further commitments. The attempt to build up direct relations between Calcutta and Ava soon failed; for the King of Burma would not appoint a resident envoy to a mere viceregal government, and in 1840 Burmese hostility forced the withdrawal of the British Resident. Another war was only a matter of time. It came in 1852 over the question of the maltreatment of two British merchant captains at Rangoon. Lord Dalhousie, against the thunders of Richard Cobden and the peace party at home, maintained that Britain could not afford "to be shown the door anywhere in the East" and, after a brief campaign, persuaded the home government to sanction the annexation of Lower Burma. Like Raffles, he believed that British rule would be a blessing to an oppressed people.

In Holland also liberalism was raising its voice against the treatment of native peoples. In this case it was the exploitation of the Javanese cultivator by means of the immensely profitable culture system that was the object of attack. In theory he was amply safeguarded, but in practice the worst forms of economic oppression were rampant, and remained so despite the efforts of the Liberals, until the publication, in 1860, of Douwes Dekker's novel *Max Havelaar* stirred the public conscience in Holland and opened the way for reform. Incidentally Dutch concentration upon Java and neglect of the Outer Settlements provided James Brooke with a fruitful field for an adventurous career dealing with piracy in western Borneo, and Britain with a further opportunity for expansion.

France's efforts to dominate India did not terminate with her defeat in the Seven Years' War. They were only finally abandoned with the defeat of Napoleon. Just before the outbreak of the French Revolution the brilliant Suffren was urging Versailles to make Burma the center of French activities against British India. After the Napoleonic wars, however, France's attention was turned to Cochin China, where through the efforts of a French missionary bishop, Pigneau de Behaine, a member of the Nguyen family of Hué, had made himself emperor of Viet-Nam. The Court of Hué, suspicious of French intentions, pursued a policy of isolation. It met the growing challenge of the West by an intense revival of Chinese classical culture and a bitter persecution of Christians. Such a policy played into the hands of the French inter-ventionists and ultimately led to the seizure of Saigon in 1859.

One thing led to another. From Saigon the French proceeded to conquer Lower Cochin China. This in turn enabled them to obtain control over the weak kingdom of Cambodia. Access to western China up the Mekong was the ultimate aim of these moves. Chambers of Commerce in Britain were at the same time campaigning briskly for the opening of the Irrawaddy route via Bhamo. But this chapter of French expansion came to an abrupt end, for the Doudart Delagree-Francis Garnier expedition of 1866-68 dispelled what Garnier appro-priately termed "la monomanie du Mekong" and soon afterwards the Franco-Prussian War brought the empire of Napoleon III to a sorry end.

With the opening of the Suez Canal in 1869 the European forward movement in Southeast Asia attained a new pitch of intensity. There was an unprecedented demand for tropical products and for opportu-nities for capital investment. The Dutch, aware of their neglect of their Outer Settlements, were apprehensive of possible European or American intervention. France, after her humiliation in 1871, yearned to salve her wounded pride by extending her overseas empire. Britain, still anxious to restrain her own would-be empire-builders, became deeply concerned at the activities of French ones, especially when they affected Upper Burma, Siam or Malaya.

In 1871 the Dutch obtained a free hand in Sumatra by ceding to Britain their possessions on the Gold Coast of Africa. Their immediate objective was the conquest of Acheh, the last powerful patron of piracy. The overall plan was to bring as much as possible of Indonesia under effective control, and press on with its economic exploitation.

Three years later Britain abandoned the policy of nonintervention in Malaya. The mass immigration of Chinese to the tin-bearing dis-tricts in the western states had brought about an intolerable state of affairs before which the native rulers were powerless. So a protectorate system was evolved whereby Malay sultans accepted British Residents, who undertook to reorganize the administration of their states on a modern basis. The experiment began in three states, Perak, Selangor and Sungei Ujong, and it was some time before the need was felt to extend it further. The European development of Malaya on a big scale began only when the internal combustion engine created an immense demand for rubber.

In exploring the Mekong the French discovered the wonders of ancient Khmer culture and the uselessness of the river as a commercial highway to western China. But Jean Dupuis, in supplying the Chinese with arms for the suppression of the Panthay rebellion in Yunnan, demonstrated the practicability of the Red River route through Tongking. "Tongking the key to China" became the watchword of Jules Ferry and the Colonial party. A premature attempt to seize control failed in 1873, but before the softening-up methods relentlessly applied to the court of Hué, Annam became a French protectorate. Then between 1883 and 1886 the definitive conquest of Tongking took place.

The results of all this were momentous. King Thibaw of Burma had so badly compromised himself in dealings with Jules Ferry that, notwithstanding the latter's fall in March 1885, Britain took the precaution to extinguish the Burmese monarchy and annex the kingdom together with its tributary Shan states. France used her new position to gain control over the Laos kingdom of Luang Prabang, then under Siamese suzerainty, and to elbow the Siamese out of all their territories to the east of the Mekong. These moves precipitated a crisis which strained Anglo-French relations almost to the breaking point. For the French Colonial party loudly proclaimed that control over the Menam valley was essential to the economic welfare of French Indochina, and in July 1893 the famous "Paknam incident" was staged with the object of provoking Siam to react in such a way as would enable the French to take all they wanted.

But Siamese restraint and British diplomatic pressure on France saved the day, though Siam bought her independence only by large cessions of territory in the Mekong valley. Ultimately in 1896 Britain and France agreed upon a joint guarantee of the independence of the Menam valley; before that happened, however, they stood a second time on the brink of war over a petty quarrel between their respective boundary commissioners on the upper Mekong which caused an hysterical outburst in France against Britain not unlike the one produced by the Fashoda incident in 1898. Actually Siam's independence hung precariously in the balance for some years. Then their growing realization of the German threat caused Britain and France to compose their differences by the Entente Cordiale of 1904. One of the features of this agreement was a joint confirmation of Siam's independence. She was then the only independent state of any importance left in Southeast Asia.

The French forward movement in Indochina also affected Malaya. As early as 1882 British fears of French intervention there had been aroused by surveys carried out by French engineers for a projected canal across the Isthmus of Kra, and by the pressure brought to bear upon King Chulalongkorn in this connection. Thus the extension of the residency system to further states, and the formation of the Federation of 1896 were not entirely due to internal affairs and administrative convenience. And by that time it was not only the danger of French intervention that alarmed Britain, but the fact that both Russia and Germany were seeking to profit from Siamese weakness to extort concessions in the Malay states theoretically under her suzerainty. It is against this background that the diplomatic moves must be seen which ultimately resulted in the transference by Siam to Britain in 1909 of her suzerain rights over Kedah, Perlis, Kelantan and Trengganu.

All this territorial acquisition was accompanied by an intensive search for exploitable natural resources, by vast capital investment and the production of foodstuffs and raw materials for the world market. The most spectacular development was in rice production. Nothing else in the economic history of Asia can match the immense expansion of rice cultivation in the Irrawaddy delta, the lower Menam valley and the deltas of the Mekong and the Red River of Tongking. Burma and Thailand became great teak exporting countries. The petroleum wells of Burma, Indonesia and Borneo became important in world economy. So also did Indonesia's exports of coffee, sugar, tea, indigo, tobacco and pepper, and the tin produced in increasing quantities in Malaya, Indonesia and Burma. Burma's great Bawdwin mine came to rank first among the world's lead mines, and was almost as important for silver. And finally in the present century all these countries, notably Malaya, began to cultivate rubber on such a scale as to outrun the world demand for the article.

Before they could realize what was happening the peoples of Southeast Asia found their familiar life of domestic self-sufficiency gone beyond recall and their livelihood dependent upon external markets and fluctuations of world prices. Traditional modes of life based upon subsistence agriculture and local handicrafts tended to break down. In the rice-growing areas, dependent upon the uncertainties of monsoon rains, agricultural indebtedness rose to alarming proportions, causing acute distress and social unrest. Everywhere the influx of foreign immigrants, Chinese and Indian, swamping the labor market, monopolizing certain professions, and acting as universal middlemen and money-lenders, operated to the disadvantage of the native peoples. And their xenophobia, always a factor to be reckoned with, received much stimulation.

The intensification of economic imperialism created new demands for administrative efficiency, for modernization of transport and communications, for scientific research and public health measures. The implementation of such a policy involved not only the development of increasingly bureaucratic forms of government, based on Western models, but also the introduction of Western education to such an extent as to divorce it from indigenous modes of life and thought. Its products became the leaders of national liberation movements. Acute schizophrenia was not uncommon; most of the native peoples felt deeply the contempt for their culture and color shown in varying degrees by Westerners.

On the other hand among the Western administrators, teachers, researchers and missionaries there were those who found their delight in the study of the religions, cultures, languages, literatures and history of the peoples among whom they worked. Southeast Asia owes a great debt to the Western scholars who discovered the greatness of its ancient cultures, scientifically explored and explained them, and, indeed, rescued from ruin and oblivion its ancient monuments and artistic treasures. Men such as Krom and Stutterheim for Indonesia, Peliot, Parmentier and Coedès for Indochina and Siam, Furnivall and Luce for Burma, to name only a few, have given the peoples of those countries a new awareness of the greatness of their cultural heritage, and the West a new respect for it.

With the coming of the twentieth century two new factors begin to have an overwhelming effect. There is awakening in the East and a change of heart in the West. Under the impact of the West civilizations long static became infused with a new dynamic. Much of Asia was affected, India, China and Japan in particular, and events in one country tended to have repercussions in the rest. It has been somewhat ineptly described as the "revolt" of Asia. It should rather be seen as a movement of renascence, of resurgence, highly complex in its composition. For while the introduction of Western education and techniques wrought in the East the same scientific revolution as was changing the West, there was at the same time an anti-Western appeal to traditionalism, which in Southeast Asia showed itself in Islamic and Buddhist revivalism. Everywhere there was emotional ambivalence and the most complete divergence of opinion regarding aims and methods. The supreme fact was that Asia was becoming aware of herself as never before. Thus the Japanese defeat of Russia in 1905, the Chinese revolution that began in 1911, and the growth of the *swaraj* movement in India thrilled the Southeast Asian countries with the sight of Asia casting off her chains.

The European change of heart was partly the result of the new democratic movements in Europe and all that they meant in revolutionizing life and outlook there, and partly in response to the new situation in the East. At the beginning of the century the Dutch publicly announced the inauguration of a new course, the Ethical Policy, or "Government of the Indies for the Indies." Decentralization of control and the promotion of social welfare were its main features. Burma, a province of India, shared in the constitutional reforms that were the British response to the Indian demand for *swaraj*. She had never willingly been joined to India. Hence one result of the introduction of a democratically elected legislature in 1923 was a growing demand for separation from India. This she achieved in 1937 with almost complete control over her internal affairs. In the French and Dutch colonies on the other hand there was no transfer of control. Dutch policy was to "kill home rule by kindness," as British policy in Ireland was once described. France employing mercantilist methods of running Indochina for the economic advantage of what she euphemistically termed *la mère-patrie*, pursued the policy of assimilation and intensified measures to promote French culture. Her rigorous repression of political agitation and her intransigent opposition to popular sentiment are the real explanation of the Communist success in gaining control over the nationalist movement in Viet-Nam. Nowhere else in Southeast Asia did this happen.

What the political history of Southeast Asia in the present century would have been, had Europe not weakened herself by two world wars is anyone's guess. The historian is only rightly concerned with what actually happened, and he is confronted by the fact that in the second war Japan's spectacular victories inflicted irreparable harm on the political prestige of the white man in the East. Hence in the new world which began to emerge in 1945 there was not only the desire but also the will to end white dominance. Naturally, the achievement of political independence by Burma, Indonesia and the countries previously forming French Indochina opens a new chapter in the story with which I am concerned in this paper. What it really means is that these countries have now assumed control over a process—call it westernization or modernization—over which previously they had none. They have now the task of adjusting its impact to their own traditional cultures.

commentary

U BA NYUNT

University of Rangoon

The period of European impact upon Southeast Asia, beginning with the Portuguese conquest of Malacca in 1511 and stretching over a long period of nearly four and a half centuries, was fraught with momentous results in the form of changes, some gradual and some revolutionary, in every aspect of life. The period of impact can be divided into three distinct phases. The first phase up to about the eighteenth century was that of European commercial and missionary activity. Europeans in Southeast Asia then were primarily traders and secondarily missionaries. There was not much significant result of the

impact during this phase. The beginning of the nineteenth century
ushered in the second phase of European political and territorial
expansion and it lasted until the end of the century. By that time the
impact had aroused Southeast Asia to protest and struggle against
European political and economic dominance. That was the third phase.
Changes wrought during these three phases created a number of
problems some of which are far from being solved today. Any attempt
to understand these problems, let alone to solve them calls for a study
of the past.

In view of the fact that the Portuguese conquest of Malacca can be
accepted as the first manifestation of European power in significant
measure it is possible to give great importance to that date. However,
it might be well to keep in mind that the Portuguese entry is largely
significant as the herald and harbinger of much more serious waves
of European conquest and consolidation. It is evident that the Portuguese did not become a major force in the region. At best they became
one more element in the welter of contending and conflicting factions
and forces in mainland and island Southeast Asia. As the proclaimed
raison d'etre of the Portuguese was the idealistic extension of the cru-
sades with state support and encouragement of Christian missionaries,
an examination of the failure of these missionary efforts might be
interesting. The work of the missionary ordinarily would tend to call
for a peaceful exposition, demonstration and establishment of the
superior worth of the religion propagated. The Portuguese effort however was a conjunction of military force and missionary zeal and as
such was destined to fail from the outset. Missionary process also
requires a comparatively unsophisticated and even primitive culture
for significant success, but the culture which met the Portuguese missionary advances was far from primitive. It was a culture based on
a solid foundation of Hindu and Muslim influences and a culture which
could boast of such splendid architectural monuments as the Angkhor
Wat, the Borobudor and the Pagan temples. Therefore the Portuguese,
though they became an important factor in the sixteenth-century Southeast Asia scene, never became the major force. The additional factor
that must certainly have operated to the disadvantage of the Portuguese
missionary effort was its timing. The Portuguese missionary effort had
been immediately preceded by the successful Muslim missionary effort.
History has shown us in the examples of the original Arab, Seljuk,

Ottoman and Mameluke explosions of power that new converts to Islam are at the very least as completely integrated and sure of themselves as the most fanatic and ruthless Jesuit or Dominican.

The failure of the Portuguese in the mainland kingdom of Southeast Asia becomes even more evident when one recalls the role to which they were reduced in Arakan, Burma and Siam. They became mercenaries generally acting as small but valuable auxiliaries in the interminable struggle for power in these regions. The possibility of their dominating the mainland kingdoms was very remote largely because these kingdoms were not solely dependent on inter-island trade or overseas trade. The superiority of their boats which gave the Portuguese the advantage of overwhelming armed superiority and mobility was of no significance on the mainland. Further, the religion which the Portuguese found entrenched in the mainland of Southeast Asia was Hinayana Buddhism. This religion was assessed by a very matter-of-fact British officer after the First Anglo-Burmese War who concluded that as a fighting religion, as a help in the mobilization of native resistance against foreign aggression, it was a very poor one. Strictly speaking, as far as the ideology is concerned, the passiveness of the religion would tend to support this assessment. However, the Buddhist nations of the mainland have not displayed any lack of the will to fight long and hard through the centuries. It was not only the Portuguese missionary effort that failed, but the later British and Dutch efforts also. Great Britain, a non-Catholic state, had always subordinated the interest of religion to that of the state and commerce even before the great mutiny of 1857 in India. After the mutiny it became the formal British policy to leave unmolested and undisturbed in so far as they did not infringe on the rights and privileges of the British, the native religions and religious establishments. The Dutch also appeared to have adopted the same attitude.

Another factor perhaps in the failure of the missionaries was the lack of understanding shown by the earlier Protestant missionaries. Most of them were god-fearing and pious individuals but they proceeded on the assumption that the native beliefs and faiths which they were asking people to forsake and cast aside were barbaric superstitions without any ability to stand up to critical examination or without the ability to produce civilized modes of behavior. After a while they became bitter and frustrated individuals. The failure of

Western missionary efforts points to the fact that Western impact on religion in Southeast Asia did not produce any significant results.

Another important feature of the impact of the Europeans upon Southeast Asia was the effect that European rule had on the class structure of the various colonial areas. The native societies at the time of European conquest were roughly divided into two categories. There were small ruling groups of families exercising autocratic sway over a vast social base of peasants. The official class was an appanage of this ruling group and, being dependent on wayward official favor, was seldom given the chance to achieve the tradition of continuity of delegated power and was therefore not very significant in the social pattern. There was a fundamental clash between the material interests of the ruling group and the peasant masses but the overriding factors which superseded this basic antagonism were the social and religious functions of the monarchy in these traditional subsistence economies and the similarity of race and speech and faith. The effect of this social set-up was the weakening of the resistance powers of these colonial peoples. It was only when the colonial powers swept aside these ruling classes and substituted themselves as the new masters that there emerged the possibility of increasing and making ever more effective national unity and solidarity. It will be observed that the peoples of Viet-Nam for instance were completely powerless against French military might when they were led by the emperors but that once they had got rid of this weakening social element they united in resentment against the patronizing condescension of the French and their ruthless economic exploitation. The colonial peoples in their respective resistance movements against Western dominance required leadership and fortunately leadership came from amongst the Western-educated natives. Colonial education systems which aimed to provide a fairly large section of administrative personnel at lower levels, offered sufficient Western education to produce frustration as well as a desire for further studies. Political ideas, economic theories and administrative methods of the West were studied by these frustrated few and from amongst them came the leaders. However, the view that nationalism in Southeast Asia is solely the work of the educated few cannot be entertained; for nationalist movements sprang essentially from the people and the educated few provided the leaders only. In passing, mention must be made of the impetus given to national movements against Western domination by the Japanese victory over Russia in 1905 and the Chinese revolution of 1911.

Another important aspect of the European impact on Southeast Asia was on the ideas and culture of the local inhabitants. The imposition of military and political control would not in itself have affected the attitudes and ideas of the people since they had no participation in the previous native administrative scene. However, the people gradually realized that the small identity of interest which the previous native rulers had shared with them was no longer existent. These foreigners were rulers who regarded the interests of the European homelands as being paramount in every case. The administrators and the merchants made it obvious that as far as possible they would remain aloof from the affairs and troubles and desires of the indigenous society. The natives who previous to the European entry did not possess a strong and definite sense of national unity and solidarity were forced into greater unity by European treatment which lumped all of them in the single category of a conquered native race. The Europeans based their assumption of superiority and separate identity on the superior progress they had made in the development of political systems. Part of this political development was of course the evolution of democratic forms of government and inevitably the native peoples were asked to admire and therefore to study and desire these forms of political advance. Together with the sweeping away of the native ruling groups and the realization of the aloofness of the Europeans this contact with the cherished social heritage of the European led to the birth of new attitudes toward national solidarity and political freedom.

Culturally the European impact acted on native society in several ways. The cultural activity which had a mass basis and in which there was mass participation stood up better to the impact of the Europeans but in the fields of theatre, literature, dancing, architecture and sculpture the situation was quite different. In these fields of cultural activity there had always been heavy reliance on the patronage of the native ruling classes. The new rulers were uninterested in these native cultures, preferring their own, and consequently the essential patronage and the prestige attached to this patronage died out very quickly. The French perhaps were the one colonial power which tried to make available French culture but even then there was not available the material and financial resources for success. Even if Western culture had been made available or consciously imposed on the peoples of Southeast Asia, it is doubtful if such a policy would have made any appreciable impression particularly in the field of art. For, "from the dawn of European history, at least from the time of the beginnings of Greek art more than 2500 years ago, the mental conceptions underlying Western and Eastern art seem to have been as the poles apart." European art gives expression to one's aesthetic tastes and indulges in the representation of animal and plant kingdoms while Eastern art tries "to define something beyond and above," and has a spiritual appeal. The result therefore of this attitude of the colonial powers in regard to culture has been, in Southeast Asia generally, gradual loss of the roots that native society had in its historical and cultural past. Perhaps one should, however, bear in mind that against the vast weight of official indifference, a few brave individuals like Peliot, Coedes, Luce, Blagden, Krom, etc., have made themselves the benefactors of the Southeast Asian peoples by their lifework on the rediscovery of ancient Southeast Asian cultural glories.

The social effect has been to produce, in this generation when the West has once again withdrawn from close control, a generation which finds it difficult to achieve the emotional balance and integration which would have been natural if it had been firmly rooted in strong native cultures of continuity and vitality. The revival of national cultures in the various countries in postwar Southeast Asia should be considered as an endeavor in the right direction to restore this balance and integration. This revival has become essential; for only a thorough knowledge and appreciation of national cultures would enable Southeast Asian peoples to understand, adopt or adapt whenever necessary, aspects of other cultures.

At this juncture the positive and constructive effects of the European impact on Southeast Asia should be taken up. Where the transfer of power has been achieved with a degree of smoothness as in Burma, there is a growing tendency amongst the natives to observe and appreciate in some measure the positive contribution of the colonial powers to the area. It is not within the scope of this commentary to enlarge on the improvements in transport and communications, on the revolution of the administrative systems, and on the apparatus left behind to mobilize more efficiently the material and man-power resources of the area. It might be stated generally that Southeast Asia has been left by the Europeans a much more viable and important unit of world society than might have been possible under the traditional types of administration. A special feature has been the organization of the individual states to the end that one special region or city has come into dominance over the traditional political units of the region. In Burma for example, through the centuries up to British entry there have been traditionally two regions or poles of power. The northern pole was centered round the Sagaing-Ava-Mandalay region. The southern pole was in the coastal region down the Sittang and Irrawaddy mouths. Today the building up of Rangoon has placed it in an overwhelmingly dominant position in the country. This contention is proved by the fact that when, in 1949, Burma's present government was considered to have control only of Rangoon, it was still in possession of sufficient prestige and resources to survive, augment its strength, and then proceed to reimpose control over the country. The country's exportable wealth could only be sold through the communication system of which Rangoon was the nodal point. The steamers and ocean liners could only be handled effectively by the modern facilities available at Rangoon. Rangoon was also the administrative nerve center, the shopping and distribution center, and had the largest collection of professional, cultural and trained personnel in the country. Like Rangoon, cities such as Singapore, Manila and Batavia have become the living symbols of the vast political and social revolution which has resulted from the impact of the West upon Southeast Asia.

Finally, there is the very difficult question of how life in the colonial areas has affected the attitudes and prejudices of the colonial Europeans and how this set of prejudices and attitudes has evoked corresponding reaction in the attitude of the Southeast Asian to the West generally. That is also a very important sociological factor. The commercial exploitation of Southeast Asia has resulted in adding to the national income of the European countries. European standards of living, which had already been raised by superior industrial technology, became higher, and the gulf between them and Southeast Asian living standards widened more and more. When one remembers that in the West there is class snobbery based on income and superior purchasing powers then it becomes inevitable for the Westerner to look down in increasing degree on the poverty of the Southeast Asian and/or the dirt, ignorance, and the lack of civic consciousness attendant upon this poverty. The Southeast Asians, after an initial period of quiescence about the beginning of the twentieth century, became increasingly aware of the disparity, the huge inequality, between what life was for the Europeans and what it was for themselves. This accentuated antiforeign feelings and is perhaps responsible for the attractiveness of the Japanese wartime slogan, "Asia for the Asians," and it may perhaps also explain why Southeast Asia as one whole is sympathetic to the aspirations of present day Asian countries.

Aftermaths of colonialism

WALTER H. MALLORY

Council on Foreign Relations

The colonial period in South and Southeast Asia which began when Vasco da Gama arrived in India more than four hundred and fifty years ago came to an end in the flames of World War II. It was the bid of an Asian power for supremacy which provided the final stroke to shatter the old structure. But there were fissures which would have brought it down in the end in any case. Japan's temporary conquests and eventual defeat only served to hasten the inevitable. Promises by the United States to the Philippines and British policy in India had already laid the basis for a transfer of sovereignty. But in Indonesia and Indochina it took Japanese occupation and military revolt to win the final decision. There are still islands of European influence—Malaya, North Borneo, New Guinea—but most of these also are yielding to the urge for freedom.

The attainment of these age-old aspirations is a cause for rejoicing. The new order is better for the new states and in the long run for the former colonial powers too. It now puts relations on a basis which frees the spirit of man from artificial inequities and makes real cooperation between the peoples possible; presuming, of course, that both sides are willing to forget the past—the old imperial countries, past glories; the new countries, past grievances.

My purpose here is to consider the aftermaths of the shift from colonialism to freedom in the particular area of South and Southeast Asia; but before doing so it may be useful to pause for a few moments to have a look at the world situation as a whole. For while most of the area under review has attained emancipation, other areas have had very little recent change in their status, and still others have actually retrogressed.

In 1953 the United Nations received reports on sixty non-self-governing territories and to this must be added eleven trust territories. All told there are probably 200 million people still under old-style colonial rule.

Africa has continued its slow progress toward greater freedom with some faster progress in North Africa and the Middle East where Libya, Syria and Lebanon have become independent nations since World War II. But, on the other hand, a new form of colonialism has swept over eastern Europe. And the picture is not all bright even for Asia. While freedom has been achieved in the South, this new colonialism has been making great progress in the North. Outer Mongolia has been integrated with the USSR, and China itself is day by day being drawn more closely into the Russian orbit. Meanwhile, Communist China has conquered Tibet by force of arms, engulfed North Korea and is in the process of extending her sway over an indeterminate part of Indochina. Whether this tide has now stopped or will sweep southward to overwhelm the recently liberated countries too, we do not know. So our satisfaction at the end of colonialism in that particular region must be tempered by the thought of losses elsewhere, and by an awareness that the new wave is not so very far away.

In terms of population some 600 million people in South and Southeast Asia and Africa have achieved their independence since World War II; while 100 million in Europe and perhaps 600 million in North and East Asia have fallen under the Communist heel—a net loss to freedom of considerable size.

There has been an effort to disguise this new colonialism. But an examination of what has actually happened shows it to be the same old wolf despite its new semantic garb. In the first place, these new colonies have been erected in the shadow of great military power. Secondly, although they are called "peoples" governments, they are composed of minorities which, having gained power, accept direction from outside. Third, the economy of the new colonies is integrated with Moscow and serves world Communism rather than the individual states.

Is not this the modern equivalent of what happened in South and Southeast Asia during past centuries? Did not India and Indonesia and Indochina and the Philippines come under the aegis of alien powers as the result of military action or overwhelming military strength? Did not these peoples, and their conquerors, erect governments which were subservient to the mother country? And did they not encourage a type of economy which would serve the empire rather than nourish the subject peoples? What, then, are the essential differences between the relations of the USSR to the Baltic States or to Poland and the former relations of Indonesia to the Netherlands?

So many centuries of the old colonial rule covering so great an area and over such vast and diverse populations have left profound effects. They touch every aspect of life and thought; and in the present essay we can do little more than list some of them and comment briefly on the most important.

The psychological aftermath of colonialism is basic to all the other aspects for it governs the attitude of the people not only toward their former rulers but also toward the new situation in which they find themselves. In the first place, I have the feeling that most Southeast Asians are not yet quite sure that they are really free. Generations of foreign control have made them extremely suspicious; and the speed and ease with which freedom was finally won (in most cases without military action) have made them wonder whether the former colonial powers have really gone home for good.

In a recent interview the Prime Minister of Indonesia said:

> Anti-colonialism and anti-imperialism are not slogans monopolized by Communists, but are living realities in the minds of the masses of the people of Asia and Africa. Unfortunately these sentiments are generally ignored or minimized by the Western world. The presumption that they are merely Communist slogans indicates an ignorance of the psychological impact on the feelings prevailing today among the Asian and African nations which only recently emerged from colonial status into independence.[1]

The fact that we are devoting this session to the aftermaths of colonialism would indicate that here in the United States, or at least in Washington, we are not as unmindful of this subject as Mr. Sastroamidjojo accuses the Western world of being. Nor have we any doubt that colonialism still occupies the minds and stimulates the fears of

[1] Written interview with I. H. Gordon, International News Service, released 2/7/55.

the peoples of South and Southeast Asia. Indeed, unless these new countries evolve stable governments, develop the will and the means to defend themselves, and provide a reasonable standard of living for their people, it is not at all sure that they can keep the freedom which they now enjoy. The devoted effort that most of the countries are making is evidence that this danger is recognized.

The political aftermath was more complex and manifested itself differently in every country. Many of the leaders who worked for freedom—Nehru, Sukarno, U Nu,—are still in power and have large popular support. This has lent stability to the new regimes in their most trying years. But there may be a definite limit to the time that a democratic government can be safely ruled by one man. George Washington thought that eight years was about enough. Certainly top leaders cannot be attracted if denied the opportunity to hold the top posts; and while one would hesitate to advocate the French system, there is a happy medium somewhere between that and the life tenure of a Lenin or Stalin.

The new countries have followed Western democratic forms in adopting their constitutions. Most of them had had some practice, even while they were colonies, in parliamentary procedure; but only in the Philippines had there been elections on a national scale. In some countries there will be the urge to continue or revive ancient forms and practices. For example, in Indonesia traditional *adat* law has operated alongside Western codes. It is felt that the former expresses for Indonesians such universal values as the principle of mutual aid, the social function of man and property in the community, and the principles of representation and consultation in the system of government, that it should not be abandoned but assimilated into Western concepts. In most of these countries the central government has been remote from the people, and the local communities have evolved forms of self-government, or have come under petty sultans and princes who have ruled them. These indigenous political practices have operated under or parallel to the central administrations and were often encouraged in order to provide a buffer between the colonial powers and the people. Now if the constitutions of the new states are to be made to work, these old forms must be molded somehow into a modern guise, or if they are not adaptable they must be discarded. The erection of the full machinery of popular government will, therefore, take time and involve problems of adjustment and adaptation which will, meanwhile, put a severe strain on stability and efficiency.

The operation of any state depends in large measure on the training, experience and devotion of its permanent civil servants. With the end of the colonial regimes each of the new countries was left with a civil service of sorts, but they varied greatly. In the Philippines, India, and Pakistan, the training of these officials had been carried to a high degree and the civil and military services included men of the first rank. At the other extreme, only junior personnel had received any training at all in Indonesia, and there were few even of these. When the British left, it was estimated that only about ten per cent of the civil servants were withdrawn, and the new governments of India and Pakistan were able to proceed with only minor adjustments. The same was true in the Philippines and to a somewhat less degree in Burma and Ceylon. In Indonesia it was necessary to build from the ground up, and the problems of training, discipline, and morale were almost insuperable.

The colonial powers in the course of their long rule brought together disparate races, tribes, religions, and cultures and put over them all a frame of government. It was these alien governments which held the peoples together; and now that they have been superseded by self-governing states which subscribe to the theory of self-determination, strong divisive forces have been released. This was at first apparent in India where the vaunted adherence to contemplative and humanistic theories was insufficient to counterbalance the religious intolerance of Hinduism and Islam, and the two states of India and Pakistan have resulted, while Ceylon has also been split off to form a third independent country. In Indonesia several of the outlying regions are reluctant to accept a central government in Java. The racial minorities in Burma are not yet fully agreed on Burman leadership. It seems quite possible, therefore, that the next years will see further divisions, and that the racial, cultural, and religious minorities through this whole region may force a breakdown into smaller political units.

In the social sphere the departure of the colonial administrations also left grave problems. Most of the countries have dense populations, a high birth rate, poverty, and low standards of health. Literacy in some areas was as low as ten per cent. In addition, all of them had been affected by World War II. The Philippines and Burma had suffered severe destruction and, along with Indonesia, had been occupied by the Japanese for several years. While India and Ceylon escaped war damage and occupation, they had made a great contribution to the war effort and all were left with serious economic problems. To be sure, social, educational, and health services were taken over by the new regimes without interruption (with the exception of the departure of the Dutch doctors from Indonesia which left 80 million people with only about 1100 physicians—in one area one surgeon for a population of over a million). But there was, of course, confusion and uncertainty and it has taken a truly herculean effort to bring these populations through to their present improved status. I think we in the West, who have only dry statistics to guide us, have little appreciation of the accomplishments which have been made in a few brief years. There are still areas where progress has been slower, and, of course, it has not been uniform in every field. While India has made great strides politically and has assured the government's stability through national elections, Indonesia has made great progress in education and already has increased the literacy of her people to a marked degree.

The departure of the colonial powers has had important effects in two other respects. It has greatly stimulated the interest in and the urge to return to ancient cultural mores, and it has greatly weakened the unifying effects of language.

All people who have an indigenous culture seek to perpetuate it and to build it up. If they are colonials, however, they are taught to lean on the mother country, and they adopt alien ways more readily, especially when the apparatus of education and government is in alien hands. But once they are cut adrift the need for the stabilizing influence of old customs, laws, and beliefs is keenly felt. People need a history, modes of life, and some ancient accomplishments to which they, or at least their politicians, can point with pride. Most of these countries must go a very long way back to the days when they ruled themselves. Meanwhile, during intervening centuries the world has moved ahead in science and technology, in political philosophy, and in knowledge about health; and thus many of their ancient forms and practices do not fit their present needs. They were reluctant to accept the ways of the West which were forced upon them, but they realize now the difficulty of competing with the West with sixteenth-century methods. This has engendered a state of frustration in intellectual circles which will long persist.

The language difficulty is perhaps a facet of this larger problem of adjustment. All of these new countries, of course, speak different languages, but each of them in turn uses a number of languages inside its national borders. In the colonies the language of the mother country was taught in the schools and provided a common means of communication for the educated classes. English was the language of the Philippines, Burma, India, Pakistan, and Ceylon; Dutch was taught and spoken in Indonesia and French in Indochina. English was also used in Malaya, Hong Kong, and more than any other Western tongue in Thailand and China—so it served to facilitate communication between the separate countries in the whole region as well as inside the countries. Now this is all radically changed. The Philippines after fifty years of English has chosen a difficult and little known tongue, Tagalog, one of its many languages, which now fortunately employs a Roman alphabet but in no other way resembles English. Indonesia, after centuries of Dutch, has stricken it from the curriculum and is developing Malay, a most inadequate language, into Bahasa Indonesia as the official tongue of the country, with English as the second requirement. The other countries have likewise chosen one of their local dialects for first place, with English as second. Thus they have all, without exception, arbitrarily hampered, at least temporarily, intercommunication between the various sections of their population and have set back more permanently the ease of contact with their neighbors. The effects of this radical change may not be so apparent now as they will be after the knowledge of the former language dies out, and before the new languages gain truly national currency. For their international dealings in the future, these countries must learn an additional tongue since they cannot expect other nations to master their purely local forms of speech.

Centuries of colonial rule have resulted in a most unsatisfactory economy in South and Southeast Asia. If these new countries are to become truly independent, viable, prosperous states, a radical shift in the orientation and, indeed, in the basic elements of their economic life will be necessary. Many of their leaders are conscious of this and are striving to understand their predicament and to find a way out of it. But they are greatly hampered by a lack of practical experience; and, even more, by what might be called the colonial mind. For there is no doubt that they have suffered by being tied to distant and often unsympathetic overlords; and that that experience has colored their ideas about capitalism, industrialization, the relations of management and labor, and many other matters about Western economic life. Thus the development of new economies, which will be hard enough in any case, is made doubly difficult because of resentments, vague social objectives, and politics which may have very little to do with production and trade.

There are four basic facts about the economies of the former colonies with which we are dealing today. Their per capita income is lower than that of most of the other countries of the world. They are, for the most part, raw material producers dependent on only a few basic products and thus at the mercy of the world price of these products. They suffer from a shortage of capital. They have been built up as sectors of the economies of the mother countries so that their trade has been funnelled through the metropolitan centers, and the control of that trade has been closely held by nationals of the colonial powers. In Indonesia, for example, the products of that far-flung chain of islands have been collected by Dutch-owned vessels which have brought them to Djakarta for transshipment, so far as possible, to Holland. Thus if a European wanted to buy tin or rubber, he would go to Amsterdam, not to Djakarta. In the same way, if an Indonesian importer wanted to buy paper he would have to deal with Amsterdam and had no direct connections with paper mills in Finland or Canada. The freight, insurance and middlemen's profits thus went to Netherlanders. Similarly the Philippines was linked with the United States; and India, Pakistan, and Burma with England.

At present all these new countries are seeking to increase their output, to diversify their production and to establish direct contact with their customers and suppliers. These endeavors are of such a fundamental nature that they are sure to result in great changes in the political and social as well as the economic structures of their societies.

Americans have not yet forgotten that the United States was once a colony of Great Britain, but they may forget that freedom was won long before the industrial revolution reached its height. Thus by the time the United States was ready for development, fear of England and resentment against the colonial regime had subsided. America turned to Great Britain, and to other European countries, for the capital to build and expand its economy to the benefit of both sides. But it is very doubtful if any such working arrangement with England could have been made in 1783. And we are quite wrong in expecting that the Indians or the Indonesians will promptly and cordially establish with the West economic ties which seem to them to resemble the very shackles which they have so recently struck from their countries' business.

Sutan Sjahrir, first Premier of Indonesia, once said:

> As long as there is Anglo-American capitalism and imperialism, we cannot achieve 100% independence, however much we try. Because of this, the fate of the people of Indonesia is bound up with international conditions and developments, and more than any other country we need a changed basis of society . . . .[2]

This great leader thus identifies capitalism and the United States and Great Britain as the real enemies of the independence of Indonesia. This is a case of guilt by association. Actually it was the Dutch colonial policy which was at fault. America had nothing to do with it, and capitalism was an instrument of Dutch policy, not itself the cause of Indonesian woes. Sjahrir and many other Asian leaders fail to see that capitalism when properly used and controlled can have as beneficial effects in their own countries as it has had in the West. I mean, of course, modern capitalism—not the uncontrolled laissez faire of the last century in Europe which gave the excuse for Karl Marx's outdated and impractical theories.

This fear of capitalism, coupled with the shortage of capital, has led in most of the new countries to the espousal of socialism as the best vehicle for improving the standard of living of the people. But socialism involves the nationalization of at least a part of the economy. The Communists, of course, advocate complete nationalization; but the Asian leaders in the countries with which we are concerned do not want to go that far. But there has been a good deal of nationalization with resulting confusion and a lack of stability in sectors of the economies which are threatened by nationalization. This hampers planning; and of course these and other uncertainties impede investment even of local capital, let alone of funds from abroad. All of these countries seek, and require, if they are to develop in any reasonable space of time, foreign capital, either private or government loans. Up to this

---

[2] Quoted by Gumar Goshal, *People in Colonies* (Sheridan House, New York, 1948), p. 220.

moment there are no clear evidences that the political and ideological struggle inside the new countries has progressed to a point where any estimate can be made of the outcome. The present tendency is to temporize and seek the best of both possible worlds. So the economies are mixed with the degree of government control constantly shifting, and there is no sign that the adequate supply of new capital for the enormous development which everybody wants will be found.

While to the Westerner it seems clear that the new countries need the application of capital to bring about the development which both desire, it is well for him to remember that the economic system which worked wonders in his homeland has gained a very feeble following in Asia. The masses there did not embrace the competitive mentality which is the driving force of the free enterprise system, but remained in a state of economic servitude. The indigenous peoples of Southeast Asia have not taken a directing part in the competitive economy which has grown up, but have left this to the Westerners themselves or to the Chinese and Indian minorities within their midst. So the application of capital, even if satisfactory conditions are created to attract it, will not be enough. Capitalism to work must have a favorable climate. People must believe in it and lend their support to it. It is hard to think that lack of confidence in a system which has proven so successful elsewhere stems from some Asian distaste for material progress. More likely past practice has not brought a sufficient share of the profit to the local peoples themselves. In any case the end of colonial rule has left these populations with little experience of the free enterprise system, except as labor in its lowest ranks at small pay, and with very little evidence of a desire to put in the thought and energy which is needed to direct and develop it.

In speaking of the aftermath of colonialism there is the temptation to think that the old, unhappy days are gone forever. While it is unwise to make predictions about the long future, it seems clear at this moment that those Western nations which had colonies in South and Southeast Asia have made a solemn decision to give them up for good. But what of the USSR and the Chinese and other Communists? It is a fact, I think, that the Asians are not yet quite sure that they are really free; but many of them, doubtless from long habit, seem to fear their former oppressors rather than those who might well be their future ones.

For example, Ambassador Panikkar in a recent book wrote:

Imperialism meant something totally different after Lenin's definition of it as the last phase of capitalism and his insistence that the liberation of subject peoples from colonial domination was a part of the struggle against capitalism.[3]

In other words, imperialism is now something that only non-Communists indulge in; but when Communists behave in an imperialistic manner that is "liberation of subject peoples from colonial domination." This, Professor F. S. C. Northrop calls "colonialism by definition." In commenting on this thesis, he has said:

This impotence of definition to transform facts makes one wonder also whether the Vasco da Gama era came to its end, as Ambassador Panikkar maintains it did, when merely the British, French, Dutch, Portuguese and Americans departed from Asia. May it not be necessary, before the historian can write *Finis* on what Vasco da Gama started, for European Russia to depart also, and for contemporary China to be guided by the norms of the peacemakers of the classical Asian spiritual tradition rather than by those of Europe's Marxist Moscow?[4]

A change of the Communist heart is fervently to be hoped for, but meanwhile this is the hour for vigilance, for mutuality, and for a steadfast defense of freedom from attack from whatever source. Then the spark of liberty which the Asians have lit can gradually be fanned into a flame that will not only benefit the masses of Asia, but help to enlighten the whole world.

[3] K. M. Panikkar, *Asia and Western Dominance* (John Day, New York, 1954), p. 264.
[4] *Far Eastern Quarterly* (Feb. 1955), p. 264.

commentary

J. S. FURNIVALL

Advisor to the Government of the Union of Burma

Mr. Mallory's statement of present day trends in the lands of South and Southeast Asia that were formerly under foreign rule is both admirable and extraordinarily concise, and most readers, I suppose, will accept the picture of the modern East which Mr. Mallory has presented. Some, however, may share my hesitation about following his argument. How far are these conditions the aftermaths of colonialism? And what is the colonialism of which these conditions are an aftermath, a second growth? Are they, strictly, an aftermath, a second growth of the same crop? Should we not consider rather more closely the nature of the crop from which this aftermath has sprung?

Mr. Mallory dates the colonial period in Asia from the arrival of the Portuguese. Was it not then, rather, that the colonial period ended? A colonist is by definition a settler in a foreign land, and a colony is a settlement of foreigners. There were foreign settlers and settlements in Southeast Asia long before the coming of the Portuguese. Indians and subsequently Muslims had long settled in these lands and founded colonies from which their religion and culture gradually spread among the surrounding peoples. But, from Portuguese times onward, one may almost say that there were no Western settlers. Formerly England had settlements and plantations. The settlements were colonies, where the settlers carried with them the status of British citizens. But the plantations were merely crown colonies, colonies by courtesy, or rather for convenience, lumped together with the true colonies under the Colonial Office because there was nowhere else to put them. These lands were not colonies; they were possessions. Not so very long ago, a small Burman friend asked me about a question in an examination paper: "To whom do the countries of Southeast Asia belong?" He knew the proper answer for Burma, Malaya, and Indochina. But Siam? That stumped him. It is quite a new thing to describe these lands as colonies. If you look up colony and its deriva-

66

tives in the largest Oxford Dictionary, I do not think you will find a definition which really covers them.

If these lands were colonies, who were the colonists? At a stretch one might possibly say the Portuguese and Spaniards. The Dutch made a very brief and unsuccessful attempt at colonization, and they have always liked to think of their India as a home from home—that is one explanation of their reluctance to leave it. But the English, French and Americans—colonists? No! England used to have colonies before they either broke away or became dominions, acquiring practical and even legal independence. The settlers there were colonists, and a colonial had a certain glamor. He might be crude, unused to the niceties of civilization in the older lands, such as commuting or strap-hanging. But the colonial was a he-man, a free denizen of the wide open spaces; to the mere stay-at-home, every colonial was a Davy Crockett. I remember a suggestion made by Mr. Churchill that there would have been no war if Hitler had recognized in Mr. Chamberlain and his umbrella a Davy Crockett in disguise—a very effective disguise. Why, then, has colonialism become a term of reproach? Who, I ask again, were the colonists?

The Westerner who put in a few years in the tropics until he had made enough money to live at home in comfort was certainly not a settler, a colonist. M. Jules Harmand, if I remember rightly, says in *Domination et Colonisation* that in Indochina, "*le vrai colon, c'est l'Annamite.*" But the Annamese was a native, and not a foreign settler. The Indian and Chinese immigrants who in recent years have settled in these lands in such large numbers comply more nearly with the definition; one does speak legitimately of Indian and Chinese colonies. But the Western colonist is not a man; it is a *business firm*. This was foreseen over a hundred years ago by the Dutch statesman, Du Bus de Gisignies: "We must colonize Java," he said, "not with men but with capital."

Is it correct even to claim that the West colonized the East with western capital? There is a tendency to overlook the fact that, as noticed by Mr. Bekker and others "all these countries have always had export surpluses larger than any possible payments for services . . . they must have exported capital."[1] Most of the large firms, at least

[1] Konrad Bekker, "The Point IV Program," *The Progress of Underdeveloped Areas*, ed. B. F. Hoselitz (Chicago, 1952), p. 237.

until quite recently, grew up from modest beginnings by the accumulation of local capital. The important contribution of the West to oriental economy was not capital so much as *capitalism*. But this term is used so vaguely that it needs definition. By capitalism I mean, at least for the purpose of this commentary, *the system of directing production on rational lines with a view to achieving the maximum surplus or profit over the economic energy expended, together with the habit of employing this surplus or profit for the further increase of production.* Europeans introduced capitalism as an economic system. There is much to be said in favor of capitalism as an economic system. But it tends to develop into more than that; it tends to result in capitalism as a social system and in the transformation of the social order into a business concern. For close on two hundred years the Western world has been engaged in a *social* effort to resist this tendency. But in these lands the foreign rulers did not; perhaps, merely because they were foreigners, they could not resist it. I know no better picture of the result than that given by the eminent Dutch economist, Dr. J. H. Boeke: there was "a total absorption in the Exchange and Market; a capitalist structure with the business concern as subject, far more typical of capitalism than one can imagine in the so-called 'capitalist' countries which have grown slowly out of the past and are still bound to it by a hundred roots."[2]

Here it may be useful to distinguish between India and Southeast Asia. When the Portuguese arrived and still later, when the English came, Indians were ahead of Westerners in many forms of economic activity; the English came as humble traders seeking the favor of oriental potentates; modern India, like modern Europe, grew up after the industrial revolution; and it had the protection of caste against permeation by capitalism. In all these matters India differed from Southeast Asia, with the partial exception of Java. To Southeast Asia Europeans came as conquerors, superior not merely in force of arms but in the strength derived from the industrial, commercial and capitalist revolutions. Not until the opening of the Suez Canal in 1869 was there intimate contact with the West; the impact was more sudden and more violent, and the shield of caste was lacking. Hence it is frequently misleading to draw parallels between India and Southeast Asia.

[2] Dualistische Samenleving, De Economist, 1935, p. 781.

It is true however that India and most of Southeast Asia resembled colonies in not being self-governing. But they differed from colonies in being under *alien* rule and subject to an *alien* economic system. They were possessions, and to refer to them as colonies is a modern euphemism. This is not mere frivolous verbal quibbling. How far do the conditions described by Mr. Mallory derive from colonialism and how far from capitalism? Capitalism, one should note, does not imply merely foreign capitalism. It has often been observed that, when Indians or Chinese, or other Asians or Africans substitute reason for custom in their economic relations they carry it to far greater lengths; within their range of vision they are far more rational than Europeans because they are not subject to the same social inhibitions.

There are, I suggest, two simple tests for comparing the relative influence of colonialism and capitalism. Thailand never lost its political independence. So far as modern conditions in Thailand resemble those in other parts of Southeast Asia there is *prima facie* ground for attributing them to capitalism rather than to colonialism. Now if we go one by one through the points raised by Mr. Mallory we shall find that there is an essential similarity between conditions in Thailand and those elsewhere; the difference is one of degree and seems due to the fact that foreign rule made less resistance than home rule to permeation by capitalism. Or one may apply another test by comparing the lands of Southeast Asia with the older colonies. Independence, according to Mr. Mallory, has released strong divisive forces. Did it release divisive forces in the thirteen colonies of this country? It is true that when they stopped scrapping with King George they began to scrap with one another. But they were divided under foreign rule, and independence released unifying forces, just as independence has made possible the union in Burma of states previously divided. (It is interesting to note that this comparison has already occurred to Prime Minister U Nu.) Moreover, when other colonies attained their independence was there any psychological residuum, a feeling that they were not yet free? Had this feeling any basis in fact? How about Canada? It took nearly half a century from the confederation to establish not merely a feeling of independence but the fact of independence. And now there is a feeling in Canada of shirtsleeves to shirtsleeves in three generations, of colony to freedom and back again to colony. "At one time Canadians watched London for changes to come; now they worry about Washington, and many feel that they have something to worry about."[3] And people worry about Washington in Southeast Asia. The chief criticism which these new governments have to meet at home (at any rate in Burma) is that they are stooges of the Anglo-American bloc, which, of course, they strenuously deny.

They are worried about Washington but, as may be seen from the speeches of U Nu and of the Socialist leader U Kyaw Nyein, they are more worried about Moscow, and fully realize the dangers of the new Communist imperialism. Yet they have, I think, more sympathy with communist *ideals* because they have seen too much of capitalist *practice*. From economic individualism they instinctively react in the direction of socialism, not necessarily, though not excluding, the text book socialism of state control over production, distribution and exchange, but of socialism as the reintegration of a society ravaged by unrestricted capitalism—or, if you prefer the term—colonialism. And, much as they dislike and fear Communist methods and Communist domination, they will, and do, respond more readily to the claim of social duty rather than to the illusion of individual prosperity. Mr. Mallory has given us a very clear account of present conditions and trends in Southeast Asia, but these, I suggest, are not so much the aftermaths of colonialism as the reaction against a particular form of colonialism which the countries there diagnose rightly as imperialist capitalism. Most of them have now obtained political independence. But, like Canada, they still "worry about Washington," despite the help that Washington so generously offers and that they so gratefully (if sometimes reluctantly) accept. Here, I suggest, is an aftermath of the new colonialism as of the old. In this country, America, we can see the flourishing aftermath of the old colonialism. I hope that, with time and patience, we may see in South and Southeast Asia a no less prosperous aftermath of the new colonialism.

[3] W. T. Easterbrook, Hoselitz, *op. cit.*, p. 62.

The progress of nationalism

RUPERT EMERSON

Harvard University

More than twenty years ago I had the pleasure of speaking on nationalism to a group of Indian students at Benares. On that occasion I found that the reception accorded to my remarks was sharply divided into two parts, and I fear that what I write today will achieve the same fate, at least so far as Asian readers are concerned. At Benares I opened with warm praise for the Indian nationalist movement and expressed my hope that Indian independence did not lie too far in the future, and those parts of my remarks were received with understandable enthusiasm. I then moved on, however, to suggest that on the basis of European and other experience nationalism was not an unmixed blessing and that it embraced within it real sins and dangers which I hoped the leaders and the people of the new and rising India might find it possible to avoid. It was here—I suppose equally understandably—that the enthusiasm markedly cooled, perhaps because it was felt inappropriate for a Westerner to indulge in warnings to Indians concerning their own problems, perhaps because the nationalist movement represented so all-absorbing and sacred a cause as to make any suggestion of criticism unacceptable.

My purpose now is to attempt a somewhat similar analysis of nationalism, indicating at the outset what seem to me some of its major virtues and advantages, but going on to point out some of its shortcomings and defects, and more particularly to suggest that for a vast and deeply important array of questions it is essentially irrelevant in the sense that it does not present even the beginning of a clue

71

to the answers. If I were to try to sum up my central theme in a few words, it would be something to the effect that the nationalism which has been the guiding star of Asian peoples seeking independence and an equal status in the world becomes a grossly inadequate guiding star once independence and equality have been won. To look to it as giving the answers is likely to be at best a futile and at worst a damaging and dangerous procedure.

I should like to make one point very clear at the beginning. It seems to me that it ill becomes the Western world to look censoriously at Asian nationalism. The West itself not only has rioted in nationalism in the past, but in the present is on the whole quite unable to live up to the admirable sentiments which some of its spokesmen express or to heed the warnings which they issue. I have no intention of indulging in the perhaps profoundly wise but also highly irritating theme that Asians are foolishly or foolhardily anachronistic in pressing their nationalisms at a time when the objective conditions of the world demand not further splintering and divisions but unity and coherence. However true this contention may be, it is certainly one which applies to the world as a whole and not peculiarly to Asians or Africans. Indeed, it would seem on the face of it that this is a moral which deserves to be applied at home by peoples who are relatively long established in their nationalism rather than by those who are still just tasting the first fruits of it. Coming at the matter from another angle, it is perhaps flattering to Asians to set out with the premise that they are endowed with a larger measure of wisdom than the rest of mankind, enabling them to see and to pursue the unity which others have missed, but it is my inclination to assume that they are merely fallible human beings like the rest of us and that their nationalism will tend to develop in much the same fashion, even taking into account the differences in time, place, and background.

The catalog of the virtues of nationalism can, I think, be presented with reasonable brevity, not by any means because they are few and unimportant but merely because they are well known and highly advertised.

Leaving many doctrinal disputes aside and stripping the matter to its bare bones, I would incline to see nationalism everywhere as essentially not the xenophobic and self-protective effort of an old society and way of life to save and perpetuate itself, but rather as the striving of a society threatened by the intrusion of alien forces to reconstitute itself in order to achieve a new place of dignity and equality in a changing world. If the first reaction of a society attacked by external forces is likely to be a somewhat blind and instinctive defense of the old order, nationalism, as I see it, is a very different kind of response to the challenge of disruption and disintegration. It is typically the response of those elements in the society which have been uprooted from their traditional status and patterns of life, which have moved far into the new world which has been thrust upon them, and which recognize the necessity of a fundamental recasting of the old-established social structure. It is one of the gravest evils of colonialism in its various guises that it works to destroy the self-confidence of those upon whom it is imposed. The nationalists are those who have achieved a new confidence in themselves and their people, in part certainly because they have successfully undertaken a reappraisal of their own society, but in very substantial part also because they have achieved a mastery of the ideas and tools, the institutions and outlooks, of those who have asserted a temporary superiority over them.

Nationalism, then, is a positive and creative response to the shattering impact upon Asia of the modern West. In consequence it means the appearance of a new élan, a new dynamism, in a society which has come to insist on taking the control of its destiny into its own hands. Associated with this dynamism is the stirring of a new and broader sense of unity among the masses whose past role has normally been one of passive acquiescence in, or of ingenious and time-honored evasion of, the dictates of their distant and unfamiliar superiors at the center. The nation is, after all, the people, and nationalism is a new sense of popular self-awareness, spreading down from a newly emergent elite to the people as a whole. To borrow the useful phrase of a recent analyst, nationalism is one of the principal manifestations of a process of social mobilization in which people and peoples who have hitherto passively submitted to the operation of history are now mobilized to participate actively in its unrolling. How deep into the masses the new dynamism and active sense of national unity have penetrated, and perhaps even the focus of the national attachment, is a matter which it is often extraordinarily difficult to determine except in a time of crisis when choice and action become virtually inescapable. Obviously we have here a swiftly changing scene, and one which varies from country to country and from region to region within countries. Certainly the aftermath of the second World War in South Asia, in Indonesia, Indochina, and Burma, and in the rise of Pakistan, demonstrated irrefutably that it had reached much further down than most observers would have estimated. But even at the present day it is still only plausible to assume that there are substantial segments of the population of every country, particularly in the great body of the peasantry, which remain largely untouched by the modern currents and which would far rather linger undisturbed in their old ways than expose themselves to the adventures and hazards of the new.

Even when this has been said, however, I would suggest that the new nations which are at least in the process of creation are themselves some part of the answer to the charge that Asian nationalism is merely an assertion of an outdated parochialism in a world which should be a single close-knit entity. The effective social horizons of the great bulk of mankind throughout history have been confined to the family or village, to the tribe, caste, or some other sharply limited grouping. If nationalism is deplorably far from lifting the social horizons to the range of the whole of humanity, it does work to open a much greater expanse of community than the ordinary individual had previously experienced. Furthermore, it tends to establish a direct relation between the individual on one side and the nation and the nation-state on the other, no longer mediated, or at least not to the same degree, through perhaps a hierarchy of lesser groupings and communities. These things are obviously the result of many currents in the contemporary world which work to promote both the sense of individual identity and of solidarity with the nation: the changes in economic life, the transformation of political and administrative structures, the revolution in transport and communications, not to mention ideas and ideologies; and it is my contention that nationalism is itself a product of these currents. Nor is it only a product. Once nationalism has come into the saddle, it becomes in its own right, at least for a time, the driving cause of further social mobilization and revolutionary change.

Once nationalism has established enough of a hold over the minds and hearts of its own people to be able to challenge the imperial forces, it moves into the great and in some sense decisive battle to overthrow alien domination and encroachment. This battle is a decisive one in the sense that, when it has been won, the nation is free to mould its own destiny within the limits of its capabilities and of the relentless pressures of a clamorous world; but it is very evidently not the end but only the beginning of the road. Where all nationalist energies have hitherto been thrown into the essentially negative task of breaking the bonds of alien control, now, as the South Asian countries have been doing for the past years, they must turn to the positive and creative task of setting the national goals and establishing the institutions of all kinds through which they may be realized.

It is precisely at this point, as I see it, that the utility of nationalism begins to dwindle. To put the matter somewhat paradoxically, nationalism triumphant becomes at the same moment irrelevant in a considerable number of vital spheres. Certainly the virtues of which I have been speaking do not vanish nor are they of small importance. The achievement of a sense of national unity, the breaking down of local and other barriers through the widening of social horizons, the dynamism and political activism which have been injected into the society, the sense of revolutionary élan, the new appreciation of the national worth and dignity, the devotion to the common cause—these are all matters of profound importance to the future of any nation. But it must be recognized that they are assets which tend to fade away and become tarnished once the first great victory of the national revolution has been won and private interests begin to intrude upon the sense of public devotion. President Sukarno has more than once pointed with dismay to the decline in national morale which followed the attainment of Indonesian independence, and the same is surely true in greater or less degree elsewhere. The fine bright flame of revolution inevitably burns itself out before long, and the more humdrum tasks of peaceful reconstruction and advance, so slow to show results, may seem a shabby substitute for the stirring days of violent and heroic action.

There is no need to elaborate here on the familiar theme of the difficulties which so many individuals and groups in South Asia have faced in making the transition from militant nationalist opposition and perhaps from actual warfare to the chores and responsibilities of carrying on everyday life. These range from the problems of youngsters whose lives had been largely spent with weapons in their hands fighting a guerrilla war to the immense readjustment required of, say, the Indian National Congress in its attitudes, organization, and mode of operation as it transforms itself from its earlier accustomed role of enemy of the government into the role of being itself the government. On the whole these difficulties have been met and surmounted in such fashion as largely to discredit the prior warnings of prophets of doom, but the continuing insecurity and scattered local revolts in Indonesia, the still troubled state of some parts of Burma, and various aspects of the tangled situation in Indochina, all bear witness to the fact that the transition is by no means an easy one.

There is another quite different facet of the issues arising from nationalism which deserves a brief glance. It is one with which South Asia is quite familiar. Although it is usual, and on the whole well justified, to see nationalism as primarily a unifying force within each of the national societies, it must be recognized to operate also as a divisive force under certain not infrequent circumstances. Both through its natural operation and through deliberate manipulation it may serve greatly to accentuate the minority problem where there is marked racial, ethnic, or religious diversity. So long as there is an essentially undiluted rule from above, as most strikingly in the old-style colonial regime, even basic diversities among the people ruled may be regarded as of no particular consequence. As soon, however, as a claim for self-determination is put forward in the name of the nation, fundamentally revolutionary elements are introduced. The nation is the people, but who are the people for this purpose? What is the "self" which demands its rights? The nature of nationalism itself forces a separation of the sheep from the goats, which may up to that time have been kept effectively under cover. In India the Moslems swung increasingly to the drive for a separate Pakistan; in Burma the Karens insisted upon a separatism of their own; and everywhere in Southeast Asia new tensions arose in relation to the Chinese. Perhaps most difficult of all, now that India and Pakistan have gone their different ways, is the future of Malaya where the two major racial communities confront each other with an almost equal division of numbers. It may be that the present Malayan electoral alliance holds within it the seeds of future unity, but there is also the very real possibility that two nations will emerge, each laying claim to the country as a whole.

Such issues as these are not, however, the ones I have in mind in putting forth the proposition, which must have a profoundly heretical ring to the ardent nationalist, that nationalism is in great part inadequate and irrelevant when a society is faced with the substantive problems of independence. Perhaps the best approach to what I have in mind is contained in the comment which has been made from time to time, half jokingly but also not without seriousness, that nations are best defined by the negative process of demarcating them from their neighbors; that is, not by seeking out the positive attributes which make this particular nation what it is but rather by laying out the bare fact that, for whatever reason, the French are not German or Italian, the Thai not Burmese or Malay. I do not want to belabor here this somewhat odd approach, but I think that it will be evident to anyone who makes an honest inquiry into it that it is fantastically, indeed impossibly, difficult to determine in any precise and operationally significant terms the special and distinctive attributes of any nation. The flag can be waved, the grand symbols of the nation's history, traditions, and heroes stand ready for the patriotic orator, and the national culture is a monument to the unique achievements of this particular nation—but it is a highly dangerous process to single out as peculiarly constituting the national essence any of the variant strands which enter into the making of a nation. Every nation is the product of many contradictory forces. Every nation is made up of peoples, classes, communities, and groups which have sometimes collaborated, but have also not infrequently warred against and conquered each other or otherwise come into fundamental conflict and opposition. In a famous phrase Renan said: "The essence of a nation is that all the individuals have many things in common, and also that all have forgotten a good many things." The things which must be forgotten on behalf of national unity bulk almost as large and important as those which must be remembered; or, to put it in a perhaps more meaningful fashion, the national memory embraces as well those things which must be forgotten as those which must be remembered. The France of the *ancien régime* is as much a proper heritage of France as is the France of the Revolution. India has a Hindu past, a Moslem past, and a British past, to name only three of the multitude of elements which enter into the making of today's India. Indonesia is Moslem, but it is also secular nationalist, and there are many Indonesians who would stand on neither of these but would give allegiance to the still newer creed of Marxism. Given these conflicting and often irreconcilable strands which are embraced within every nation, I believe it can be said that a liberal nationalism must of necessity abstain from the temptation to define the nation and its values with any precision. It is only with the coming of totalitarianism that the effort is made by arbitrary fiat to exclude certain groups and elements from the multi-colored heritage of the nation, in place of liberalism's implicit acknowl-edgment that the truer national unity rests upon the acceptance of diversity.

Approaching the same matter from a more familiar standpoint, it can certainly be said, as it often has been, that the most vigorous and effective stimulant of a sense of national unity and identity is opposition to a common external enemy. In a colonial situation this boils down to the simple statement that the central rallying point for the nationalists is the struggle against the imperial power from which they seek to free themselves. Although the national heritage and glories are sung, what is of key importance is not that there be agreement on the positive values of the nation but that there be a rallying and joining of forces against the alien. I do not at all mean to imply any basic difference between a colonial and any other people in this respect, but merely to suggest that the discovery and identification of the common enemy is more self-evident under colonialism than in most other circumstances.

If there is at least some measure of validity in these comments, then the next stage is the presumption that the one clear and concrete point of application of nationalism is where the common enemy, actual or potential, is involved. Is it too farfetched to suggest that the per-sistence and the emotional impact of the issue of colonialism in South Asia are derived in part, though by no means wholly, from a sense that if nationalism is to retain its passionate hold, it is also necessary to retain the image of a hostile external object at which it can be directed? To cite a single example, does such an attitude explain some part of the importance of the West Irian question for Indonesia? More generally, I incline to the idea that the questions for which nationalism has at least the start of an answer are those which carry over directly from the days of dependence and which refer to that dependence.

Let us glance briefly at some of the major types of problems with which an independent nation is confronted and try to make out the bearing of nationalism on them. One point certainly is indisputable: nationalism demands the attainment of full sovereign self-government, and insists that decisions which are to be made shall be made by instrumentalities of the nation's own choosing. This is by itself an immensely important determination, but no more can be read into it than precisely what it contains. What I mean by this is that neither the content of the decisions nor the nature and structure of the instrumentalities by which they are reached are contained within nationalism.

To take the last point first, it seems to me obvious that even at the high level of the general structure of the political, economic, and social institutions and systems to be put in force by the newly independent societies, there applies what I might call the principle of national indeterminism, and the same holds for already independent countries like Thailand or Afghanistan if and when they embark on revolution or basic change. Nationalism by itself offers no dependable criteria to guide the choice between the different systems which might be brought into operation. If nationalism represented essentially an effort to return to earlier traditional roots, it might be expected that the search would be for institutions organically related to the national past, although here as elsewhere the national past of every society offers a great diversity from which to choose. There is no single traditional national pattern which inescapably establishes itself as the one which must be followed. In fact, however, it is the almost unbroken experience of the nationalist victories of our days that the drive is not for a return to an older heritage but for the adoption or adaptation of alien forms characteristic of and derived from the alien societies whose imperial sway has just been broken. Here, certainly, nationalism establishes no vantage ground from which to choose between the different types of systems and institutions which the modern West offers in relative profusion, such as variant forms of liberal democracy and of authoritarianism and totalitarianism.

On the face of the brief record to date it appears that in the political realm the institutions of the former mother country have a great influence in determining constitutional patterns—the Philippines, for example, follow the American presidential system, while India and Indonesia have adopted parliamentarism. It is, of course, already clear that these borrowed institutions are caught up in a continual process of change and evolution to fit them more closely to the local needs and genius. In this connection one might speak, in a different sense, of a national determinism at work since no one could argue with the proposition that the institutions and systems which emerge will be the resultant of the forces operating within and on the societies concerned. But for those who must make the decisions the determinism involved in some underlying and inherent necessity can be revealed only by accident and carries no certainty of conviction; and, as in all human affairs, the decisions which are taken themselves significantly affect future developments.

It might be contended that the doctrine of national interest gives the answers on the assumption that those solutions which best advance the national interest will and should be adopted. The hitch in this contention, as I see it, is precisely the same as the one I have been suggesting. The national interest is little, if anything, more than a blank check which still needs to be filled in, and the figures which might be written on it may quite legitimately vary enormously. Communism or socialism, democracy or authoritarianism, traditionalism or Westernization, theocracy or a secular society, and many other alternatives and combinations can be and have been plausibly put forward by substantial groups within every society as embodying the true national interest. Nationalism cannot produce the answers to cleavages such as these existing within the body of the nation itself.

What I have been saying as to institutions and systems in the large applies equally to the lesser and more nearly day to day decisions which every society must make. Let me illustrate by a few concrete examples. In the nationally highly important sphere of language, should India go all out for Hindi as the national language or let English in fact linger on as the Philippines appear to be doing, or should there be a yielding to the demand for linguistic states? Should Indonesia conciliate its threatening separatisms by a turn to federalism, and, if so, what is the proper division of powers and functions, or should it stand firm by the decision to build a single unitary republic? In the economic sphere what should be the relation of private and public enterprise? Nationalization has an appealingly nationalistic ring to it, but in particular and concrete instances does it actually represent the national interest? How much play should Burma and other countries give to foreign investors and entrepreneurs? The resounding nationalist formula might be: None whatsoever; but with what assurance can this be said to represent the best interests of an expanding and developing economy?

In all these and any number of other matters, large and small, the national interest is no fixed point on the horizon but is the inevitable battleground of groups equally embraced within the nation. For South Asia, no less than for other parts of the world, there is always the danger that particular and partial interests, or the adherents of one among several competing ideologies, will succeed in wrapping themselves in the national flag and get away with persuading the rest of the society that they have a justifiable monopoly of the hallowed symbols of the nation.

On the whole the issues so far discussed have been primarily domestic in bearing. When one turns to the international scene nationalism bulks somewhat larger as a relevant force, but for a great number of the issues of foreign policy it is of as little concrete use as it is at home. The foreign affairs counterpart of the domestic demand for self-government is the insistence that the nation not be sold down the river or subordinated to alien interests; but this statement contains at best only the barest bones of an approach to most actual policy issues. Does the national interest dictate alignment with one of the two great power blocs or a policy of neutralism? Does SATO lay out the desirable path, or should there be a striving toward a close alliance, perhaps even some sort of federal union, of South Asian states? Burma rejected the Commonwealth while India, Pakistan, and Ceylon decided in its favor—is the one position more properly nationalist than the other? International organizations, present and potential, are likely to raise questions which involve the surrender on a cooperative basis of some measure of sovereignty, but I would deplore, as would, I am sure, many Asians, the blanket *a priori* answer that nationalism precludes any such pooling in the common interest.

Nationalism as it looks out at the rest of the world has always had two faces which might, in its European guise, be personified as those of Herder and Hitler, Mazzini and Mussolini. The one sees the nation and the achievement of national freedom as the stepping stone toward a peaceful and collaborative world order; the other thrusts the nation forward as the summation of all human values, to which the interests of the remainder of mankind may legitimately be sacrificed if what appears to be the national interest is thereby advanced. Which of the two faces will the nationalisms of South Asia adopt as their own?

There is, I am wholly confident, no reason why the choice should fall to the side of Hitler and Mussolini. In the ultimate analysis it may be that nationalism must stand condemned because it blocks the path to the world community through which alone peace can be assured. I am sure that this is not necessarily so, and there have been many among the Asian nationalist leaders who have denied it with full sincerity and conviction. Nationalism is not only a builder of unity within each of the peoples it has touched; it has also the potentiality of freeing peoples to join voluntarily together for the salvation of all of us.

commentary

HTIN AUNG

Rector of the University of Rangoon

Professor Emerson has expressed an anxiety lest Asian readers should accord a cool reception to his statements. On the contrary, as an Asian, I congratulate him on a fair appraisal of the forces of nationalism in South and Southeast Asia. However, his approach to the subject is that of a political theorist, and therefore he has attempted to generalize and has looked beyond the actual practice, to the theory of nationalism in South and Southeast Asia. As a plain lawyer, however, I will make my comments more on facts than on theory.

I do not think that it is true of all nations in South and Southeast Asia that the idea of nationalism came only as an aftermath of colonialism. At least it is not true of my own people, the Burmese. Just as England because of her insular position, was fertile ground for the early and rich flowering of nationalism, Burma because of her geographical position became acquainted with the idea of nationalism many centuries before the British conquest of the country. Hemmed in on both sides by powerful neighbors, China and India, the Burmese in their long history have always been conscious of their nationality and have ever endeavored to preserve their individuality, although always grateful for the rich cultural gifts from those two powerful neighbors. The early kingdoms of Burmese history, the Pyu Kingdom of Prome and the Mon Kingdom of Thaton were perhaps "international" in outlook and in tradition, but with the establishment of the Kingdom of Pagan, the Burmese withdrew to the upper valley of the Irrawaddy, which served as a shell into which the Burmese could retire to escape from foreign interference. Thus the policy of Burmese kings after Prome was to withdraw their peoples from the dangers of the outside world. To cite but one instance, King Kyansittha of Pagan (1084–1112) refused for his daughter the offer of marriage from a powerful Indian prince of a kingdom in what is now East Bengal, because of the fears expressed by his ministers that the marriage might result in an influx of Indians into the country. This was in the latter half of the eleventh century, when Buddhism had just become the official religion of the kingdom, when Indian monks were teaching the scriptures in the monasteries, and when Indian artisans were helping in the building of the countless pagodas of Pagan.

In times of great national unity and resulting strength this admittedly narrow nationalistic policy of the Burmese kings expanded into a dream of internationalism. The Burmese kings always had a plan to unite the whole of the Indo-Chinese peninsula and the neighboring islands into a great state which could act as an effective buffer between India and China, and which could also take its full part in the great world in a position of equality with India and China. The Burmese chronicles claimed that at one time the Kingdom of Prome was in effect an empire, within whose domain were included the whole of the Indo-Chinese peninsula, and the islands later known as Sumatra and Java. Prome at the time was directly on the trade route between India and the Malayan regions, because the Hindu merchant-adventurers at first hugged the coast in their voyages and only later did they dare to cut across the open sea, comprising the Bay of Bengal and the Gulf of Martaban, and according to legends and folktales, the kings of Prome themselves were merchant-adventurers whose delight was to sail the unknown sea. All this showed that even at Prome, there existed a dream of a Southeast Asian empire. After Prome, Burma was three times united under three great dynasties, and at the peak of its power, each dynasty attempted to translate the dream into reality. Anawrahta (1044–77) of Pagan, Bayinnaung (1551–81) of Toungoo, and Alaungpaya (1752–60) of Ava and his immediate successors were the kings who made this bold attempt. The Burmese attempts to conquer Siam were in pursuit of this policy of uniting Southeast Asia into a state. But under Bodawpaya (1781–1819) of Ava, this idealistic nationalism became imperialistic, resulting in a period of narrow nationalism making the Burmese unduly proud and aggressive. This fierce national pride enabled the country to meet and defeat four separate invasions by the Chinese (1769) but also prompted the army to conquer the Indian kingdoms of Assam and Manipur. The Burmese thus left the protection of their shell, and came out to the strange new world of imperialism and found themselves face to face with the British power in India. It was vital for them to draw back quickly into their shell, but their fierce national pride blinded them to the danger. The extreme and exaggerated nationalism of the period is best illustrated by these two stories, which have now crept into Burmese folk-lore:

> The master of the house said to his servant "Look out of the window. I hear the footsteps of some people." The servant looked and replied, "Sire, there are no people in the street, only three foreigners."

> The quiet of a village was broken by shouts of "A man has fallen into the well!" The villagers came out in alarm, but the first to reach the well looked into it and cried out "Be calm, my friends, it is not a man, but a Chinese!" The Chinese from the bottom of the well shouted back in anger, "If I am not a man, am I a bird? Am I a bird?"

Such fierce pride naturally had a fierce fall, and Burma was conquered by the British after three wars—the Anglo-Burmese wars of 1824, 1852, and 1885.

In my opinion, the introduction of Buddhism into Burma was not a cause of, nor did it affect, Burmese nationalism. However, the fact that Burma fell very little under the influence of Hinduism and was not affected by Islam at all, made it possible for Burmese nationalism to develop unhindered. With Islam, as with Christianity, religious zeal led to religious crusade; and just as the idea of nationalism did not arise when all Europe had the conception of a Christendom, so nationalism could not find a logical place in the world of Islam. Thus in Islamic Indonesia, the idea of nationalism could arise only as a consequence of colonialism. Hinduism, with its emphasis on caste, encouraged class-consciousness in place of nationalism, and therefore, in Siam and the lands beyond, and in the Indonesian islands before the introduction of Islam, Hinduism was an effective check against the coming into being of the idea of nationalism.

However, in Siam, other factors played to bring about the birth of nationalism. In the thirteenth century, pushed by the Chinese, the Thai-Shans overran the whole of the Indo-Chinese peninsula founding in 1229 the kingdom of Assam in the north, and in 1350 the kingdom of Siam in the south, and interfering in the small Burmese kingdoms into which Burma broke up after the fall of Pagan in 1287. Although the Thais called themselves "The Free" and prided in their love of individual liberty, they had no conception of nationalism and they mixed freely with the Burmese, the Mons and the Khmers. The long wars with the Burmese did nothing to rouse the national spirit of the Thais of Siam, and in the varying fortunes of war the Thai chieftains on the frontier often sided with the Burmese and as equally often raided Lower Burma when opportunity occurred. This absence of ideas of nationalism is illustrated by the fact that in the folk-lore and legends of Siam, the Burmese kings Anawrahta and Bayinnaung were always portrayed as the greatest heroes of all time. But the fall of Siam's capital Ayuthia in 1767, ushered in a new era in the history of Siam. Ayuthia had been sacked before, just as the Thais had sacked the Lower Burma capital of Pegu. But the new kings who reigned at the new capital of Bangkok preserved the ruins of Ayuthia to keep alive the memory of the Burmese conquest and thus arouse a spirit of unity and nationalism among the Thais. When Burma had been conquered by the British and Indochina beyond Siam had fallen to the French, it was to the interest of the colonial powers to keep alive the anti-Burmese feeling among the Thais so that an understanding and friendship between the Burmese and the Thais should not become easily possible. Thus European writers on Burma and Siam tended to give undue emphasis to the sack of Ayuthia, and colonial officials never failed to mention Ayuthia whenever the subject of Burma and Siam came into their conversation. Even some American visitors to the region seem to have been influenced by this outdated colonial propaganda. Last year, I led the Burmese Fulbright Board to Bangkok on a courtesy

visit, and when I sat down at a banquet given in our honor by the
Ministry of Foreign Affairs, after giving a speech expressing deep
gratitude to the Thai government, an American diplomat sitting opposite leaned forward, gave me a knowing wink, and whispered, "You
didn't mention Ayuthia." The other day also, in Washington at a din-
ner, an American consular official asked me whether I had ever been
to Bangkok, and when I said I had, he winked and whispered—"You
didn't sack it, did you?" Only recently with the waning of colonial
rule in Southeast Asia, has it been possible for the Thais to forget
Ayuthia and clasp the hand of friendship held out by the Burmese.
Thus, although as a general rule, colonialism is the enemy of nationalism, we find colonial powers using the very idea of nationalism to
further their purposes.

Although the colonial powers must have realized the danger to them
of the rise of a nationalistic spirit, they encouraged racial consciousness
among the minority groups of the various South and Southeast Asian
countries, with a view to limit the influence and the power of the
majority groups. Thus in Burma, the Chins, the Kachins, the Karens,
and the Shans were prompted by the colonial government to give
emphasis to their racial differences from the Burmese, and to ignore
their racial affinities. The factors uniting the various Tibeto-Burmese
tribes were first, Buddhism tinged with the native and pre-Buddhist
worship of spirits, and second, the Burmese language which was the
common heritage of all the Burmese peoples. Both these factors the
British government attempted to destroy and substitute in their places
racial consciousness and racial suspicion. The Shans were racially
different from the Burmese, but the two racial groups had mixed and
mingled for the past ten centuries, and the Shans had been deeply
influenced by Burmese culture, Buddhist religion, and the Burmese
court. As a result, the British government found it difficult to alienate
the Shans from the Burmese. With regard to the Chins, the Kachins,
and the Karens, they belonged with the Burmese to the Tibeto-Burmese
racial group, but they were still not yet deeply influenced by Burmese
culture, and on them the government concentrated. The colonial government was assisted by foreign missionaries, who hoped to introduce
Christianity to these more primitive peoples, and to wean them out
of Burmese cultural influence. In spite of the repeated demands of
the Chin people, the British government prohibited the teaching of the

Burmese language in Chin schools right up to 1941. The foreign missionaries, however, were more successful with the Karens, and the missionaries at once began to evolve the myth that the Karens did not belong to the Tibeto-Burmese group of races, but were either members of the Mon-Khmer racial group, or even one of the lost tribes of Israel. Linguistic research recently conducted by Professor Luce and other European and American scholars has proved beyond all doubt that the Karen language is merely a branch of the Tibeto-Burmese group of languages. As early as 1890, foreign missionaries advised the British government to arm the Karens and use them against some Burmese rebels in Lower Burma, and from that time onwards, the Burma military police and the British army in Burma recruited Chin, Kachin, and Karen military policemen and soldiers, at the same time refusing this privilege to the Burmese and the Shans. When the "dyarchy" or dual control form of government was introduced, and when a more representative form of government was introduced into Burma after the separation from India in 1937, the British government reserved for the rule of the British Governor the so-called frontier areas which really constituted Highland Burma. When the British were negotiating with the Burmese political leaders in 1947 over the issue of independence, some British officials made in secret fruitless endeavors to influence the representatives of the frontier areas to reject the proposed federation with Burma.

The period 1890–1905 marked the lowest ebb of nationalism not only in Burma but in the other countries of Southeast Asia. The colonial powers consolidated their power and glory of conquest, and the sudden improvement of living standards as a result of the impact of Western trade and industry dazzled the conquered peoples. In all the regions of Southeast Asia, native cultures were overwhelmed by the new culture of the colonial powers. But the well-trumpeted victory of Japan over Russia and the emergence of Japan as a great world power aroused the dormant nationalism of the Burmese and inspired nationalistic ideas in the other Southeast Asian countries, and like a giant awakened, nationalism turned militant against colonialism. This militant nationalism was further inspired and encouraged by the appearance of national leaders in India, especially in Bengal. But in Burma, in French Indochina, Malaya and the neighboring islands, leaders were lacking. In Burma, a social-political organization, the Young Men's

Buddhist Association modeled on the Young Men's Christian Association, came into being, which was typical of the new nationalistic plan adopted all over Southeast Asia—a plan itself influenced by the example of Japan—namely to revive national cultures and institutions by remodeling them on Western culture and institutions. The Young Men's Buddhist Association was much less religious than its model, the Y.M.C.A., but it did a great service to the country by the foundation of Y.M.B.A. schools, which conformed to the requirements of the Colonial Government Directorate of Education and took the examinations conducted by the Directorate, but which gave also lessons in the Buddhist scriptures unlike the government schools. In this also the Y.M.B.A. was merely copying the practice of the mission schools, which conformed to the government syllabus, but which also gave bible lessons. By this time, the monastic schools which were the backbone of education under the Burmese kings, had died out, through lack of encouragement by the new government, and the Y.M.B.A. schools purported to take their place in the social life of the Burmese people.

The war of 1914–18 postponed the inevitable clash between the new nationalism and the colonial governments, for the peoples of South and Southeast Asia were still loyal to their colonial governments, and had not yet learned to dream of open rebellion and full freedom. In fact, when one looks back one is surprised at the hold the colonial governments had on the loyalty of the conquered peoples. French Indochina was fully loyal to the French and Burma was fully loyal to the British during the war, and there was a tacit recognition that Germany was the aggressor. Even the most ardent nationalist in Burma did not wish a British defeat, and the Y.M.B.A. school children vied with missionary school children in singing "Rule Britannia" and in hating Kaiser Wilhelm. But the end of the war saw the resurgence of militant nationalism. The labors of Mahatma Gandhi and the Indian Congress inspired the whole of Southeast Asia, and dreams of seizing power from the colonial government by protest and agitation came into being. In Burma, in December 1920, came the great university strike, which was the first open challenge of nationalism to British rule. The University College, Rangoon, had been a college affiliated to the University of Calcutta, but now it was to become the first university for Burma. The University of Rangoon Act gave entire control to the government, and there was to be no autonomy for the university. Before Rangoon, the British government, when establishing universities in India, had followed the tradition of academic freedom and autonomy of British universities and naturally the Act was taken by the Burmese as a repressive measure. The students of the newly established university went on strike, and very soon all the schools throughout the country were on strike. The people gave their full support to the undergraduates and the schoolboys, and the government was forced to amend the University Act. Many of the striking schoolboys never went back to government schools, and new schools were founded by financial support from the public. These new schools and the Y.M.B.A. schools came to be known as the national schools, and later the government was constrained also to give recognition and state aid to these schools. It was the first conflict and the first victory of the nationalists against British rule, and the anniversary of the strike is now celebrated as Burmese National Day. It was a glorious victory, but it left unhappy effects on the schools and the university, which have lasted even to the present day. In India also, the universities became involved in politics about this period, and the Indian universities are also feeling the effects even at the present day. In Burma the Y.M.B.A. movement was eclipsed by an openly militant national movement for freedom, and the General Council of Burmese Associations (G.C.B.A.) was formed. The emphasis was on "Burmese" and not on "Buddhist" which was perhaps an admission that Buddhism, by its very nature could not inspire a militant movement. Yet at this very moment, Burmese monks entered the political arena and became involved in militant nationalism. In vain the elders of the order explained that no Buddhist monk should take part in politics of any sort, and the younger monks were carried headlong in the tide of militant nationalism. For this the colonial government itself was indirectly responsible, because it had withdrawn the patronage given to the Buddhist monks by the Burmese kings, and that patronage involved the right of maintaining discipline in the order through its elders. Many of those young monks were patriots, but they did untold harm to the prestige of the order, and it is interesting to note that when the final struggle for national freedom against the Japanese, and then the British, came, Buddhist monks were not involved.

When the second World War broke out in 1939, the countries of
Southeast Asia were on the whole in sympathy with their colonial
governments and fully recognized Nazi Germany as the aggressor, but
loyalty was lacking, unlike in the first World War. They did not
want a German victory, but at the same time they were ready to take
the first opportunity either to strike a hard bargain with their colonial
governments in return for aid against the enemy or to break away
in open rebellion. When Japan entered the war, the hopes of the
nationalist leaders ran high, for was not Japan their inspiration and
their model? Japanese propaganda played on these hopes, and promises of liberty were freely given. Everywhere the victorious Japanese
armies were received as liberators, but soon they proved that they came
really as conquerors. The promised political freedom did not come,
and instead the harsh rule of the Japanese military police was the key-
note everywhere. The nationalist leaders in every country had to
co-operate with the Japanese, but they were biding their time. When
in 1943 victory was no longer certain to the Japanese, the Japanese
endeavored to revive militant nationalism and leveled it against the
colonial powers who were fighting back for their lost territories. But
at the same time the Japanese endeavored to control it by re-empha-
sizing their idea of a "co-prosperity sphere" in which independent
Asian countries would co-operate with each other, under the leadership
of Japan. The old battle cry of "Asia for the Asians" was used
again. But it was too late. Militant nationalism joined the forces of
the colonial powers to drive out the Japanese, and then proceeded to
free Southeast Asia from the same colonial powers.

One phase of militant nationalism was economic nationalism. After
just one or two decades of colonial rule, the Southeast Asian countries
found that the new trade and commerce benefited others but not their
own nationals. It was a trite remark of history books written by European officials of the colonial government that the opening of the Suez
Canal brought prosperity to Burma, but no mention was made of
the fact that the Burmese cultivator by the year 1910 was much poorer
than his counterpart under the Burmese kings, and the benefits of
the new commerce went to Europeans, Indians, and Chinese who had
come to the country to accumulate wealth and then return to their
own countries. It was laissez-faire according to the colonial governments, but it was economic exploitation to the nationalists. The result

was the rise of economic nationalism. In Burma, this economic nationalism had a history of its own. When the British finally conquered Burma in 1885, they seemed to have wavered between varying
forms of administration suitable for the country, but finally chose to
make it an administrative unit of the Indian Empire. It was most illogical and, for the colonial government, it was most unwise. It was to cause
great resentment when the new nationalism came into being, and at
the same time, it gave a reason for the nationalists to demand step
by step the same measure of political freedom as given to India.
Above all, it opened the door of unrestricted immigration into Burma.
Without restraint of any sort, Indian merchants and Indian laborers
could come into Burma at will. Rangoon was just another Indian
port from the point of view of the administration, and thousands of
Indians had merely to buy a ticket, board a steamer at Madras or
Calcutta, and soon they were in Rangoon. Burma was the land of
gold to the Indian merchants of the early centuries of the Christian
Era, but to the Indian immigrants of the twentieth century, it must
have seemed a sitting duck with flesh and eggs of gold. Chinese merchants also came in, but luckily for the country not in great numbers.
Big European firms controlled the import of Western goods and the
export of Burmese rice and timber. Indian and Chinese petty merchants
profited from the leavings of the European firms. The Indian moneylenders with their usurious rates of interest soon had the Burmese
cultivator on his knees, but when the Burmese cultivator through debt
had to cease to be a small landholder and became a farm laborer,
his trouble did not end as he then had to compete with the Indian
laborer whose standard of living was lower. When the rich oil fields
of Yenangyaung were developed, their liquid gold enriched only the
European shareholders of the Burma Oil Company, the American and
Scottish technicians, and the Indian coolies. By the year 1930, the
plight of the Burmese cultivator was pitiable indeed. To add to his
woes, the world depression of 1929 reached Burma in 1931. The result
was the rebellion of 1931. It was a peasants' rebellion, born of sheer
desperation. The nationalist leaders had no hand in the rebellion,
and they had no great influence over the rebels, and even if they had,
they would have advised against the rebellion, for even with the more
militant nationalists in other South and Southeast Asian countries, it
was realized that it was then not possible to obtain political freedom

from the colonial powers by an appeal to arms. The Burmese rebellion of 1931 was perhaps the nearest Asian counterpart to the Peasants' Revolt in medieval England. Armed only with swords and sticks, the Burmese cultivators had no hope or chance of victory, but the rebellion was a protest against both the British official and the Indian immigrant. In the wake of the rebellion came the British proposal to separate Burma from India, so that it would become a political unit on its own. Coming as it did at the height of anti-Indian feeling, the proposal was welcomed by some of the nationalist leaders, but others were suspicious. They thought that the British wanted to slow down the pace of political reforms in Burma, so that when Dominion status finally came to India, Burma would not be in a position to demand equality of treatment. In fairness to those leaders, it must be admitted that the British did propose in 1919 to leave out Burma from the dyarchy reforms of India, and Burma was ultimately included only after nationalist protests. The attitude those nationalist leaders had to take was a most difficult one. At home they were against Indians, but at the same time they admired the political leaders of India and wanted to hitch their wagon of political freedom to the star of India. However, in 1937, Burma became a separate administrative unit of the British Commonwealth, and was given the same constitutional reforms as given to India. The Burmese nationalist leaders who were in the new Cabinet under the reforms swiftly introduced immigration laws, which were resented by the Indian immigrants, but which were appreciated by the nationalist leaders in India itself. However, the Japanese invasion resulted in a general exodus of Indians and Europeans, and to a lesser extent, of Chinese, from Burma, and when Burma attained her independence in 1948, the immigration problem had solved itself. The poverty of the masses in Burma and other countries of South and Southeast Asia stood out against the background of twentieth-century industry and commerce, and naturally inspired the nationalists to aim at economic freedom as the next goal after the attainment of political freedom. After the second World War, with independence gained and the colonial enemy no longer in the field, economic nationalism came to the fore, and all over South and Southeast Asia, the ideal was nationalization of industry and trade. Admittedly the new national governments made some mistakes in pursuing their policy of nationalization of industry and trade, but their policy did stabilize the economy of their country, which had been disturbed, distorted, and disintegrated by the long years of colonial rule and the catastrophe of the Japanese war.

As Professor Emerson pointed out, the achievement of independence by the South and Southeast Asian countries was followed by a period of disunity and internal strife. However, perhaps it will not be fair to blame nationalism for that. A great change is always followed by a period of readjustment, and just as the loss of independence by the South and Southeast Asian countries was a great upheaval, the regaining of that independence was an equally great upheaval. Just as powerful allies tend to quarrel among themselves after the final victory in a great war, the nationalist leaders after independence of their countries found themselves without the old unity and mutual trust. But that does not mean that South and Southeast Asian countries would keep their peoples in perpetual fear of the bugbear of colonialism. It is certain that not one of the newly independent Asian countries really fears the return of her old colonial master, and not one of the colonial powers concerned hopes to regain her lost territory. I do not think that the newly independent countries are really bitter against those countries from whose colonial rule they have just escaped. At least I can say of the Burmese that they have only warm regard and affection for the English people. Even during the fever pitch of nationalism, before the gaining of independence, the Burmese had a high regard for English culture and institutions, and in 1942 the retreating British soldier and civil official were assisted and helped by the Burmese, and there was never treachery or bitterness from either side. If some Southeast Asian leaders still speak of the danger of imperialism, it is because the meaning of the word has changed.

Professor Emerson suggested that nationalism had two faces, and his words created in my mind's eye a picture of a monster with two faces, one angry and distorted, with the desire of trampling on all other nations for the greatness of his own, and the other face smiling and kindly, with the intention of leading his nation to live in peace with others. I do not think that this is a true picture of nationalism. Nationalism when it aims at destroying other nations ceases to be nationalism at all. Nationalism is like liberty. One loves liberty only when one values not his own liberty but the liberty of others. I cannot shout "I am a free Burmese," and then park my car at a crossroad.

Nationalism is the foe of imperialism, but although it may seem a paradox, nationalism when it becomes militant, can lead a country toward imperialism. But that does not mean that nationalism and imperialism are merely variations on the same theme.

Nationalism in South and Southeast Asia was militant only against colonialism, and as the countries become more and more used to their new status of sovereign states, this mood must pass. Nationalization of commerce and industry has definitely slowed down, and in Burma two British firms, namely the Burma Oil Company and the Burma Corporation (a mining company) have resumed their operations in joint venture with the Burmese government, and the recent pronouncements of the Burmese government make it clear that foreign capital will be welcome in the country. The growing pains of independence seem to be rapidly disappearing if we take South and Southeast Asia as a whole. In Burma racial conflict and racial misunderstanding have given place to racial harmony, and an appreciation of the fact that Burmese culture and Burmese nationality belong to all the racial groups and not to one particular group. Professor Emerson suggested that the Karen insurrection was due to the nationalist desire of the Karens to have a separate state. In actual fact, the Shans, the Kachins, and the Kayahs have been given separate states, and the Chins declined the offer of a separate state, being satisfied with a Chin Special Division, yet they are as proud of their Burmese citizenship as the Burmans themselves. Moreover, it was agreed from the beginning that there should be a Karen state. The dispute was as to the actual territorial limits of that state. Happily that has now been settled. The various racial groups of the country now realize that Burmese national culture is a common heritage like the Burmese language, and that each racial group has contributed and will continue to contribute to the preservation and development of that culture. As illustrations, I may mention these: (1) There has been a revival of interest in ancient Mon culture both among the Burmese and the Mons themselves, because it has been found that Mon culture originally served as the base for the new superstructure of Burmese civilization of the Pagan period. (2) Recently at a small Karen village on the Salween was found a cherished tradition of the dance forms of the Burmese court of the later nineteenth century. In the same way, the controversy over the language question and linguistic states in India will be solved by the realization that

Indian culture is neither Aryan nor pre-Aryan, neither Hindu nor Muslim, but a compound of all these. This multiracial nationalism with its multiracial cultural traditions is surely familiar to the American members of this audience. In the United States, there are many racial groups, and each seems proud of its own racial origins, but all are proud of their American citizenship and the American way of life.

I believe that nationalism, shorn of its militant coating, will remain the guiding star of South and Southeast Asia, for without nationalism, no country can prosper. The dangers and limitations of nationalism are fully realized by the South and Southeast Asians, but it is not because they are endowed with a larger measure of wisdom than the rest of mankind, but because of the stormy part their region has played in the aftermath of the second World War. They insist on the equality of all sovereign states, as recognized in the Charter of the United Nations, but at the same time, like the characters in *Animal Farm*, they know that some states are "more equal" than others. The states of South and Southeast Asia, except India, are small, and they fear aggression as only small states can fear. They want time, capital, and technical assistance from richer countries to develop their lands. In addition, they have a sense of unity, of understanding, and of similarity among themselves. All these factors will guarantee that South and Southeast Asian nationalism does not become militant and aggressive. The Bandung Conference, in my opinion, is a happy augury of the further achievements of nationalism in South and Southeast Asia.

Problems of political development

RICHARD L. PARK[1]

University of California (Berkeley)

There is a beguiling compactness in the term "South and Southeast Asia" that belies the variety of experience residual in the political units comprising the region. Twenty years ago it would have been reasonable to expect a greater level of precision in any discussion of problems of political development relating to that region, but since then the struggles between British, Dutch and French imperial policies, on the one hand, and the aspirations and demands of the several nationalist groups, on the other, have given a framework for analysis that has scope and definition. Ten years ago, at the end of World War II, the situation changed markedly: the awakening of a whole continent to its independence was apparent. However tortured were to be the years to full nationhood one could afford in 1945 to be idealistic about the "golden era" that was to arise with the rejection and expulsion of foreign rule from the continent of ancient lineage.

The analytic task before us now offers few opportunities for the use of resounding clichés and overstuffed generalizations. Every one of the countries in South and Southeast Asia is occupied with experiments in the processes of government, the ramifications of which lead to yet more experiments and to their resulting institutional consequences. Although change is characteristic of all operative political systems, the rapidity and (occasional) eccentricity of such political movements in Asia run on at an accelerated pace that defies leisurely summarization.

[1] The author wishes to thank Richard S. Wheeler for his assistance in the preparation of this paper.

It may be that most of us in the West (and indeed we may share the illusion with many Asians) are so impressed with the familiarity of Western-style political institutions to be found throughout Asia that we fail to recognize the radical adaptations that are rendering some of these institutions familiar in name only. One of the purposes of this essay is to evaluate the degree to which the political principles and practices of constitutional and parliamentary government have established firm foundations in the region concerned.

It would be presumptuous to present an attempt at comprehensiveness in approaching "Problems of Political Development" in South and Southeast Asia. There are, however, a series of questions that have occupied the minds of close observers of the region and these would seem to be worthy of further discussion and study. A few of these have been selected for comment, on the understanding that contrary views, a choice of different questions and a selection of other specific experiences would be expected from other observers.[2]

Time may be the master healer, but most of the leading political elements in Asia today are unwilling to bind up their economic and social wounds and wait for the inevitability of years to bring national well-being. One of the legacies of nationalist enthusiasm during the struggles for freedom is a long list of promises to the people that must be met, at least in part and quickly, if those who organized for freedom are to remain in power. In several countries, notably India, Burma and Indonesia, the local Communist party, or authoritarian parties of the extreme right, are among the serious contenders for political power in the event of failure of the existing governments. This is only part of the story of time.

Of paramount importance is the necessity for sustaining the atmosphere of national self-confidence and vigor that came with independ-

2 The following books may be consulted for more extended discussions: Rupert Emerson, *Representative Government in Southeast Asia*, Harvard University Press, 1955; Sydney D. Bailey, *Parliamentary Government in Southern Asia*, Institute of Pacific Relations, 1953; *Problems of Parliamentary Government in Colonies*, The Hansard Society, 1953; Sir Ivor Jennings, *The Commonwealth in Asia*, Oxford, 1951; George McT. Kahin, *Nationalism and Revolution in Indonesia*, Cornell University Press, 1952; Virginia Thompson and Richard Adloff, *Minority Problems in Southeast Asia*, Stanford University Press, 1955; William L. Holland, ed., *Asian Nationalism and the West*, Macmillan, 1953; Phillips Talbot, ed., *South Asia in the World Today*, University of Chicago Press, 1950.

ence. Even though raising the standard of living in India, or developing a literate society in Burma may be tasks for many generations,
the element of hope that comes with dramatic, creative strides in at
least a few directions is as essential as are the thorough plans for
evolutionary change and development represented in Five-, Six-, and
Seven-Year Plans. Both the long-range planning, and the short-range
symbolic pilot achievements are borne by the whirlwind, and effectiveness plus drama are the marks of their grounding in success.

Prime Minister Nehru emphasized the importance of time in a
speech before the Lucknow Conference of the Institute of Pacific Relations in 1950: "We have suddenly arrived at a stage when we have
to run. Walking is not enough—and in running we tumble and fall
and we try to get up again. It is no good anybody telling us to walk
slowly . . . . It involves risks and dangers but there is no help and
no choice for it, for there is a torment in our minds . . . ."

Politics cannot escape the popular pressures that insist on social
and economic reform. It is in the realm of politics that the leadership
and discipline necessary to effect reform legislation take place. It is
here that ideas and dreams are forged into potential realities. Thus we
should not be surprised that in countries such as India, where strong
political leadership and a relatively stable political society are combined, there have been greater strides toward social and economic
rejuvenation than in countries such as Pakistan and Indonesia, where
political strife has hindered a comparable development.

Urgency and experiment are characteristic elements of action in the
most vital areas of Asia today. Among the most impressive aspects of
Communist China to Indian and other visitors from Asia has been the
disciplined enthusiasm that seems to pervade the countryside. For
those who experience general apathy, querulousness in political debate
and ponderous procedural delay in their own countries, the Peking
regime reflects a set of positive attitudes that are persuasive of imita-
tion. It may be that China's ability to harness her population to a
pattern of constructive work is a more compelling lure to Asians than
the philosophy of Marx and Lenin, as interpreted by Mao.

The Hansard Society in London, devoted as it is to the study of
parliamentary government, is as much concerned with the developments of institutional forms of government in India, Pakistan, Ceylon,
Burma and Indonesia, to name a few, as it is to the examination of

similar experiences in the Atlantic community. One of the truly remarkable consequences of west European imperial connection in South and Southeast Asia has been the impact that Western political ideas and institutional forms have made throughout the area. The rule of law, cabinet responsibility, representative government, parliamentary procedure and political parties are now established principles of government in Asia. Even in Communist China, as in the Soviet Union, at least the outward forms of parliamentary or constitutional government are to be found. As always, however, appearance and reality often are separated by wide gaps.

It would be difficult for anyone to enunciate a universally acceptable definition of parliamentary government, to include criteria understood by all to be essential to its theory. In origin, both constitutional and parliamentary government stem directly from the Western political tradition. Many of the rules of procedure and the forms of operation can be traced back to historical circumstances that must seem highly remote to an Indonesian politician, for example. However, the beauty of the parliamentary tradition has been its ability to encompass a wide variety of local circumstances and to adjust, within given theoretical limitations, to quite different objectives. A study of British, French, and Dutch experience, to say nothing of American adaptations and drastic changes, would lead one to be less ready to criticize the experimental parliamentary regimes in Asia.

As a matter of fact, parliamentary government has been effective in very few countries, and it would be well to resist judging Asian experiences against any preconceived norm, particularly the classic case of Great Britain. Sydney Bailey[3] has suggested a principle that might better be recognized as the general rule: "Parliamentary government is not a precise piece of constitutional machinery but a method of resolving the conflicts of society in a controlled manner."

In order for such sophisticated forms of government to operate in any country, the state itself must be viable and secure. This is one of the reasons why most of the countries of Asia are concerned by the prospects of armed hostilities, for it is felt that any widespread conflict would affect Asia directly and that such conflicts would strain democratic government to the breaking point. Similarly, as a domestic

[3] Sydney Bailey, *Parliamentary Government in Southern Asia*, p. 11.

issue, both Communist and other disruptive political and social elements remain as a constant threat to the peace and security of the
countries concerned. In India, for example, where an excellent record
may be cited on behalf of vigorous, constitutional government, it has
been found necessary to retain a Preventive Detention Act for use by
the executive branch of government in preventing potential outbreaks
of violence against the considered best interests of the state.

Although students of civil liberties may be shocked to realize that
such preventive detention is practiced in times of peace in a country
that purports to be democratic, long second thoughts should be given
to the effectiveness with which disruptive elements have been dealt
and to the present relative stability of Indian society. The phrase "in
times of peace," also, might be subjected to scrutiny. Who is to say
that the years from 1947 to 1955 were peaceful in the usually accepted
sense of the term? It is, indeed, remarkable that parliamentary government has needed so few protective props in the socially revolutionary
postwar years in Asia.

Nevertheless, there are certain special problems that continue to face
most of the governments of South and Southeast Asia in the operation
of parliamentary government. India, Pakistan, Ceylon, Burma and
Indonesia all have problems relating to national unity. The most
dramatic of these cases, of course, is that of Pakistan where the physical
division of the state adds thorny issues to politics that are yet to be
solved in a satisfactory manner. At this juncture, with the unification
of West Pakistan and on the basis of a newly-elected Constituent Assembly, a constitution for Pakistan may be in the offing. But if the
case is more dramatic in Pakistan, the same category of difficulties
may be found in the other countries also. These states are concerned
with working out constitutional principles that are acceptable to a
great variety of religious, racial and linguistic minorities. If the
founding of Pakistan helped to solve part of the minority controversy
involving Muslims in undivided India, there are now two minority
problems in Indo-Pakistan: the Hindus, particularly in East Pakistan;
and the Muslims in India.

Federalism, as a principle, is accepted in India, Pakistan and Burma,
but is a matter of considerable controversy in Indonesia. There are
those in unitary Ceylon who advocate a federal scheme even for that
small country. It is probable that some form of federalism will develop

in most of the countries of South and Southeast Asia because of the varieties of peoples involved, and because of difficulties in transportation and communication. At the same time, in every case where the federal principle has been accepted, the weight of authority and power is retained by the central government. Some measure of a planned economy and of national development in resources, human and material, has been accepted by all these countries. It is for this reason that a pattern of federalism as understood in the United States finds few advocates in Asia. Indeed, the terms "welfare state," "socialism," and "planned economy" have affirmative connotations in Asia rather than the reverse, and they relate to a centralization of power.

Nowhere have the constitutional fathers of South and Southeast Asia been more thorough than in their insistence on the granting of fundamental political and civil rights. In the past there have been so many instances of racial, social, political, and religious discrimination in their societies (not only during the periods of imperial control), that the guaranteeing of fundamental rights to all citizens finds few—if any—detractors. Of course, these rights tend to be more closely related to ideals than to realities, in Asia as well as elsewhere. But as guides to governmental action and as sign posts to the forces of public opinion, the ideals are important components of the constitutional, democratic tradition. It has been pointed out, on the contrary side, that there is a danger that the enumeration of fundamental rights may lead to their acceptance as the maximum, rather than the minimum, freedom that the citizen may expect. The courts may be expected to assist the citizen in this respect. And, fortunately, the law is highly revered as a social control and as an institution of freedom in most of Asia.

Minorities and their protection, as well as their merging into the general political community, continue to vex most of the countries under consideration. In India, certain communities, notably the Anglo-Indians, untouchables and backward tribes have been given a strictly limited opportunity for protected political representation during a transition period. Pakistan has introduced special electorates for Hindus as a minority safeguard. In Burma, minorities are given special representation in the Upper House, as well as weighted representation to the Karen community in the Lower House. Ceylon has constructed her parliamentary constituencies in such a way that the minority communities are assured of some representation. With the possible exception of Pakistan, however, it appears to be the objective of these states to build a political community in which the need for special safeguards for minorities will be unnecessary. It may be assumed that it will be many years before such an eventuality will become a reality.

On the whole, the formal procedures of parliamentary government have met with considerable success in South and Southeast Asia in the postwar years. Few serious suggestions have been raised for altering, fundamentally, the principles and institutions of this form of government.

One of the obstacles hindering the full acceptance of parliamentary government throughout the mass of the population in Asia is the gulf that separates the ruling elite and the ordinary citizen. For the most part, the men who run the countries of South and Southeast Asia are sophisticated, educated, experienced men who are well informed concerning the Western tradition. In some instances, these same men have a learning and insight relating to their own people and its tradition that matches their Western orientation. But at best, the rulers are men with hands in two or more worlds, and it is this political ambidexterity that tends to separate them from their own people.

The problem is particularly acute in these crucial years of nation-building because of the fact that almost all of the top leaders received their education in Europe and find themselves at least partially committed to the European ideas and institutions with which they are familiar. In Asia's villages, there is no comparable commitment. Through education, political experience, better communication and social camaraderie, the gulf between the rulers and ruled may be expected to close in the years to come. But the chances are that the movement in ideas and institutions will be a two-way passage, with indigenous experience gradually gaining a greater foothold as parliamentary traditions are severely adapted to local needs and wishes.

The time for the creative political theorist will come in due course. A reading of the Constituent Assembly Debates in India does not reveal a searching for fundamentals of the character to be found in the situations following the American, French and Russian revolutions. The chances are that the relatively easy transition from imperial control to freedom in South and Southeast Asia did not raise the same kind of issues that faced post-revolutionaries. But there can be little doubt about the fact that we have witnessed a major revolution in Asia in our time; in due course a political theory to match the challenge for radical response will arise. One exception to the general rule has been Pakistan, where the search for an Islamic state theory has been a most potent force in recent years. For those who are satisfied with effective institutions of government, and who are untidy about the theoretical underpinnings of those institutions, the bitter dispute in Pakistan over theoretical matters may appear chaotic and even unnecessary. But political experience would seem to point to the ultimate importance of a close union between institutions and political philosophy. It may be ventured that the ruled, as opposed to the rulers, in Asia are more concerned with their society's purposes, and thus with philosophy. The tremendous impact of Mahatma Gandhi in India is to be reckoned with by those Asians of more pragmatic and secular persuasion.

An independence movement is not the best breeding ground for political parties in the Western sense. In the search for unity in opposition to the ruling imperial power, the Asian nationalist movements exerted every effort to bring all factions together into one independence-bound organization. The Muslim League for Pakistan, the Indian National Congress, the Nationalists in Indonesia and Ceylon and the Anti-Fascist People's Freedom League in Burma were built on the principle of unity. After independence, as was natural, these movements tended to break down, with groups of minority views leaving the parent body to form new political groupings. However, the impetus given to the majority group in the original movement by the tradition of the past has allowed certain individuals and their followers to dominate the political scene in South and Southeast Asia since independence. It is this circumstance of history that has given most of the area a relative stability that a well-organized political party system might have hindered.

Even today, with the possible exceptions of Pakistan and Indonesia, the parties of independence have no major rival in their local political arenas. Where the Communist party and socialist groups have some strength, as in India, Burma and Indonesia, for example, the rivals' strength is small in comparison to that of the ruling party. Much of the success of the legislative and planning programs in these countries can be traced to the large, disciplined majorities held by the party in power in the respective parliaments. The hard test of parliamentary government, of course, will come when this situation no longer prevails. One finds a preview of the complexities of hard-boiled party and opposition party politics in both Pakistan and Indonesia.

There have been several minor governmental problems arising from the novelty of party government in Asia that have made the task more difficult. For example, the tradition of collective cabinet responsibility has been challenged in almost every country under consideration. Also, the secrecy of cabinet meetings has been broken on several occasions, not always by minority-party members. In addition, the definition of the respective responsibilities of ministers of government, members of Parliament, and senior civil servants continues to confuse efficient self-government. There is nothing particularly unique about Asia that brings on these problems for they are commonplace in Europe and the United States also. But the precedents being set by these pioneers in modern Asian government are too important to be by-passed.

There are those who feel that providing sound government, which is to say good government, is the primary responsibility of the civil service. Although the generalization may be unnecessarily broad and unfair, it is suggested that in most of the countries of South and Southeast Asia administration, rather than politics, holds the higher status in public esteem. The aspiration of most students of excellence is a post in government, which is to say within the administration of government. Politics, as such, involving work for a political party, holds little chance for personal security and as yet offers only modest social status except in the highest realms.

Probably because of the large majorities held by the ruling parties, the assumption seems to prevail that there are right and wrong, correct and incorrect public responses to issues facing the political community. The function of government, then, is to study the facts and come up with correct solutions, following which legislation is to be passed and the laws enforced. In general, this is the frame of reference of many civil servants. The situation is compounded in South and Southeast Asia by the distance separating the rulers and the ruled. "The masses" too often is accepted as a term connoting a pliable group that needs to be taught what is right and wrong. As a politics of diversified policies of government gains a greater foothold in Asia, it is to be expected that the power of the "masses" will rise, and the dominance of the professional administrators and their ministerial colleagues will decline.

The developmental nature of the work being undertaken by the governments in Asia does call for superior service from the professionals. But the change from a civil service of imperial control to a public service in the building of welfare states calls also for a change in the orientation of public administrators. For the most part, this change has not yet taken place. In formerly British-controlled areas, the system of local district officers representing the long arm of the professionals in government has been retained with only minor changes. As a matter of fact, the district administrative system has a grand tradition of efficiency and sensitivity to local needs. However, these local administrators are not political, and they respond lightly to local political advice; thus, as far as most local government is concerned, a *politically* irresponsible, powerful element tends to retard the development of local self-government—which is to say politically-oriented government.

The problems of political development in South and Southeast Asia are those with which we should be familiar, for, on principle, they are ageless problems without geographical limitation. It is far too early to hazard bold generalizations about the ultimate nature and forms of government that will evolve in this vast region. A magnificent opportunity is now present, however, for the adaptation of the traditions of parliamentary government (traditions that have served so many bountifully elsewhere) to the ancient cultures of Asia that strive today for tomorrow's fulfillment.

commentary

G. L. MEHTA

Ambassador from India to the United States

While I wish to congratulate Dr. Park sincerely on his illuminating essay, I have a grievance against him in that he has said very little with which I do not agree, and it is, therefore, difficult for me to make any comments in a spirit of controversy. All that I intend to do, therefore, is to supplement and amplify some of the points touched upon by Dr. Park.

In the first place, I think it is necessary to realize that it is yet too soon to judge the trend of political development in South and Southeast Asia. This is not only because countries in this region attained their independence less than a decade ago, but also because of the international situation. What is called the cold war has in many ways affected domestic political situations and relations. For instance, soon after the attainment of independence by some of these countries, the local Communist parties tried to organize insurgent movements which, however, rebounded on them. A popular government having come to power on the crescendo of a national movement could not be easily upset and could rally public opinion. Moreover, the fact that most Communist parties are presumed to have affiliations with movements outside the country and are understood to take instructions from abroad has weakened their position in countries which have just emerged from a dependent status and value their hard-won freedom. But, above all, economic and social conditions have influenced and are bound to influence profoundly political trends in these countries. Poverty, unemployment, low purchasing power, absentee landlordism, smallholdings and fragmentation of land, vagaries of the monsoon, dependence of economies on a few raw materials—these and similar conditions and problems intimately affect the political environment. The difficulties of Burma in regard to disposal of rice, of Indonesia about disposal of rubber, the divergence in economic conditions between East and West Pakistan, the volume of unemployment in India are all issues which are far deeper than those of constitutional machinery and forms of government. The people of these lands will judge a political system by the manner in which and the speed with which it removes social and economic disabilities and insures equality of opportunity. It is not necessary to be a Marxist in order to realize that economic conditions and social relations are fundamental in a political system. The community, in Prof. Barker's words, "thinks justice into existence."

We must, therefore, realize, as Dr. Park has pointed out, that political development in Asian countries even though democratic in character need not necessarily be of the same pattern as the Western types of parliamentary or presidential forms of government. While the democratic concept in the sense of sovereignty of the people is vital, its forms and mechanism need not be the same in all countries. It is essential to emphasize this because there is sometimes a tendency to interpret the democratic system in rigid terms and equate it with certain forms of government and administration which have developed in many Western countries. While in Britain measures of democratic reform followed the industrial revolution—indeed, universal suffrage might be called the product of the steam-engine—forms of representative government have been established in Southeast Asian countries first, while industrialization has yet to develop. Asian countries will have to evolve their own patterns of democracy. Their historic background, their traditions and culture, their economic conditions and ways of living are radically different from those of the Western world. Their economy is based primarily on land, and the village is still a predominant factor in the lives of millions of human beings. It is obvious that Western democratic institutions cannot be superimposed on Asian countries. Transplantation of such institutions without the social and economic milieu might mean copying only the obvious and the superficial while leaving out the essential. To broadbase the structure of representative government on a population that is poor and largely illiterate is by no means easy. There is the continuous temptation of preferring totalitarian methods and of exploiting the masses by forming popularly irresponsible cliques. We in India, however, have chosen the hard but straight path of democracy. Despite the warnings of pessimists and doubts of sceptics about the advisability of adopting universal suffrage, the Indian constitution embodies this

principle and the electorate has till now vindicated the trust reposed
in it. In our general elections in the winter of 1951–52, nearly 107
million persons voted out of a total electorate of 172 million. Since
then we have had general elections in three of our states. In Travancore-
Cochin, in the southwest of India, in 1954 the percentage of people
who voted was 88.6; in the northern state of PEPSU (Patiala and East
Punjab States Union) the percentage was 88.8; and in the more recent
Andhra elections this year, the percentage was 74.9. There has not
only been widespread and intense public interest, but also a fine discrimination and judgment on the part of the electorate which has
surprised many people. No wonder foreign observers have said that
India has taken to democratic politics.

I should like to pass on to problems relating to national unity
mentioned by Dr. Park. Although nationalism has been the vital
force in Asian countries, there are racial and communal differences and
regional loyalties which impede and hamper national unity. So far
as India is concerned, we have a constitution which is fundamentally
secular in character and recognizes no differences based on caste,
creed, color, race or sex. This is also true of Burma and Ceylon which
have a Buddhist majority, Indonesia which has a Muslim majority
and the Philippines which has a Catholic majority. Members of minority communities occupy not only important posts in our central and
state cabinets but also hold high diplomatic posts (the first Indian
Ambassador to Washington after independence was a Muslim); they
hold appointments in civil services as well as the defense services.
Special efforts have been made to assist the backward communities
through educational opportunities and economic assistance. Because
of its size and diversities, India has adopted the principles of federalism in its constitution which has three categories of power—Union,
State and Concurrent. There has been in India a demand for states
based on the linguistic principle, and a commission is examining the
whole question of states' reorganization and is expected to submit
its report this fall. It is true that in the past, certain disintegrating
tendencies thwarted Indian unity. But whatever the merits and demerits
of reorganization of states on a linguistic basis, there cannot be any
question of a breakdown of government or administration since all
the states are integrated in the Indian Union. The financial powers
and control of the Union government, the needs of modern defense

and the demands of national planning would all tend to prevent any centrifugal tendencies. No doubt, India like other modern countries has, and will have, practical questions of co-ordination between the center and the states and of sustaining and encouraging local initiative and enterprise while maintaining national cohesion and the broad pattern of the national plan.

Dr. Park has rightly referred to the need for leadership and discipline because a constitution is, after all, an instrument of the will of the people. I hope I can say without immodesty that the leadership in India since independence has been of a caliber which has not only held the country together but has been laying strong foundations for its future progress and has been setting it firmly on the path of economic and social development. But Indian leaders want to lead, not to drive the people, to persuade them and not to coerce, to govern and not to enslave. Let me also add that the transfer of power which took place in many Asian countries was in the nature of a constitutional revolution; it involved no breakdown of government or administration as happens after a violent upheaval. So far as India is concerned, the transfer of power has in some respects been taking place for over three decades both in the legislative and the executive branches. There was an administrative machinery, an efficient and loyal army, industry and trade, civic bodies and municipal politics, and an educated middle class. Above all, India has had a tradition of tolerance and compromise which are the essence of democracy.

I shall now pass on to the question of political parties. As Dr. Park has observed, parties which led the national movements in Asian countries head the governments because of their past services and their prestige, although this is not true of one or two countries in the area like Pakistan. Political parties in democratic countries have been based on divergent principles and are divided on important issues of policy. But, frequently, nowadays, many issues of foreign policy and questions of economic development cut across party lines even in countries where the democratic system of government has existed for a long time and, where, in the past, party controversies have been sometimes bitter. It is recognized that in a country's international relations, there should, as far as possible, be a common or bipartisan approach. Even in regard to domestic issues, the conception of what might be called a welfare state is broadly accepted by conservatives and socialists, Republicans and Democrats. It has, indeed, been suggested by some socialist writers that this is one of the reasons for the ebb tide in the fortunes of socialist parties in Europe. In countries of Southeast Asia, however, there has not yet been enough time to develop a party system in the sense in which it is understood in Western democracies. The national parties provide a broad platform for working on common lines. Except those who believe in totalitarian methods whether of the right or the left, various parties do and can work together for common constructive programs of economic and social development. No doubt, there would be many differences of opinion and approach between different schools as well as personal rivalries for leadership. But since any party coming into office would be faced by the same problems of a stagnant economy, unemployment, low purchasing power, lack of capital resources, economic inequalities and social disabilities, it would have to address itself to these questions directly irrespective of ideological doctrines, party slogans and preconceived notions. As Professor Harold Laski once remarked, those who speak of the right and left wings are apt to forget the flight of the bird. In India, the fact that the Congress party, which was led for nearly thirty years by Mahatma Gandhi and has since been virtually headed by Prime Minister Nehru, is in a majority at the center as well as in all the states, has been a factor leading to stability, especially in the early stages of representative government. But this does not mean in any way a one-party government. There are several opposition parties in the central (or federal) Parliament as well as in the state legislatures; there is a free press which is quite alert and there is an increasingly vigilant public opinion. So far as the constitution is concerned, there are ample safeguards against any kind of oligarchy or any denial of fundamental rights. Under the Supreme Court of India, there functions an independent judiciary. There are, no doubt, differences in approach to social and economic problems even within the Congress party. This is unavoidable; even in advanced democratic countries with a much longer tradition of party politics, such differences do exist; we hear, for example, of the "liberal" and "conservative" wings of the Republican party or the "conservative" Democrats of the South and the "liberal" Democrats of the North. Many people believed that the Congress party would dissolve within a few years after the attainment of independence and that it would not be able to stand the test of a general election. But because of a leadership which is by and large sober, devoted and farsighted, and because of a general sense of discipline, the Congress party is still active and will unitedly contest the general elections at the end of 1956.

While on this subject, I should like to mention some interesting trends. While the rightist parties, that is, those who do not accept fully the conception of a secular state or are not in favor of measures of social reform for the Hindu community, made a poor showing in the last general elections, the leftist parties did much better which is not surprising in view of the poverty and economic hardships of the people. Nevertheless, since the general elections, the present government has gained strength for a variety of reasons. Through the Five-Year Plan, a sustained and concerted endeavor is being made to raise the standards of living and provide an element of hope which is essential for the survival of democracy. Revolution by consent is India's approach to realization of social justice. The community development project has been India's answer to regimentation of rural life.

But that is not all. Contrary to forebodings and apprehensions that India's policy of nonalignment would play into the hands of the indigenous Communist party, the expression of friendship by Soviet Russia and the Peoples' Republic of China have, if anything, placed the Indian Communist party in a dilemma. It can also be maintained that the part which India has played in bringing about a certain measure of understanding and harmony between countries and the international status which she has attained during the course of the last eight years have undoubtedly strengthened the Nehru government.

Political institutions, after all, are a vehicle for the energies of the people, they are a means of expression of the general will, they are an instrument of social and economic forces. The democratic system of government is by no means perfect but its very imperfections are capable of scrutiny and improvement. There may be dangerous germs in the democratic body politic but there are also active resistant elements which do function and can counteract. Democracy can be successful only if it is a living organism which can continuously come to terms with its environment. Otherwise it might meet the sad fate of the French nobleman who when told that the French Revolution had broken out remarked that he had decided to ignore it. We might, therefore, well remember Madison's warning that "any system of government, meant for duration, ought to contemplate these revolutions and be able to accommodate itself to them." And the revolutions which permeate Asia today are far more complex and widespread than anything in Madison's time. For, the very foundations of our social and economic system are being challenged and democracy has to prove equal to that challenge.

Evolving political institutions in Southeast Asia

JOHN F. CADY

Ohio University

It is manifestly presumptuous to treat briefly a topic so diverse and complex as the current evolution of political institutions in the various countries of Southeast Asia. Even if all of the relevant facts were known, which of course is not the case, space does not permit the many qualifications and exceptions which would need to be cited. Our awareness of the dynamics of political life is even more fragmentary than our knowledge of factual developments. One must also attack the moot question of what sort of norm to apply in attempting an assessment of evolving political institutions.

And yet because the subject is one of such overriding importance it is worth exploring, even if briefly and tentatively. It is highly important that an effort be made to evaluate current political trends in Southeast Asia before the countries involved reach a point of no return, when the topic will become nothing more than an academic exercise.

The Moribund State of Indigenous Political Institutions

The first generalization which I wish to hazard is that the indigenous political institutions of the countries of Southeast Asia based on the pattern of the God-king of India are either dead or dying. The evolutionary trend in Burma, for example, is clearly away from such ancient concepts. Successive efforts to revive the Brahmanical traditions of

113

divine kingship have been confined, since World War I, to obscurantist elements of the population or to occasional political opportunists desperate to bolster their political fortunes. Indian-trained numerologists and astrologers still enjoy in Burma wide popular prestige, and their lore is apparently staging a revival around the seat of the old royal court at Mandalay, but few political leaders of postwar Burma look to such sources for solutions to real economic or political problems. The visitor to Burma is even surprised by the extent to which current efforts of the government to support Buddhism on the ancient pattern of the court are discounted by politically sophisticated circles in Rangoon as being overexpensive and largely beside the point. Few if any educated leaders counsel return to the monastic system of education in vogue a century ago.

The same decline of traditional political standards can be seen in the postwar attrition of the authority of the Shan Sawbwas. Burma's Shan princes are caught in the cross fire of popular repudiation of their hereditary sovereignty and the concurrent efforts of the central government to assimilate the Shan states administratively with the rest of Burma.

Similar deterioration of older political institutions is also occurring in the Islamic parts of Southeast Asia. The Malay sultans are losing influence. In 1946 they staged an effective counterattack against repudiation of their authority under the British proposal for a Malayan Union, but they are comparatively quiescent in 1955 in the face of an equally thoroughgoing impairment of their political position. In Java, Darul Islam appears to be, to the outside observer, only the dead hand of the past even though the nonpolitical religious orientation still possesses considerable vitality.[1] A serious attempt to revive Islamic political institutions would run counter to the need to bridge across ethnic and religious differences and would also aggravate the already staggering problem of adjusting governmental administration to meet present day demands of world political and economic relations.

Much the same judgment holds for Indochina. Few informed persons would question the conclusion that the authority of ex-Emperor Bao Dai, himself a sophisticated Westernized Vietnamese, was a spent force

---

[1] The unexpectedly strong showing of the orthodox Nahdatul Ulama in the Indonesian elections of 1955 reflected the strength of basic religious loyalties rather than any articulate political demands.

long before his repudiation by plebiscite. When in 1946, Bao Dai abdicated his throne and assigned to the emerging Republic of Viet-Nam the care of the bones of his royal ancestors, he repudiated not only his crown but the very Confucianist basis of his kingship. French efforts to establish his authority after 1949 were foredoomed to failure on more grounds than one.

Kingship in Thailand is at present emasculated of any political initiative, although it continues to serve as a useful symbol of governmental authority. It may be that in the future some civilian alternative to military dictatorship at Bangkok, perhaps stemming from an educated middle-class organization backed by real economic power, may be able successfully to exploit the royal tradition and take over control governmentally, but in all probability such a movement would be more Westernized than the present military regime. Divine kingship of itself is no longer creatively potent in Thailand. In the absence of any domestic alternative to royal authority in Cambodia and Laos, kingship may survive for some time unless eliminated by outside influence. It would nevertheless be hazardous to predict that either of these governments is capable of independent survival for long in its present form. King Norodam's recent resignation to become political party leader indicates the direction of change. As for the Philippines, the extant political institutions and traditions are of Spanish and American origin, not indigenous at all. Spanish *cacique* domination of the government still persists, but under threat of insistent demands for economic and social change. Observable trends are clearly away from the moribund anachronistic remnants of traditional governmental forms.

The same degeneration of traditional governmental forms is apparent at the middle and lower levels of authority. The hereditary *myothugyi* in Burma is gone beyond recovery. The regents of Java too long mortgaged their authority to the Dutch for them to escape the progressive attrition of their power under independence. The authority of the Confucianist Indochina mandarin officials evaporated with the destruction of the Annamite kingship, and the powers of the village notables, undermined by French rule, is also one beyond recall. Similarly the disintegration of the highly structured social order within which village "democracy" functioned in pre-European times renders almost impossible its revival. Local self-government is ebbing away also because political decisions and the funds to implement them come from the center, which, through improved means of transportation and communication, can now exercise fairly effective control of outlying areas. Introduction of the "atomized" democracy of the liberal West based on "one person, one vote" can only assist in destroying the essential social basis on which rested the traditional influence of the village elders and the petty local chiefs. The loss of local governmental vitality is far advanced even in Thailand, which never suffered the imposition of colonial administration and which has also escaped the revolutionary impact of the postwar period.

Positive Aspects of Postwar Political Evolution in Southeast Asia

At least four positive political factors can be identified which have been operative within the revolutionary movements of postwar Southeast Asia. The most important is a belligerently assertive nationalism. It has served as an essential weapon for the attainment of independence and also as a means of unifying the country once freedom was achieved. The second factor, and an encouraging one, was a strong predilection, shared by most of the youthful nationalist leaders, for liberal constitutional government and the wide enjoyment of individual liberty. Third in importance has been the vogue of some form of planned economy involving state control of foreign trade and sponsorship of industrial development. A fourth and final factor interrelated with the others, has been the insistent trend toward unitary control, motivated in part by nationalist concern to counter pressure for provincial autonomy and political disunity generally, and in part by the need for central direction of economic planning. All four of these factors are largely alien to the indigenous political traditions of the several Southeast Asian countries, although some traditional methods have sometimes cropped up in their implementation. These four dynamic factors will be considered in turn.

Nationalism

The desire for freedom from foreign rule was well-nigh universal among the indigenous inhabitants of Southeast Asia. But nationalism differed qualitatively from place to place. In areas where emancipation was accomplished either by force or threat of force, as in Burma, Indonesia, and Viet-Nam, leadership in the nationalist movement fell into youthful revolutionary hands. The accidental circumstances attending the Japanese occupation and withdrawal, made it possible for the Thakin group in Burma, for Sukarno, Hatta, et al. in Indonesia, and for the many youthful Vietnamese nationalists as well as Communists associated with Ho Chi Minh to vault into prominence. Full-throttled nationalism served also as an integrating cohesive element within the several emerging states. Once freedom was achieved, nationalists felt impelled to counter the demands of differing ethnic groups and regional units to seek autonomy in their own right. Nationalism was in a very real sense therefore the universal political factor. In 1955 the co-operation of rival communal groups in Malaya under the Alliance party banner was achieved on the basis of nationalist demands for early independence. Ngo Dinh Diem attracted his first flicker of popularity in South Viet-Nam when he started in 1955 to talk back to the French and to Bao Dai.

Nationalism in itself was nevertheless notoriously deficient in definitive political content. One strong but frequent inarticulate demand associated with the independent movements was the reaffirmation of the validity and worth of indigenous cultural values. This demand stemmed in part from an assertion of cultural independence and in part from a deliberate effort to revitalize national morale. The emphasis was socially constructive, but it was usually not immediately relevant to the solution of concrete economic and political problems. It could be obstructive of progress. Many of the youthful Western-oriented nationalist leaders paid little heed to the need for cultural revival. U Nu of Burma has been a notable exception. As political leaders, the younger nationalists nevertheless exploited all expressions of patriotic sentiment, cultural and otherwise, as a means of mobilizing mass support for a variety of radical objectives, including plans to "nationalize" the country's resources.

The Vogue of Liberal Constitutional Government

The demand for political freedom for the individual was also strong. Most of the nationalist leaders who found themselves in control following the Japanese withdrawal were the products of a generation which had struggled to gain from colonial masters the boon of representative government. For them, the progressive achievement of self-government under some form of the parliamentary system had been historically the very touchstone of political progress. The demand for independence itself had usually been based on the radical principle that sovereignty resided in the people, to whose freely elected representatives the executive power must be held responsible. Where protection of personal liberties could not be based on customary law, such guarantees have been incorporated in the new constitutions.

Thus it happened that in fashioning the governments of the several newly independent regimes, the majority of the political leaders accepted as desirable the familiar liberal institutions characteristic of their respective colonial rulers. In the Philippines and Burma, the governmental pattern was already set by successive constitutions acquired in the course of the previous decades. The Dutch had made a beginning of representation in the Volksraad, although the number of Indonesians acquainted with the character and operation of parliamentary forms of government was pathetically small. In prewar Malaya and Indochina, virtually no steps had been taken to introduce liberal governmental institutions which could have provided a pattern and a training agency for self-government. The Thai revolution of 1932 reproduced the forms, although not the substance, of free government. But even so, the educated leaders who had been denied experience in constitutional government nevertheless tended to accept liberal representative institutions as the norm of political progress. In one respect only, that of the guarantee of property rights and of freedom in the economic field, did Southeast Asian champions of freedom reject the pattern of the liberal West.

Emphasis on Planned Economic Development

Opposition to free capitalism in Southeast Asia is not difficult to understand. It derived from the close association obtaining between imperialism and capitalist exploitation. Foreign investors before the war had been in many countries the most inveterate enemies of self-rule. The attainment of political independence therefore, stimulated economic nationalism and the urge to end foreign economic control. State capitalism was a natural recourse because nearly all of the prewar financial and industrial capital resources within the several countries had belonged to aliens, citizens of the metropole or resident Chinese and Indians. Except in the Philippines the new government leaders, themselves propertyless, had no personal stake in safeguarding property rights. They also attacked landlordism, even though indigenous, as an evil. If planned economic development was to be realized without the risk of foreign capital domination, the state presumably must itself provide the essential funds and much of the administrative talent. Domestic savings could theoretically be realized by state monopoly of staple exports or from the profits of expropriated industries. Import curbs could ensure that productive goods received priority.

Although the pursuit of Marxist ends has been an act of faith by political leaders in North Viet-Nam and Burma, the concern of the economic planners of Southeast Asia has been essentially nationalist rather than Marxist per se. The Soviet Union provided, of course, the outstanding example of forced-draft economic development and embodied the theoretical goal of a classless society devoid of exploitation. It afforded therefore a possible pattern by which needed industrial expansion could be achieved quickly without incurring bondage to foreign business interests, as well as a program for the abolition of landlordism through state monopoly of the land. But one of the most thoroughgoing Southeast Asian programs of state interference with private economic activity occurred in anti-Marxist Thailand, as a counter-move against the threat of Chinese domination of all business activity.

The policy of state-directed economic development, whether deliberately Marxist or not, has had and will have far reaching effects on the evolution of political institutions. In the first place it saddled fledgling governments with onerous responsibilities extending far beyond the minimal services afforded by prewar colonial regimes. In a situation where dependable and experienced administrative talent was in very short supply, the new regimes undertook to staff their armed forces, to initiate financial controls, to conduct domestic and international trade, to rehabilitate and operate transportation and other services often under difficult circumstances, to send purchasing missions abroad, and to execute construction contracts of large dimensions. Youthful leadership attained on the basis of emotional opposition to imperialism and answerable to no considered public opinion was usually not calculated to provide needed business experience, however honest its intentions. In actuality inexperience as well as politics have been the causes of widespread corruption and maladministration in most countries.

Because the concentration on planned economic development occurred in the context of an overriding emphasis on national ends, compromises with the Marxian demand for public ownership of the means of production have been frequent. If essential industries could not be developed on a national basis, concessions were made to private initiative or even to the utilization of foreign capital and management. This has been done not only by Burma and Indonesia, but in the early period, by Viet-Minh also. Execution of planned economic development revived two unfortunate aspects of traditional patterns of government, namely, the royal trade monopolies and the association of government in the popular mind with the exercise of arbitrary power. Such older practices were in sharp contradiction with the novel ideal of governing through deliberate assemblies operating on a democratic basis. Efforts to achieve economic self-sufficiency have also disregarded the large potential savings which might have been realized through an attempt at co-ordinated regional development. The deservedly praised Colombo Plan, is not a regional program, but rather a scheme for assisting the realization of a collection of national plans.

Unitary Governmental Control

The final dynamic factor, namely, the trend toward highly centralized governmental authority derived in the first place from concern on the part of nationalist leaders that no "toe in the door" openings be conceded to the retiring colonial authorities which might suggest their possible return. Burma rejected the Scheduled Areas proposal contained in the British White Paper of May, 1945, and Indonesia similarly challenged the Dutch-sponsored Federation scheme. The prolonged furor in Indonesia over continued Dutch control of Irian in New Guinea, exceeding by far the intrinsic importance of the area itself, obviously stems from anti-imperialist considerations. Other instances include Vietnamese nationalist resentment over the misguided attempt of Admiral d'Argenlieu and his supporters in June, 1946, to repudiate previous promises to exclude the colony of Cochin China from the limits of the emerging republic.

Unitary control was also needed to bridge across, both militarily and politically, the multifarious differences of ethnic origin, of religious and cultural affiliations, of geographical diversity, and of governmental experience found in all of the Southeast Asian countries. Such problems of disunity cannot easily be solved. In order to counteract the British Scheduled Areas proposal for Burma, U Aung San in 1947 had to promise autonomous states for the hill peoples. It will not be easy later to integrate the peripheral regions. Similarly the Indonesian rejection of the Dutch-sponsored Federation scheme did not cancel the problem of coming to terms with particularist interests in many parts of the island empire. One of the many unfortunate aspects of postwar French improvisation in Indochina has been the encouragement of territorial disintegration by the concession to sectarian groups of private armies and de facto territorial autonomy.

Unitary government has been promoted politically through government-sponsored parties designed to function throughout all sections of the country and within mass organization groups. If political tensions were great, the development of comparable party organizations by rival groups could be officially hampered, thus making political freedom a kind of luxury to aspire to in the future, rather than something to enjoy immediately. Even political leaders who cherished a genuine regard for democratic values and methods were often loathe to subject their treasured economic development programs as well as their own political power to the risks inherent in free political associations and elections. Scheduled elections were therefore usually staged under circumstances involving negligible risks to the party in power. For those not committed to democratic ideals, it was an easy further step to espouse what was in effect the Communist principle of democratic centralism. The seeming advantages of arbitrary control by an elite group at the center were obvious. It would avoid the necessity of soliciting popular acquiescence in official policy, and, if the Soviet pattern were followed, authority could be uninhibited in its use of sanctions to throttle criticism and to crush obstructionary efforts.

On the other side of the ledger was the need for political stability. Where nation-wide party organizations are lacking, the traditional tendency to cluster politically around rival leaders to the disregard of issues and principles presented in many areas of Southeast Asia, Indonesia in particular, the threat of multi-party confusion and political chaos. Any effective government is probably better than anarchy, and the most admirable of constitutional forms can be vitiated by political irresponsibility.

It appears fairly obvious, in conclusion, that of the four dynamic factors operating in postwar Southeast Asia, nationalism was not in itself pro-democratic, while two others, planned economic development and centralized control, tended to cancel out the principle of free government. And yet it is precisely the latter that must be posited as the norm of political progress.

The Norms for Assessing Political Progress

The time-honored dictum that the people who are subjected to a particular government are the best judges of its excellence comes from Aristotle. It implies the corollary proposition that any effort to achieve governmental progress of an institutional nature must provide some systematic method for registering the grievances of the people. Magna Carta and the Bill of Rights are cases in point. Political progress inheres, not in any particular static constitutional form, but rather in the degree of opportunity afforded within the framework of law to make known the representative views of the governed and thus to seek amelioration of injustice and tyranny. A considerable measure of freedom of expression and of political association is obviously a necessary prerequisite, therefore, in any progressive political system. A particular government is free and democratic, in the words of Professor Emerson, to the extent that citizens, however humble, are aware that they can participate meaningfully in government and that their expressed wishes will be taken into account.[2]

The norm must in every case be a relative one, for the ideal is never perfectly achieved. No government however arbitrary is entirely immune from the impact of public opinion, and, conversely, the most thoroughgoing provision for democratic participation is subject to abuse. Governments can only approximate justice, and all forms are

[2] Rupert Emerson, *Representative Government in Southeast Asia* (Cambridge, Harvard Press, 1955), pp. 13-14.

capable of degenerating into demogoguery, tyranny, or chaotic rebellion if the views of thoughtful citizens cannot be constructively heeded.

It does not follow, of course, that political forms are all of equal validity in terms of their contributions to human freedom and progress. Especially valuable are those institutions distilled from generations of experience personally or vicariously shared. The same, if artificially imposed, can be meaningless. Substantial progress, in fact, can only be measured in terms of institutional development rather than in hand-to-mouth improvisations, however clever, to meet immediate difficulties. This is particularly true of established practices which afford to the average citizen regular opportunity to voice his grievances and to review governmental performance. Periodic elections of representatives qualified to act as spokesmen for the people and guaranteed the freedom to do so, plus courts competent to interpret the law, free from executive interference, are among the most venerable institutions of human liberty. Elections can therefore be regarded as a good habit even though ill understood and sometimes abused. Democracy achieves real vitality when the people become aware that political liberty as such is too precious a part of their birthright to be bartered away for the pottage of temporary governmental stability or even forced-draft economic development.

In the light of such a norm, how can one evaluate the political evolution of the governments of Southeast Asia?

Encouraging Aspects

The most encouraging aspect of the immediate postwar situation in Southeast Asia is the fact that the Western-oriented leaders such as Sukarno of Indonesia, Nu of Burma, Magsaysay of the Philippines, Diem of Viet-Nam, plus the emerging political leaders of Malaya, hold in high regard democratic principles of government. They and their followers illustrate the basic truth that persons capable of entertaining political judgments cherish the right to express their aspirations and their grievances. Such democracy affirms that human dignity and economic and social betterment are conditioned in the long run on the individual's freedom to formulate and to express considered opinions.

The postwar gains have been tangible as well as theoretical. Filipino leaders in 1953, for example, subjected their devotion to free government to the acid test of staging an election free from intimidation and violence, which unseated the party in power, with the losers accepting the popular verdict in good grace. Regular elections have recently been held in Malaya and Indonesia, while Burma will hold its second general election in 1956. Premier Diem is also planning to hold a series of elections in South Viet-Nam. The staging of all-Viet-Nam elections as provided under the Geneva agreement, if honestly conducted, could also constitute an important achievement for the democratic process, notwithstanding the fact that a strong case can be made against Communist abuse of democratic liberties as a means of sabotaging their future exercise.

A second major contribution to the validation of democratic institutions in Southeast Asia has been the efforts of the top political leaders to demonstrate that popular government was expressly designed to enable people to make their preferences effectively known. The interest which Magsaysay, for example, has demonstrated in ameliorating the lot of the peasants, even if not fully effective, sounded a new and wholesome note in Philippine politics. The genius behind the Pyidawtha drive in Burma relates to its encouragement of popular initiative for self-help at the village level and also to its promotion of public understanding of the long-term phases of the national welfare program. Human freedom and dignity can survive in such a political climate even in troubled times.

Discouraging Aspects

One of the most discouraging aspects of the politics of Southeast Asia relates to deficiencies in political organization and education. Party organizations must become something more than coteries of co-operating office-seeking politicians. They must be capable in some measure of defining the issues and policies with which they are identified. Equally difficult is the task of communicating these alternative policies to politically inexperienced peoples in simplified terms which they can understand. Difficulty arises also from the fact that basic popular loyalties usually relate to religious and group associations or at best to commitments to striking personalities. Such communal issues tend to overshadow the reasoned definitions of basic political issues unrelated to popular fears and suspicions.

This perennial problem of political education, present, everywhere, is particularly critical in Southeast Asian countries because the situation does not admit of indefinite delay in finding solutions for urgent problems of livelihood and political integration. Whereas Democratic processes need time to mature, an overcautious policy will not suffice to find effective solutions within the time allowed. Hope lies in the fact that, although an immature body politic cannot be expected to fashion or even to understand proposed solutions to complex problems, it can, if left free, evaluate results and distinguish between honesty and fraud. It is probably far better in any case that a government be held answerable periodically to popular appraisal, even though imperfect, than for it to be free from such obligations entirely. The door to popular judgment must, therefore, not be closed. There is also the probability that the need for speedy solutions has been overestimated.

Another major difficulty arises from the age-old tendency of persons who find themselves in political control to undertake to perpetuate their personal power at the expense of the development of the institutions of freedom. Such tactics can always be rationalized on the assumption that the maintaining of stability and security of the state are the primary obligations of any government. This consideration has been re-enforced by stressing the importance of realizing economic development programs, which might suffer delay or possible repudiation at the whim of an unappreciative electorate. A high sense of urgency, itself a concept more Western than indigenous to Southeast Asia, seems thus to preclude the slower but sounder method of educating popular demand. The positing of modest objectives short of optimum expectations and more likely of achievement would be far less likely to leave inflated hopes unsatisfied.

Arbitrary power can also hide behind the smoke screen of the allegedly spontaneous support of synthetic mass organizations of workers, peasants, veterans, or other special interests. These frequently function not as autonomous self-governing agencies, but rather as direct extensions of the political authority of the group in power. The ultimate weapon of autocracy is, of course, resort to military power, a situation currently present in qualified form in Thailand. Military factors may, unfortunately, play an important role in the future political development of Viet-Nam. Military influence has been dangerously present in recent political developments in Indonesia, and it reared its head at fearful cost during the course of the Burma rebellions. Militarism is potentially present wherever power is arbitrarily exercised and political institutions are of uncertain vitality.

The stake of democratic institutions is particularly vital in the area of education. Here the outlook is not everywhere encouraging. Ambitious plans for educational expansion have faltered for lack of facilities and staff. Even more essential than mass literacy is the capacity of higher education to stimulate independence of thought, creative achievement in terms of social progress, and withal the development of a body of informed opinion which governmental authority cannot safely or wisely ignore. Actually, rote dictation of lecture materials for subsequent examination use, as practiced, is more likely to breed student frustration than ability to think objectively. Development of technological aptitudes, furthermore, is not enough for a free society. How to make educational activities contribute to the improvement of political institutions is therefore one of the perennial problems which admits of no easy solution. Operating in reverse, political intrusions alien to educational ends and largely Communist inspired, continue to bedevil efforts in many parts of Southeast Asia, adding a further handicap to the sheer lack of physical facilities and teaching personnel.

The popularity in Viet-Nam allegedly enjoyed by Ho Chi Minh owes much to nationalist anti-French sentiment and something also to Ho's efforts in 1945–46 to attract support from liberals as well as nationalists. He conducted local elections, attacked illiteracy, and initiated flood-control measures and famine relief. But invariably Ho's disciplined Communist cadre retained the positions of power; it took over complete control in 1949 following the Communist victory in China. Under the familiar Communist pattern of "democratic centralism" introduced by Ho, all decisions of the popularly elected bodies at the lower echelons were subject to review at successive levels of those above, so that decisions were made in the end only by the top Communist directors riding at the peak of the pyramid of indirectly chosen councils. The Communist party in time effectively infiltrated echelons at all levels. In the absence of any elections whatever in the French administered areas, Viet-Minh was able to capitalize on its alleged democratic character. In actuality the locally elected Councils under

Ho's scheme became the instruments of the party in power, while the mob psychology of Peoples Courts provided a poor substitute for the majesty of law. Here the French failure to satisfy in a prompt and generous fashion legitimate Vietnamese nationalist demands operated to betray the cause of genuine political liberty. It may still be possible to salvage something from the wreckage.

In the broadest context, constructive evolution of political institutions in Southeast Asian countries is dependent in part on the effective continuance of world cultural exchange. The United Nations provides a wholesome climate of world opinion and experience in which to recognize the inadequacies of parochialism and also to discount tawdry rationalizations of one's own shortcomings. In its efforts to establish a norm for human rights and to improve labor standards and health conditions, as well as in providing a world forum for airing political grievances, the United Nations is in fact a projection on a world scale of the democratic ideal. Even more significant from a long range point of view will be the continued international exchange of students and faculty, business and cultural missions.

Without question, the peoples of Southeast Asia are today exposed to the impact of world forces as never before in their long history. This fact alone forbids return to the despotic traditions of their monarchical past. But whereas the negative nationalism of anti-imperialist sentiment has accomplished the liberation of Southeast Asia from foreign rule, genuine political freedom there still awaits achievement. It is far from assured. Fortunately the peoples of Southeast Asia do not lack friends who wish them well in this challenging undertaking.

The role of
political parties in Indonesia

SOEDJATMOKO

Secretary, Indonesian Council of World Affairs

If, in discussing political parties, one attempts to determine their role in a given country, apart from their history, ideology or party programs as such, one in fact embarks upon a roughly charted course in the field of political science with few landmarks and guideposts. To undertake such a study with regard to a country like Indonesia, only recently come into nationhood, its political institutions young and not yet consolidated, its literacy rate low, and only its ignorance and poverty great, is an even more hazardous venture into almost virgin territory. Personal observation and experience, limited though they inevitably are, mere hunches and tentative ideas are all that can guide us into this field, and no more than a very provisional value can be attached to the impressions and generalizations derived from such a study.

In presenting this essay the writer is fully aware of its limitations in this connection. That he has the temerity to present it nevertheless, is to a large extent due to his realization that the Indonesian experience in parliamentary government may afford some interesting insights to the student of political science into some political relationships and the process of political evolution in general, due to the coincidence of revolution, freedom, and a diffuseness of power in that country.

128

It is also due to the stimulating experience of having participated in and observed Indonesia's first general elections.

Development of Multiparty System

The year 1908 is usually accepted as the beginning of Indonesia's nationalist movement. It was the year in which Budi Utomo (High Endeavor) was established, by some young Western-educated men of the feudal class. Though it originally set out with an educational and nonpolitical program, it gradually evolved into a more political nationalist organization. The first political mass party, however, was established in 1912, when the Association of Moslem Traders reconstituted itself as the Sarikat Islam (Moslem Association). It is not without significance that this first mass party, which spread through the country like wildfire, was a nationalist party organized on the basis of religion.

It was from some of the branches of the Sarikat Islam that in 1920 the Indonesian Communist party sprang. The following years saw a struggle between the Sarikat Islam and the Communist party for control of the nationalist movement. In 1927 the Indonesian Nationalist party was established with Mr. Sukarno, now President of the Indonesian Republic, as its chairman. With the emergence of the PNI as the first purely nationalist mass party, the future pattern of Indonesian politics was set.

Henceforth Indonesian political parties could be categorized into three main groups according to their general bias: religious, nationalist and Marxist. Furthermore the multiparty character of the political system was to become a permanent feature. Judging from the provisional returns this multiparty character is not going to be affected by the recent elections, although the numbers of parties represented in parliament will be considerably reduced. During the Japanese occupation all political parties were disbanded although subsequently kinds of semipolitical public service organizations were set up by the Japanese with a view to involving the Indonesian population as much as possible in the Japanese war effort. Part of the Indonesian leadership seized upon this opportunity to preserve at least some semblance of nationalist organization, while the other part took to underground work.

The proclamation of independence was the fruit of the joint labors of both these movements.

Political Parties and Parliamentarism

After the proclamation of independence the political parties re-appeared as the direct result of a government decree issued on November 3, 1945, three months after the proclamation of independence, on the advice of the Working Committee of the Central National Convention which stated that the government "favors the establishment of political parties, because with the existence of political parties all currents of thought which are to be found in society may be canalized into a regulated course." The decree further stipulated that those parties should serve "to strengthen our struggle for the defense of our independence and the preservation of the security of the nation."

Within a few months the establishment of the major political parties had become a fact. Consequently, the membership of the revolutionary Central National Convention grouped itself accordingly, and a further step was made toward the full development of parliamentary democracy in Indonesia.

In itself, this development was not new. Political parties had existed even during the colonial period. They were the main vehicles of growing national awareness. And even during that period there had been repeated attempts of the then existing parties to create shadow parliaments apart from the colonial "People's Council," through the establishment of combinations and concentrations of parties. In 1922 the so-called Radical Concentration was set up, a combination of the political parties based on the principle of nonco-operation with the colonial government. Later on, in 1927, the PPPKI, and in 1938 the GAPI were also set up. Subsequently, in 1941, the nationalist party combine, the GAPI and the Muslim Party combination MIAI, joined together in the establishment of the Indonesian Peoples Congress (Kongres Rakjat Indonesia), which was later on broadened again by the participation of trade unions in the Indonesian Peoples Council (Madjelis Rakjat Indonesia).

The desire for parliamentary government therefore is deeply rooted in the development of the political parties themselves. Understandably so, since the struggle against colonialism of necessity took the form of a struggle for more democratic rights.

In that sense parliamentary government has been a product of the political parties, although technically, after the proclamation of independence, it was parliament, i.e., the National Convention, which created the political parties.

Political Parties and Their Mass Support

The recent tremendous turnout at the polls, of more than 80 per cent of the number of registered voters, has brought out some interesting developments regarding the composition of the mass support of each party. It is rather unlikely that the number of regular members plus the number of sympathizers of all the parties together could account for the immense returns, or in other words that this could be considered a reflection of the degree of popularity of the political ideologies and party programs.

The elections have shown that the non-Communist political parties, that is those non-Communist groups which have proved to have mass following, are by no means political parties in the usually accepted sense of the word. Mass following has proved to consist to a large extent of aggregates of people in the villages grouped around the dominating factors of their daily life; the village headman and the religious teacher. Popular vote in the villages was in the first place a show of allegiance to either of the two, or to both. Hence the surprisingly large turnout of the villages at the polls, often above 90 per cent of the registered voters, larger even than in the towns (70 per cent) with their more politically conscious populations. Hence also the almost complete insignificance of campaign issues like corruption in government, high prices, economic development, etc., on the village level. It was only among the small minority of literates and politically conscious people that these issues helped determine the vote, and that the usual modern campaign techniques proved to be moderately effective. The numerical strength of the political parties as shown by the election results, or more precisely the political power of the particular elite groups leading those parties, is therefore, not so much, and not only a reflection of the measure of acceptance of either ideology or leadership, but also a reflection of such groups' ability to manipulate the traditional power relationships within the village.

It would be wrong however to think of the village vote merely in terms of allegiance to the traditional centers of power. After all, the village structure and its economy are in transition, breaking down as a result of the incursion of modern money economy, modern life and communications, and also as a result of the increasing inability of the village to provide for its inhabitants, and the general dynamization of the villagers as a result of the struggle for independence and of independence itself. The Indonesian village is undergoing a transition, the political consequences of which will increasingly make themselves felt. On the village level, therefore, increasingly substantial groups do not any longer fit into the old way of life and social structure; often they are in latent or open conflict with the old village hierarchy. These groups then constitute a now dynamic or potentially dynamic political force.

The provisional election results seem to indicate that the Communist party has managed to monopolize a considerable segment of these new dynamic forces in the country thus securing for itself, with the gradual breakdown of the old social structure, an even stronger position in the future. This does not mean that the entire Communist vote consists of such elements. Wherever possible, the Communists have made skillful use of all the social pressures to which the collectively and hierarchially thinking village population is exposed. Nevertheless the control by the Communist party of an important part of these new forces is one of the central facts emerging from the recent elections. It also emphasizes the failure of the Socialist party which should have been in the best position to compete with the Communist party in this field.

Be that as it may, it is evident that ideology and party program play a limited role in the composition of the party's membership, and that on different levels of political sophistication different techniques and tactics to attract support are being used, often based on the existence of the traditional power relations within the village. This of course is not surprising, especially in a pluralistic society like Indonesia.

With regard to the role of ideology in the party system one cannot escape noting how great the similarity between the different party programs is, even among the programs of parties which do not belong to the three categories referred to before: religious, nationalist and Marxist.

Almost all political parties profess to adhere to a more or less socialistic program. It can be said that, as far as political ideologies are concerned, Indonesian political life is left of center because of its general emphasis on anti-imperialism and anti-capitalism.

One's choice of a political party among the three main currents of thought is in general determined by the mental and psychological climate prevailing in a particular party. Within each of those three main categories there are of course a number of parties. The particular choice of one party over another within each category is most often determined by one's personal sympathy or loyalty to a particular leader. In general the choice is not made on the basis of specific stands the parties have taken on particular political issues. Political issues are rather fought out within each party. Political parties, therefore, represent in the first place, mental and psychological climates rather than clearly defined political opinions. With an increasing degree of political sophistication this situation is bound to change and political ideologies together with concrete political issues will in the future increasingly determine the choice of political parties.

Political Parties and Their Organization

Having indicated the limitations of the importance of political ideologies in the operation of the parties, it becomes clear that the problem of the organization of the party as a mass party is, in the first place, a problem of organizing a mass vote.

It is in this connection that control of the government civil service, i.e., the machinery of the Home Affairs Ministry, the Ministry of Religion and the Ministry of Information, is a major political asset, especially in a country such as Indonesia where traditional authoritarian government has been the rule for so long. Control of these strategic assets does of course not obviate the necessity for party organization as such. Political parties in general are rather loosely organized entities. Dues only play a limited role in the finances of the party. Conversely, party discipline is also limited. Within each party, with the possible exception of the central core of the Communist party and the small Socialist party, political power is diffuse. This, of course, also follows from the earlier observation that political parties represent mental and psychological climates rather than clearly defined political ideas.

Political Parties as Vehicles of the Nationalist Upsurge

After these general observations regarding the relationship of political parties and their ideologies, mass support, and organizational structure, we now have to deal with the interrelationship between political parties and the environment in which they operate, and in which they themselves are at the same time operated upon.

All these political parties operate on an emotionally strong and irreversible groundswell of nationalism. It is this which determines their general direction and scope of action. No political party can afford to ignore it. In this respect Indonesian nationalism is part and parcel of the tremendous historical forces which are in the process of changing the position of the peoples of Asia and Africa in the world.

While, therefore, all the political parties can only become or remain effective political forces to the extent that they remain the vehicles of this nationalist upsurge, at the same time, as political organizations responsible for the conduct of the affairs of the state, they are confronted with a set of problems whose solutions require, in many cases, a different frame of mind, a different mentality and even a different emotional outlook. These are problems in the fields of economics, finance, development, efficient administration, and the conduct of international affairs.

It is not surprising that those parties which are inclined to give priority to such problems lack popular appeal. In this connection the importance of general education is quite evident. There is little doubt that an increase in the level of education will bring about significant changes in the popular pattern of political behavior. In fact, it can be said that general education will increasingly constitute a political factor of the first order.

It is the difference in priority given to the pressing demands of nationalist sentiment and the requirements emanating from the responsibility for the conduct of the affairs of the state, which provides another yardstick for the differentiation between the political parties and their prevailing mental climates, between the personalities of the politi-

cal leaders, between factions and even more important, between generations within political parties.

Political Parties and Their Environment

Another, and perhaps one of the most important observations one
can make on the basis of Indonesia's ten years' experience in government, is that political power in this country seems to be quite diffuse.
Neither cabinet nor parliament, nor the two together are the exclusive
or dominant repositories of political power, nor do they fully reflect
the pattern of political forces within the country. Political power seems
to be widely distributed among the political parties, government bureaucracy, the army, all diffuse within themselves, and outside these
institutions, over large, often inarticulate bodies of opinion or emotion,
often of a regional, or local character. Several reasons could be
adduced to explain this situation. In the first place it has to be
realized that the revolution which gave rise to the Indonesian Republic
did not start as a centrally led uprising, but was largely a spontaneous
outburst taking place almost simultaneously all over the country. It
was only gradually that central leadership became effective. In the
same way the Indonesian army was welded together from largely independent units and armed bands, each bringing with it its own particular history and sometimes its own political outlook. The political
parties also reflect this development in their loose organizational
structure.

Secondly Indonesia's geographical situation—it is a sprawling
archipelago of about 3000 islands with inadequate means of communication and consequently different levels of political sophistication—has
also contributed to the diffusion of political power. It has led to
regional differences in political action and hence often to different
emotional frames of reference.

The third important factor has been the generally low level of
bureaucratic and organizational efficiency, characterizing both the
government apparatus and the political parties. This has made the
effectuation of central authority an extremely difficult process. Conversely, administrative inefficiency of the central government has
created a political problem of its own, e.g., regional dissatisfaction with

the central government, because of alleged insufficient attention to provincial problems.

A fourth and very important factor is imbedded in the Indonesian cultural pattern. By age-old custom decisions in the village are made as a collective act. All important elements within the village participate in a meeting (musjawarat), where all decisions are achieved not by majority vote, but by a process of talking things out until a common understanding is reached (mufakat) which is subsequently carried into effect under collective authority. Related to this custom is the general reluctance to overdo things, to outrage a fundamental "sense of proportion and order" in social and political behavior. Political attitudes among the political elite still strongly reflect this basic pattern.

All these factors account for the slowness of the process of political decision making. There is a complex, even though inarticulate system of checks and balances, knowledge of which can only be acquired through close familiarity with the Indonesian scene both as a whole and in its constituent parts. No cabinet can be found willing to make an important decision without allowing its members to consult their parties, where again as we have seen, the same diffusion of power is reflected. In fact, cabinet decisions of any importance are often preceded by party decisions. The same is the case with the factions in parliament. These factors also account for the slowness and comparative uneventfulness of some of the more serious political crises which have been experienced. The two army crises, in October 1953 and in July 1955 are cases in point.

With these factors in mind it is understandable that government decisions and policies, and equally, party decisions, have to conform to a broad general consensus which can often only be felt rather than explicitly heard. They have to be taken with careful recognition of this complex system of delicate balances. Politics in many ways—and the election results will not fundamentally change this—will have to be played by ear rather than by the arithmetical process of toting up votes in parliament.

Whenever this intricate system of indefinable checks and balances is disturbed, long drawn out conflicts, sometimes in the form of armed rebellion, have occurred. In these conflicts it is often not the concrete issues about which no agreement could be reached which are important, but rather the underlying sentiments and attitudes.

Such conflicts, therefore, in the course of their existence, undergo continuous changes both as to substance and form of expression, and also as to the position of the sometimes many parties to the conflict. Needless to say in such a situation a sense of timing is of extreme importance and an essential element of wise statesmanship. One cannot say that these problems would disappear if there were strong central authority and determined leadership. The factors mentioned before will make it, for sometime to come, almost impossible for such authority to establish itself.

Limitations to the Role of Political Parties

From what has been said before regarding the diffuseness of political power, the structure of membership and mass support of the political parties and about the nature of political parties as representing psychological and mental climates, it should be clear that the political parties at this stage of their development do not and cannot entirely encompass all factors of national political life.

We have already seen that the low level of administrative efficiency of the apparatus of the central government is partially responsible for local or regional dissatisfaction, sometimes expressing itself in political terms, e.g., in the form of local patriotism and defiance of the central government.

This situation has been further aggravated by the incursion of the political parties into the government bureaucracy. Since an important part of the politically conscious minority is in one way or another connected with the government apparatus, this development has, maybe unfortunately, been more or less unavoidable. The combination of political instability and a politicking bureaucracy however has not helped to increase the effectiveness and efficiency of the central government.

Apart from this, however, it should be recognized that regional desire for political, cultural, and economic self-expression in the different areas of Indonesia, is a political fact of the first order. It constitutes an element in political life cutting right through all political parties, often binding individuals of one particular region closer together than they feel themselves bound by their own party allegiance, thereby creating problems both inside and outside the parties with which they are not always in a position to cope. Yet their future development will to an important extent depend on their ability to do so.

Of a similar nature is the problem posed by the existence of religious minorities. Here again we are faced with a problem cutting right across many of the parties. Insufficient attention by the party leadership to this problem, especially in view of the often high degree of political sophistication and influence of these minorities, and the fact of their concentration in certain areas, might prove to be highly dangerous to the cohesion of the parties concerned and to the unity of the state.

Furthermore, while in the past political parties have often avoided taking a stand on concrete political issues—though they were sometimes used to unseat a cabinet—the new parliament, and with it the political parties, will now be inescapably confronted with them.

Land problems, economic development, the degree of autonomy of the regions and the speed of its implementation, foreign investment, and foreign aid, are some of the problems which will have to be faced and which undoubtedly will have a profound influence on the future development of each of the political parties.

More than ever before, political parties will be forced to take a position, and in doing so to clarify and further define their policies. Since this may run counter to particular interests or established emotional attitudes within the parties, it is clear that this will put a considerable strain on the cohesion of the politically conscious membership, and consequently on its mass support, since we have seen that the motives to join a party operate on a different level from the concrete political issues which will now have to be faced. It will also bring with it the possibility of a clearer territorial delineation of the sphere of greatest influence of several parties.

The future role of the political parties, and hence the future of the parliamentary system in general, will depend on the ability of the parties to rebuild themselves gradually into effective instruments of political power, able to cope with the concrete issues of the nation. To that end it will be necessary to develop the ties which so far have held party membership together into something more politically manageable.

In facing up to these problems which come with their attainment of power, the political parties, however, cannot afford to overlook the fundamental balance they have to maintain with the impatient and essentially revolutionary demands of colonial nationalism.

These are some of the problems which have put definite limitations to the role of political parties in Indonesia, and which so far they have in many cases not really come to grips with.

To the extent then, that political parties still are unable to cope with them, it is up to the political wisdom of the government to deal with them. It would prove a lack of statesmanship if a government in deciding upon its course of action were only to take into account parliamentary majorities.

Extra-parliamentary factors, such as the ones mentioned above, are bound to continue to play a role of considerable importance. Disregard of them, or inability to cope with them will lead to extra-parliamentary political crises. Political power being as diffuse as it now is, too much emphasis, for instance on centralism, on one particular area, on one particular religion, or on one particular ideology, upsetting the delicate system of political balances, may lead, and in some cases has led, to armed rebellion, and eventually to the breakdown of the national political structure, either through separatism or through chaos without a clear and open break.

In this connection the position of the army has proved to be of great importance. Like the political parties themselves, the army was a product and an instrument of the revolution. As such the army, too, next to the political parties, considers itself the embodiment of the national ideals. The army has therefore always felt that it shares equally with the political parties the responsibility for the welfare of the nation. This has led to an uneasy balance between the role and responsibility of the political parties and those of the army, as each of them saw it. This balance has so far not been able to find adequate expression within the parliamentary framework. Hence the army has in the past often been, and will for sometime in the future continue to be, one of the extra-parliamentary factors to be seriously taken into account in plotting the course of the nation.

There is in Indonesia one more political factor extending beyond the scope of the political parties which should be briefly mentioned here—the President. Despite the fact that his constitutional position places him outside the political arena, his personal authority and political acumen have almost inevitably made him and his opinions one of the very important political data, which no political party can afford to ignore.

We now can draw the following conclusions regarding the role of political parties in Indonesia.

1. The political parties in Indonesia have been the most important expression of the awakening of national political consciousness; they were the main instruments in the struggle for freedom and parliamentary democracy.

2. At this stage of their development they still represent psychological attitudes and mental climates rather than articulate political opinions, although they all operate on the basis of a strong nationalist tide. Hence the comparatively insignificant role of ideologies as distinctive factors in the political spectrum, and the important role of personalities. Loosely organized, the political power of parties is concentrated in, but widely distributed among, the politically conscious elite. The ability of parties to bring large masses to the polls is not yet a measure of their effective political power, although, of course it provides a basis for the gradual building of such power.

3. In this situation the political parties do not as yet encompass all political developments of the country. Consequently, parliament does not fully represent all of the political factors at play.

4. Extra-parliamentary political developments will, therefore, continue to play an important role for some time to come. The art of government lies in the ability to gauge and cope with these extra-parliamentary and extra-party factors; government policies and decisions cannot solely rest on parliamentary considerations. Without having developed the point before, one could also say in this connection that the fight for increasing political awareness, for democratic government and for Indonesia's introduction into the twentieth century, will to a large extent have to be waged within the political parties themselves. In fact the political parties will be important agencies through which the social and cultural changes necessary to this end will be effectuated.

If Indonesia's political parties are eventually to represent the whole range of political opinion within the country and if the sound development of Indonesia's parliamentary democracy is to continue, the political parties have a tremendous task to fulfill within themselves in terms of political education.

Problems of political integration in Southeast Asia

BRIAN HARRISON

Hong Kong University

The historical causes of political disintegration in Southeast Asian societies have been fully though not, of course, exhaustively examined and described.[1] I shall not attempt to discuss the question how far what we are here concerned with should really be described as problems of *re*integration.

It may be helpful to look first at some of the universal aspects of the problem before discussing it in its Southeast Asian context. For we are really concerned with particular cases of a general problem— that of unity and diversity in politics; or, we might say, the problem of state unity and national diversity.

Most states, if not all, have had to face this problem at one time or another and in one form or another. National integration is clearly a matter of degree; the national state represents, after all, an only more or less stable balance of centripetal and centrifugal forces. A culture has been compared to "a series of *more or less* efficiently intermeshed gears,"[2] and we may perhaps usefully apply the comparison also to national integration.

[1] J. S. Furnivall, *Colonial Policy and Practice* (Cambridge University Press, 1948).

[2] Cora Du Bois, *Social Forces in Southeast Asia* (University of Minnesota Press, 1949), p. 18 (the italics are mine).

National diversity—the complex of differences of political, social and religious ideas, of language, even of race, within a nation state— is then an almost universal condition. Naturally, where diversity is least the possibility of integration will be greatest. Thus in the West a unitary form of state is an indication that national diversity is comparatively unimportant. Yet even in a unitary state we do not expect to find complete national cohesion, rather a comparatively high degree of cohesion.

A federal state allows for a greater national diversity than does the unitary state. The component parts or groups of a federation desire union but not unity;[3] they wish to form a single nation for certain purposes but not for all purposes. The value of the federal system is therefore that it achieves a working compromise between unity and diversity, a balance, more delicate than that required of the unitary system, between centripetal and centrifugal forces.

National diversity may be, or may become, so wide and so uncompromising that it cannot be contained within a federal system, much less within a unitary one. The result then may be partition; complete disintegration, that is, of the original unit. Partition is a confession of failure to achieve reconciliation of major differences within a single state system.

The forces of integration and disintegration are perpetually at work in all states—here one counterbalances the other in a more or less delicate equipoise; there one outweighs the other, creating a disequillibrium that may lead to disunion.

In the West the development of the forces of integration has been a slow one; they could not be called into being at will; in the last analysis they have had to await the formation of a general disposition toward integration in the minds of the majority of the people concerned. This is not to deny that the forces making for integration have been nursed and strengthened by national governments as a matter of conscious policy. But policy of itself could only assist what was, after all, a mental process; somehow men's minds and wills had to be fired by the desire and the determination to achieve integration among themselves. Nationality, citizenship—these, in the West, were ideas in

---

[3] A. V. Dicey, *Introduction to the Study of the Law of the Constitution* (Macmillan, 1927), p. 137.

the minds of man for a long time before being translated into terms of certificates and dossiers on the desks of officials.

Whereas in the West the growth of a sense of nationality was a gradual process culminating in the full emergence of the sovereign nation state of the present day, with its national signs and symbols, in the East, while mechanism of the modern nation state is being more or less faithfully reproduced, complete with signs and symbols, the sense of nationality is only at an early stage of development. We need not, of course, assume that the countries of the East should or must follow the pattern of historical or institutional development in the West. And because development along a certain line was very slow and gradual in the West, it does not necessarily follow that it cannot be, or ought not to be, very fast in the East. And if we find that in fact it *is* fast, there is no need to regard this as somehow improper. Still, it does not seem at all likely, in view of the conditions actually discernible today, that the pace of national integration in Southeast Asian countries can be very rapid.

The factors that make for national integration have often been discussed. A common language, a common religion, a common racial origin, a common historical and geographical environment, a common will—these are usually mentioned as being desirable or even necessary.[4]

A common language is clearly one of the most important factors favoring political integration. That it is not an indispensable factor is shown by the examples of Switzerland, Canada and the U.S.S.R., among other states. And the achievement of national status by one of several possible languages or dialects may be largely a matter of historical chance, depending not so much upon linguistic principles as upon the outcome of political and social forces.[5] However that may be, there can be no doubt of the integrational value of a common language—as, for example, among the Chinese people. In India, which lacks this advantage, official policy aims at establishing Hindi

---

[4] *Nationalism: A Report by a Study Group of Members of the Royal Institute of International Affairs, London* (Oxford University Press, 1939), p. 254 ff.

[5] Rupert Emerson notes a tendency toward *ex post facto* reasoning in regard to national language, in "Paradoxes of Asian Nationalism," *Far Eastern Quarterly*, Vol. XIII, No. 2 (February 1954), pp. 131–142.

as a national language in the interests of integration, and in order to counteract "linguistic regionalism."[6]

In Southeast Asian countries linguistic regionalism remains a formidable obstacle in the path toward national integration. It is true that in several instances Japanese wartime occupation had the eventual effect of promoting integration in this as well as in other respects; this was so in the Philippines and Indonesia, though not in Burma. In Indonesia the use of the *bahasa* spread rapidly during the Japanese occupation. This, it has been noted, "had important effects in stimulating a consciousness of unity among the indigenous peoples of the East Indian archipelago, and in making the term 'Indonesian' something more than a mere appellation of convenience."[7] A common language grows out of unity and itself stimulates unity. In this and in other respects we need not, of course, underestimate the unifying effect of the previous period of Western colonial rule.[8]

A relevant question here is the extent to which a foreign language such as English can act, or can be accepted, as a primary or secondary aid toward integration. The use of English as a second language in Indonesia is interesting. In Malaya, of course, English approaches much more nearly to primary status, but British postwar policy of "encouraging a spirit of common nationality among the communities on the basis of a common language, namely English,"[9] has aroused opposition from members of at least one community, the Chinese.

Language as a key factor in the integration of Southeast Asian societies naturally features prominently in educational policies, which are themselves vitally concerned with integration—political, social, and cultural. In a recent work of particular value for this whole discussion, Virginia Thompson and Richard Adloff lay proper emphasis on the importance of education in the newly independent states as "a major means of creating national unity and of training future citizens among

---

[6] Marshall Windmiller, "Linguistic Regionalism in India," *Pacific Affairs*, Vol. XXVII, No. 4 (December 1954), pp. 291–318.

[7] F. C. Jones, *Japan's New Order in East Asia* (Oxford University Press, 1954), p. 373.

[8] J. F. Halkema Kohl, "Colonial Nationalism," *Indonesia*, Vol. VII (1953–54), pp. 36–61.

[9] Victor Purcell, "The Crisis in Malayan Education," *Pacific Affairs*, Vol. XXVI, No. 1 (March 1953), pp. 70–76.

ethnically diverse and very largely illiterate populations."[10] But education is a slow process, and there is therefore a special need for urgency in the planning of national education programs and for the provision of schools, teachers and equipment. However, the difficulties in the way of national educational schemes in Southeast Asia generally are enormous; shortages of money and of trained teachers are encountered everywhere.

The spread of modern education is bound to have disturbing and disintegrating effects at first; these effects can only be remedied by *more* education. But it is where wide ethnic as well as linguistic diversity exists that the disintegrating effects of education can be greatest, and the practical problems of education in its task of nation building most difficult.

This brief discussion of education brings us to consideration of another of the factors already mentioned as favoring national integration—that of a common racial origin. The absence of this factor, as is well known, constitutes a formidable obstacle to integration in Southeast Asian countries. In the sphere of education it presents the major problem of bringing the education of Chinese (and Indians) within a national scheme. Education organized on a communal or racial basis has been, and continues to be, a serious obstacle to integration. With regard to Chinese independent schools, the problem which they would in any case present for a national educational policy is complicated and intensified by the part they play as agencies of Communist indoctrination. It is this latter aspect of the problem which impresses itself most urgently on the governments of Southeast Asia, whose reaction has frequently been to resort to repressive measures. This is understandable enough, but constructive measures are clearly also required if progress toward integration is to be made. It is important that the problem of Chinese education in Southeast Asian countries be tackled no less vigorously in its national than in its extranational aspect, for success in regard to the first is most likely to bring success in regard to the second.

But how is this particular problem of integration to be tackled? In Thailand, according to Thompson and Adloff, the government "is determined to continue, if not intensify, its present policy toward

[10] Virginia Thompson and Richard Adloff, *Minority Problems in Southeast Asia* (Stanford University Press, 1955), p. 8.

Chinese education in the hope that eventually it can force the majority of Chinese children in the country to attend Thai schools."[11] A different answer is suggested by Malaya where in 1951 a Special Committee appointed by the Legislative Council accepted the principle of free education in national primary schools, with instruction in English and Malay as well as provision for the teaching of Chinese and Tamil, such primary schools to lead on to English secondary schools.[12] In Burma, well acquainted with the problem of linguistic regionalism, the policy announced as early as 1946 was that of permitting the Indian alien minority as well as the national minorities to use their vernaculars as a main language in the primary school stage, the main language at the secondary stage to be Burmese.[13]

Where the problem of educational integration is not so complicated by ethnic and linguistic diversity, there is more scope for the encouragement of school societies, local school management committees and parent-teacher associations, as a means of creating the concept of a common citizenship through the practice of community service.

These are only some of the educational aspects of the problem of political integration in a multiracial society. Another difficult aspect of the problem is that of citizenship and nationality—especially again in relation to the Chinese. Generally speaking, government policies in Southeast Asia are torn between a desire for political integration and a suspicion that the Chinese cannot or will not be integrated. Within the limits of this generalization, policy in any one country naturally tends to be determined by the numerical strength of the Chinese rather than on general principles. In Malaya, as a result of a series of policy modifications since the war, citizenship is now automatically accorded to any Chinese or other non-Malay born in the Federation, one of whose parents was also born there. This has been described as "the most realistic approach to the problem yet attempted

---

[11] V. Thompson and R. Adloff, *op. cit.*, p. 48. See also R. J. Coughlin, "The Status of the Chinese Minority in Thailand," *Pacific Affairs*, Vol. XXV, No. 4 (December 1954), p. 383.

[12] A revision of this policy is reportedly planned by the new Alliance government of the Federation of Malaya.

[13] "This liberal policy has saved the language question in Burma from becoming the problem that it represents in Malaya." (V. Thompson and R. Adloff, *op. cit.*, p. 89.)

in any Southeast Asian country."[14] Since 1953 the law in Thailand has been that a child born of non-Thai parents is classed as alien, but if the mother is Thai the child is Thai, unless already registered as alien.[15]

But as long as the traditional attitude of Chinese governments toward overseas Chinese persisted—the attitude that a Chinese, whatever his status in another land, is always a citizen of China—the gaining of citizenship by Chinese in a Southeast Asian country did not necessarily indicate acceptance on their part of a single national allegiance. In the interests of real political integration attempts have therefore been made to resolve the issue of dual nationality by inducing the alien minorities to make the positive choice of accepting or rejecting a local citizenship which would involve a definite renunciation of the citizenship of their original homeland. Efforts of this kind have been made in Indonesia and in Burma but so far they have not met with much success.

The positive choice of citizenship is a difficult one if only because of uncertainty as to what a choice really implies. However strong their sentimental attachment to Chinese nationality may be, overseas Chinese may feel reluctant to register their names in the local embassy of the present government of China. There is also the question how far local citizenship is intended to carry with it full possession of all rights and privileges of nationality; and how far, on the other hand, discrimination against former alien minorities is to continue despite acquisition of citizenship. Are they to be treated as second-class citizens? Will restrictions be retained, for example, on landownership and on the pursuit of certain occupations?[16]

A co-operative attempt to resolve the dual nationality issue in regard to the two and a half million Chinese in Indonesia was made at the Bandung Conference in April, 1955, in the form of a treaty between China and Indonesia; and Premier Chou En-lai declared, at the plenary session of the conference, that his government was willing to settle the dual nationality question with all other governments concerned. Under

[14] V. Thompson and R. Adloff, *op. cit.*, p. 36. See also Francis G. Carnell, "Constitutional Reform and Elections in Malaya," *Pacific Affairs*, Vol. XXVII, No. 3 (September 1954), pp. 216–235.

[15] V. Thompson and R. Adloff, *op. cit.*, p. 44.

[16] See R. J. Coughlin, *op. cit.*, p. 381.

the arrangement, which calls for positive choice of nationality by Chinese in Indonesia within two years, Indonesian nationality must be either accepted or renounced by declaration before a representative of the appropriate government. Those who fail to make the choice within the period will have it made for them: The child of a father of Chinese origin will be classed as a Chinese national. Whether this arrangement will succeed where others have failed remains to be seen.

The question of dual nationality is one of the extra-national aspects of the problem of political integration, and it seems likely that no real solution of the question can be found until the national aspect of the problem itself is solved. It may be important, in other words, that overseas Chinese and Indians should be pressed, if not forced, to make up their minds about which nationality they prefer, but it is more important that they should *want* to have the nationality of the country which is their permanent home. This cannot be brought about by registration or declaration. People cannot be cornered into loyalty; their loyalty must somehow be won.

Another factor in the problem of racial diversity in Southeast Asia is the presence of a number of national as well as alien minorities. The case of the Eurasian minorities is comparatively clear-cut. For since these carry little weight politically or economically within their own countries, and since extra-national considerations carry even less weight, it would seem that complete integration of the Eurasians, painful as the process may be to some of them, is only a matter of time. It is in Indonesia that their present position is perhaps most difficult, if only by reason of the contrast between the present and the past. Eurasians in Indonesia qualified for Dutch citizenship; they came to belong politically and socially to the Dutch world, and by 1930 they constituted 56 per cent of the total population classified as "European." After the war most Eurasians were committed to the Dutch side in the struggle for Indonesian independence. In 1949, when Indonesia gained independence, Eurasians were given a two-year period in which to opt for citizenship, but at the end of that period only about 11 per cent of the total community had declared for Indonesian citizenship.[17]

A stiffer problem for political integration is set by the more fully national minorities, such as Karens and Arakanese in Burma, or Am-

[17] Paul W. van der Veur, "The Eurasians of Indonesia, Castaways of Colonialism," *Pacific Affairs*, Vol. XXVII, No. 2 (June 1954), pp. 124–137.

bonese in Indonesia. About four of the eighteen million people of Burma belong to such minorities. Indonesia contains "many sub-races of Indonesian stock, each with its own language, customs, social structure and, in certain cases, religion."[18] Where such minorities feel themselves to be so distinct from the national majority that they demand some form of local self-government, the federal system may, on purely institutional grounds, be the answer. In Burma it was the answer applied to the compact Shan, Kachin and Chin minorities in their frontier areas which had already been under separate administration from the rest of Burma under British rule, but not to the widely scattered Karens, nor to the Mons. It was the answer applied to the Indonesian Republic as a whole from December, 1949, until a unitary constitution replaced the federal one some seven months later.[19] The federal system, in the precise meaning which it has for constitutional lawyers in the West, is not likely to suit conditions outside the West without some modification or adaptation. But the decisive objection to the federal scheme as applied to Indonesia was not that it was unsuitable but that it was Dutch. A reaction in favor of the practical value of the federal idea may perhaps be foreshadowed in the reported intention of the new Indonesian government formed in August, 1955, to grant increased autonomy to provincial areas.

Geographical diversity often accompanies the political separatism which impedes full integration. Especially in Burma, Indonesia and the Philippines, difficult geographical barriers to integration have to be surmounted. In Burma, for example, Arakan is largely isolated from the rest of the country by a long range of hills—and, partly in consequence, it has been the seat of a strong separatist movement.[20] Because of its vast extent, not to mention its geographical complexity, the territory of Indonesia must inevitably present great difficulties for political integration under a centralized government. In the island republic of the Philippines separatism is favored by extreme geographi-

[18] L. G. M. Jacquet, "The Indonesian Federal Problem Reconsidered," *Pacific Affairs*, Vol. XXV, No. 2 (June 1952), pp. 170–175. Other minorities of some importance are the Thai of Tonkin and the Malays of Thailand.

[19] Actually, according to George McT. Kahin, in William L. Holland (ed.), *Asian Nationalism and the West* (New York, the Macmillan Co., 1953), p. 111, the federal system remained intact for only a scant six weeks.

[20] V. Thompson and R. Adloff, *op. cit.*, pp. 151–158.

cal fragmentation. The colonial regimes of the past certainly laid valuable foundations for integration when they began to draw such wide areas together by modern means of communication. Transportation and communication systems are of key importance not only for economic progress but also for political advance; yet in large parts of Southeast Asia they remain sadly inadequate.

Turning again to the problem of alien minorities in Southeast Asia, it is well known that these form not only racial but also economic obstacles to political integration. Economic and ethnic diversities often coincide. The contrast between the economic situation of the Chinese entrepreneur in Malaya or the Indian Chettiar in prewar Burma, and that of the indigenous Malay or Burmese peasant, has often been noticed. The problem of reducing such wide contrasts in economic status is an extremely difficult one. How far and how soon can indigenous peoples hope to participate in the valuable economic activities now or formerly carried on by Chinese and Indians? Can these alien minorities be replaced as the small man's moneylender, as the financier of the Southeast Asian peasant? The co-operative system, so far, has not been able to replace them.[21] Burma's Land Acts of 1948 released perhaps a quarter of the country's best riceland from the grip of the Chettiars,[22] but the hold of the Chinese on Southeast Asia's economy in general remains. On the Malayan aspect of this problem it has been remarked that a nation can only be built on a basis of approximate equality of status among the members of all races; that "the political status of the Chinese and the economic status of the Malays should be simultaneously developed towards equality."[23] With the spirit of that observation one must surely agree, while admitting the great difficulties in the way of establishing and maintaining even a rough equality.

Apart from the position of alien minorities, the economic structure of the dual societies of Southeast Asia tends in itself to retard political integration. The division between town and country represents not only a division of economic interests between the immigrant groups

---

[21] See Prof. Dr. J. H. Boeke, "Three Forms of Disintegration in Dual Societies," *Indonesië*, Vol. VII (1953–54), pp. 278–295.

[22] V. Thompson and R. Adloff, *op. cit.*, pp. 83–84.

[23] T. H. Silock and Ungku Abdul Aziz, in William L. Holland (ed.), *op. cit.*, p. 330.

and the indigenous (the Chinese minorities as a whole are becoming increasingly urbanized), but also a division among the indigenous themselves. According to one view, "as they advance economically, the leading classes become more pronouncedly urban in character . . . . The rural elite deserts the countryside," and "in general, the rural masses in dual societies are growing poorer and poorer."[24] J. H. Boeke even doubts the possibility of social-economic integration at all in the heterogeneous societies of Southeast Asia, in which, he argues, the two social systems of capitalism and pre-capitalism exist, and will continue to exist, side by side but separate from one another, having no positive or organic connection.[25]

Economic diversity in Southeast Asia is often accompanied not only by racial but also by religious diversity. Religion may sometimes, however, act as a powerful integrating force, as in Burma or Indonesia as a whole. It is well known that in Burma in the past, "political and social life . . . from the palace down to the village, centered around the Buddhist religion."[26] After a postwar period of reaction, the government of Burma in 1950 established a central Buddhist organization responsible for promoting religious unity in the country.[27] But many Karens in Burma are Christian, as are many Ambonese in Indonesia. The Mujahids in northern Arakan, the Malays in southern Thailand, and the Moros of Mindinao in the Philippines, form religious as well as racial minority pockets. In Indonesia the vast majority (perhaps nine-tenths) of the population of eighty million are Muslim, but even within this majority religious cohesion is not complete. One observer notes "the existence of three Muslim political parties besides the Masjumi, all aiming at a Muslim state, all hoping for Muslim unity in Indonesia, and all opposed," and he adds that "the same divisions are . . . reflected in the purely religious field."[28]

The existence of a common or general will—however this may be defined—is perhaps the factor most vitally necessary for national inte-

[24] Boeke, op. cit., p. 283 ff.

[25] Boeke, ibid., p. 293.

[26] John F. Cady, "Religion and Politics in Modern Burma," Far Eastern Quarterly, Vol. XII, No. 2 (February 1953), pp. 149–162.

[27] The Buddha Sasana Act of 1950. See Cady, op. cit., p. 160.

[28] Leslie H. Palmer, "Modern Islam in Indonesia," Pacific Affairs, Vol. XXVII, No. 3 (September 1954), pp. 255–263.

gration. Movements for national independence can create great internal political cohesion, but this tends to weaken once independence is achieved, with the result that there is a loss of national *élan*. If this national spirit is to be recovered and strengthened, the people must somehow begin to feel a sense of active participation in the political life of the state—that participation which was for Aristotle the very essence of citizenship. Western observers are perhaps inclined to attribute greater importance to the operation of democratic institutions than can be justified by actual conditions in some Southeast Asian countries, but even where it is true that participation in parliamentary elections cannot result in the expression of a general will because no such will exists, elections may be one of the means of creating a general will. This can be so, however, only where elections have a genuinely national significance. Where either the qualifications of the electors or the responsibilities of the elected are unduly restricted, the nation-building value of democratic machinery must remain limited.

It is sometimes suggested that the practice of active participation in the political life of the community be encouraged and developed in Southeast Asian countries at the village level. Economists point to the nation-building value of community projects in India and Ceylon which stress voluntary participation, self-help and mutual help.[29] Self-help is certainly the best help, and the village community may contribute powerfully to the growth of a national spirit by encouraging an increasing acceptance of group as well as individual responsibilities. It may well be that village community projects offer a real hope of reconciling the individualist emphasis of Western political and social ideas with the traditional group and family emphasis of Southeast Asian societies. With regard to the more purely political aspect of the village community as a factor in integration, the point is sometimes made that in some Southeast Asian countries the practice of democracy has long been established as part of village life. However true that may be, it is still a question how far "village democratic experience can be translated in any direct fashion to the national scene."[30] At

[29] H. Belshaw, "Some Aspects of Economic Development in Under-developed Countries in Asia" (New Zealand Paper No. 2, 12th Conference of the Institute of Pacific Relations, Kyoto, September 1954).

[30] Rupert Emerson, "Problems of Representative Government in Southeast Asia," *Pacific Affairs*, Vol. XXVI, No. 4 (December 1953), pp. 291–302.

the same time it is hard to see how political integration can be achieved without the establishment of an effective relationship between the village and the national government.

The spread of experience in local government bodies may assist political integration, even if only to a limited extent. The comparative lack of success of local government in India and Burma in past years has been commented on, and it seems clear that unless it is coupled with real local responsibility—the power of making and carrying out important decisions—local government can have only a very restricted value as a school of political education.[31]

National elections to a representative assembly can certainly promote a process of political integration by nurturing a common will, a national spirit, a public opinion. The Philippine presidential election of 1953 was "the calmest and cleanest election since independence" largely because of the pressure of public opinion in favor of a free and fair election.[32] But elections do not make a democracy; a far more essential feature of Western democracy—the feature that gives reality to the elector's choice—is the existence of an organized opposition within the state. Paradoxical as it may seem, if people are to get used to the idea of a common will within a framework of democratic institutions they must get used to the idea of an organized constitutional opposition to the existing government. The opinion has been expressed, however, that the peoples of Asia "do not as yet have any conception of the possibility that there could be an organized and legal opposition to the established authority.[33]

A number of other factors may seem to favor the existence of authoritarian government in the countries of Southeast Asia. In a way, national diversity strengthens a tendency toward single-party government; the pressing need of the moment may seem to be for a government strong enough to solve complex social and economic problems—which tend to take priority over internal political problems. But a healthy process of political integration can hardly take place unless the authoritarian form of government is superseded by a genuinely

[31] Hugh Tinker, *The Foundations of Local Self-Government in India, Pakistan and Burma* (London, Athlone Press, 1954), p. 333 ff.

[32] Willard H. Elsbree, "The 1953 Philippine Presidential Elections," *Pacific Affairs*, Vol. XXVII, No. 1 (March 1954), pp. 3–15.

[33] Philippe Devillers in William L. Holland (ed.), *op. cit.*, p. 258.

democratic one. Sound integration requires that the wide political gap between the small Western-educated governing elite and the mass of the population be bridged. In this connection, the absence of a substantial indigenous middle class is sometimes considered to be a serious obstacle to democratic political integration in Southeast Asia.[34] That may be so, though it is worth noting that in the Philippines, where "that backbone of Western democracy, the middle classes as we know them, does not exist,"[35] the electoral system at any rate has worked impressively well.

Another supposed obstacle to the proper working of elections is a low literacy rate, as for example in Indonesia, where "perhaps only two-fifths of the people are literate."[36] But India's success in running a massive general election leads one to doubt whether illiteracy—or a variety of languages and creeds—need be incompatible with the working of democracy.

But the hardest part of the problem of political integration turns on the position of the alien minorities, especially the nine or ten million Chinese. The Indian minority in Southeast Asia, it has been remarked, "no longer constitutes a problem, for it has so shrunk in numbers and economic importance as to have ceased to arouse hostility";[37] though, it may be added, the problem of integration—even with regard to small minorities—is one not merely of reducing hostility but of increasing co-operation. The Chinese, on the other hand, are increasing in numbers, even where, as in the Federation of Malaya, immigration is restricted; in Malaya and Singapore together they have become a majority, slightly outnumbering the Malays. But an increasing proportion of these Chinese are local-born, and the overseas Chinese as a whole are becoming more rooted in Southeast Asia. In Singapore (a special case because of the fact that the Chinese constitute an overwhelming majority) nearly three-quarters of the population is local-born, and, more significant, more than half are under twenty-

[34] Rupert Emerson, *op. cit.*, p. 296; Lennox A. Mills, *The New World of Southeast Asia* (University of Minnesota Press, 1950), p. 305.

[35] Henry L. Mason, "Problems of Philippine Independence," *Indonesië*, Vol. III (1949–50), No. 5, pp. 447–467.

[36] Herbert Feith, "Toward Elections in Indonesia," *Pacific Affairs*, Vol. XXVII, No. 3 (September 1954), pp. 236–254.

[37] V. Thompson and R. Adloff, *op. cit.*, p. 285 ff.

one years of age. The prospects for integration everywhere improve
as the younger generation grows up.

The approach to the problems of integration must itself be integrated
if it is to succeed; it must be a planned approach from a number of
different angles. It is not really possible to isolate one aspect of
national integration (social, economic, cultural, or political) from the
others. One point seems clear; "the minorities, both ethnic and alien,
are in the region to stay, whether the national majorities like it or
not."[38] Repressive or discriminatory measures against minorities will
not encourage integration, but rather will prevent it. Finally it may
be added that the whole problem is essentially one for internal solution; progress toward a solution in each country will depend upon how
far the people can succeed in coming to peace with themselves. Stability, continuity, and integrity in government and public affairs are
key conditions making for political integration. Steady development,
such as India and Burma have had in the past few years, is required.
The prospects on the whole are good.

[38] V. Thompson and R. Adloff, *op. cit.*, p. 286.

Burma: the political integration of linguistic and religious minority groups

KYAW THET

Rangoon University

The local conception of political integration is of some importance largely because some of the problems of political implementation are significantly affected by, perhaps even created by, the methods and ends of the particular method of integration. It may easily be understood that the problems of political integration faced by the British in a Burma conquered by force of arms and annexed by proclamation with the end of inducing a lesser breed to wave the Union Jack at the happy prospect of indefinite economic, political and social inferiority to a ruling class setting wearily out from the minor public schools to bear its share of the white man's burden would not perhaps be identical with those faced by the national leaders of independent Burma. Political integration as it is being implemented in Burma today is not of the type which has been made evident in the incorporation of the Baltic states into the Soviet Union. Neither is it of the type which made Burma a part of Queen Victoria's empire. There the technique and the tempo of integration were always dominated by the availability of overwhelming force and the willingness to use it. These methods have not had general public acceptance in this country, and this particular state of mind holding true of all sections of responsible opinion, the problems are in Burma seen in a different light and have so been handled.

It may be postulated at this stage that revolutionary liberalism is a necessity of the government and not a choice and that this Union never commanded the resources to prove that it had rejected the older types of political integration as of choice. The Union of Burma has demonstrated over the past seven years through mutiny, ambush, and insurrection, that it commands in relation to all opposing dissident groups overwhelming and viable resources, and yet it still adheres to the liberal approach which already to some appears excessively circumspect and tedious. Time and circumspection have however been accepted by the responsible people as integral factors for the success of any worthwhile political integration in Burma. As Prime Minister U Nu in the speech to the regimental commanders of the Burma army said "Before we decided on our final choice of these two roads—democracy or dictatorship—we pondered deeply . . . . We studied them from all aspects and then only we discarded dictatorship and chose democracy. We made our choice not haphazardly but after serious consideration."

Historically the problems of political integration have always existed and never been adequately solved in Burma. The Burmese kings who ruled just 70 years ago were perhaps fortunate in that although they faced some similar problems, at least, they escaped the new ones brought in by Burma's entry into world society and economy.

The first problems of political integration in Burma are those raised by geography and demographic distribution. In the nation state that is known as Burma today, society was overwhelmingly influenced by the rate and pattern of the peopling and settlement of the country. The process of settlement has been comparatively recent; scholarship and tradition both agree that the chief races and types who at present inhabit the area only began coming into Burma about the early centuries of the Christian era. According to the very carefully checked census of 1783 carried out by the Burmese king Bodawpaya there were only four million people in Burma at that date. About a hundred years later, after the British had taken over, it is estimated that the population had only increased to about seven million. These figures would therefore indicate that the process of settlement was if anything a matter of small groups and tribes trickling in.

The physical geography of the area in turn influenced the pattern of settlement. Burma is roughly the shape of a diamond with the southern base blunted to the deltaic zone around the Gulf of Martaban. From the southeast a long tail forms the Tenasserim division which physically is made up of the fairly long but narrow coastal plain with a central mountainous spine which is shared by Thailand on its eastern side. In the north there is an arc of forbidding mountains, snow clad on the higher slopes and densely jungled on the lower. This mountain system in the northeast merges into the central mass of the Southeast Asian peninsula, the Burma portion of which is known as the Shan plateau and is regarded as the eastern highlands of the country. Then again curving out in a southerly direction from the north mountain area are two mountain ranges, the Arakan and the lesser and more traversible Pegu. The intervening valleys are those of the Irrawaddy and Sittang rivers, which, having a network of approach tributary valleys both west and east, serve to provide access to and from the side regions of the country. Finally west of the Arakan range is the rather inaccessible Arakan coastal strip.

Into this isolated backwater, off the main trade and travel routes of the world, physically protected from being swamped by the two great neighbor cultures of the Indic and Sinic worlds, into the remote valleys and spurs, the nooks and crannies and corners, trickled and eddied a medley of tribal groups. The general direction of the movement was always to the south, the immigrants desperately withdrawing from the political domination and the threat of ruthless integration that continued proximity to Tibet and Tang China implied. The harshness and exactions of the Tibet and China of these days must not be underrated in an assessment of the motivations of those immigrants, but we may safely assume that in part they came away because of desires to formulate and hold their own attitudes and values and to live in the context of their own cultural patterns.

Broadly speaking the peoples of Burma who are regarded as indigenous today are divided into three main groups: the Monkhmers, the Tibeto-Burmans and the Thais. The order of arrival has not been in sequence and was never very orderly, in fact there has been much confusion and overlapping. The result therefore has been the cutting off of many kindred groups by streams and waves of other groups who were themselves affected by the same process. When to this devel-

opment is added the fact that some of these groups wandered into
isolated corners and cul de sacs, the groups who started off with the
same type of culture have now variously developed in the special way
of isolation and also in the diverse manner which exposure to different external factors must result in. In the beginning the various
groups seemed to have had a fairly similar level of culture, all primitive in equal degree with no consciousness of being either a majority
or minority cultural group. They could probably be classified as
primitive hill culture groups. About the second or third centuries after
Christ the first groups crossed the Rubicon between the essentially
primitive, hillside clearing and burning, dry cultivation and the wet
cultivation on the plains. The present day representatives of these
groups are the Mons and the Burmese, the close cousins they left behind on the hills are today the Was, Palaungs, Danaw and the Riang
on the side of the Mons and the Marus, Lashis and the Atsis on the
Burmese side. The Mons, the earlier group on the plains, and the
Burma Mons finally settled down in the south, around the mouths of
the Sittang and the Irrawaddy rivers. The Burmans on the other hand
settled down in the central zone of the area which has been rather
dry and rainless throughout history but which does include the two
irrigated districts of Kyaukse and Minbu.

The southern group first came into contact with the Hindu merchant
adventurers who were sailing all over the seas of Southeast Asia in
that period. The Mons soon acquired many of the graces, arts, skills,
techniques, and culture of the Hindus who were soon establishing small
colonies in the Mon area. The Burmans of the north on the other hand
though at a less polished level of culture had multiplied in numbers
and increased in strength and, hearing of the superior aspects of the
Mon culture of the south, were soon urgently desirous of emulation.
With the greater energy of their less sophisticated culture they swept
down in conquest and made a very thorough job of transplanting
en masse the whole physical basis and apparatus of the Mon culture.
The Burmans under the leadership of their kings but with the whole-
hearted co-operation of their subjects took to the borrowed culture with
all the enthusiasm of the fresh converts that they were. In time the
whole of the plains peoples belonged to the same cultural group, with
myths and traditions, values and attitudes, hopes and aspirations sufficiently similar to reinforce the pressures toward uniformity of culture

which similarities of physical and climatic environment and the common dependence on rice were producing. In the meantime beyond the foothills, in the horseshoe shaped areas of high peaks and ravines which framed the northern portions of the country the lesser groups, never achieving the cohesion and solidarity necessary to effect a radical change in their social patterns, went their own ways, vegetating in their remoteness and showing little signs of ever breaking out of their primitive parochialism. There were scores of little dialects hardly understood a day's march away.

In the twelfth century another major group came into the picture. They were the Shans, the Burma representatives of the Thai race. They infiltrated into the area now known as the Shan states and though seemingly possessed of fissiparous tendencies the favorable terrain and the fairly large valleys of the Shan plateau enabled them to establish sizable principalities where at one time a non-Buddhist culture was thriving. These Shans in the course of time began to come down onto the plains and soon became a serious threat to the political hegemony of the Mon-Burman group. When the Tartar terror swept into Burma in the thirteenth century the Shans acted as their auxiliaries and remained behind to set up Shan statelets on the plains. Within two centuries they were swept out of the plains and thrust back into their highland homes. When they went back they were, in almost every aspect of cultural significance, part of the plains cultural group. Once Burmese hegemony was re-established the setting up of close administrative links between the Shans and the plains, assured a cultural uniformity through the plains and the Shan highlands.

Mention must now be made of another group, the Karens who are divided into two distinct sections: the sgaw and the pwo. This group has been considered to be related to the Shans, but it has also been conjectured that the Karens came into the area much earlier than the Shans, in such scattered driblets, with such a noncohesive penchant for wandering off into remote corners and hilltops and jungle clearings that, in the period when the Mon-Burmese group was busily engaged in building up its areas of power the Karens, although present in the same areas in quite impressive aggregate numbers, were almost totally ignored and when noticed were normally treated with the smug airs of conscious superior righteousness and power.

Toward the end of the tribal migrations, early in the eleventh century came the first known attempts at political integration. Major tensions and antagonisms had arisen out of the conquest of the Mon country in the south by the Burmese kings of Pagan. The third king of the
dynasty, Sri Tribhuvanadityadhammaraj, firmly imbued with the sacro-
sanct and socially accepted principal of monarchical rule, attempted
integration by marrying his daughter to a Mon royal prince and naming
the issue as the heir over the prior claims of an elder but non-Mon son.
This attempt might have achieved the same measure of success achieved
by James Stuart's accession to the throne of England but in Burma
the integration was confined to the top, just a royal gesture, and
proved to be superficial for the Mons went their own way soon afterwards.

Through the remaining period of the Burmese kings even such
imaginative persuasion was unknown. The attempts at integration
were of the crudest sort and in the regions easily accessible. The
strictly limited objective of the kings was to impose a more or less
formal subjection to his house. The limited technical and manpower
resources of the state, the deep jungles and mountains enabled the
numerous and diverse groups to go their own way. In the eighteenth
and nineteenth centuries, coinciding with the coming of the Europeans,
there was a substantial increase in the strength of the Burmese state
and somewhat closer integration was sought. The Thais in the east were
sought to be brought in by the king's custom of marrying the daughters
and sisters of all the more important Shans chiefs or saophas. The sons
were brought in as pages and squires to be brought up as Burmese
princes. A feudal system of integration was the end result. In the less
accessible and poorer north the Burman state posted frontier officials
who issued chiefs' appointment orders. Nominal integration seems to
have been achieved. For example in 1830 the Daipha Gam, the paramount chief of the fabulous Hukawng valley, married the widow of
the Burmese myowun or governor of Mogaung as a means of consoli-
dating his position.

The impact of the British conquest and occupation resulted in bringing into the open the issue of the minorities. In a sense the British left
a difficult legacy by accentuating the distinctions and differences between the various groups, but it must also be said that they left a valid
tradition of effective political hegemony with control from Rangoon,

a sketchy but uniform system of statewide education and a modern communications network which ultimately should prove to outweigh the difficulties they created and left. The first contacts of the British were with the plains peoples, and the law and order government which the British soon imposed encouraged the Karens to emerge from their jungle hideouts to form in time the nucleus of the first real modern minority group. In the process they were aided and abetted by the missionaries who in providing them with the cultural basis of another major religion, alien and different from the Buddhist basis, inevitably encouraged them to regard themselves as apart from the other inhabitants of the country. In the taking over of the northwest the British decided on the policy of regarding the whole Chin area as a separate charge which was to be isolated from Burma proper. They set out to conserve or fossilize the many quaintnesses of the primitive culture with only such British-type administrative reform as was considered fitting on the part of the representative of the great Victorian culture. The only contact the Chins were encouraged to have with the plains people was as mercenaries who were used eventually to police the totally disarmed Burmans. The same pattern was also adopted in the northern region, the Kachins were encouraged to consider themselves apart and the administrative system was shaped towards this end. In the Shan areas the British, who were reluctant to embark on another and expensive campaign of conquest, were content merely to demonstrate their superior strength by means of flag marches, and to accept the submission of the hereditary chiefs and princes and to incorporate them more or less peacefully into the British Empire. This peculiar process, however, meant that whereas in the rest of Buddhist Burma the indigenous monarchical element was swept away with the exile of the king, the Shan states still retained as part of their culture pattern the exaggerated behavior patterns which the continued presence of a ruling chief implied. The red Karen area was likewise incorporated into the British Empire by a version of diplomatic arrangement. Here too the area was cut off as far as possible from Burma proper, and therefore another nucleus was formed for the eventual emergence of yet another minority group.

With the coming of the British, other minorities appeared. Burma had been conquered as an extension of the Indian empire, and naturally Indian troops were used in the conquest. After the normal processes of what is euphemistically and hypocritically called pacification, Indian and half-breed Indians were imported in increasing numbers to help man the lesser office jobs. Indian traders, craftsmen, and laborers soon enjoyed a privileged position in Burma by virtue of their familiarity with the various methods and techniques of their British masters, and they began coming in large numbers into the country. In the peak year of 1927 over 400,000 of them came in. Initially they had no thought of staying permanently in Burma but they soon did, and in the urban centers of the south and in the ricelands there were soon large Indian settlements.

The other minority that appeared with the British was the European half-breed. This group tried to fit itself as closely as possible to the European cultural group, and even though conscious of frustrations caused by a lack of any real acceptance by the group they tried to remain aloof as far as their limited economic resources would allow.

Still another minority group were the Chinese, who flocked in under the Pax Britannica, to handle so effectively the processing and distributive jobs of the new-style economy. The local cultural pattern and the lack of interest of the Manchus, enabled them to become absorbed in the caste free society but with the advent of the Kuomintang government and the greater ease of communication this desirable trend was halted and the Chinese became a more and more intransigent cultural minority.

When the time came for the British to hand over power to the representatives of the indigenous peoples, the British, who to a certain extent had come to hold themselves responsible for the integrity of the minority areas they had helped to create and preserve, stipulated in their preliminary negotiations for the transfer of power that the Burmese should offer adequate guarantees for the preservation of the rights—cultural and otherwise—of these minorities. These stipulations however were not as difficult as they might have been. In the first place the hill peoples had not been very enamored of the type of rule that the British had offered. On the one hand they had been encouraged to respect and look up to their tribal chiefs and leaders, who were given much authority over their own peoples. However, these same chiefs were required to subordinate themselves utterly to a number of frontier officials. The system thus aroused the antagonism of the most powerful elements of these minority groups. The Burmese leaders, conscious of the great weakening that partition had caused in the much larger unit that was British India, were determined that the minority groups were to be given anything reasonable, and it has throughout been in this kind of mood that relations between the state and the cultural minorities have been evolved. This determination created at the very outset a situation somewhat reminiscent of A. V. Dicey's classic statement that federalism ". . . requires for its formation two conditions . . . there must be a body of country so closely connected by locality, by history, by race or the like as to be capable of bearing, in the eyes of their inhabitants, an impress of common nationality." On the other hand there must be ". . . a peculiar state of sentiment among the inhabitants of the countries, which it is proposed to unite. They must desire union, and must not desire unity."

There were also other factors which reinforced the trend toward the recognition, federal in form, of the inherent democratic rights of the various minorities. In the first place the National Front, called the Anti-Fascist Peoples Freedom League, which had been set up to hasten the transfer of power, had been set up on as broad a basis as possible. All of the participating groups, regional, economic, religious, tribal, and linguistic had been assigned equal rights and responsibilities. When that organization came into power it was inevitable that the representatives of the various minorities should expect and receive equal degrees of power and responsibility. The first concrete step toward sharing power and responsibility, as a step forward in political integration, was taken at what has now come to be known as the Panglong Conference, held nine years ago. From the accounts of witnesses and participants, there seems to have been very early a general awareness and acceptance of the distinctiveness of the various groups. Then the sense of the imminent fulfilment of the aspirations of all, seems to have steadied and sobered all of the participants. On the heels of this came very fast an awareness of the interdependence of the various peoples of Burma. Out of all these feelings and attitudes, out of the emotionally charged atmosphere, the Burmans, the majority group, gave due recognition to the linguistic, cultural, and emotional sense of distinctiveness which had assured survival and given identity to these minorities. The minorities on their part signified their acceptance of responsibility for the Union by pledging their resources to the tasks of building up the Union. This sense of agreement and mutual understanding was implemented in the Constitution of the Union of Burma. Under the constitution the various indigenous minorities were to elect the members of their own state governments, who were to be at the same time members of the Union Legislature. The heads of state were to be cabinet ministers of the Union government.

The constitution of Burma is in a sense both a manifestation of the basic problem of the political integration of minorities and an attempted solution. The most explosive force created by the imposition of British colonial rule was nationalism. This explosive force injected into the basic problem of man's relation to organization, which is the very heart of political integration, has considerably complicated the situation. The spirit of independence making its appearance in the modern form with the American Revolution, has become in its manifestation of nationalism one of the essential factors in the relation of the state and the minorities. Nationalism is a decentralizing impulse which, in so far as it breaks up colonial systems, acts as the champion of minorities. Within itself however the mastering mood is one of centralization and this clashes with the interests of minorities. The paradox becomes even more pointed and the confusion of attitudes chaotic when it is remembered that while politically man is busily creating new nation states, he is at the same time reaching out for union among and across nations. However, on reconsideration the paradox becomes meaningful and the confusion only a seeming confusion. Man reaches out for integration into larger and larger units because he is forced to act on the fact, whether unpleasant to him or not, that the world is now a much smaller place in terms of space and communications barriers; on the other hand he creates new nation states because in the creation of the larger units which might one day develop into a single world unit he has to fight for and establish a position of recognition and guarantee both *de facto* and *de jure* in the sense of proper constitutional safeguards for minority rights. This latter process has been even more inevitable because of the effects of the violent and widespread outbreak of nineteenth-century imperialism. The various imperial powers generally proceeding on the assumption that all minority groups, or even subjugated groups, outnumbering the imperial power concerned, represented obsolete, inferior and in varying degrees redundant cultures which deserved consignment to oblivion in as decently speedy a manner as the political and administrative conditions would allow. This interpretation of the recent emergence of the nation states as one more manifestation of the problem of the relation of the state to the minorities, is in itself a basic guide to the solution of the problem. The problem after all is a question of forms of power, the use and control of tendencies toward abuse and inequity.

In the free world the ultimate rationale of the free man is the release of personality. Man is frustrated and rendered less creative by the atmosphere of ponderous organization and remote controls. He inevitably and invariably works toward the ends of resolving affairs and relationships into more comprehensible and manageable proportions. Even while he values the material basis of the good life, the analysis of human society which a shrinking world has forced upon the more thoughtful of his kind, makes him realize that he must take into account the endless permutations and combinations of interdependence and the imperative necessity of unity to survive. In the application of these thoughts in Burma the first salient problem must be how to drive home the fact that in many spheres of activity and at certain levels of association and organization the whole nation state is the minimal unit if it is to survive in the conditions of the present day world.

The next problem must be to consider how far the recognition of differences is a strategy in the integration of loyalties. The problem is how to give factual recognition to the cultural and other diversities in the national area by evolving a pattern of relationship which, while evoking additional psychological strength for the nation state from the minorities by an absence of oppressive coercion, will at the same time retain a degree of control sufficient to prevent the same minorities from becoming centers of fissiparous and disintegrative tendencies.

One basic factor in the situation has not yet been touched upon: that of the numerical ratios in the minorities pattern. The 1955 census figures are not yet completely available but it is possible to project the 1941 figures to give us a reasonably adequate guide.

We would then have in a total population of 18 million, a Buddhist group of 84 per cent. Of this group 90 per cent would speak Burmese, alone or as one of the two tongues spoken in the locality. Next comes an animist group of nearly 5 per cent, which could be split up into the numerous linguistic minorities in the north. Then come, with approximately 4 per cent each, the alien groups who are Hindu or Muslim, all speaking the tongues of India and Pakistan; but then again

99 per cent of them speaking Burmese as well. We then have the
Christians with 2.3 per cent. Two thirds are Karen speaking, about a
third from the northern hill tribes and a very small proportion Burmans and Anglo-Burmans. It is safe to assume that 98 per cent of the
Christians speak most adequate Burmese.

It will be immediately obvious from these statistics that the Burmese-
speaking majority is so large in proportion that the purely technical
business of making Burmese the official language for the Union is a
comparatively simple one. It is also simplified by two other factors.
One is that where the minority in question has progressed sufficiently
the literate members (excluding always the Indian and Pakistani
groups) use the phonetic Burmese script. The second factor is that
English is invariably understood by the politically advanced members.
Under the terms of the Union constitution while Burmese has been
made the official language English is also recognized. This basic
situation is of considerable help in the task of political integration
and has immediate relevance to the first problem I have put forward,
of driving home the necessity of having the whole nation state as the
minimal unit in many essential fields of activity. A legacy from the
British has stood the Union in good stead. Most of the frontier minorities were kept by the British, whether deliberately or not is still uncertain, in a remarkable state of physical isolation which in turn produced an equally remarkable absence of political consciousness or
even acquaintance with the workings of a modern state. As a result
a tradition of all affairs of state being directed from the capital,
Rangoon, was part of the political training of the minorities. When
independence came it was therefore easy to write into the constitution
clauses ensuring central control over education, finance, revenue, police,
defense, and foreign policy. The few individuals who might have
protested in the name of the minorities were disarmed by being asked
to become part of the central control as ministers, generals, permanent
secretaries, or ambassadors. Today, eight years after independence, a
glance at the list of ministers and officials will show that this method
of political integration is still being used and successfully.

In the other spheres, basically it is a question of persuading the
minorities that they will not be victimized because of their differences,
and that as far as possible the state will protect their right to be different. This right is guaranteed at once by the preamble of the

Union constitution, almost in the words and completely in the classical tradition of the American and French Revolutions. It must be remembered, lest there be any careless shrugging away of the actual efficacy of constitutional guarantee, that this Union constitution is the first one in the history of all the races in the Union, and that into its making have gone all of their highly charged emotions, and all of their understanding of true liberty. To the Burmans it has validity and meaning and it is certain that right at this moment they intend to honor its terms.

The theory and reality
of economic development

B. B. DAS GUPTA

Central Bank of Ceylon

Economic development is fast becoming a well-developed branch of economics. Much thinking has been done on it in recent years and the literature on it is growing. But still it can hardly be asserted that there is a complete or established theory of what development is or what forces generate and stimulate it.

Development is a complex, almost mysterious process. It requires a whole constellation of favorable forces. The primary economic factors have been and are being well discussed, although here also we are not sure that we know all the factors or the precise role that each plays. But development is more than an economic phenomenon. It depends on social, cultural, and political factors as well. For instance, it is hardly expected to flourish if social attitudes are hostile to saving, adoption of new techniques or occupational mobility, or if there is political disorder in the country. In England it seems to have been triggered by a wave of scientific inventions, but why these inventions took place in England rather than in any other country is difficult to explain. Even climate seems to play its part, for it is perhaps more than an accident that the temperate countries of the world are more developed than the tropical countries. The role of these extra-economic factors in development is, however, difficult to assess and even more difficult to control.

We are of course primarily concerned with the economic factors. Let us consider what particular shortcomings in these factors are cramping development in the countries of Southeast Asia.

There are broadly two conditions necessary for an expansion of production, (1) more or better factors of production and (2) market
opportunities. One is the supply and the other the demand side.
Mere availability of factors or resources is not enough; they will not
be harnessed for production unless the output can be marketed at a
profit. The two conditions are, however, not unrelated. A good market
tends to evoke a larger supply of factors of production, while a larger
supply of factors in turn would, by reducing costs, tend to widen the
market. But in the short period at least, they may be considered as
largely independent of each other.

There is no doubt that in Southeast Asia market limitation is a serious obstacle to development. The home market is small because
national income and national spending power are small. The home
market cannot, by itself, sustain any large increase in production,
although production must, in most fields, be organized on a large
scale to ensure competitive efficiency. Market limitation cramps particularly the growth of manufacturing industries, because the poorer
a country, the less is the proportion of its income that it spends on
manufactured goods. In Ceylon, for instance, the average consumer
spends 59.91 per cent of his total expenditure on food and only 2.54
per cent on clothing and 0.14 per cent on shoes.[1] The level of incomes
is so low that these percentages would not be likely to be much altered
even if incomes rose moderately. In other words, people would still
continue to spend the bulk of their income on food. In this situation
a producer will obviously think twice before he launches into any
ambitious scheme of production of manufactured goods. The home
market is of course not equally limited in all the countries of the region.
In India, although per capita income is small, the total volume of purchasing power seeking goods is, because of the size of the population,
much larger than in Ceylon. Consequently the size of the home market
is less a hindrance to development there than in Ceylon.

The external market also has limitations. The demand for many of
the primary commodities in which the region specializes is becoming
weak and uncertain because new sources of production, natural and
synthetic, are being tapped in other countries. The elasticity of export
demand for one commodity, rice, seems to have already fallen below

[1] Report of the Ceylon Consumer Finance Survey, 1954.

unity. The export outlook for manufactured goods is even less promising because of severe competition from highly industrialized countries and restrictive trade policies in most importing countries. In this respect Japan had an advantage over countries which are seeking development now. She had fewer competitors and tariff barriers to reckon with during her developmental stages.

Actually, the market problem though difficult should not preclude a satisfactory rate of development. The export market for some of the primary products, as for instance tea, is still good. Production of these commodities can still be profitably expanded. In the home market, although the expansion of one industry may be limited by the size of the market, the simultaneous expansion of a large number of industries which buy one another's products, will automatically create its own market. This kind of group advance will also, if it is localized, increase the external economies enjoyed by each firm and so reduce costs. This is one reason why industries tend to be gregarious. It is cheaper to run a factory in a place where there are many factories than where there are very few.

There is another way in which the home market may be enlarged for home producers, namely by capturing what is at present supplied by foreign producers. This is possible in quite a few fields, particularly in the field of small-scale industries. These light industries use a technology which is labor-intensive and capital-saving, but which nevertheless is no less efficient than the capital-intensive and labor-saving technology used in the industrialized countries. In countries where capital is scarce and costly, but labor is plentiful and cheap, this technology is obviously, both from the production and the employment angles, the most desirable. There seems particular scope for it in the production of such goods as textiles, footwear, domestic hardware, glassware, ceramics, umbrellas, soap, and biscuits. Japan has gone a long way in converting big factory industries into decentralized light industries, and her example may profitably be followed by the countries of Southeast Asia.

Thus market deficiency, though important, does not seem to be the root cause of the stagnation of the region. Actually, production has not even risen to the level of the existing market, the potential market lying completely untapped. The root cause seems to be on the supply side in factor scarcity. There is no scarcity of labor and land, on the contrary even much of what is available remains idle or underused. But there is a great shortage of capital and entrepreneurship. In the literature on economic development, the capital shortage has been much highlighted, but not so much the entrepreneurial shortage. Yet it seems to be no less serious a handicap.

Capital (resources saved from consumption) does not by itself or automatically produce anything. It must be harnessed for producing capital goods and the capital goods in turn harnessed for producing consumer goods. This is the investment process and it requires the services of some agent or intermediary who initiates, organizes, takes risks, and sometimes also manages. In underdeveloped economics such sponsors or entrepreneurs are an extremely small tribe and this is one important reason why development is so slow. How else can we possibly explain the fact that even when capital, technical skills, and markets are all assured, as for instance in the case of many small-scale industries catering to domestic demand, new enterprises are still not coming into existence? It often happens that after someone successfully starts a new industry, many more flock to it. Apparently they also previously had capital and other facilities, but lacked ideas, courage, or knowledge. Someone has to show them the way and spark them into action. There is no dearth of gamblers in Southeast Asia, but gambling is quite different from taking calculated business risks.

It is not easy to see how this shortage of entrepreneurs can be overcome. Education can do much, but the best school for businessmen is business itself. It is by operating in the business world that one gets knowledge and ideas about business. Here also we face the familiar vicious circle. No entrepreneurs, therefore no development. No development, therefore no entrepreneurs. One method which will help to break the circle is to encourage foreign entrepreneurship to work in partnership with local entrepreneurship. The foreign entrepreneurs will bring ideas and techniques and also train local entrepreneurs. These advantages are lacking if foreign capital comes only as loan capital. In Ceylon joint ventures are becoming increasingly popular and may well make an important contribution to development. In this connection it should be pointed out that the training scope for private businessmen will be less, the more businesses are taken by the public sector. This is an aspect of public ownership and management of industries which is often forgotten.

Capital shortage is the other basic handicap. Of course, even without increasing capital equipment some increase in production is possible by improving organization and methods and the quality of labor and management. But its scope is limited. For a large advance in production, particularly if it is to exceed the rise in population, capital formation on a large scale is indispensable. In fact the chief difference between developed and underdeveloped countries is that capital equipment in relation to labor is very high in the former and very low in the latter.

Unfortunately here again we have the abominable circle. Capital formation requires saving. In poor and underdeveloped countries saving capacity is low. But low incomes and low saving power are themselves due to low capital equipment. The circle can only be broken by either a big and austere program of domestic saving or a generous inflow of foreign saving. Neither method is easy.

Actually, the capital situation and outlook, although certainly bad, does not seem to be as hopeless as it is often made out. A small amount of capital is already available. But even this is not being effectively mobilized and invested because of lack of entrepreneurship, markets, and other factors. It is of course quite insufficient for an ambitious all-out advance in agriculture and industry, which only will fully solve the market problem. But this limited available supply can be augmented in various ways.

Private voluntary saving, personal and corporate, in the region is necessarily low because incomes are low. But this stream can perhaps be moderately increased by suitable fiscal and other incentives. The increase will take place almost entirely in the upper income groups, the lower groups having little or no saving capacity. It is true that growing contacts with higher consumption standards prevalent in rich and developed countries and the growing appearance of new and tempting varieties of consumption goods in the market are weakening the propensity to save. But in Eastern countries with strong traditions of nonostentatious, even austere, living they will probably not do great harm. The tradition of plain living should, where possible, be strengthened by moral persuasion and suitable tax discouragement of conspicuous consumption.

A second source of capital is compulsory saving by taxation. It cannot of course take much out of existing incomes, because they are so low. High taxation when incomes are low will ruin the desire to work, save, and invest, and consequently defeat rather than promote development. But when incomes are rising, public finance can become a valuable instrument for siphoning off the rise and reserving it for additional development, instead of allowing it to be frittered away on consumption. In fact in underdeveloped countries where the marginal propensity to consume is high, without taxation it will be impossible to ensure that increments in income will be largely saved. It is essential to ensure this because the scope for development by cutting consumption below the present level which is already very low, is extremely limited. Development must therefore mainly come out of future rises in income. These must be largely saved, voluntarily or compulsorily. Happily, underdeveloped countries are fully aware of this and public finance has been actively used in siphoning off rises in income. This has taken place particularly in the export sector where real income has often conspicuously risen by improvements in the terms of trade. In this way in Ceylon for instance export duties have become an important development weapon. However, the course of the terms of trade is largely unpredictable. In any case all countries are not likely to gain equally from it. But as long as the terms of trade are favorable the increments in real income from them may well be an important source of development capital. The imposition and collection of compulsory saving by the state does not necessarily mean that it will also use the saving for production itself. It need not do the investing at all, but may pass the saving to private hands for investment.

Thirdly, deficit financing may be used to release resources for development. In the economics of this region however, this must be used very cautiously because of the inflation it may cause to domestic prices or the strain it may impose on the balance of payments. Even when the investment is on the production of consumption goods, the output may not rise sufficiently or quickly enough to match the rise in money incomes because of various bottlenecks and shortages. When the investment is on the production of capital goods or social overheads, any resulting rise in the output of consumption goods will necessarily take more time. Mild and occasional inflation may, however, give a stimulus to investment without causing much social distress or injustice, but carried beyond a point it will lessen and misdirect investment and also cause great social hardship.

Fourthly, the "disguised saving" which is now feeding and maintaining the "disguised unemployed" may be diverted to capital formation. There is a considerable amount of disguised unemployment or surplus labor in the region, particularly in rural areas. In Ceylon for instance in 1953, 386,000 workers representing 14 per cent of the employed were reported as working less than 20 hours a week.[2] If fully employed for 48 hours a week, their work could have been done by 160,833 persons; in other words, 125,167 persons were surplus and unproductive. The withdrawal of this surplus will not reduce output, on the contrary it will very probably increase it. In effect, therefore, the correctly required laborers are "saving" and using the saving to maintain the underemployed. If the underemployed were used for capital formation, say in projects like road, irrigation, and house construction, but maintained by the same saving, the saving would be better utilized.

This proposal has its limitations. For instance, the laborers who are left behind may increase their consumption and the saving may not materialize at all. Or the saving may be difficult to collect and transfer to the investment workers who may work at a different place or demand a money wage instead of the subsistence which they got before. Also, the transferred workers will have no tools and machines to work with if they depend only on this saving, which means that their productivity will be low. To provide them with equipment additional savings from other sources will have to be obtained, and this may not be easy. However, in spite of these limitations, the method can still make a material contribution to capital formation and is already being actively tried in the countries of the region.

Lastly, there is foreign capital. Provided it is obtained on reasonable nonexploitation terms and in sufficient quantities, nothing obviously will be better. Development can then take place without any great squeezing of consumption, that is to say without many tears. But the difficulty has been that foreign capital in many cases not only has sought high profit investments but also has taken most of the profits out instead of ploughing them back. It has also shown no particular

[2] *Ibid.*

interest in training local people in managerial and technical skills. The only gain to the borrowing country in such cases has been some employment and some tax revenue. No wonder, therefore, that some underdeveloped countries have been closing the door to foreign capital. However, a more realistic attitude is developing both in the borrowing and the lending countries. The borrowing countries are becoming more conscious of their need, and the lending countries of their enlightened self-interest in aiding the underdeveloped. New international financing institutions are also being created. In this climate a bigger flow of foreign capital on mutually advantageous terms can be confidently expected.

The capital flow should be both in terms of loan and investment capital. Loan capital will be useful in developing the infra-structure or the basic utilities. Investment capital will bring with it technical, managerial, and entrepreneurial skills.

Summing up regarding capital, it is true that individually none of the sources discussed may bring much, but together they should guarantee enough to make a good start on development. Subsequently if the incremental saving ratio is kept high, the rate of development will automatically rise. It is perhaps better that development should be slow but steady rather than involving heroic sacrifices from the present generation. After all, the present generation also has some right to consume. Needless to say, whatever the rate of development, its effect on the level of living will be completely neutralized if population is allowed to rise at a faster rate.

This paper cannot possibly discuss every issue on development, but a word may perhaps be said on certain questions which are often discussed.

One is, should development be planned or unplanned? Obviously no dogmatic answer to this is possible. It will depend fundamentally on how far the planners can correctly measure social needs and preferences and how far their anticipations about production techniques and results remain true. A change in market demand or in techniques will upset the plan. Even with given techniques, the increase in aggregate output from an increase in aggregate investment is difficult to forecast because a good deal will depend on the project composition of the investment. If the investment is chiefly on social overheads, the returns for some time will be low. Any elaborate exercises made on the basis of a fixed general capital-output ratio will thus be some-what risky. In the underdeveloped countries the shortage of competent planners and essential statistics make planning particularly difficult. In this respect we can almost say that the countries which need planning have no planners, while the countries which have planners need no planning. However, planning has certain advantages. It helps to define ideals and measure achievements. It also helps to make the country more development minded. But the plans made should not be too forward looking, too pervasive, or too rigid.

Another question often raised is whether investment should be mainly private or public. On this also no general answer can be given. The private sector will not undertake certain types of investment, although the social marginal productivity in these cases may be high. How commercial investments should be shared between the private and the public sectors is largely a question of relative efficiency. The state can mobilize more capital, but not necessarily better entrepreneurship. On the other hand, the dissociation of rewards and penalties from the suc-cess and the failure of the undertaking, may cause misdirection of investment, inefficiency, and waste. It may be mentioned that Ceylon's experience with state commercial ventures has not been a happy one. The government has now decided to withdraw from this field and step up its assistance and encouragement to the private sector by such devices as tax incentives, the creation of a Development Finance Cor-poration, and an Institute for Industrial and Scientific Research, and so on. Another point is that there is a limit to the size of the total investment which the state can handle, because it cannot suddenly increase the size of its administrative and technical machine. Conse-quently even voted funds may remain largely unspent. This has hap-pened in Ceylon, the underexpenditure on capital account being as much as 32.8 per cent in 1952–53 and 29.5 per cent in 1953–54.

Lastly, should development concentrate on agriculture or on indus-try? The answer obviously is whichever of the two offers higher marginal net returns. Only then will national resources be best utilized. Marginal net returns depend on marginal cost and on marginal reve-nue. Even if costs are low, but the market is poor, net returns may not be relatively attractive. Markets may of course be internal or external. Assuming there is no export market, the market for one commodity will be the producers of other commodities. Thus ultimately agriculture will have no market unless industry is developed and industry will have no market unless agriculture is developed. Thus the marginal principle will automatically ensure diversified development. It should be remembered that both the cost and the market positions may be quite differently altered by large changes in investment than by small marginal changes. As already mentioned, one factory alone in a region may not pay, but fifty factories may. Further, net returns in money terms are incalculable or irrelevant in such fields of investment as social overheads.

From the cost angle, the region with its abundant supply of land and labor but scarcity of capital would seem to be naturally more fitted for agriculture than industry. But the market situation seems already to demand also a moderate and selective development of industries. The position of course differs in different countries. In Ceylon, export agriculture, particularly tea, still earns good net returns. In Burma and Thailand, however, the chief agricultural export, rice, is highly depressed. But these countries also may perhaps develop other agricultural and extractive exports such as timber and minerals. Not only export but home market agriculture also has in certain cases good net return prospects, as, for example, rice in Ceylon. These particular fields will bear further development. By and large, however, the net return position of agriculture relative to industry is now becoming such in the region as to justify a stepping up of industries, particularly of the small-scale type. Agriculture must still be expanded wherever it has better scope. But this expansion will itself necessitate and permit industrialization. The higher agricultural productivity will provide capital and market for new industries, while the industries will absorb the surplus labor which agriculture must release in its process of improvement. Thus industrial development will complement agricultural development and the process of industrialization will be gradual. The alternative ideal of creating overnight an industrial state may be glamorous but would hardly be realistic or cheap in terms of human suffering.

commentary

LIM TAY BOH

University of Malaya

In the introductory paragraphs of his essay, Dr. Das Gupta discusses briefly the concept of economic development. The remainder of his paper deals with the factors influencing economic development in Southeast Asia.

His emphasis, in the introduction, is on the difficulty of precise definition of the concept of economic development and of controlling economic and noneconomic factors in development.

On the conceptual problem of economic development, I agree with Dr. Das Gupta that the various conventional measures of development have their limitations and arbitrary elements, and that on the whole the usual measure of economic development, in terms of a rising average level of productivity per head of population, is a sound one, since the basic objective of economic development is to raise living standards. It is true that this concept has several arbitrary aspects.

In the first place, it refers to standards of living narrowly defined in the material sense, and does not include the broader political, social, and cultural aspects of development. It is a much narrower concept than that of welfare. Secondly, the index commonly used to measure the average level of productivity is the per capita national income, the computation of which involves somewhat arbitrary procedures. For example, estimates of subsistence output, which forms a significant part of the national product of an undeveloped economy, are inevitably very rough, not only because of the difficulties of getting accurate statistical information, but also because of the use of arbitrary devices of valuing the output. Moreover, the size of the national product is affected by the relative importance of subsistence output in the economy.[1]

Thirdly, the average level of per capita national income is a relative concept, as there is no absolute level which divides a highly developed

[1] Cf. Willard L. Thorp, *Trade Aid, or What?* (Johns Hopkins Press, Baltimore, 1954), pp. 154–155.

179

from an underdeveloped economy. In practice, countries are regarded as underdeveloped because of their low per capita national incomes in comparison with those of highly developed countries like the United States, Canada, the United Kingdom, Australia, and New Zealand.

Fourthly, the per capita national income of a country is merely an average figure and does not show what has happened to the distribution of income between different social classes. In assessing economic progress, it is also necessary to take into account improvements in income distribution as well as increases in per capita income. However, in spite of its limitations, the concept of average per capita national income can be taken as a rough but significant index of economic development, provided it is qualified to take account of changes in income distribution. Such an index refers, of course, to the long-run trend of productivity and not to temporary changes. Windfall rises in the national income and temporary changes in the terms of trade would thus be excluded.

It refers also to the aggregate product including both consumer and capital output. An increase in the average national product due to an increase in capital output would be regarded as a sign of economic development, since from the long-run point of view, an increase in capital equipment will tend to increase the output of consumer goods.

Finally, the concept refers to the growth of production relative to that of population. The rise of average productivity depends, therefore, on the rate of increase in production relative to the rate of growth of population. A decline in population accompanied by a rising average national product implies an improvement in productive efficiency due to either the adoption of improved technology or the use of capital-intensive methods of production.

I turn now to the factors influencing development, which Dr. Das Gupta discusses under the headings of demand and supply. On the side of demand, the chief obstacle to development, according to him, is the limitation of market opportunities both at home and abroad. On the supply side, the factors are the shortage of enterprise and the shortage of capital. Of these two sets of factors, those on the side of supply are regarded as more critical. Both are, however, purely economic factors. Dr. Das Gupta is, of course, aware of the importance of social and cultural factors, and although he does not elaborate on the role of such noneconomic factors, he is careful to emphasize the point that development is not a purely economic phenomenon.

Social and cultural factors are highly important because they affect the motivating force of economic development. The factors discussed by Dr. Das Gupta might be described as the conditioning factors of development. He does not make a clear distinction between such factors and the motivation of development. It seems to me that any adequate theory of economic development must explain why, given the existence of favorable conditioning factors, such as good market opportunities and the availability of productive resources, development has not proceeded as rapidly in some countries as in others, and why, if it did take place in some countries, it did not take place much earlier. The phenomenon cannot be fully explained by theories which are formulated in terms of the influence of conditioning factors. Thus, theories which are based on the influence of such factors as population growth, capital accumulation, and technological progress do not give us the full answer to the problem, because such factors are not strictly autonomous or independent variables in the process of economic development.[2] They are conditioning rather than motivating factors. They set the limits to the maximum rate of growth, but this maximum will not necessarily be achieved in the absence of some motivating force which generates development.[3] What is crucial is to determine what this force is which sets in motion the process of development.

Dr. Das Gupta is on the right track when he emphasizes the shortage of enterprise as one of the serious obstacles to development in Southeast Asia. In highly developed capitalist economies, the acceleration of economic development has been due primarily to the activity of entrepreneurs, who have undertaken the risks of investment. In the underdeveloped countries of Southeast Asia the entrepreneurial class is very small, with the consequence that the capitalist sector constitutes a relatively small part of the whole economy. In recent theories of economic growth, attention has been focused on the motive which influences entrepreneurial behavior and on its diffusion, which is essential to the emergence of a large entrepreneurial class. The basic thesis is that it is the will to develop, or the urge to expand, or the

[2] I. N. Kaldor, "The Relation between Economic Growth and Cyclical Fluctuations," *Economic Journal*, March 1954, pp. 65–67.

[3] *Ibid.*, p. 69.

spirit of enterprise, which is the motivating force of entrepreneurial activity.

It is this spirit of enterprise which has changed the methods of production in capitalist societies and accelerated the rate of development.

This analysis draws attention to the critical role played by entrepreneurial psychology in economic activity, and suggests that economic development is the product primarily of social and cultural forces and cannot be accounted for solely in terms of economic and technological factors. Capital accumulation, the supply of natural resources, and labor and technological innovations constitute the conditions under which entrepreneurs operate. They set the limit to the potential rate of development. But if the will or urge to develop is weak, the maximum rate of development cannot be attained.

Development, it has been pointed out, is a state of mind. People have to develop themselves before they can change their physical and economic environment. This is a slow process and, to a large extent, accounts for the hitherto slow rate of development in Southeast Asia. For habits of thought and conduct are even more serious than economic obstacles. The key factor in development is, in short, the motivation of the people themselves. Unless something happens to change motivation, a static economy will not turn into a dynamic economy. Even if development were started with state or foreign aid, it would not become self-generating.[4]

Social and cultural factors play a fundamental role in development, because they influence human attitudes and motivations and help or retard the emergence of a sufficiently large body of entrepreneurs. They are also significant in another respect: They determine whether the social, political and administrative framework is favorable or unfavorable to development.

I shall now turn to the economic factors, to which Dr. Das Gupta has given detailed attention.

The first factor discussed by Dr. Das Gupta is the limitation of market opportunities in the underdeveloped countries of Southeast Asia. He points out that for many of the countries in South and Southeast Asia, both the home and the external markets are too limited

---

[4] Eugene Staley, *The Future of Underdeveloped Countries* (Harper & Brothers, New York, 1954), p. 215.

to provide stimulus to rapid development. So far as the home market is concerned two factors are largely responsible: (a) the smallness of the population and (b) the low purchasing power of the majority of the people. Of these two factors the more important is the low purchasing power of the masses. India, for example, has a large population, which means that it has a large potential market. But because of the low per capita income, the actual demand is very much below the potential demand. It must also be remembered that population is growing rapidly in all the countries of this region. Even if the market is relatively small in many of the individual countries, the fact that population is growing rapidly means that the home market will expand in future, provided there is adequate purchasing power. The significant implication of this argument is that if the purchasing power of the masses could be appreciably raised, the home market would be enlarged. This is precisely what economic development can achieve, because the increased employment and purchasing power generated by development would provide favorable conditions for expanding the overall home demand to match the increasing output of consumer goods. The case for a program of public investment, in fact, rests on the increase of employment and purchasing power, which is favorable to the expansion of the home market. Of course, the problem is much more complex in practice, for there is no guarantee that the increased flow of purchasing power will be distributed between the different components of the increased output in such a way that the increased supply of each product will be matched by a corresponding demand for it. This is because in the real world the price mechanism does not bring about a rapid and smooth adjustment of market conditions to changes in supply. There is therefore a need for the careful planning of the pattern of economic development so as to produce the types of products that will be absorbed.

The important point, however, is that the size of the home market and economic progress are interdependent. Professor Nurkse probably had this in mind when he advocated the enlargement of the home market by the simultaneous expansion of a large number of industries which buy one another's products.[5] The multiplier effect on incomes

[5] R. Nurkse, *Problems of Capital Formation in Underdeveloped Countries* (Basil Blackwell, Oxford, 1953), p. 13.

and purchasing power of such a process of development will also tend to stimulate demand in other sectors of the economy.

The enlargement of the market depends not only on the expansion of purchasing power but also on the development of communications which link up isolated sectors of the economy into larger home markets. Of particular importance is the linking up of the subsistence sectors of underdeveloped countries with the more developed urban sectors to ensure the extension of markets into the rural areas.[6] Given the link and the removal of physical barriers, the development of industries will lead to the creation of markets in the rural sectors for the products of the industrial sectors.

It is clear that the limitation of market opportunities is not as serious an obstacle as is sometimes supposed. A more serious obstacle to rapid economic development in the countries of this region is the difficulty of achieving a surplus of basic foodstuffs to meet the increased demand from the urban industrial sector. Economic development generates increased income and demand for basic foodstuffs through the drawing of surplus labor into employment in the industrial sector. This increased demand must be matched by an adequate increase of food surplus available for exchange. Whether this will be achieved or not depends on (a) the increase in productivity, on the one hand, and (b) the limitation of food consumption by the peasants, on the other. In Southeast Asia, there is usually a large number of underemployed workers in the rural areas. If they are drawn into employment in the urban sector as a result of rapid economic development, the problem of achieving a marketable surplus of food becomes of critical importance. If the reduced population on the farms produce the same amount of food as before, they must not increase their consumption, otherwise they will not achieve a larger food surplus for the industrial sector where the demand for food has increased owing to increased employment and incomes. Progress in the industrial sector, in short, depends on an increase of food surplus in the rural sector, and this latter in turn depends on an increase in productivity without a corresponding rise in the food consumption of the rural population. In other words, the rate of industrial development depends on the elasticity of supply of food surplus in the rural sector, and

[6] Charles Kindleberger, *International Economics* (Richard D. Irwin, Inc., Homewood, Illinois, 1953), p. 382.

this latter depends in turn on improvements in agricultural productivity on the one hand, and on the stabilization of food consumption in the rural sector on the other. In a market economy, any failure to achieve an adequate food surplus is likely to manifest itself in inflationary tendencies, which may frustrate the development of the industrial sector.[7]

The implications of this analysis for economic development may be briefly stated:

(a) Agricultural development must keep pace with industrial development if economic progress is to be sustained. This is the basis of the case for a balanced and integrated program of agricultural and industrial development.[8]

(b) An increase in food consumption in the rural sector may have to be checked in order to achieve an accumulation of marketable food surplus adequate to meet the expanding demand for food in the industrial sector.

The significance of these implications becomes clear when we consider them in relation to Dr. Das Gupta's point about the utilization of "disguised saving" as a means of capital formation in underdeveloped countries. Dr. Das Gupta discusses the problem of capital shortage in some detail, because he considers the shortage of capital and enterprise as critical factors in the development of Southeast Asia. His emphasis is on the difficulties of achieving a rate of saving adequate to maintain a high rate of economic development. He does not make explicit the distinction between real saving and money saving, especially in relation to the mobilization of domestic capital. Most of the points raised by him relate to the problem of increasing money saving to finance capital formation.

His discussion of the utilization of underemployed or surplus labor in the rural areas for capital formation is based on the concept of "disguised saving," which he regards as an additional source of financing capital formation. This approach seems to me to be misleading because it fails to bring out the basic problem of utilizing surplus labor. For the crucial factor is the achievement of an adequate marketable

---

[7] W. Arthur Lewis, *Economic Development with Unlimited Supplies of Labour* (The Manchester School, May 1954), pp. 161–162.

[8] Cf. Marcus Fleming, "External Economies and the Doctrine of Balanced Growth," *Economic Journal*, June 1955.

food surplus to feed the workers diverted from agricultural production. Capital formation through the utilization of underemployed rural
labor is only possible if (a) food production does not fall as a result
of the diversion of surplus labor from agriculture, and (b) food consumption per head of the remaining rural population does not increase.

Dr. Das Gupta assumes that the output of food will not be reduced
in the process. This is by no means certain. Where agriculture is carried on in a subsistence economy, production is organized on the
basis of the joint effort of the members of the family. Underemployment may exist in such a system, because owing to primitive methods
of cultivation, the yield per worker is low. But the diversion of the
surplus labor to other occupations does not necessarily mean that the
remaining population will produce the same output either by working
harder or by improving their organization and methods of production.[9]

Dr. Das Gupta is, of course, aware that the necessary amount of real
saving in the form of an adequate food surplus may fail to be achieved
because of an increase in the food consumption of the remaining rural
population. Moreover, there is also a possibility of an increase in the
demand for food by workers diverted to the production of capital
goods.[10] Thus even with the existence of surplus labor, capital formation may be retarded by an inelastic supply of food available for the
workers engaged in the capital goods industries. The central problem
of capital formation and industrialization in a closed economy is the
achievement of an adequate rate of real saving through improvements
of productivity and the limitation of consumption; and the most important aspect of this problem is the improvement of agricultural productivity and the restriction of food consumption.

In the light of this analysis, the financial aspects of economic development fall into their proper perspective. Dr. Das Gupta raises the
problem of increasing both voluntary and compulsory saving as a
means of releasing financial resources for economic development. But
the significance of voluntary and compulsory saving lies in their effect
in reducing consumption. The fundamental problem is one of physical
shortages, especially of basic consumer goods, rather than one of
financial shortage. Shortage of finance assumes significance only because the existence of physical shortages makes it necessary to restrict

9 F. C. Benham, "The Colombo Plan," *Economica*, May 1954, p. 100–101.
10 Cf. Willard L. Thorp, *op. cit.*, pp. 168–169.

consumption demand in order to adjust it to a relatively inelastic supply. If the supply of basic consumer goods were perfectly elastic, the shortage of finance would not be a serious problem in capital formation, since it can be offset by the creation of money, without causing a serious inflation. But such a situation does not exist in the real world. It is for this reason that there are limits to the possibility of financing a program of public investment by incurring a budgetary deficit. The danger of deficit financing in a closed economy is precisely that of inflation arising from the expansion of purchasing power in the face of a relatively inelastic supply. In an open economy with an elastic export demand and a high propensity to import, deficit financing on an appreciable scale is likely to lead to serious difficulties in the balance of payments.

This is probably true of most of the countries in South and Southeast Asia. India is perhaps the only exception. Her Second Five Year Plan contains a much bolder program of development than that for the first five years.[11] But this larger program of development is planned on the assumption that food production is relatively elastic, so that deficit financing on the scale envisaged in the Draft Plan Frame[12] will not give rise to serious inflationary tendencies. Moreover, in contrast to the other countries in this region, India is much less dependent on foreign trade, especially on the import of consumer goods.

Next, I should like to comment briefly on the points raised by Dr. Das Gupta on the role of foreign capital in development. I have no doubt that there is a great need for foreign capital in the countries of Southeast Asia, where, owing to low national income levels, there are serious difficulties in the way of achieving a rate of domestic saving adequate to maintain a high rate of capital formation. The import of foreign capital enables capital formation to take place without a drastic reduction of the consumption of the people. It also relieves the pressure on the balance of payments by providing badly needed foreign exchange. Moreover, the inflow of foreign capital usually brings with it organizational and technical knowledge, which is essential in raising the level of productivity in underdeveloped countries.

[11] See *Second Five Year Plan—The Framework* (The Publications Division, Ministry of Information and Broadcasting, Government of India, Delhi), 8.

[12] *Ibid.*, The "Draft Plan Frame," prepared by Professor P. C. Mahalanobis, gives a draft outline of the Second Five Year Plan.

Nevertheless, it must be emphasized that foreign capital is only one factor in economic development. Unless capital formation is financed largely by domestic saving, the process is not likely to be self-generating.

Another point which requires emphasis is that if foreign capital is to play a constructive role in the economic development of Southeast Asia, it must operate on terms which provide for (a) the ploughing back into investment of a more substantial part of the profits than was the case in the past, and (b) the training of local personnel to take over some of the responsibilities at the managerial and technical level. This implies a revolution in the outlook and attitude of foreign private investors, but is nevertheless necessary in order to remove the distrust of foreign capital on the part of nationalists in this region, a distrust which arises from the association of foreign capital with economic exploitation and domination.

Dr. Das Gupta mentions the creation of international financial institutions to stimulate the flow of foreign capital into underdeveloped countries. Such international agencies are important and we may hope they will lead, on the part of foreign investors, to a new approach to investment in underdeveloped countries, and, on the part of the governments and nationals of underdeveloped countries themselves, to the creation of incentives, as well as stable political and administrative conditions, that will attract the flow of foreign capital into this region.

On the problem of industrialization in underdeveloped countries, Dr. Das Gupta raises the following points:

(a) the interrelation between agricultural and industrial development and the need for industrialization as a complement to agricultural development.

(b) the greater scope in the countries of this region for the development of small-scale or light industries, producing consumer goods for the home market.

(c) the advantage of using labor-intensive methods of production from the point of view of increasing employment opportunities and economizing the use of capital.

With these points I am in general agreement. I have already elaborated on the first point in my discussion of the case for a balanced and integrated growth of agriculture and industry. Dr. Das Gupta's emphasis on the complementary development of agriculture and industry is therefore sound.

On the second point, I have only a brief comment to make.

There is no doubt that in most countries in this region, the scope for the development of light industries is much greater than for heavy industries. In fact, with the exception of India, the region is not favorably endowed with the natural resources essential for the development of heavy industries, such as those producing iron and steel, motor vehicles, etc. This probably explains why India is the only country which gives high priority to heavy industries in her program of development outlined in the Second Five Year Plan.[13] In the other countries, public policy is likely to be concerned mainly with the encouragement of light industries. This is in accordance with the recommendations on industrialization contained in the reports of the two International Bank missions on the economic development of Ceylon and Malaya.[14]

The last point raised by Dr. Das Gupta in his discussion of industrialization relates to the creation of employment opportunities through the adoption of labor-intensive or capital-saving methods of production. This is a very important point, in view of the urgent need of solving the problem of underemployment and unemployment in this region. One of the striking features of industrialization in the West was the introduction of capital-intensive methods of production, which raised the level productivity but reduced the ratio of labor to capital employed in industries. In the case of underdeveloped economies faced with a serious problem of surplus labor, there is a real danger that the rapid introduction of capital-intensive methods may in the short-run aggravate the problem of unemployment. The current emphasis on the development of rural and cottage industries in India's Second Five Year Plan[15] is an indication not only of the loyalty of Indian economists and social thinkers to the Gandhian ideals of rural development, but also

[13] *Second Five Year Plan—The Framework*, cited, pp. 14–15.

[14] International Bank for Reconstruction and Development, *The Economic Development of Ceylon* (Johns Hopkins Press, Baltimore, 1953), pp. 42–44; *The Economic Development of Malaya* (Government Printer, Singapore, 1955), p. 27 and pp. 84–86.

[15] *Second Five Year Plan—The Framework*, cited, pp. 15–16.

of their concern with the problem of underemployment in the rural areas.

Japan has shown us the possibility of raising agricultural productivity per acre of land by the exploitation of labor-intensive methods of cultivation. If the same technique can be developed in industries, it would be possible to increase not only industrial productivity per unit of capital but also the volume of employment.

Dr. Das Gupta mentions the question of diversifying production, but does not discuss the basic issue involved. In popular discussions of the need for the diversification of the economies of countries in Southeast Asia, the tendency has been to prescribe diversification as the solution to the problem of economic instability arising from the dependence of export economies on a fluctuating world market. The objective of the policy advocated is to increase the range of production for the home market and cushion the economy against the effects of price fluctuations in the export market. But it is seldom appreciated that diversified production for the home market as a substitute for specialized production for the export market would involve a loss of productivity and a deterioration in living standards.[16] Malaya, for example, has been able to achieve a relatively high level of per capita income largely because of her specialization in the production of exports for the world markets. The abandonment of her export industries in favor of production for the home market would result in a serious fall in her national income.

It is true that the production of rubber and tin for export has led to the lopsided development of the Malayan economy. But the case for a more balanced development through diversification does not imply the inevitable abandonment of specialized production for export. The objective of diversification from the point of view of a balanced economy should be the complementary development of a wider range of production for both the home and export markets. Such a policy would ensure that diversification is not achieved at the expense of increased productivity. This is undoubtedly the basis of the recommendation of the International Bank's mission for a program of

---

[16] Eugene Staley, *op. cit.*, p. 294. See also President's Materials Policy Commission, *Resources for Freedom*, Vol. I, p. 73.

raising the productivity of the Malayan natural rubber industry on the one hand and for diversifying Malaya's agriculture and industry on the other.[17]

There is only one other question, raised by Dr. Das Gupta, which I want to comment on. This is the question of the relative scope of public investment and private enterprise. Although the relative importance of the public and private sectors in development varies from country to country, there is no doubt that the general trend of economic policy is common to the whole region. A striking characteristic of postwar economic development in this region is the steady enlargement of the public sector, and judging from the emphasis on the importance of public investment in the development plans of the individual countries, the trend is likely to continue in future.

One major reason for the expansion of public investment is, of course, the realization by the nationals of the various countries that private enterprise alone has hitherto not succeeded in bringing about a sufficiently rapid rate of economic development in this region to catch up with the growth of population. Indeed, the predominant view reflected in all the development plans of the individual countries is that without a well planned public program of development, it is impossible to create an environment favorable to the rapid expansion of private investment.

But while emphasis is laid on the importance of expanding the public sector, the contribution of private enterprise to the creating of a dynamic economy is fully realized by the authors of the various development plans. There is general agreement, for example, on the essential role of private enterprise in the field of small-scale or light industries. There is also general agreement on the role of public investment in the development of basic services and utilities, like electric power, water supply, transport and communications. But between the field of small-scale industries and that of basic services, there is an area of development in which the precise line of demarcation depends mainly on political and social considerations. In the Second Five Year Plan of India, the role of the public sector is given greater emphasis, because India aims at the achievement of a socialist pattern of society.

[17] International Bank, *The Economic Development of Malaya*, pp. 21–22.

In Malaya, on the other hand, the scope given to private enterprise is much wider.[18]

But whatever the respective scope of public investment and private enterprise in each country, the crucial question in economic development is whether there are in existence the necessary social and cultural institutions to foster the emergence of a sufficiently large class of entrepreneurs or leaders capable of sustaining the process of development by their skill and energy. This does not mean that the economic policy of the government is not important in speeding up the process of development. In fact, the relatively slow rate of economic progress in this region was, in the past, due partly to the failure of the colonial governments to adopt constructive programs of development. The laissez-faire policy of the colonial administration was associated with economic stagnation and lopsided development. Nevertheless, it must be emphasized that the success of development depends basically on the response of the people to the challenge of their physical and economic environment.

In the last analysis, it is the human factor that is decisive in ensuring an acceleration of economic growth in Southeast Asia. For it is the skill and industry of the workers, the enterprise and energy of the leaders, and the will of the people to control the rate of population increase that determine whether natural resources, capital accumulation and technology will be utilized in achieving a rate of development that will outstrip the growth of population.

[18] *Second Five Year Plan—The Framework,* cited, p. 21. International Bank, *The Economic Development of Malaya,* pp. 86–87.

The development and utilization
of labor resources in Southeast Asia

ABDUL AZIZ

University of Malaya

Analysis of the Main Concepts

The vastness of the subject and its extreme diversity in Southeast Asia are both temptations toward a sterile nebulosity having no direction. Therefore careful definition of the concepts involved and a fairly clear outline of the framework of the discussion is necessary if that discussion is to reach the optimum degree of fruitfulness.

There are three concepts to be determined: labor resources, their utilization, and their development.

The labor resources are understood to be the factor of production—labor. In Southeast Asia the most important distinction is between urban labor and rural labor.

Urban labor includes industrial labor, the factory workers, the administrative and clerical (or white-collar) workers, and the commercial classes. In Southeast Asia these last two groups have roles that give them a much greater significance than their counterparts in the non-Asian world. Thus administrative workers have much greater political and social significance, while the commercial groups very often play special roles in political situations, especially where they appear to be associated with racial factions. Furthermore, in general, the economic, political, and social elite of Southeast Asia tend to be urban folk, although the greater proportion of the population is always rural.

Rural labor means primarily agricultural labor. Thus the Woy-
tinskys state that of the 410 million persons making up the total labor
force in Asia and Oceania, 310 millions or 75 per cent are in agriculture.[1] They also state that about 60 per cent of the world agricultural labor force as compared with less than 40 per cent of the nonagricultural labor force is to be found in Asia and Oceania.

The great characteristic of this labor is its diversity of occupation
rather than its specialization. As Patel says this characteristic is aptly
summarized in the 1901 Census of India Report which states "The
small agriculturist is frequently a cultivating and non-cultivating land-
owner, a tenant, a farm servant, and a field laborer all rolled into one;
owning land which he partly cultivates and partly lets out for rent,
hiring other land from someone else, and eking out his earnings by
working on the land of others."[2]

Thus, not only is a great variety of jobs being done by the workers
in a village or in a family but at different seasons the same person will
be doing different jobs. Economic, social, or political changes may
also influence people to change either the intensity of their work or
the very occupation itself.

The rural labor force can be divided into three main groups: the
subsistence farmers who may be owner-occupiers or tenant-occupiers,
and who are rather outside the price system of the world economy; the
farmers who devote some or all of their economic resources to the
production of cash crops; and wage workers on plantations organized
on a capitalistic basis.

In discussing the utilization of labor resources the first task is to
realize the situation that exists at present. The main problem can be
stated in the form of a question: "Is there full utilization of current
labor resources in South East Asia?" A negative answer, even though
it be a partial negative, means that there is underemployment of resources.

The Indian Famine Enquiry Report states that "Perhaps the most

---

[1] W. S. Woytinsky and E. S. Woytinsky, *World Population and Production*
(New York, Twentieth Century Fund, 1953), p. 365.

[2] Census of India (1901), Pt. 1, p. 205, quoted in *Agricultural Labourers in
Modern India and Pakistan*, by S. J. Patel (Bombay Current Book House, 1952),
pp. 98–99.

important, and in many ways the most intractable of all rural economic problems is that of underemployment."[3]

Although economists are not yet completely agreed on the final nomenclature, it can be stated that three concepts are involved in the idea of underemployment of labor. The first is that underemployment which occurs, according to a United Nations Committee of expert economists, whenever there are workers "so numerous, relatively to the resources with which they work that if a number of them were withdrawn for work in other sections of the economy, the total output of the sector from which they were withdrawn would not be diminished even though no significant re-organization occurred in their sector and no significant substitution of capital."[4]

In fact, the concept of underemployment can be subdivided into seasonal and chronic underemployment.[5] Seasonal underemployment occurs when a portion of the total potential working hours of the labor force are not fully utilized through the year, although they may be in full utilization at certain periods, such as the harvest period. Chronic underemployment is the simple case where even at the time of peak labor requirements there are still workers whose subtraction would not affect total output.

The second concept involved in underemployment is disguised unemployment. This was considered by Joan Robinson, one of the earliest economists to use the term, to be associated specifically with the disease of an advanced industrial country.[6] Thus she says, ". . . a decline in effective demand which reduces the amount of employment offered in the general run of industries will not lead to 'unemployment' in the sense of complete idleness, but will rather drive workers into a number of occupations—selling metal boxes in the Strand, cutting brushwood in the jungles, digging potatoes on allotments—which are still open to them. . . . In those occupations which the dismissed workers take up, their productivity is less than in the occupations that they

[3] Famine Inquiry Commission (Final Report), 1945, p. 302–3.

[4] Measures for the Economic Development of Under-developed Countries (New York, United Nations, 1951), p. 7.

[5] See, Chiang Hsieh, "Underemployment in Asia," International Labor Review, 65, 1952, pp. 703 ff.

[6] Joan Robinson, Essays in the Theory of Employment (London, Macmillan, 1937), p. 82–101.

have left. . . . and it is natural to describe the adoption of inferior occupations by dismissed workers as disguised unemployment."

However, this phenomenon has been found by the Navarettes to occur in countries which are neither very advanced nor very industrialized, such as for example Mexico.[7] They found that as a result of cityward migration of agricultural labor workers had to engage in activities of very low productivity. "They become, for instance, pedlars of all kinds of goods and services requiring little or no capital outfit, such as vendors of fruit, chickle and cigars, lottery tickets, newspapers or else car washers, boot blacks, porters, waiters, and shop assistants. The remarkable feature of this type of underemployment is that it is continually nourished by the vast reserves of hidden underemployment in rural areas." The meaning is clear to anyone familiar with occupational patterns in Southeast Asia.

The third concept involved in underemployment is potential underemployment. This must be considered especially in connection with the development of labor resources, which will be discussed shortly, for as a result of a development program, containing both major and minor reforms, it may happen that certain resources become redundant or underemployed.

In its elementary form the introduction of labor saving devices, work-simplification schemes or any raising of the intensity of work per unit of time, will tend to create underemployment if the other resources remain fixed. Furthermore, any fundamental changes in the agrarian structure, such as a change in the average size of farms, or extensive mechanization of agriculture, would certainly create conditions where a great number of workers could be released from the agricultural sector without affecting output.

The primary aim in the development of labor resources should be to examine the main techniques that are available for such development. It would be very valuable if experiences regarding the application of such techniques in the different countries of Southeast Asia could be exchanged.

The main aspects of the development of labor resources appear to be: (1) Increasing the productivity of labor. Not only are the tech-

[7] A. Navarette, Jr. and I. M. DeNavarette, "Underemployment in Undeveloped Economies," *International Economic Papers*, No. 3, ed. by A. T. Peacock et al. (London, Macmillan, 1953), p. 235–239.

niques in agriculture, manufacturing and commerce capable of much
improvement, but the productivity of labor can be raised by improving
the quality and quantity of capital, land, and organization that are
combined with labor in the process of production. (2) Elimination
of underemployment of labor. This involves not only fiscal policy,
investment, and the increase in effective demand, but may also include
the reorganization of the control of national economic resources. (3)
Improving the mobility of labor. Mobility can be between occupations,
industries, or different geographical areas. (4) Improving the conditions of both urban and rural labor. This includes creation and extension of labor codes, wage regulations, and better machinery for industrial relations as well as the development of the co-operative movement,
together with land, marketing, and credit reforms.

One Aspect of the Supply of Labor Resources— The Demand for Income

One aspect of labor economics deserves more attention than it has
been accorded in the past. In theoretical terms this means an investigation of certain characteristics of the supply curve for labor. In particular the interaction between quantities of effort (labor) and the price
offered for such effort (wages).

There are many influences on the supply of labor. These may range
from the health, age-structure, and sex-ratio of the population to social
attitudes regarding work or money. However, all influences can be
separated into two groups, namely: changes in the rate at which
income can be earned (e.g., changes in wage rates for workers or
changes in product prices for farmers) and all other influences on
the supply of labor. This essay is solely concerned with the first
group.

In simple terms the problem may be stated thus: "Is a worker
willing to do more work, less work or the same amount of work,
if the rate at which his efforts are rewarded is changed?"

For example, a daily paid rubber tapper is willing to work 22
days a month for a wage of $5 per day. Suppose the wage rate is
increased to $10 a day. Then the problem is to know whether the
tapper will work for more or less than 22 days a month. If he is
willing to work for 30 days, then in the language of economists, the

elasticity of his demand for income in terms of effort, is high. On the other hand if he is only willing to do less than 22 days of work a month, his elasticity of demand for income in terms of effort is low. In this latter instance it will be clear that he prefers increased leisure to increased income. Thus in 11 days he can earn the same income as before. He can now have 19 days of leisure per month compared to 8 days of leisure before.

At this point, the question, legitimately, may be raised as to the importance of considering this apparently trivial matter.

The justification for bringing up this problem rests on these reasons. First, this is a major item in the theory of labor economics. Second, although hardly any field studies have been carried out on this aspect of labor economics, several influential economists and agricultural economists appear to have reached definite conclusions about it. Third, if the reasoning of some of the aforementioned economists is carried to its logical conclusion then the whole idea of economic development of the so-called backward countries becomes rather hopeless.

It is this third reason that is so compelling. If it is true that the "lazy natives" will do less work every time their productivity is raised, or the prices of their products are increased—then what future is there for agricultural development, land reforms, or improved marketing systems? Every real increase will be taken out in more leisure. Total production will never rise and rising standards of living will remain a mirage on the horizons of statisticians.

That some influential groups of thinkers, economists, and agricultural economists do hold such views can be seen from the following examples which are taken from a collection of well-known texts.

These authorities may be divided into three groups: those who believe that people (incidentally, they always refer to them as "natives" or "backward people") will do less work if wage rates are raised, and vice versa; those who disagree with this group, and who either believe that a really significant change in wages can act as an incentive to more work, or who believe that other factors, such as the general availability of consumer goods, or elements of social prestige, are more influential in causing changes in the willingness to work; and those who warn against *a priori* reasoning in this field, who suggest that each category of workers needs to be carefully studied, and who believe that willingness to respond to income incentives should be the object of scientifically designed inductive investigation.

One of the leading American agricultural economists, John D. Black, is illustrative of the first group. Speaking of workers who are said to have backward sloping supply curves—the higher the wages, the less labor they supply—he says, "Such behavior traits are most likely to be encountered amongst common laborers in tropical or near tropical countries where needs for shelter and clothing are easily supplied."[8] Parochialism carries him to add further that "In only a few social groups in this country (i.e., the United States) however, is such behavior predominant." Similarly P. L. Yates, writing about small rubber producers in Southeast Asia, states that "The native like peasants everywhere, tends to produce more rather than less when the price begins to fall."[9]

The classic example, however, of this group is perhaps, to be found in one American writer who has several books on Southeast Asia to her credit. "The Malay Social Organization makes it possible for a householder to get his work done for him free by his dependents and in general the Malays do not commercialize their product, and work as little as possible and in very small units. They survive quite pleasantly on a diet of bananas, durians and coconuts."[10] Even Alfred Marshall says ". . . experience seems to show that the more ignorant and phlegmatic of races and individuals, especially if they live in a southern clime, will stay at their work a shorter time, and will exert themselves less while at it, if the rate of pay rises so as to give them their accustomed enjoyments in return for less work than before."[11]

Perhaps Marshall was not aware of the following quotation from Adam Smith, who may be taken to represent the second group of authorities on this subject: "That a little more plenty than ordinary may render some workers idle, cannot be well doubted; but that it should have this effect upon the greater part, or that men in general

[8] J. D. Black *Introduction to Economics for Agriculture* (New York, Macmillan, 1953), p. 536.

[9] P. L. Yates, *Commodity Control* (London, Jonathan Cape, 1943), p. 115.

[10] Virginia Thompson, *Thailand the New Siam* (New York, Macmillan, 1941), p. 604.

[11] A. Marshall, *Principles of Economics*, 8th Ed. (London, Macmillan, 1947), p. 528.

should work better when they are ill fed than when they are well fed, when they are disheartened than when they are in good spirits, when they are frequently sick than when they are in good health seems not very probable."[12]

Also representative of this group is I. D. Greaves, a modern anthropologist, who has made a very careful study of the economic behavior of a group of socially backward people and who states, "In fact, what is condemned as laziness or dislike of work on the part of the natives has often been in essentials a reluctance to expend a large amount of effort upon inefficient and poorly remunerated forms of labor.

"A policy of increasing the productivity value of native labor rests, of course, on the assumption that higher wages will be an incentive to voluntary effort. If you believe that a higher rate of pay would be 'a direct encouragement to idleness,' which amounts to saying that the native's demand for leisure is elastic and all the other elements in his standard of living are fixed beyond the lure of avarice or vanity, then the longer you want him to work the less you must pay him. But in practice this is exactly the situation which gives rise to labor difficulties. There are no complaints of the members of any race refusing to take well-paid positions, or those of less onerous kind. The Malay, for instance, who will not work on a plantation willingly becomes a policeman or a chauffeur; the best Philippine labor left agricultural for artisan employment; neither in East or West Africa is there difficulty in obtaining natives for the more skilled occupations; and in all places where the higher grades of employment are open to them it is lack of training and not unwillingness that restricts their numbers. In parts of Central America where landowners had long complained that voluntary labor was insufficient or unobtainable, a foreign company has found it possible to work large banana plantations with free labor paid a higher rate than that prevailing for other occupations in the neighborhood, and both well managed and fully equipped with capital facilities."[13]

---

[12] Adam Smith, *Wealth of Nations* (London, Everymans Library), Bk. 1, ch. VIII, p. 74.

[13] I. D. Greaves, *Modern Production Among Backward People* (L. S. E. Studies No. 5, 1935), pp. 163–5.

T. S. Simey is also representative of this group. He attacks the view expressed in a report of the Economic Policy Committee, headed by Professor F. C. Benham, issued in the West Indies in 1945 which states, "The main explanation appears to be most people do not want to work long hours in a hot climate. They prefer to have a lower standard of living and more leisure; they are not educated to appreciate a higher standard of living and would rather take life more easily than add to their material comforts.[14] To this Simey replies, "This argument is of course merely the old staple diet of the West Indian political warrior. Natural indolence, served up in a slightly new form to meet the modern tastes. To the present day student of social affairs, however, it cannot appear to have any more secure foundations than pure prejudice, since no 'attitude studies' of the modern type have yet been carried out amongst the masses of the West Indian peoples, and such explanations of their motives as these are significant only as a demonstration of the form which the folk-lore of the upper classes takes in contemporary society." He also points out that, "It is absurd to call a West Indian or Irishman lazy when the former have been in demand as laborers for the building of the Panama Canal, and in the war time, for the cultivation of the farms of the United States, and the latter have won an outstanding reputation for themselves for hard work on the farm and civil engineering projects all over the world."[15]

The third group—or those who warn against *a priori* reasoning on the subject—are best represented by L. Robbins: "Any attempt to predict the effect of a change in the terms on which income is earned must proceed by inductive investigation of elasticities, (i.e. elasticities of demand for income in terms of effort). The attempt to narrow the limit of possible elasticities by a priori reasoning must be held to have broken down."[16]

Taking a similar point of view J. R. Hicks in a rigorous theoretical analysis states, "It has sometimes been thought that change in wages will always change the willingness to work in an opposite direction;

[14] T. S. Simey, *Welfare and Planning in the West Indies* (Oxford University Press, 1946), pp. 135–6.

[15] *Ibid.,* p. 139.

[16] L. Robbins, "On the Elasticity of Demand for Income in Terms of Effort," *Economica,* No. 29, June 1930, p. 129.

but there is no logical justification for this point of view."[17] And another careful student of labor economics, L. H. Fisher, suggests that
the sex and age composition of the labor force should be borne in
mind when analyzing the supply of agricultural labor. Thus the total
labor force may diminish with rising incomes, because the women and
children are able to live at home on the income of the able-bodied
males.[18]

Finally, as a result of a field survey in Antigua, Rottenberg concludes
that "Most writers treat both aggregate supply of labor in a particular
trade and the supply of labor offered by an individual as though they
were mainly functions of price. Where social-prestige factors intensify
occupational reservations, however, price changes and relative prices
may have a negligible influence on labor supply."[19]

During the past seven years this writer has had a number of opportunities to study this problem in so far as rubber and padi farmers in
Malaya are concerned. In very general terms the following conclusions
have been reached: (1) The concept of the "lazy native" with his high
preference for leisure to income is not true. (2) The situation is very
complex, and as is the case of all human relations, it is very subtle.
There are many district categories of labor. Each category has a different behavior pattern in response to price or wage changes. (3) Often
potential income changes have to be substantial enough to start a
change in the willingness to work. However, once this change has
been started, quite small potential changes in income can alter the
labor supply situation. (4) The direction of the change is as important
as its acceleration. Thus willingness to work in a boom-to-slump situation is different from willingness to work in a slump-to-boom situation. (5) The nature and range of all other factors that can have
influence on the willingness to work need much study.

This paper is being written and offered in the hope that one or
both of two effects may be accomplished: first, that the dangerous
implications of the "lazy native" concept may be noticed, and that in
so far as possible the realities of the situation may be clarified, and

---

[17] J. R. Hicks, *The Theory of Wages* (New York, Macmillan, 1932), p. 98.

[18] L. H. Fisher, *The Harvest Labour Market in California* (Harvard University
Press), Ch. 1.

[19] S. Rottenberg, "Income and Labour in an Undeveloped Economy," *Journal of
Political Economy*, Vol. 2, 1952, p. 101.

second, some constructive work in this sphere may be carried out both in pure theory and in case studies in the field.

These are some of the questions that need to be answered: What is *income* and what is *leisure* in the context of the economies that are to be found in Southeast Asia? What are the *other factors* (besides income variations) that influence the supply of labor, and how does underemployment fit into the picture? What particular techniques will be most useful for making case studies in this field?

commentary

W. KLATT

Economic Adviser and ILO Consultant

Definitions have been given and theoretical classifications have been provided in previous essays. However, there may be room for a report on one or two case studies. The main topics to be dealt with are related to the rural section of the population and the agricultural wing of the labor force, sometimes forgotten in an era of rapid industrial development. The main areas from which examples will be taken are East Bengal and Burma, sometimes overlooked at a time when attention is mainly directed to the achievements of the larger countries of Southeast Asia. Yet, the pace at which Southeast Asia will progress may well be determined in some of the less conspicuous parts of the area and in the spheres of activity least observed by the outside world.

If we include India, Pakistan and Japan, we are dealing here with a total area in which well over a quarter of the world's population, i.e., more than six hundred million people try to make a living from less than five hundred million acres of crop land. This means that on average the produce of three-quarters of an acre only is available per head of population. If we define Southeast Asia in the more narrow sense of this book, the pressure of population is somewhat less intense. But while approximately twice as much land is available per head of population, yields are a good deal lower than in the more advanced parts of this area. The area is too large to permit of broad generalizations, but there are certain features common to most of it. Throughout the area the rural population accounts for at least three in four, sometimes even four in five of the total population. The villages provide a home to local traders and craftsmen as well as to those who till the land. The cultivators' share in the total labor force amounts usually to two-thirds, but in some of the least industrialized areas, such as East Bengal, it amounts to at least three-quarters of the labor force.

Even if the accuracy of these data may be questioned in each individual instance, the preponderance of the villager in general and the agriculturist in particular is overwhelming. Any survey of the labor force, its size, its forms of employment, and changes in its composition would therefore not be complete without an assessment of the agricultural sector. Administrators, intellectuals, traders, and industrialists may play a more prominent part in the economic and social setting of Southeast Asia. Yet, their ties with the villages are usually close; many of them are not more than one generation removed from village life. No wonder that towns often give the appearance of villages that have grown beyond their bamboo or cactus fences without having lost entirely the characteristic features of rural communities.

Surveys of agricultural labor and rural working conditions are scarce throughout most parts of the world. In Southeast Asia the understanding is beginning to grow that the planning of economic and social changes is closely tied to an understanding of the position in the rural communities. To give only a few examples: In India the results of a statistical enquiry into the conditions of agricultural labor undertaken in 1950–51 were published in 1954.[1] In Pakistan a survey of labor conditions in agriculture was carried out recently, under the auspices of the International Labour Office, by Sir Malcolm Darling who has been associated with that part of the Indian continent for many years. When his report becomes available, it will add substantially to the knowledge of labor conditions in one important area of the region. In Burma the government is at present engaged in carrying out a similar survey, again with the assistance of the International Labour Office.

[1] Government of India, Ministry of Labour, *Agricultural Labour, How They Work and Live* (New Delhi, 1954).

Where the statistical services are well developed, as in India, a quantitative survey based on a representative sample may be possible. In most parts of Southeast Asia the services necessary for an enquiry of this kind are not yet sufficiently developed. Certain salient features are, however, so pronounced that they can be given at least in qualitative, if not in quantitative, terms. Often the impressions of a survey team checked against the information of experienced men in the field are the best that can be obtained. So far as may be judged from enquiries into the occupational pattern of villages in East Bengal and in Burma, it would appear that one-fifth to one-quarter of the village population may be engaged in nonagricultural activities. The division between agricultural and nonagricultural employment is of course not rigid. Trading and handicrafts are in any case closely tied to the needs of the village communities, and occupational activities are therefore interwoven and interchangeable.

As far as the agricultural labor force is concerned, one has to include cultivators and tenants as well as agricultural laborers in the narrow sense. Any other grouping would be artificial since the lines of division between these various forms of occupation in agriculture are fairly fluid. Generalizations are more dangerous here than elsewhere, but it may be of some interest that in Burma the agricultural laborers seem to account for between one-third and two-fifths of the total agricultural labor force. In East Bengal the position appears to be not very different. The size of holdings of course determine largely the size and the composition of the agricultural labor force. The smaller the farms, the more they depend on family labor and vice versa.

In some communities the owner-occupiers and tenants try to maintain a social status different from that of the laborers, but any such segregation tends to break down where the land available is so limited that cultivators and tenants may have to seek supplementary manual work in order to support themselves and their families. On the other hand, there are, of course, also agricultural workers who own some land and thus stand somewhere between the landless laborer and the owner-occupier.

This is no place to go in any detail into the very complex history of postwar reforms of agrarian patterns, but this aspect cannot be ignored entirely. Where land reforms have taken place and the worst features of landlordism and moneylending have been eliminated, as for instance in Burma, the village community appears more homogeneous in its social composition than it might be otherwise. Tenants tend to gain by comparison with owners, and laborers sometimes gain by comparison with both. It would be wrong to conclude that land reforms create an egalitarian society. While breaking down traditional class barriers, they tend to open the way to new forms of farming and to free technical skill and national leadership, thus laying the ground for a new economic and social disequilibrium.

The amount of underemployment or hidden unemployment among cultivators and tenants varies a great deal from area to area. It is clearly related to the amount of land available and the type of crop grown. If plantation crops are disregarded, throughout most parts of Southeast Asia paddy is grown on wet ground and wheat, pulses, and oilseeds are grown on dry land. The overall labor requirement to cultivate the land and to grow and harvest the crop is of the order of two hundred man-days for ten acres—that is under present conditions of farming. To this have to be added the days needed to repair the house, the bunds, and the implements, to collect firewood for the kitchen and fodder for the animals, and to cart the agricultural surplus to the market. This adds up to almost uninterrupted employment from one end of the year to the other. There is not enough work, however, for the breadwinner of the family, if the holding is substantially smaller than ten acres. Many farmsteads are of course smaller. In fact, throughout Southeast Asia the average size of holdings is nearer five than ten acres.

In these circumstances underemployment can be averted only if the level of intensity of farming can be raised or supplementary or alternative employment can be found outside agriculture. The survey of villages in Burma seems to suggest that under present conditions of farming there is much less idleness among cultivators and tenants than is sometimes assumed. This implies that farm output and productivity of farm labor cannot be raised substantially without the application of farm requisites additional to those available at present. Employment outside of agriculture tends to be available more readily near urban centers than in remote areas. This shows the close interdependence of agricultural and nonagricultural development. Since the war, building and other nonagricultural activities have been at a fairly high level throughout Southeast Asia. As a result villagers have found it easier than in the past to secure supplementary employment and thus additional income. It may be estimated that in Burma as much as twenty per cent of the villagers succeed in finding supplementary work during some part of the season.

These activities rarely contribute substantially to reducing seasonal unemployment which is a special phenomenon of the monocultures of Southeast Asia; it occurs in paddy fields as well as in plantations. While there is no panacea for this ill of the agriculture labor situation, it can be said in general that any broadening of the occupational pattern tends to reduce the seasonal fluctuations of agricultural employment. Rural and cottage industries usually provide imperfect remedies only. Rice mills absorb only a small part of the seasonally unemployed. Against this, double cropping and mixed farming tend to even out the labor curve.

Under conditions of partial underemployment and seasonal unemployment the national output is naturally smaller and the remuneration of labor is consequently poorer than it would be otherwise. In the rice economy the wages of regular laborers are usually paid in kind; elsewhere they are often paid partly in kind and partly in cash, the latter form of payment being applied in particular where wages are based on piece rather than on time rates. Sometimes a certain part of the payment is made in the form of meals, occasionally even in the form of clothing or cigars (cheroots). In Burma daily wages of agricultural laborers without special skill amount to approximately 2s.3d. sterling (or 0.30 U.S. cents) for men and 1s.6d. sterling (or 0.20 U.S. cents) for women; to this must be added the value of meals which raises wages at times by as much as fifty per cent. When piece work is done, payment may increase to twice the time rate. In East Bengal agricultural wages are of the same order or slightly lower.

At income levels of this order the agricultural workers clearly belong to the most underprivileged. Industrial workers of low skill earn twice as much and skilled workers may earn more than three times as much as agricultural laborers. The discrepancies between the incomes of owner-occupiers and tenants on the one hand, and traders, brokers, and industrial manufacturers on the other hand are of a similar order. In these circumstances it is not surprising that the contribution of farming to the national income is much smaller than the share of the agriculturalist in the total labor force might suggest. This discrepancy is well known from other economies, but it is not as wide in Europe and America as it is in Southeast Asia.

It is hardly surprising that at income levels as low as those quoted the bulk of rural earnings is spent on daily necessities, most of all on food. If the cost of food consumption in rural communities of Burma is evaluated at prevailing retail prices, some eighty per cent of the total net income is usually spent on food, the remainder being expended fairly evenly on clothing, shelter and other daily necessities. Three-quarters of the total income is spent on cereals which in turn provide approximately three-quarters of the daily calorie intake. While the diet is overburdened with starchy foods, its content of animal protein is low. As rice is highly milled in large parts of the area, the diet lacks thiamin and cases of dry and wet beriberi are common. After weaning the consumption of milk is insignificant. The absence of milk causes shortages of calcium and riboflavin which are not met sufficiently in any other way. These deficiencies are responsible for short stature, low body weight and high frequency of angular stomatitis and other nutritional illnesses.

Frequently the rural income is not sufficient to make ends meet. Approximately half the village population may be estimated to live with the help of loans. These are relatively small in the case of landless laborers, but a loan of no more than £7 (or 20 U.S. dollars) may in extreme cases be equal to one-third of the total annual earning of an agricultural laborer. In the case of cultivators and tenants loans are often twice to three times as high without necessarily being spent on means of production. On the contrary, frequently one-half to two-thirds of the loan is spent on consumer goods and social functions, and only the remaining half or one-third is used for the purchase of farm requisites. At the interest rates that still prevail in many parts of Southeast Asia, loans of this order and spent in this way frequently spell disaster to the villagers and their families. As a rule the vicious circle of indebtedness caused by low production that leads to new indebtedness cannot be broken without help provided from outside the rural community.

In considering the future prospects of the rural economy and of improvements in labor and living standards, it is important to be clear from the outset about certain factors that will not change for some time to come. First of all, the communities of Southeast Asia will remain predominantly agrarian. Unless substantial outside help is given over a long period, most countries of the area may find it a task beyond their means to do more than employ in a productive manner the annual increase in population. In Burma, for instance, it is reasonable to forecast a regular annual increase of at least 75,000 men of working age by the end of this decade. In East Bengal where the annual rate of increase in population is as high as one and a half per cent, an addition, year by year, to the labor force of at least 200,000 men may be expected. This is a formidable growth of the employable population. On a modest estimate it would cost at least £600 (or 1,700 U.S. dollars) per man to absorb this new labor force outside agriculture; it may be as high as £1,000 (or 2,800 U.S. dollars). It may prove too costly to do this. Consequently, the agricultural labor force may grow rather than shrink.

In these circumstances it will be imperative to direct attention to the necessities and possibilities of increasing farming activities and improving rural earnings. This will be all the more important, since the increasing population will have to be fed. Unless farm output increases at an annual rate of approximately one and a half per cent, it will not be possible to maintain even the low levels of consumption and standards of living that prevail in the region at present. Any substantial improvements in the composition of the diet and thus in the condition of health will require an annual growth of farm output of three per cent or more.

It is understandable that countries that have recently gained, or are in the process of gaining, their national independence look upon industrialization as an expression of their political aspirations. And indeed, industrialization there must be. But it is perhaps not too early to point out that this process, which is costly and painful in the best of circumstances, is likely to take place most smoothly if it is divorced as little as possible from the existing patterns of economic activities. Setbacks in living standards will be unavoidable unless sufficient emphasis is given to productive investment in agriculture. This applies in particular to countries whose income abroad is derived mainly from this source. Even if economic activities are expanded largely with the aim of raising the production and productivity of the predominant industry, that is farming, and thereby in the interests of consumer goods most in demand, that is food and textile fibres, the process will be far from easy. Unless it is accepted that capital investment be paid, at least initially, by the taxpayers of other countries, it will mean a fairly long period of reduced rather than improved living standards.

When trying to assess the possibilities of increased farm output, the human element must be taken into consideration first of all. In Burma and in East Bengal, as well as elsewhere in the region, the view can be heard at times that the cultivator is lazy and conservative and thus incapable of introducing changes into his farming practices. This contention is not borne out by village surveys. On the contrary, the villager shows imagination and adaptability to a significant extent where he is given inducements. Moreover, he can be found busying himself throughout the year, mostly working hard with the outmoded equipment at his disposal. If he is found at times resting before the day is over, it should be borne in mind that he is faced, day after day, with work in a trying climate and that his body is weakened by diseases which do not occur or have been eliminated in the farming areas of the temperate zone.

Village surveys also suggest that the cultivator shows initiative where it is likely to bring a tangible return. He need not be considered a mere object of government planning, but on the contrary, he can be entrusted to become an active participant in any program directed toward progress in farming. Therefore, government action can happily be limited to laying down overall planning targets while the interpretation of government policy may be left to the village community. Help is, however, needed from outside. As a rule farm output and productivity of farm labor cannot be raised readily without the application of farm requisites not available at present. Seeds, fertilizers, and insecticides come to mind; but of the many technical devices applied in modern agriculture none seems more capable of making an impact on farming in the initial phase of modernization than the tractor.

At present cultivating and seeding are rarely done at the right time and little land is utilized for a second crop during the dry season. In Burma as in East Bengal it can be found that there is a vicious circle here that has not yet been broken.[2] At the end of the season the

---

[2] W. Klatt, "Agricultural Planning in East Pakistan," *Pacific Affairs*, Vol. XXV, No. 3, September 1952.

soil is in deplorable condition because of the lack of draft power when it is needed most, between the end of the old and the beginning of the new season. The draft animals are too weak to pull any equipment heavier than the outmoded tools now in use. In the absence of sufficient fodder for draft animals, there is no hope of breeding heavier animals; and in the absence of sufficiently strong draft animals there is no hope of growing fodder as a second crop. This vicious circle cannot be broken without additional power. It can only come from outside in the form of tractors. Of course, in countries in which human labor cannot find alternative employment easily, it cannot be the function of the tractor to replace man. On the contrary, it is to create the conditions for additional productive employment of man in a farming industry that is more intensive than it can be in present conditions.

The advantages of turning agriculture, the largest single operational unit of the area, into a modern industry are manifold. The first advantage lies obviously in the size of the industry. The number of people likely to be affected in their employment pattern and living standards even by minor improvements in farming practices is bound to be much greater than can be hoped for as a result of setting up a steel mill. Moreover, as the bulk of the annual additions to the labor force are country-bred, any improvements of production methods achieved in the villages are likely to have the most far-reaching effects on the technical skill of the generation that will have to supply the workers for other industries. Lastly, since agriculture is usually the main earner of foreign exchange in this area, any modernization in this sphere is likely to improve the competitive position of the export industry.

It should not be forgotten, however, that productivity in industry tends to be at least twice as high as in agriculture. This means that the investment in farming should not go beyond the needs of the indigenous population increased by the requirements of the export market. Any human, physical, and financial resources that can be spared after the need for rationalizing the farming industry has been satisfied are best utilized outside agriculture. For some time to come capital is likely to be scarce while the increase in the working population will continue to be substantial. In these circumstances it will be advisable to concentrate on investment in industries that are extensive rather than intensive in their capital requirements. The industrial development in certain countries of Latin America and the Soviet orbit where industrialization has been bought at heavy expense to the consumer should be a warning to the countries of Southeast Asia. In industries where the investment per head of the labor force is low, the share of human labor and thus of wages tends to be high. These are the industries most suitable at this stage for most parts of the region.

Next to agriculture, the development of those industries that are nearest the consumer demand will probably yield the most satisfactory national returns. Most countries of the area have passed the stage where clothes are produced from imported cloth; but in many cases domestic weaving is still based predominantly on yarn bought at the cost of scarce foreign exchange. Here then is the next line of a possible progress in industrialization. Again the advantages are manifold. Existing village skill in this sphere is plentiful; capital investment per worker is cheaper than in less labor-intensive industries; the consumer market is large, unsatisfied, and expanding; and last but not least the possibilities of domestic supplies of textile fibres are far from being exhausted. Fears that a development of this kind might be detrimental to the British and Japanese textile industries and might thus jeopardize the chances of Southeast Asian exports to these countries would seem unwarranted, provided agreement can be reached on a division of labor between the traditional and the new textile producers.

While skill and initiative are more plentiful than is sometimes thought, much training will be needed before an industrial labor force deserving of the name will be available. The lack of technical education is likely to cause considerable delays and setbacks. In Burma where the state of literacy is relatively high and women play a full part in the country's affairs, the development is likely to be much faster than, for instance, in East Bengal where the rate of literacy is very low and women are still precluded from any but domestic activities. In Burma the ease with which the lower industrial skills are acquired by untrained men and women is most encouraging. By comparison, in East Bengal and other countries with similar educational handicaps it may be necessary to have recourse to somewhat unconventional practices in education. In fact, it may be necessary to spread education without attempting to erase illiteracy. The traditional form of education may have to be supplemented or indeed replaced by teaching through radio and film. If this were done in direct relation to the daily affairs of the villager and his family, the results might well be startling. General education among villagers might become a by-product of teaching modern farm techniques instead of being considered its prerequisite.

When all these measures have been given the places of priority which they deserve, there will remain the problem of providing the higher technical and administrative skill without which no modern industrial country can hope to handle its own affairs. It is indeed gratifying to see that the programs of foreign assistance, whether they are provided under the auspices of international organizations, such as the agencies of the United Nations or the Colombo Plan, or national institutions, such as the Ford Foundation or the Johns Hopkins University, recognize to an increasing extent that here lies the most rewarding contribution that the outside world can make to the development and utilization of the labor resources of Southeast Asia.

Demographic influences on economic development in Southeast Asia

B. W. HODDER

University of Malaya

In this examination of demographic influences on the economic development of Southeast Asia, I will focus not on the effects of spatial distributions and population density patterns—interesting though these may be—but rather on the economic consequences of population trends; and more particularly on those demographic determinants relating to the rate of natural increase of population, migration, and age structure.

First, the rate of natural increase in population is high. In some areas very high: in Brunei, Singapore, and the Federation of Malaya it is over 30 per thousand a year. Elsewhere, rates of from 15 to 20 per thousand are usual—rates which, if maintained, would increase the present population of 180 million by more than half over the next thirty years. The chief reason for this high average rate of natural increase is that birth rates are very high and death rates fairly low. Southeast Asia has left behind the era of high birth and high death rates which kept the size of population small up to 1800. The region is now experiencing what has been called "a medieval birth rate with a modern death rate."

No immediate fall in these rates of population growth can be expected. On the contrary, they are likely to rise. For as health and economic standards improve, death rates will continue to fall without any immediate likelihood of a comparable reduction in the birth rate. The force of this argument, admittedly, varies from country to country.

In Burma, the relatively low rate of growth of population is caused by a high death rate—still twice that of any other country in Southeast Asia (indeed, her infant mortality rate of 200 per thousand is one of the highest in the world). Burma, then, has greater scope for reducing her death rate and so must face the possibility that her rate of population growth may soon rise steeply. The Philippines, on the other hand, can reasonably hope for at least no significant increase in her relatively low rate of natural increase because it is a function, not of a high death rate, but of a low birth rate.

Does this generally rapid growth of population in Southeast Asia stimulate economic development? Or is it an obstacle to such development? There are firm grounds for maintaining that the high rate of population growth, at least in this underdeveloped corner of the world, tends on the whole to limit economic development. In terms of capital, certainly, the high rate of population growth is costly. If we assume that about 4 per cent of the national income must be saved to provide capital for a 1 per cent increase in population, it follows that in some countries of Southeast Asia up to 15 per cent of the national income must be saved for demographic investment, that is, merely to cope with the additional population without any increase in the average standard of living. In Singapore and the Federation of Malaya the population is growing at a rate of 3 per cent to 3½ per cent a year so that these countries require a net domestic capital formation rate of 12 to 15 per cent merely to provide the increased population with a per capita endowment of capital assets. Even the most cursory examination of rates of domestic capital savings in the countries of Southeast Asia makes it clear that they are insufficient, relative to the rate of population growth, to allow any significant increase in the average standard of living. Without outside help the countries of Southeast Asia can do little in the way of economic investment. In Singapore and the Federation of Malaya the rate of domestic capital formation is only about 10 per cent. In Indonesia and Indochina it has been negligible and in the Philippines only about 2 per cent. Burma, it is true, appears better off in this respect. Her rate of natural increase is relatively low and her rate of domestic capital savings is relatively high—18 per cent in 1954–55. But this advantage is to some extent offset by the high potential for population growth in Burma referred to previously.

I come now to the second demographic factor—migration. This does not affect significantly the tendency in the foregoing argument to identify the rate of natural increase with the rate of population growth. Southeast Asia is nowadays little disturbed by migrations of people into or out of the region. Admittedly, this is a quite recent phenomenon. For after the middle of the nineteenth century large numbers of Indian and Chinese laborers moved into the region and before 1900 the rate of population growth in certain countries was a function more of migrational surplus than of natural increase; in Malaya indeed the population frequently increased in the face of an excess of deaths over births. Now, however, natural increase has everywhere taken over as the main determinant in the rate of population growth in Southeast Asia.

From our point of view the chief interest of this recent history of mass immigration lies in its effects on the racial, sex, and age composition of the population rather than on its size. Indian and Chinese immigrants—disproportionately male and of the young adult age groups—form only small proportions of the total population today, but they have provided much of the labor force for the mining and plantation industries in Southeast Asia, attracted foreign capital, and contributed energy and skills. In varying ways they continue to play a vital role in the economic development of the region.

Thirdly, the age structure. One of the most important demographic implications of the high rate of natural increase in Southeast Asia is that the region has a large number of children in proportion to the population of working ages. Whereas the age median in the United States for instance is 29, in Southeast Asia it is about 18. The proportion of the population under 15 years of age varies from 37 per cent in Burma to 43 per cent in the Philippines. The average percentage of the total population in the region excluded, at least in theory, from the effective working population is 40 per cent whereas in many Western countries the figure is often between 22 and 30 per cent. In practice, on the other hand, this theoretical burden of child dependency is lightened by the low age at which children enter the effective working force. For this reason a large family is frequently regarded as an economic asset.

The high proportion of children in the total population limits capital formation, already made difficult, as we have seen, by the high rate at which the population is growing. The needs of the whole community have to be satisfied by a small working population so that little is left for purposes of investment. Moreover, where infant mortality rates are high, an unusually large part of the investment made in the bearing and rearing of children is wasted because so many of them never live long enough to enter the labor force.

At first sight it would seem that another consequence of the bottom-heavy age structure would be a shortage of labor. But, on the contrary, underemployment is a characteristic of Southeast Asia. In spite of the fact that the ratio of dependent to economically active population is high, there is no widespread shortage of labor. In so far as the problem of labor supply in Southeast Asia *is* quantitative, it is not that there are too few economically active persons available but that there are too many to be supported by the economic structure, weakened as it is already by the rapid rate of population growth and by the high ratio of child dependency.

These three demographic factors must clearly all affect deeply the nature, extent, and sequence of planning for economic development in Southeast Asia, but it is on the rate of growth of population that attention is commonly focussed. It has been said that the problem of economic development is, in its simplest terms, how to increase production at a rate in excess of the rate of population growth. The central problem in the demographic-economic relationship is a corollary to this—that a too rapid growth of population should not dissipate the benefits of economic development.

What measures are being used to meet this problem? There are two main lines of approach, one demographic, the other economic.

The demographic approach includes a direct attack on the natural increase by the use of birth control measures. The value of these in reducing birth rates is very much a matter of opinion. At the World Population Conference in 1954, however, only a minority supported the large-scale artificial restriction of births. It is perhaps for long unlikely to be effective in underdeveloped Southeast Asia where educational and economic standards are still low, and cultural, particularly religious, prejudices are difficult to overcome. This is not to dismiss birth control as a potentially effective measure. Obviously birth control measures must be known and available to the people. But the more fundamental and difficult task is to make the people of Southeast Asia want to use them.

The economic line of approach to the problem is directed at developing production at a rate greater than the rate of population growth. In so far as this approach affects the demography of the region, it does so only indirectly.

I will deal with only two important measures under this heading—the increase of agricultural production and the development of industrialization.

The increase of agricultural production implies both its areal extension and intensification. The areal extension of agricultural land, or agricultural colonization, has three main aims: to increase the total food production, to relieve population pressure in the area from which colonists come, and to encourage economic development in the area to which colonists go. Thus in Indonesia, official support for agricultural colonization in the islands outside Java is designed to increase the total amount of food produced within Indonesia, to relieve population pressure in Java and, finally, to assist in the development of the more sparsely peopled islands. Such a redistribution of population by internal migration is based on the assumption that certain parts of Southeast Asia, such as Java, are overpopulated, and that others, like Borneo, are underpopulated; or to express it in another way, that there are too many or too few people in some areas to allow the fullest economic development. We cannot examine here the problem of the optimum population concept; admittedly it is a vague, ambiguous, and even sterile idea, but it is in some form or another implicit in any discussion of overpopulation and underpopulation. What must be emphasized, however, is the value in this connection of the concept of 'nutritional density' of population: that is, the density of population per acre of padi land. As one writer has pointed out, although simple areal densities in Lower Thailand and the Tonkin delta are similar, the first, with a nutritional density of under one person per cultivated acre can hardly be considered overpopulated, whereas the Tonkin delta, with a nutritional density of about three persons per cultivated acre, is undeniably overpopulated.

Although pioneer agricultural settlement is commonly successful in raising the total amount of food produced within a country, and is also commonly successful in assisting economic development in the new area, there is, I suggest, no evidence that the redistribution of population for agricultural colonization in Southeast Asia has anywhere appreciably lessened population pressure in the country of origin. The numbers involved have never been large enough over a short enough period. In 1953, the Indonesian government moved some 50,000 colonists from Java to sparsely peopled islands, chiefly Sumatra and South Borneo. Such a figure constituted less than one tenth of the natural increase in Java during that year. However, it is hoped within a few years to move as many as 500,000 a year out of Java; the government feels that this is the only practicable solution to its problem of overpopulation.

All schemes for agricultural colonization have to face the dilemma that if the shift of population is large enough and speedy enough to reduce significantly population pressure in the place of origin, then the rate of immigration into the new area might seriously strain its capacity for absorbing extra people. And unless it is planned and controlled it can hinder rather than assist development: the sudden impact of a half million refugees from North Viet-Nam hampered for some time normal agricultural operations in the Saigon-Cholon area of South Viet-Nam.

As for the potentialities in Southeast Asia for pioneer agricultural expansion, most authorities contend that the available arable land is by no means fully utilized, even if one assumes the continuance of present methods of growing rice. Certainly the proportion of total land cultivated is often quite low. In Thailand the cultivated area accounts for only 8.6 million out of 51.2 million hectares. It is often asserted that Burma has plenty of available land for development and that the large island of Borneo is almost empty. But it is wrong to suggest that there are vast open spaces waiting to receive colonists in Southeast Asia. Apart from the difficulties I have already mentioned, the successful opening up of new agricultural lands depends on a host of factors including an adequate knowledge of the local climate, weather, and soil conditions, as well as a complex of economic and social considerations, including the provision of essential services (notably communications) and the availability of capital. Clearing operations are especially difficult and expensive in this tropical environment. Moreover, it is becoming increasingly difficult to find colonists, for in most parts of Southeast Asia population pressure is not yet so

critically severe as to make people want to move away from their traditional homes. Land tenure conditions and climatic and health hazards in
the receiving areas, too, are frequently discouraging to prospective migrants. Colonists today demand high standards of economic and social
security from the moment they arrive in the area to be opened up.
An instance of modern standards in agricultural colonization is given
in the recent agreement referring to the employment and settlement
of Filipino workers in British North Borneo. Provision for migrants
there includes a model labor contract conforming with the requirements of both governments as well as of the International Labour Organization. Colonists are guaranteed the opportunity to acquire land
and become independent farmers.

Southeast Asia can no longer afford to be a safety valve for the
overpopulated parts of Asia. It is unlikely that large-scale migration
into the region from the neighboring densely populated countries of
India and China is either likely or desirable in the future. On the
other hand, there is scope for internal migrants to play a substantial
part in the economic development of the region.

As for the intensification of agricultural production, I will not say
very much about it here, vitally important though it is. The intensification of agricultural production is very much a matter of applied research, affecting both the methods and techniques of farming and seed
and plant selection. For example, the improvement of strains to suit
local peculiarities of soil, climate, moisture, and terrain frequently
may have remarkable results: in Java, one third of the island's padi
planters now use an improved seed on United States technical advice.
A yield one third higher than before is now obtained.

The extension and intensification of agricultural production constitute important measures to meet the demographic-economic problem
in Southeast Asia. The nature and relative emphasis of these measures
must vary from country to country. In densely populated Java the
emphasis is on intensification by various means whereas in Sumatra
the extension of agricultural land is of first interest. In some countries,
a combination of these measures is emphasized. Thus in the Philippines
it is planned to increase the production of food crops from 7.3 million
tons in 1955 to 11.3 million tons in 1959. A large part of this increase
will come from the extension of agricultural land: 2 million hectares
of public land will be distributed during the five years. Production

increases, however, will also arise from improved farm practices, soil conservation, and improvements in irrigation, but above all, in this particular part of Southeast Asia, from the extensive use of fertilizers. It should be pointed out here that the importance of the increase of food supplies as a measure to meet the demographic-economic problem is sharpened by its repercussions on human energy. It is estimated that economic progress is impossible until the available calories per head of population exceed 2,000 per day. Further, a marked development of energy and capital accumulation is unusual until a level of 3,000 calories per head per day is reached. In most Southeast Asian countries, however, the calorific intake per head per day is less than 2,000. Total food supplies have in most countries not kept pace with the growth in population numbers.

I come now to industrialization, meaning not only the development of primary or secondary manufacturing industries but also the mechanization of agriculture.

One of the commonest arguments for promoting industrialization in the region is that it will be accompanied by urbanization which, by Western analogy, brings about a decline in fertility. Certainly, the relevant social transformations are more easily effected in towns than in rural areas. But on the other hand, such a decline in fertility must lag well behind the expected declines in death rates previously referred to so that no immediate reduction in the rate of natural increase of population could be expected. Analogies between Western countries and the countries of Southeast Asia are dangerous because the potential for population expansion in Southeast Asia is greater than it ever was in Western countries at the early stages of their industrialization. In this connection, it can be pointed out that Singapore and Malaya, the two most urbanized countries in the region, have among the highest rates of natural increase of population. Urban-rural differentials in fertility in Southeast Asia are not yet evident.

Urbanization is also believed to reduce population pressure on the land, for urbanization is frequently a function of migration from rural to urban areas. But it can lead to increased pressure of population because there is often a disproportionately large number of young adults in these peasant migrants to the towns, and because it hastens the decline of rural industries. Moreover, urbanization itself often leads to severe problems of population pressure in the urban centers.

As in many parts of the world, the larger cities and towns are growing more quickly than the medium-sized and small towns. It is from the four foci of Singapore, Djakarta, Manila, and Saigon-Cholon that most of the broader benefits of industrialization can be expected to radiate. And though town-planning can help to meet the problem of housing in such centers, it can do little to affect the problem of employment arising out of urban population pressure.

Industrialization has, from our point of view, two disadvantages compared with agricultural production as a measure to cope with the demographic-economic problem in Southeast Asia. In the first place, industrialization demands more capital outlay. It has been said that industrialization and capital accumulation are virtually identical processes because the application of mechanical techniques has always been more limited in agricultural production than in manufacturing industry. Southeast Asia, as we have seen, is poor in domestic capital potential. Secondly, industrialization is less effective at absorbing labor than is agricultural development. The application of those Western technological devices aimed at saving labor is unsuitable, even illogical, in the Southeast Asian context with its problems of under-employment. The high population density in those parts of the region most likely to attract and stimulate industrial development must limit the pace of introduction of any labor saving machinery.

Both these disadvantages apply not only to manufacturing industry but also to the mechanization of agriculture. Consequently such measures as seed improvement and the scientific use of fertilizers, as we saw in the Philippines, play a larger part in schemes for intensifying agricultural production than do the more expensive and labor saving measures of mechanized agriculture. Moreover, in areas of high agricultural density land fragmentation frequently makes the large-scale use of machinery impracticable. In so far as large-scale agricultural mechanization is desirable in Southeast Asian countries, I suggest it is best confined to pioneer agricultural development areas.

Much remains to be learned about demographic-economic relationships, more especially in an underdeveloped part of the world like Southeast Asia. The population seminar to be held at Bandung in the near future will examine, among other things, the need for research on the interrelationship between population trends and economic development. Much of what I have said is highly controversial, and it is difficult to be quite sure that what one says is entirely free from cultural prejudices and is not affected by a too facile analogy with Western experiences. Moreover, it must be emphasized that population is not always the most important factor influencing economic development. Certainly it is not always the determining or decisive factor. My argument, however, can be summarized in this way. Supporting the view that in general the high rate of increase of population in Southeast Asia limits economic development, I have expressed the demographic-economic problem in terms of how to keep the benefits of economic development from being absorbed by the increase of population. Though birth control may eventually play an important part in solving this problem, it cannot be widely effective for some time. Nor can the rate of population growth be lessened by any substantial emigration out of the region. Under Southeast Asian conditions, the problem can best be met, not by attempting directly to decrease the rate of growth of population, but by increasing the rate of production, both in agriculture and in industry. The increase of agricultural production in Southeast Asia is perhaps best brought about without the widespread application of mechanical techniques to the land; and industrialization in its widest sense should take second place to the increase of food production in measures to meet the demographic-economic problem. Any industrialization in the region is as far as possible to be adapted to suit the special needs of Southeast Asian countries which are poor in capital but have abundant labor. For this reason one must applaud attempts in certain countries, notably Burma and Indonesia, to promote small-scale and cottage industries which do not need large capital expenditure, and which do not aggravate present problems of underemployment.

Finally, it is held that this economic approach is the most promising though indirect way of reducing both the pressure of population in parts of the region and the ubiquitous high rate of natural increase. The extension of agricultural land implies a redistribution of population more in accord with the physical and economic potentialities of the region, and the growth of industrialization, if accompanied by any significant degree of urbanization, may effect that decline in human fertility which, I suggest, is so necessary to the fullest economic development of Southeast Asia.

commentary

R. M. SUNDRUM

Rangoon University

The most important aspects of the manner in which demographic factors exert an influence on economic development have been summarized. These factors may be defined in a wide sense to include the size of the population, the age and sex composition, the regional distribution, the rate of growth, and in addition a factor which can perhaps be best described only as the equality of the people.

One gets the impression that in the countries of Southeast Asia, all these factors are present only in a form in which they constitute obstacles to economic development,[1] and according to some extreme views, even in a form in which they are an argument against policies designed to promote economic development. Examples are: (a) population is dense, creating in some countries a shortage of land, and in most countries a shortage of capital, so that the existing techniques of production are far from the best possible. (b) The age structure has been so influenced by high birth rates that the population is bottom heavy, and the proportion of the working population to the total is small. (c) The regional distribution even within countries is unsatisfactory, because considerable areas of some of the Southeast Asian countries are sparsely populated while at the same time other areas can support a relatively dense population only at a low level of living. (d) The rate of increase is so great that such economic development as is possible out of the domestic savings of the people can hardly keep pace with the growth of the population. (e) Finally, the attitude of the people of these parts to the problem is such that little progress can be achieved which depends on their co-operation.

With such an unfavorable demographic situation, the question is then posed whether attempts at economic development are justified when the fruits of such progress will almost certainly be cancelled by

[1] See, e.g., J. J. Spengler, "The Population Obstacles to Economic Development," *American Economic Review*, May 1951, p. 341.

population growth. This is an age-old argument dating from the days of the English classical economists. To draw this analogy is useful, because it points to the assumption which is common to both types of argument that population tends to reach the size at which the standard of living of the working classes is at the subsistence level.

Perhaps I have overstated this aspect of the argument. If so, I must straightaway admit that there is so much truth in most of these propositions that no useful contribution to the study of demographic influences on economic development is possible which does not recognize them. Nevertheless, I would like to introduce some qualifications to these propositions, if only to remove some traces of the fatalism which occasionally appears in discussions of this problem.

Take first the matter of the density of the population as a factor in the impoverishment of the people and in retarding economic development. On considering this statement, one realizes that the highest densities are not in Southeast Asia, that far higher densities are to be found in the most industrialized countries, and that therefore if Southeast Asia is to be called a densely populated region, it must be in reference to its predominant techniques of production. And then one recognizes that the "primitive" methods of production are as much contributory factors to the present situation as is the density of population.

The age structure of the population has been described as one which makes for a large proportion of children and dependents. Professor Hodder has already made a qualification to this argument in pointing out that the age at which people enter employment is lower in this region than elsewhere, a factor which for example makes a large family of children an asset to a farmer although it leads to undue fragmentation of the land later on. At the same time, it must be noted also that female labor is often a large proportion in this region.

The large proportion of young people among the populations of underdeveloped countries is usually mentioned as an obstacle to economic development, because it reduces the size of the labor force relative to the total population. While admitting this, it must also be brought out that such young populations are usually more progressive; they feel to a much smaller extent the dead weight of tradition which stands in the way of speedy change required for economic development.

In spite of these considerations, the fact still remains that, something like 22.5 per cent of the Indian national income is spent on maintaining those who die before they reach the age of 15,[2] as compared to 6.5 per cent in England; and the situation in the Southeast Asian countries cannot be much different.

It has been brought out that most of these countries have high birth rates, and that this brings about a high rate of population growth except in cases, like Burma, where it is offset by a high death rate. In these latter cases, the rate of population growth is potentially high, when death rates are brought down under the influence of social welfare programs already underway. In such a case, even to keep the standard of living of the people constant requires a rate of capital formation often beyond the level of domestic savings.

Where, for example, there is a high rate of growth due to a recent fall in the death rate not yet followed by a fall in the birth rate, we can expect with some degree of confidence that the birth rate will fall in the future, if for no other reason than that traditional attitudes to the size of the family are powerful influences and that such attitudes favor a size which, over the average duration of the family, is not large. We must remember that even populations which are growing at a rapid rate at present have had long periods of steadiness. To put it differently, the period of rapid population growth is only a phase in the S-curve of demographic evolution, a phase which may be long or short, but which is definitely finite under given conditions.

Finally, we come to the argument that population factors are such obstacles to economic development that, as H. W. Singer put it at the Rome Conference on World Population Problems, "anyone who attempts to promote economic development otherwise than through population factors is barking up the wrong tree."[3] I think that it is this preoccupation with the purely demographic aspect of the matter that explains for example the stress laid by the Indian government on further research into contraceptive techniques. In his paper, Singer discussed this problem at length and I cannot add to it. I can only emphasize here the importance of directing attention to the economic aspect

[2] Estimate of D. Ghosh, *Pressure of Population and Economic Efficiency in India* (New Delhi, 1946), p. 22.

[3] "Population and Economic Development," Proceedings of World Population Conference, Rome, 1952.

of the matter. On the other hand, Professor Hodder has also come to the view that the economic aspects of future policy are more important, but he has been led to this conclusion because of the futility of more direct policy action on the growth of population.

I shall attempt to bring out some important economic influences on the demographic factors and suggest the conclusion that economic policy in underdeveloped countries can not only lead directly to economic development in spite of adverse demographic factors, but can so influence the demographic situation as to make these demographic factors reinforce the trend toward a better standard of living for the people.

In the foregoing part of my discussion, I have been enumerating the main features of the demographic influences on economic development as commonly stated and have attempted to bring in some qualifications which are necessary. I shall now try to enlarge on the thesis that these demographic factors are themselves subject to other influences, in particular to economic factors, which at once constitute the explanation of the present unfavorable demographic situation of the underdeveloped countries and in some cases point to methods of improving that situation.

It is perhaps not fair to say that these considerations have been neglected, but it must be stressed that it is only recently that their importance has been fully recognized. Thus, J. J. Spengler, writing as recently as 1951, was pleading that "A multiscience approach is required."[4] It has always been my impression as I watch, for example, method after method being proposed for the measurement of human reproductivity that there is something missing in these elaborate calculations, and that the missing factors could perhaps be of a purely economic or sociological nature. Apart from the impact on fertility of such factors as, for example, changes in price structure, there has been surprisingly little discussion, at least for this region, of even such an important sociological factor as the traditional attitude to family size among the people. One wonders whether such a concept is sufficiently stable to be made a tool of analysis and interpretation, and whether in consequence a rapid fall in the infant mortality rate

---

[4] *A Survey of Contemporary Economics*, Vol. II, Bernard F. Haley (ed.), American Economic Association.

will not to a great extent be balanced *within the same* generation by a fall in the birth rate, in the effort of people trying to stabilize their family size on the average over the duration of a marriage.

We begin then with the question of overpopulation, defined in terms of the density of population. We have already seen that questions of overpopulation cannot be decided without reference to such factors as the predominant types and techniques of production, and in consequence, to such factors as the terms of exchange within the country and between countries. Thus a predominantly industrial country can support far higher densities of population on the land than an agricultural country. In the same way, an agricultural country, like New Zealand or Holland, with a line of agricultural production having a more favorable rate of exchange with industrial products can support higher densities than primary producing countries, say, of Southeast Asia. If therefore in these countries, the population is thought to be so dense as to keep living standards low, then the obvious solution is to influence the economy by a change in the occupational structure of their people. People should be encouraged to shift from agriculture to industry, where the operation of diminishing returns is more gradual. This will make at once for a more intensive agriculture on the one hand, and for the beginnings of industry on the other.

Professor Hodder has referred to this type of solution of the problem. I would however add to his remarks only in stressing that industrialization and intensive agriculture are not alternatives to each other, but rather two aspects of the same forces tending to labor-intensive methods of production. This is clearly brought out by a study of the situation in advanced countries. See for example the summary given by F. G. H. Barter in his paper to the Rome Conference.[5]

Professor Hodder's own inclinations seem to favor the method of further extensions of agriculture, so that the same population is spaced out over a wider area and production becomes less labor-intensive rather than more. I think it should be agreed that even in long settled areas of Southeast Asia considerable areas of land are still available for cultivation and that a good part of high agricultural densities can be relieved by a regional redistribution of populations. And I agree that all plans for economic development within a country should

---

[5] "Fundamental Factors Affecting the Stage and Status of Agricultural Development," World Population Conference, Rome, 1952, p. 9 and Table 2.

be firmly oriented toward the more even development of all parts of the country and that governments can come in more actively than hitherto with assistance for internal transmigrations. So far it seems that the problem has begun to be tackled on any large scale only in Java.

But even so, it must be realized that this cannot be a lasting solution, and that it is only putting off to a later day the fundamental structural changes called for by the situation. Let me pose the problem in a different way. It is well known that in the middle phase of the demographic revolution, that is, between the two stable periods of high birth and death rates and low birth and death rates, there is a large rise in population by natural increase, due to the lag of the decline in birth rates behind the fall in death rates. It has been estimated that "at least a threefold multiplication is implicit in the processes by which peoples hitherto have achieved low birth and death rates."[6] Thus many countries of Southeast Asia, like Burma, which are just beginning to feel the impact of the demographic revolution, have to think of methods which can cope with a rise of population, of the order of a threefold multiplication. It does not seem to me that the resort to further extensions of agriculture, however useful as a matter of immediate relief, can be a long-period or ultimate solution.

Difficult as is the problem relating to high densities, perhaps even more difficult is that relating to the high rates of growth. Let me now try to analyze the manner in which economic factors influence the demographic situation and in turn the possibilities of economic development. It seems to me to be ironical that in this field of study, we can have gone so far from the earliest conjectures that we read now that "In any event until we know more about the interrelationship of increases in population and total income, it seems appropriate to consider the two as independent variables."[7] The earliest conjecture on this subject was the Malthusian postulate that the economic condition exercises a dominating influence on the growth of population. It is of course widely agreed that the Malthusian postulate was an extreme position, that the picture painted by "the broad strokes of the Malthusian brush" oversimplifies particularly in denying any place to the

---

[6] M. C. Balfour *et al.*, *Public Health and Demography in the Far East*, Rockefeller Foundation, 1950.

[7] Henry H. Villard, *Rev. Economics and Statistics*, May 1955, p. 190.

"substitution effect" in the allocation of income increases, but as one writer has said, "there is no reason to rush to the other extreme and assume that the non-acceptance of the exclusively Malthusian postulate severs the nexus between material conditions and population changes."[8]

It might be useful at this point to refer to the somewhat daring speculations of a recent book by Lieberstein.[9] His discussion is centered round the concept of the stability of the Malthusian equilibrium, and he examines the conditions under which a "displacement," such as the injection of new capital in a development program, can be expected to lead to a new equilibrium or to a cumulative development, the Malthusian equilibrium being the situation in which the size of the population is kept at the existing level by subsistence requirements acting on a high birth rate. He argues that this equilibrium is stable under small displacements or series of displacements. However, if a displacement is large relative to all the given circumstances, such as the capital-income ratio, he believes that a sudden rise to a new high level of income will alter the relationship between economic factors and population growth fundamentally, so that further progress of the economic factors will not be lost in a corresponding population growth but contribute directly to raising per capita incomes, and thereby set in motion the sort of cumulative expansion, which is the history of Western countries. The book appears to emphasize the dangers of slow development.

This is an interesting line of inquiry, which can be followed up in further research, particularly in an attempt to reduce the discussion to quantitative terms of the size of displacement that is needed to make any impression. I would like to relate this to a problem in economic theory concerning consumer behavior. This is the result of a recent research, reported by J. Duesenberry,[10] that when consumers reach a high level of consumption in the upper phase of a cycle, they tend to cling to that level as much as they can in the subsequent period. The conclusion is reached by him that "the income or consumption of the last cyclical peak will carry a special and very heavy weight in

[8] Alan T. Peacock, "Theory of Population and Modern Economic Analysis," *Population Studies*, March 1954, p. 227.

[9] *A Theory of Economic-Demographic Development* (Princeton, 1954).

[10] *Income, Saving and the Theory of Consumer Behaviour* (Harvard University Press, 1952).

determining consumption at a given (lower) level of income during a depression." He then discusses how such a conclusion helps to understand many statistical results obtained from surveys of consumption patterns in the United States. A similar hypothesis appears to underlie Lieberstein's model, that is, if an initial displacement occurs to raise income and consumption to a sufficiently high level, the effort to retain this level of consumption in the subsequent period may be strong enough to bring the question of family size within the economic calculation of large numbers of people.

The essence of the matter is really the fact that in spite of the many indirect ways in which economic factors influence the growth of population, they do not as yet directly influence the peoples of Southeast Asia in deciding the number of their children. And I think that it cannot be sufficiently stressed in any discussion of this problem that far far more important than merely making contraceptive techniques available to people and exhorting them to make use of them is the question of establishing in the minds of individuals the direct connection that exists between their family size and the prospects of further economic betterment. And so far, a promising method appears to be to enable people to experience high levels of income in order subsequently to increase and sustain their demand for higher incomes.

Now perhaps we can take up the question of whether there is anything in the quality of the people of Southeast Asia which inhibits rapid economic growth. We cannot spend too much time in this essay going into the matter, and I will do no more here than record the impression that the initiative and enterprise of these peoples has been very much underestimated in popular accounts.

This is of course most important in the field of the prevailing technology of production. In this field, we hear often the remark that if more efficient methods were employed for instance in agriculture, by way of using fertilizers, tractors, etc., productivity could be raised substantially and would enable real economic development to proceed. I think by now that sufficient evidence is available to conclude that these technically superior methods have not been employed for strong economic reasons. Thus, Wickizer and Bennet have recorded that fertilizers have not been utilized on a larger scale in rice cultivation simply because they are uneconomic at the prevailing price relationships.[11] In many areas of production, agricultural and otherwise, mechanization is still not profitable at prevailing wages and price rates. Thus, Hla Myint concludes after a study of Asian and African conditions that "peasant methods are found to have lower costs than the 'modern' scientific methods, and that is the reason why peasant production has been able to withstand the competition of the plantation system in some countries."[12]

To conclude this part of the discussion, it appears that important economic influences affect the two aspects of our problem, the capacity of a country to support its population at higher standards of living, and the factors which might reduce the rate of growth of population to a level at which economic development can be undertaken successfully to raise living standards.

With regard to the first aspect, the main problem facing the countries of Southeast Asia may be said to be the unfavorable prospect of their trading relations with other countries. With regard to the second, it would appear that the vital problem is that the important decisions regarding family size are still outside the sphere of economic calculation for the bulk of the people of this region, and that no lasting solution to the problem is possible which does not alter this situation.

Reviewing the economic policy of many of the countries with programs of economic development, we find a concentration on the purely economic aspects of development, while the theoretical literature on the subject appears to emphasize the demographic aspects. It is clear that the demographic aspects should not be overlooked in practice, and that planners of economic development should take more account of population problems than they do at present, if only to make a more intensive study of the present position and prospective trends. In particular, it seems to me that more can be done to study individual reactions to economic incentives on matters of family size and care.

It is necessary to give this word of advice, because movements in the size and structure of population are relatively slow, and therefore often do not catch the eye of the men of action, while if no action is taken, the problem can take on major proportions and become more

[11] *The Rice Economy of Monsoon Asia* (Stanford, Food Research Institute, 1941).

[12] *An Interpretation of Economic Backwardness*, Oxford Economic Papers, June 1954, p. 154.

difficult of solution. At the same time, I hope that this survey of population problems in economic development will have brought to light some aspects of the matter in which speedy action can also give speedy results.

The influence of racial minorities

VICTOR PURCELL

Cambridge University

Population figures for Southeast Asia are very approximate and it is only in Malaya that a fairly recent (1947) as well as comprehensive census has been taken (in Indonesia the last census was in 1930). Nevertheless it is possible to state the relation of minority to total populations in terms of estimates that are not likely to be very wide of the mark.

The total population of Southeast Asia is in the neighborhood of 165–170 million. Of this total, about 11 million are Chinese, the most numerous and important of the minorities. Their distribution is roughly as follows: 3½ million in Thailand in a total population of 18 million; 3 million in a total population of nearly 7 million in Malaya;[1] a quarter of a million in British Borneo out of a total of about a million; over 2 million in Indonesia in a total of over 80 million; in Indochina over 2 million in a total of about 27 million; in Burma, only a quarter of a million in a total of 20 million; in the Philippines they number between a quarter and a half a million in a total of over 20 million.

It will be seen that it is only in Malaya and Thailand that the proportion of Chinese to total population makes it possible to regard them as an immediate physical "threat," though in Indochina the

[1] The Chinese are the most numerous single community in Malaya if Singapore is included with the Federation—85 per cent of Singapore's total population of about 1,200,000 being Chinese. In the Federation, however, the Malays still outnumber the Chinese by a few hundred thousand although in several of the States and Settlements the Chinese are in a majority.

234

proximity of China itself is a factor which greatly influences the situation and makes the number of Chinese actually resident in the country of secondary importance.

The second most numerous and important minority distributed through the region is made up of the Indians. In mid-1954 there were about 1,246,000 Indians in Southeast Asia. In Burma, where they numbered 1,018,000 in 1931, they had increased up to World War II, but half a million of them had fled the country during the Japanese invasion and even now, owing to immigration restrictions, insecurity, and adverse economic conditions, the Indian community in Burma is still below its prewar numbers. In Malaya, the Indians had increased from 624,000 in 1931 to 744,000 in 1941 but had dropped to 600,000 in 1947 and have now probably recovered to about their prewar figure. The majority of Indians in Southeast Asia are Hindus from south India, but there are also Sikhs, Punjabis, and Muslims, and a few Parsees among them. About 80 per cent of the total are agriculturalists and the remainder merchants and moneylenders with a sprinkling of professional men.

Apart from the Chinese and Indians, there are numerous other minorities—the Arakanese, Karens, Shans, Chins, Kachins, etc., in Burma, the Malays in southern Thailand, the Ambonese, the Dutch Eurasians, Arabs, etc., in Indonesia, the Muslims or "Moros" in Mindanao, a number of aboriginal tribes throughout the region, and many others, several of them of political importance but not sufficiently so to justify separate treatment here.

On the face of it, the minority question in Southeast Asia would seem to be a matter of academic interest pure and simple to those not immediately involved, but in point of fact the subject is usually approached with a number of firmly held preconceptions.

For example, those nationals of the ex-colonial powers who are not yet reconciled to the idea of self-government for colonial peoples incline to feel that Western withdrawal from control of that part of the region that is now independent was premature, and are disposed to resist the extension of self-government to countries from which the withdrawal is incomplete. Such persons see the separatist tendencies of some of the minorities such as the Karens in Burma or the Ambonese in Indonesia as the inevitable consequence of the withdrawal of colonial power, and their sympathies invariably rest with the minorities in their reluctance to accept majority control (in the case of the Karens an additional sympathy is engendered among Europeans by the fact that many of them have been converted to Christianity). Adherents to this point of view are numerous among those who have taken part in the administration of the countries in question during the colonial period and among those with commercial or other interests in the region, and they are supported in their attitude by the consensus of conservative opinion at home.

This conservative sympathy for minorities, however, does not extend to the Chinese, for they are regarded as being potential spearheads of Communist expansion and a threat to the security of the major communities in which they live. This also is the approach of that section of Western opinion not in contact with the region but which is conscious primarily of the Communist threat arising from the alliance of the U.S.S.R. and China.

Since a majority of the British, Dutch, French, and Americans in contact with Southeast Asia incline to the above point of view, it is this which is given predominent expression in the press of western Europe and the United States. It is also the general view stated by the governments of the Philippines and Thailand which are in close association with the West. Opposed to it, however, is the attitude of the newly independent countries generally, and of Burma, India and Indonesia in particular, and of course, that of the Communist governments of China and North Viet-Nam. The contentions of the governments of Burma and Indonesia, in which they are supported in principle by Mr. Nehru, is that the separatism of the minorities is merely a legacy of the colonial policy of divide and rule. The fact that the revolts of the Karens and Ambonese respectively were supported by British and Dutch adventurers was a signal to the independent countries to raise the cry of imperialist intervention (despite the fact that neither the British nor the Dutch governments were involved and, indeed, it was the British ambassador at Rangoon who revealed the Karen plot to the Burmese cabinet). The feeling was widespread among Southeast Asian nationalists that the colonialists wished to revive colonial rule.

This nationalist suspicion was extended to the United States when the latter proposed to give military and economic aid to the region and is not yet dissipated. At the same time, the encouragement of

Communist and minority movements on the part of Communist China counteracted to some extent the sympathetic attraction which China exerted toward herself, and the creation of satellites within the Communist territories along the borders of Burma, Thailand, and Cambodia (autonomous "Free Kachin," "Free Laotian," and "Free Cambodian" states) was regarded as directed against the anti-Communist governments of Rangoon and Bangkok. Nevertheless the balance of attraction was toward the Communist bloc and away from the West, for the latter was regarded as the most immediate threat to Far Eastern nationalist aspirations.

The minority in Southeast Asia which, however, is vastly more significant than all the other minorities put together is the Chinese. This minority is regarded widely as an extension of China itself and as a potential fifth column in the event of a Chinese advance into the region. Many Westerners maintain that this advance has already started as an operation of the cold war. In support of the conception of an expansionist China the evidence usually adduced is (1) Chinese action in Tibet, (2) the creation of the "free" border states or movements, (3) Chinese support of the Viet-Minh insurgents in Indochina, and (4) the less certain Chinese support for the Communist risings in Indonesia, Burma and Malaya since 1948. This evidence, however, does not stand up to examination sufficiently to sustain the charge of expansionism which must therefore rely for its validity on direct evidence of fifth column activity among the Chinese minorities themselves.

In Thailand, Communism is undoubtedly widespread among the Chinese and, until they were closed down, the Chinese language newspapers generally expressed Communist sympathies. Nevertheless, there is a hard core of Chinese businessmen who are interested in the maintenance of the status quo and who, while careful not to offend Communist China, do much to neutralize the underground agitation of their "red" countrymen. At the same time the policy of the Thai government in making the Chinese community as a whole the scapegoat for the alleged expansionism of the People's Government of China coupled with the extortionate taxation imposed on the Chinese of Thailand (the head tax alone on Chinese was increased by over two thousand per cent in 1952) invites the common hostility of the Chinese toward the Thai government. Meanwhile the concentration of Viet-Nam refugees in northeast Thailand (most of them undoubtedly Viet-Minh adherents or sympathizers) gives encouragement to the Chinese Communists in the country while it increases the alarm of the Thai government.

In Malaya, the traditional British policy has been to treat the Malays as "the people of the country" (even when they are not true Malays but recent arrivals from Indonesia) to whom obligations are owed under the terms of the treaties with the sultans and to regard the Chinese and Indians as aliens even though their families have lived in Malaya for generations. Recent legislation, however, has created a large number of Chinese and Indian "Malayan citizens," while sidestepping equal citizenship and leaving the Malays in possession of an overwhelming majority vote when the first elections were held in July 1955. Although the actual number of Chinese in the Federation is nearly as great as the number of Malays, of 1,280,000 registered federal electors, 1,077,562 (84.2 per cent) were Malays, 142,947 (11.2 per cent) Chinese, and the remaining 4.6 per cent mainly Indians. (In Singapore, which as has been mentioned above is 85 per cent Chinese, the first elections under the new constitution were held in February 1955 but several non-Chinese [out of proportion to their numbers] were nevertheless elected.)

It has always been maintained by the British advocates of a "go slow" policy in Malaya that the advance toward self-government would intensify intercommunal hatreds while the complete withdrawal of the British would inevitably mean that the Malays and the Chinese would be at one another's throats. How well based these anticipations are remains to be seen, but the evidence at present available suggests that the communities, if left to themselves, would have a better chance at arriving at a *modus vivendi,* and indeed of evolving a common nationality, than they have had under post-1951 British policy which, until very recently, was palpably one of divide and rule. The existence of the United Malays National Organization-Malayan Chinese Association-Malayan Indian Congress (UMNO-MCA-MIC) alliance is a striking proof that the three communities are able to combine effectively for constructive purposes. If, however, the Malays were to regard the Chinese as a fifth column or as a spearhead for Chinese expansion such an entente would dissolve overnight and the Malays would seek new political alignments, probably with the Indonesians. But in spite of the efforts of sections of the press to split the UMNO-MCA-MIC alliance, it is likely to hold together indefinitely in view of the overwhelming success of the alliance at the July 1955 elections at which it obtained 51 out of the 52 seats to be filled by election.

There remain, nevertheless, the 5,000 odd Communist guerillas in Malaya who are ninety-five per cent or more Chinese and who have been in rebellion against the government since June 1948. The available evidence points to the fact that the "Emergency" (as the Communist insurrection is officially termed) is an indigenous movement relying on local manpower and on funds and supplies given by or extorted from the local populace and that no material aid has been received from China. Peking Radio, indeed, has given propagandist support to the movement but represents it as one of the "Malayan People" and not merely of the Malayan Communist Chinese. This is in accordance with the fiction maintained by the Malayan Communist party that Malays, Chinese and Indians are taking an equal part in the rebellion. The guerillas thus call themselves the "Malayan People's Liberation Army."

Although it is true that the Chinese Communist government exploits the overseas Chinese communities financially in much the same way that the Kuomintang government used to do, an important distinction in approach is imposed upon it by Communist theory. The KMT was openly irredentist while the Chinese People's government disclaims any intention of pushing the claim of the Chinese, as such, to any new territory. So far it has been successful in allaying the fears of Burma and Indonesia. In Burma, where the presence of large bands of fugitive KMT soldiers has offered an excuse for the invasion of Burmese territory, the Chinese government has shown great restraint and has abstained from punitive action inside the Burmese frontier; in Indonesia, the Chinese embassy has been careful not to make any overt intervention in local politics.

I come now to a matter which has been an abiding source of suspicion of Chinese intentions, namely the Chinese nationality law. This law adopts the *jus sanguinis* instead of the *jus soli*, thus claiming the descendants of Chinese through the male line as Chinese nationals for ever. The dual nationality created by the conflict between this law and local nationality laws has been a bone of contention between China and Southeast Asian countries, whether colonial or independent, for over forty years, but there has recently been evidence of the

intention of the Communist government of China to remove this source
of resentment.

On 22 April 1955, a treaty between China and Indonesia on the
question of the dual nationality of the two million overseas Chinese
in Indonesia was signed by Mr. Chou En-lai and the Indonesian Foreign
Minister, Mr. Sunario. It provides for a period of two years during
which one nationality must be chosen and the other rejected. Those
who have not made their choice at the expiry of the two-year period
are automatically to be given the nationality of the father. Persons
who opt for Chinese nationality are to be encouraged to respect the
laws of Indonesia and are not to take part in any political activity
there. (One clause in the treaty, though somewhat ambiguous, seems
to imply that any Chinese who changes his mind can return to China
and resume his Chinese nationality.)

This treaty promises to be a most important landmark in the history
of Sino-Southeast Asian relations and the way in which it works out
will be watched with great interest all over the region and not at least
in Malaya. Its signature certainly deprives those who maintain the
existence of an expansionist intention on the part of Communist China
of one of their main arguments.

A successful solution of the Chinese minority question in Southeast
Asia turns finally on whether China really has long-term designs on
the region or not. Western (especially United States) policy toward
the region has been based on the proposition that she *has;* the whole
object of Chinese propaganda has been to demonstrate that she has
not. SATO was conceived in terms of the former belief, while the
Afro-Asian Conference at Bandung in February 1955 was convened
in opposition to SATO and therefore within the supposition of a non-
expansionist China. Mr. Chou En-lai, who represented China at the
conference, scored a notable diplomatic success in giving an impression
of pacific intention on the part of China toward the Southeast Asian
region.

Those who argue a Chinese tendency to expansionism appeal to
history and recall the fact that at various times China has claimed
suzerainty over a much wider area than that she now occupies. History
also reveals, however, that there can be no real analogy between Chinese imperialism and the *Pax Romana* or even the *Pax Britannica.*
Although relationships between the central administration of China

and the border states were originally established by war, military administration tended swiftly to disappear and to be replaced by a local and indigenous administration maintaining the loosest possible connection with China proper. Whereas, in the Roman system, the tendency was to assert the authority of Rome, in that of China, it was to shake off as much as possible the responsibility for administering subject states. "Its essence," says E. B. Price, "was to permit other peoples to assert their own right of self-government."[2]

Apart from any anticipations derived from history, however, the present situation in China suggests that the Communist government has preoccupations within China proper which will occupy the whole of its attention for at least a generation. Any intervention in Southeast Asia would be bound to give rise to hostile reaction among the independent countries of the region whose own nationalism was largely stimulated by the growth of that of China. Of this fact the Chinese are perfectly aware and, so far, have intervened solely in border disputes and only when they had a colorable excuse for believing that their safety was threatened. Their complicity in starting Asian Communist and other insurrections in Southeast Asia remains unproven.

The pressures exerted on China and Southeast Asia by the exigencies of Western strategic policy and the containment of Communism are more likely to provoke than to restrain Chinese expansion, but even assuming that the West were to withdraw entirely from the region, certain basic difficulties impeding a *modus vivendi* between the overseas Chinese and the indigenous communities would remain. The superior economic position of the Chinese and their greater enterprise and industry are the greatest of these, but even in this field a compromise is by no means impossible.

Much has been made of the "economic stranglehold" of the Chinese on Southeast Asia. It is certainly true that in many branches of industry their interests preponderate and of the retail trade they have obtained something like a monopoly. But the expression "in the hands of the Chinese" suggests an equal distribution of wealth among the members of that community which is not in accordance with the facts. That this is so is sufficiently indicated by the income tax statistics for Malaya. In 1951, 10,037 Chinese in Malaya paid tax on incomes

[2] E. B. Price, *The Russo-Japanese Treaties of 1907–16*, Johns Hopkins Press, Baltimore, 1933, p. 2.

amounting to M$117,812,000 as compared with 9,624 Europeans who paid tax on M$136,071,000. Moreover the value of European investment in Malaya is double that of the Chinese. The truth is that the bulk of the Chinese are not very much better off than the Malays or the Indians so that there is not the economic gulf between Chinese and Malays that the aggregated figures would suggest. There is therefore no insurpassable obstacle to the majorities of the two communities, Chinese and Malays, forming a common front on the basis of their economic interests.

At the same time it cannot be denied that the superior enterprise and industry of the Chinese in general to the majority of the indigenous peoples is a source of friction. In postwar Burma, the decline in the numbers of Indians in the country has given the Chinese a new opening with the result that their economic importance has notably increased. In Viet-Nam, too, the withdrawal of many Vietnamese from the French-held areas has allowed the Chinese to move in and take their places.[3]

A bigger obstacle to a peaceful solution than the economic division between the Chinese and the indigenous peoples is the cultural problem. The alarm created among the Chinese of Malaya by the attempt of the government to establish "national schools" with English and Malay as the media of instruction at the expense of the Chinese vernacular schools has brought this issue strikingly to the forefront. It has been the declared aim of British policy to evolve loyalty toward Malaya while at the same time disclaiming any intention of destroying the cultures of the separate communities whether Malay, Indian or Chinese. English has acted as a solvent of cultural differences in the past, especially in India, and to a lesser extent with the Chinese of Malaya. Many Chinese settled in Malaya and educated in English

[3] "As early as May 1947 (as the writers can testify), many shops and other enterprises in Saigon which formerly had Vietnamese proprietors had already been taken over by the Chinese. As to the north, according to a French source, by mid-1948 'all the commerce of Tonkin had passed into Chinese hands.'" *Minority Problems of Southeast Asia*, by Virginia Thompson and Richard Adloff, Stanford University Press, 1955, p. 5.

The above study is recommended for an up-to-date account of the subject. The present writer's *The Chinese in Malaya*, 1948, and *The Chinese in Southeast Asia*, 1951, both published under IPR auspices by the Oxford University Press provide the basic material.

have become "Malayans"—but only at the price of losing their Chinese language and mode of thought. In the past few years, however, a unified and resurgent China has powerfully affected the Chinese in Malaya. "Where there is no direct patriotism stimulated," says the Singapore correspondent of the London *Times* on 23 March 1955, "there is culturalism instead, and the Chinese, smoked out of their self-sufficiency, leap to the defense of their language, their culture, and their interests as Chinese. Just how powerful this feeling is may be seen in the number of English-educated Chinese who are now furtively and hurriedly learning the language that was disappearing with more and more English-speaking."

The truth, I fear (and I say this after many years of experience of Chinese education in Malaya), is that the opportunity for the national school has now passed by (to have a hope of success it should have been introduced in the 'thirties) and the Malaya of the future is likely to remain multilingual. Malay, it seems will increasingly become the *lingua franca* of the country and the position of English as a common language must depend on the success achieved in teaching it effectively in the vernacular schools. The more aware among the members of all the communities still feel the need of English for the purposes of international intercourse and for higher education. In Indonesia, where the medium of instruction in schools is *Bahasa Indonesia* (a kind of Malay—first systematized by the Dutch), English has been adopted as the second language in place of Dutch.

From all the indications, it would seem that a cultural fusion between the communities of Southeast Asia is likely to be postponed to a very distant future. The communities in Malaya, for example, may well be able to achieve something approaching political and economic equality and to induce a common sense of Malayan nationality, but they are likely to continue to live in different cultural compartments for an indefinite time to come.

Touching the possibility of an eventual fusion of the races in the Southeast Asian countries, the factor of religion is also an important one. In Malaya and Indonesia the Muslim religion is a barrier preventing intermarriage between Malays and Chinese and it limits social intercourse by its taboos on pork and dogs. The Hindus are also segregated from other communities and stratified by the caste system (which, however, tends to be far less rigid in Southeast Asia than in

India). But in the Buddhist countries—Burma, Thailand, and Cambodia—as well as in sinicized Viet-Nam, no such barrier exists, and intermarriage was common until the Chinese immigrants began to bring their own womenfolk with them in large numbers in the present century and caused a barrier of another sort to rise. In these countries previous to this the Chinese immigrants were usually assimilated into the local Thai or Burmese communities within three generations.

Now that the control of the region is passing, or has passed, into the hands of the local inhabitants, the solution of the minority problems is one in which the Western countries can take very little effective share. They can, however, complicate the issue by their policies, and, maybe, with explosive results. For example, the maintenance of a chain of so-called "Communist containment" straddles the Far Eastern region which is now in a state of flux—a flux in which the minority problem is one current and the movement against Western control or interference another. Southeast Asia is in the process of finding a new synthesis and no Western policy can succeed which disregards this fact or oversimplifies the situation in terms of the "free" and "unfree" dualism of current propaganda.

The only promise of a happy solution of the Chinese minority question is that the local governments will offer the minorities sufficient inducement in the form of equality of citizenship, security of land tenure, and in otherwise giving their members a stake in the country to persuade them to merge into the general population, and that simultaneously the Chinese government will remove all grounds for suspicion that it intends to utilize the Chinese minorities as fifth columns in aid of a new Chinese imperialism.

Most of this essay has been devoted to the Chinese in Southeast Asia, and justifiably so in view of the preponderating importance of this community both politically and economically, but something should be said in conclusion of the Indian minority.

In the field of external politics the leadership of India, especially that of Mr. Nehru, is almost invariably followed by Indonesia and Burma, as also its lead in domestic policies, but this is no indication of the standing of the Indian minorities in Southeast Asia. The Indians in the region, in fact, are not feared as much as are the Chinese, but on the other hand they are not as greatly respected on account of their economic power.

India is associated in the mind of the ordinary inhabitant of Southeast Asia with the *chettiar*, or moneylender, who first entered the country in the wake of British or French imperialism and who remits to India the wealth he has obtained from the local community. Nor did the short Indian collaboration with the Japanese during the war in the shape of Azad Hind endear the Indians generally to the local peoples. In Burma, at the end of the war, three million acres of rice land were owned by Indian moneylenders as were most of the buildings in Rangoon. In its postwar measures of land reform, Burma passed a series of laws directed against the *chettiar*, in particular the Land Nationalization Act of 1948 which prohibited noncultivators from owning land and fixed the amount of compensation to be paid to dispossessed landlords at twelve times the current land tax.

In Malaya, Indians have taken a part in local politics and trade unionism out of proportion to their numbers, a fact which is no doubt due to experience gained in their own country under the British, but they are nevertheless disposed to feel the inferiority of their position. The Indian paper, *Tamil Murasu*, of Singapore (14 January, 1953) expressed this feeling in succinct language thus:

> Whatever the political position of the Chinese may be, their influence in the economic field closely rivals that of the British who rule the country. In contrast with the Chinese, the Indians of Malaya are considered to be of no consequence in any field. Although the Indians consider themselves experienced in politics and capable of leading other communities, there is not a single Indian in the Federal Cabinet. In the economic field the Indians are looked down upon as coolies, and Indian chettiars are criticized, although they lend money at a fair and legal rate of interest. Local English newspapers are ever ready to put the Indians in their place. If the Indians go to India, they are "dodgers" [of National Service]; if they immigrate they are accused of being an economic burden to the country. Such is the predicament of the Indians of Malaya who by the sweat of their brow have made the country prosperous.

Political equilibrium in Southeast Asia is unlikely to arise through the influence of the Chinese being counterbalanced by that of the Indians, and it seems that it can only be achieved through a *modus vivendi* between the indigenous peoples and the local Chinese endorsed by the government of China.

commentary

FERDINAND KUHN

Journalist

Any layman must be either brash or diffident in commenting on an essay by Victor Purcell about minorities in Southeast Asia. Mr. Purcell is, of course, an acknowledged authority; he has spent more than a quarter of a century in the area, chiefly in Malaya, and his book on the Chinese in Southeast Asia is a searchlight that has helped many visitors to pierce the murkiness of Southeast Asian problems. My comment then will be that of a reporter, not an expert—and a diffident reporter at that.

Naturally Mr. Purcell's essay puts most of its emphasis on the Chinese in Southeast Asia. But I wish he had been able to deal more fully with another minority which numbers about a million and a quarter: namely, the Indians who grow rich or struggle for a living in Burma, Malaya and Indonesia, and in smaller numbers in other countries of the region. It is not as big or as prominent in Southeast Asian affairs as the Chinese minority, but it is important all the same. Mr. Purcell has given us a hint of this in his last sentence:

> Political equilibrium in Southeast Asia is unlikely to arise through the influence of the Chinese being counterbalanced by that of the Indians . . . .

Many Americans, and British, have hoped that Nehru's India might become such a counterweight—a leader, if not a protector and defender, of the little nations across the Bay of Bengal. But such hopes, I think, are unrealistic. One reason is the existence of the Indian minority and the attitude of Southeast Asians toward it. My comments will attempt to show why these Indians, usually overlooked or underrated in American discussions of the problem, are actually a negative political influence of importance to the future of Southeast Asia.

On my first visit to Rangoon an American friend took me to the window of his office and told me to look carefully at the crowds passing outside. "You will see," he said, "that this looks like an

246

Indian city." And so it did. At first sight this was not Rangoon but
Calcutta. These swarms of men in dhotis and turbans were cooking
their food or selling their wares on the sidewalks, throwing their refuse
into the streets, squatting or sleeping outside shabby peeling buildings
that had the look, not of Burma but of India.

I find it hard to credit the 1953 census figures which showed only
54,000 Indians among the 700,000 people of Rangoon. If the figures
are correct, then this minority of perhaps 7½ per cent is surely the
most conspicuous, for its size, in all of Asia. Its members bring their
caste system, their customs, their untidiness and poverty with them.
The dynamics of Nehru's India seem not to have touched them. The
free institutions of present-day Burma are of no account to them except
as Burma gives them a chance to earn a living.

In Rangoon the Indians, generally, are coolies, dock workers, clerks,
shopkeepers and unemployed. In north Burma, in places such as
Lashio on the Burma Road and Bhamo on the Irrawaddy, the Indian
shopkeeper is a competitor of the ever-present Chinese. His standard
of living, like that of the Chinese, is far above that of the Burmese
around him, and his business acuteness is equally far ahead of that
of his happy-go-lucky Burmese neighbors.

These Indian emigrants, by and large, create an unpleasant image
of India in Burmese minds. They do not assimilate easily or gracefully
into the political or social life of the country. Of course there are
exceptions. The Indian doctors whom Burma has recruited, at relatively high pay, are a credit to both countries. The present Minister
of Commerce, M. A. Raschid, or U Raschid as he likes to be called,
is a naturalized Burmese born in India, the brother of the present
Indian High Commissioner in Canada. He, too, is an honor to the
countries of his birth and adoption; yet even this brilliant and resource-
ful official was the target of public complaints in Burma as recently
as last winter. Why, it was asked, should Burma tolerate an Indian
in its cabinet? Prime Minister Nu himself had to quiet the clamor
by a public statement that U Raschid's Indian birth would not be
allowed to stop him from serving his adopted country.

The Indian minority in Burma, generally speaking, is far from being
a kind of peaceful fifth column of Indian influence. It is an active
impediment to India in her intermittent efforts to become the political
mentor of Burma and other countries to the East. Again and again

U Nu has shown his independence of Mr. Nehru, although in a general way he has followed Mr. Nehru's policies of nonalignment. Even if U Nu were not such a brave independent in Asian politics, political necessities would force him to stand up to Nehru, as he did in recent conferences, and to take an individualistic stand in world affairs. The Burmese do not want to see their government knuckle under to their giant Indian neighbor. One reason, I am convinced, is that they do not like or trust or respect the Indians living among them.

In countries where Indians are less numerous, such as Thailand, Cambodia and Viet-Nam, the Indian moneylender and shopkeeper produce the same kind of emotional response. In Thailand, of course, the present government has shown not the slightest willingness to follow Indian leadership in Asian affairs. Among the Thais, the counterweight to Communist China is not India but the West, and chiefly the United States. Even if the present Thai government should be overthrown, and if Thailand should, improbably, move into a more neutralist position, I doubt whether Mr. Nehru's India or any other would be accepted in Thailand as the leader of non-Communist Asia.

In Cambodia, India is beginning to assert a protective role toward a small, young, predominantly Buddhist nation. When Mr. Nehru was in Cambodia last winter, he quickly saw that the country was Indian in its cultural heritage instead of being, as some Indians supposed, a mere appendage of Viet-Nam and its Chinese culture. Yet the Cambodians, who want India to take a greater interest in their somewhat fragile independence, nevertheless keep their distance in their dealings with Mr. Nehru. I do not doubt that the Indians in Cambodia are responsible for some of this reserve. The Indian army officers on the Indochinese armistice teams appear arrogant and overbearing to the gentler Cambodians. The Indian moneylenders and shopkeepers have the same greedy, grasping reputation as in other parts of non-Indian Asia.

With this poor advertisement, this built-in handicap, what chance has Nehru's India of becoming the dominant influence in Southeast Asia? Suppose Mr. Nehru meets failure in his present efforts to win the confidence of the Chinese; suppose Mao Tse-tung and his colleagues should drive Mr. Nehru into more active opposition to them; suppose that Mr. Nehru, or his successor, should then try to pull the little Southeast Asians into a closer relationship with enormous India.

Would Burma, Thailand, Cambodia, Laos—the Buddhist countries of Southeast Asia—then turn to India for help and leadership? My belief is that they will not want Indian dominance any more than they want Chinese or American. What they have seen of the Indian minority is so disagreeable that they will think twice before becoming clients, suppliants, or satellites of New Delhi.

If the Indian minorities are thus an obstacle to Indian political ambitions, the Chinese in many parts of Southeast Asia are likewise a handicap rather than an asset to Peking. For the Chinese, too, are envied and disliked from Burma to the Philippines. The discriminations against them in much of Southeast Asia are evidence of their superior commercial skill and of their unpopularity as well. I cannot believe that the independent peoples of Southeast Asia will ever encourage political or propagandist infiltration by Communist China, or that they would embrace a Chinese army if Chinese expansionism should take the form of armed aggression. The Japanese in the last war were hailed as liberators in Southeast Asia, partly because the people of the area did not know the Japanese. The Chinese, in contrast, are already well known through their millions of settlers. The knowledge buttresses the determination of Southeast Asians to stay free.

Mr. Purcell tells us that Communism is "undoubtedly widespread" among the Chinese in Thailand. He may be right, but I found no evidence to support him. According to the best estimate I could get in Bangkok, there are 3,000 active Communists among the 3,500,000 Chinese in Thailand, plus about 30,000 sympathizers. On the other hand, there are about 10,000 active supporters of Nationalist China and perhaps 100,000 sympathizers. The rest of the 3,500,000, the vast majority, are not just politically neutral but neuter. For their own good, they know they must be careful. The latent hostility of the rest of the population toward the Chinese is, I think, underestimated in the United States. It will operate as a force for resistance to any pressure from Peking, whether political, psychological or economic.

My mention of Chinese pressures leads me to a statement of Mr. Purcell about Western pressures. He has told us that "the pressures exerted on China and Southeast Asia by the exigencies of Western strategic policy and the containment of Communism are more likely to provoke than restrain Chinese expansion." Then he said it would be difficult to work out a *modus vivendi* between the overseas Chinese and the indigenous communities "even assuming that the West were to withdraw entirely from the region." The first of the statement is a sweeping indictment and the second a sweeping assumption. Mr. Chou En-lai has talked in the same way about alleged Western provocations; and U Nu, whom I deeply respect, told me in Rangoon that if he were Mr. Dulles he would withdraw all American forces from Asia and promote "cordial" relations with China.

But unlike U Nu, who feels he has to talk in this vein to Western visitors, Mr. Purcell is not the leader of a weak country with a 1200-mile frontier with Chinese territory. Does he seriously suggest that Western policies have done more to provoke than to restrain China? If so, does he mean that our British friends should quit Hong Kong and Malaya, that we and our allies should withdraw from Korea, that we hand back Okinawa to the Japanese and pull the Seventh Fleet back to the Hawaiian Islands? If this is Mr. Purcell's prescription, I think it should not go unchallenged.

And since we are talking today about the overseas Chinese, I would also question the implied suggestion that we withdraw our support for a non-Communist Formosa. I discovered in Southeast Asia that support for Formosa, and interest in Formosa, among the overseas Chinese was not just a figment of the China lobby's imagination. A withdrawal of support from Formosa would have a serious effect upon the fortunes of the overseas Chinese. When I asked the young King of Cambodia—now Prince Norodom—about the Chinese in his country, he said they were not a problem now. But, to my surprise, he said: "If you Americans want to help Cambodia, please go on supporting Chiang Kai-shek. By supporting the Nationalists you will help to keep our Chinese quiet." I felt that the King had not the slightest interest in Chiang, but rather that he was talking as a shrewd politician who knew his own people, including the Chinese minority.

One last observation concerns the future of the minorities in Southeast Asia, especially the Chinese. Fifty years from now (unless we have an atomic war) the 12,000,000 overseas Chinese will be a much larger number than now, because of their high birth rate as well as immigration. Unless the Peking government forcibly prevents emigration, as Russia has done under the Soviet regime, the Chinese population bowl will, in Mr. Purcell's own words, continue to spill southward, as it has done since prehistoric times. After all, the present-day Burmans are said to be descendants of immigrants from the cold Tibetan plateau. The Thais are descendants of Chinese who were driven south, by military and economic pressures, from south China. Today one can encounter little colonies of Nepalis from the high Himalayas living as far south and east as the Shan states of Burma. The movement of what we call Mongolian or Mongoloid peoples southward is inexorable and never-ending. To this day it is continuing in northern Burma even though the Chinese and Burmese governments have forbidden it.

Does this mean, then, that the Chinese will take over Southeast Asia, as Professor Toynbee, for one, seems to believe? Will we see, in time, a re-creation of the Ming Empire in Southeast Asia, and by methods no more violent than procreation and immigration? I would not be so fatalistic, nor would I agree with Mr. Purcell that a cultural fusion of the overseas Chinese with the Southeast Asians may be postponed until "a very distant future." It is true that nationalism is accentuating the separateness of the overseas Chinese and other minorities in the new nations of Southeast Asia, and is showing its uglier side in many forms of political, social and economic discrimination. But another force, almost as powerful as nationalism, is beginning to work in the opposite direction. Free institutions, now emerging in Southeast Asia, are a solvent of ethnic, social and religious differences. The record of our own immigration from Ireland, Italy and Russia shows that huge minority groups, once thought to be unassimilable, can become a part of American society and contribute immeasurably to it. We are not alone in this experience; the Australians with their Italian and Dutch newcomers, the Canadians with their Poles and others, have proved the same truth.

You may say that these immigrants in the West were of the same or similar racial stock, and that what worked well in America will not work in older, more rigid, Asia. Yet the Chinese in much of Southeast Asia are of similar racial stock to the people around them. Remember, free institutions are new in these ancient societies. The Chinese and Indian immigrants and settlers have never, until now, been exposed to the melting process of free schools and common citizenship. Is it not possible that the revolution in Asia, which is gradually dissolving caste barriers and religious hatreds, will also bring the minorities more closely together with the Southeast Asians among whom they live?

Free Asia in world affairs:
the use and misuse of history

PAUL H. CLYDE

Duke University

In one notable respect the topic of this essay, *Free Asia in World Affairs*, presents no problem, for the topic is so unfettered by boundaries that no matter what one may choose to say, his remarks are certain to have at least a remote relevancy to the subject. Heartened by this happy but disarming thought, I plunged blithely into the business of composing these remarks.

Reminded that as an historian I must approach this subject through the medium of history, I re-examined the *Proceedings* of the conference on Southeast Asia held in Washington by the School of Advanced International Studies just three years ago. It was a stimulating experience suggesting how rapidly and how substantially our knowledge of Asia has grown and matured. Even so recently as twenty years ago, much of the historical substance in the record of that conference could not have been written by the American scholars who contributed to it, and I have some doubts as to the contributions that could have been made by our Asian friends.

Today the resources of the free world, both East and West, in weapons of scholarship are even greater than in 1952. This growth in scholarly horizons may well prove to be the greatest of all free world assets in the years that lie ahead. The improvement in our American scholarly horizons is the more striking when one recalls that only half a century ago there was an American President who symbolized our poverty of insight by his uncertainty as to where the Philippine Islands might be.

The Youth of Asia's Free World

Fifty years ago there was a free world in the West, but there was no free world in Asia save for Japan and the buffer state of Thailand sandwiched between the Asian empires of Britain and France. In reality, free Asia was born only yesterday. As yet it has not lived through a single generation. Greater China became a full-ranking member of this free world all too briefly in 1943; the Philippines and the Associated States of Viet-Nam, Cambodia, and Laos in 1946; India, Pakistan, and Ceylon in 1947; the Union of Burma and the Republic of Korea in 1948; Indonesia and the Republic of China on Formosa in 1949; and the new Japan in 1951. This chronology acquires more precise significance when interpreted to mean that the peoples of monsoon Asia have taken their first steps in what the Chinese proverb might call a journey of ten thousand miles, have taken these steps together, and within less than a decade. If the turbulence of this past decade has not deprived us of all sense of historical perspective we should find satisfaction in the basic historical reality that a free Asia has been born and that some of it is still alive.

The Complexion of Free Asia's Birth

While in the West the phenomenon of physiological birth is accepted as commonplace, we have in practice wrapped it in all the elaborate precautions which medical science can provide. The nature of physical birth has been studied, its enemies and its friends have been identified, conditions of ideal growth have been defined and, in a word, while the future of the newborn is not foretold, it is anticipated. Its future is more certain because the historical resources of science have been utilized to that end. It would seem, however, that in the birth and growth of nations there has not been a corresponding use of history to the common purpose of creating a livable world. In a national world there has been great adeptness in the use of what is sometimes called history for destructive and chaotic purposes. This adeptness in the misuse of history may go far to explain the present state of affairs between free Asia and the world in which it finds itself, and it is to this misuse of history that I wish to address these remarks, first with some passing notes on man's inseparable relationship with history, and secondly with a few examples of how we have used history.

The Nature of History

The business of anticipating the future is one of the principal functions of history. History in essence is the memory of things said and done. It is a common ground for all of us in the sense that every normal person knows some history, good, bad, or indifferent as it may be, and all of us in the simplest decisions of the day use constantly such history as we have. There are of course two histories: first, the actual series of thoughts and events that once occurred; and second, the series that each individual affirms and holds in memory. This latter form is usually what is called the history of the specious present. There is some correspondence between the two histories and it is the business of the historian, at least in a free society, to make the correspondence as exact as possible. A complete coincidence of the two histories is never achieved in any absolute sense. A relative coincidence is always possible in any free society. Indeed the degree of coincidence is measured by man's capacity to write and to understand history and thereby to minimize his dependence on the history of the specious present or, as it is commonly called, traditional or crisis history.

By whatever name it is known, the history of the specious present is always with us. It is a product of tradition, of wishful thinking, of folklore, of the imagination, and of the emotions. It may by chance encompass some of the proven facts of evidence, but its real force and power come from what we wish to believe out of the past. Its true bases are fanciful. It is the history on which most of us act most of the time whether we be concerned with casting our ballots or with settling the problems of Asia.[1]

The Historical Foundation

The contemporary problem of a free Asia in world affairs has arisen in the immediate sense from the universal upheaval of World War II, from the concurrent collapse of colonial empires in Asia, from the destruction of the prewar balance of power, and from the resulting concentrations of power in the Soviet Union and the United States. In this immediate and pragmatic sense the problems belong to political science, to economics, and to military strategy and tactics. Their solu-

[1] For a modern and profound interpretation of history, see Carl Becker, "Everyman His Own Historian," *American Historical Review*, XXXVII (1932), 221–36.

tions must be devised by the experts in these fields of knowledge. The
difficulty that lies in this simplification is that free Asia is not primarily a creation of yesterday but rather of the past century. Its birth
may be dated within the past decade, but in reality this nativity has
been in process for a hundred years. One could perhaps date the
inception of pregnancy in 1842 when the traditional system of foreign
relations between China, on the one hand, and the outer barbarians,
on the other, was brought to an end and replaced by a Western system
of international relations. The movement, later to be known as the
impact of the West on Asia, had won its first great victory. It had
imposed on the Confucian world new rules of human conduct and
new institutions through which these rules would be carried out. From
1842 to the present moment the pressure of an ever-new, creative,
expanding Western society has been relentless upon Asia as well as
upon the West. Nevertheless, the impact of this modern world on Asia
and on the West has not been the same. The free world of the West
was a creation which Western man conceived and built for himself
through the entire span of modern history. His adjustment to the new
life was the easier not only because he was remodeling a house to which
he was already accustomed, but also because his new world was an
intellectual reality before it was a material fact. In Asia, modern state-
hood and society are not native; they were not conceived in the mind
of Asia. On the contrary they were alien concepts and institutions
intruding upon traditional cultures, and operating often in fact before
they were or could be understood in theory.

What Did the Western Impact Do?

What did the Western impact do to Asia and to the West from which
that impact came? The free world during the past quarter century has
given a few but by no means satisfying answers to this question. It
has been said that rich but moribund civilizations collapsed and were
replaced by philosophies of nationalism; that the family gave place
to the individual; that cultural bondage retreated before aspirations
to freedom; and finally that what was Eastern strove to become what
was Western. There is undoubtedly much truth in all these stock
answers. The arresting thing for the historian is that until twenty-five
years ago, this question was rarely asked at all in the world beyond

Asia. Moreover, when the question was asked there was the tendency to accept ready-made Western answers. Scant attention was given to the confused and at times incoherent voice of Asia; to the thesis that Asia was in revolution and had been so for a long time; to the hypothesis that in Asia revolution would not mean one but a host of revolutions; that behind these revolutions would be complex states of mind, perhaps misguided, befuddled by deceptions from the inside and the outside, but, most important, states of mind that were "the reflections of wholly real and even profound indigenous conditions." There was for us the easy answer which assumed that Asia's first interest was with Communism considered as a question of military conspiracy and aggression. With the very real possibilities of military aggression there has never been any question, and there is evidence that steps to meet it have been taken by the West if not always by free Asia. These military preparations, however, do not dispose of the question whether our knowledge of historical forces prepared us to deal not only with military aggression in Asia but also with the emotional, irrational forces of Asia's indigenous, revolutionary states of mind.[2]

The mobilization of the West in matters historical and intellectual to meet the complex of the new Asia, free and unfree, has not equalled the military attack on the problem. As a result the status of free Asia in world affairs is not what we have wished it to be. A basic explanation lies in our manner of using history. For example, a free world under American leadership was intellectually unprepared for a free Asia bent on finding its place in world affairs through neutralism. The first reaction to Asian neutralism was that free Asia, above all else, must be taught how to combat Communism. It was then equally shocking to discover that free Asia was not always an attentive pupil. The historian must therefore raise the question whether the reason for this unhappy clash of purposes may not lie in our dependence on the history of the specious present, in our faith in crisis history. We are now getting a little closer to the minds of free Asia. Indeed, some attention has lately been paid to the idea that free Asia expects from the free West

> positive and imaginative suggestions as to how the peaceful future of the world might be shaped and how our own vast economic

[2] George F. Kennan, *Realities of American Foreign Policy* (Princeton: Princeton University Press, 1954), 96.

strength might be so adjusted to the lives of other peoples as to permit a fruitful and mutually profitable interchange, without leading to relationships of political dependence and coercion. But it is not only the more conspicuous of the in-between countries who are looking to us for this; it is all the non-communist countries, in fact, and even all the subject peoples within the communist orbit, who know that their chances of liberation will be best if we Americans are able to develop positive and constructive purposes that serve to place the negative, destructive purposes of communism in the shadows where they belong.[3]

The Role of History

One would be naive to suggest that a correct reading of history during the past fifty or one hundred years would have dissolved all our troubles. History does not predict the future. Yet it is not at all unreasonable to suppose that if our historical insights had been somewhat deeper, our grooming for what was to happen in Asia could have involved less wasted motion and far less intellectual numbness and emotional violence. The proposition that free men could have anticipated the future far more than was done is in no sense fantastic. The unbridged chasm between the history we might have understood as against the history of the specious present in which we so largely indulged ourselves may be illustrated by impressive examples. Only a few can be mentioned in this essay. They will be limited to an area involving the historical relationship between Asia on the one hand and the United States representing the outside world on the other.

The Meaning of the Topic

The topic "Free Asia in World Affairs" considered as an historical problem is simply a convenient phrasing of what might be restated as the response of Asia to the Western impact and the concurrent response of the West to what it found in Asia. The past century during which this Western invasion of Asia developed its momentum and its power has carried all Asia along with the rest of us into what may be called man's first universal revolution. Although it is an oversimplification to say that our recognition of this revolution can be dated within the past ten years, in the brief span since World War II, there is, nevertheless, in this simplification an uncomfortable degree of truth.

---

[3] Kennan, *Realities of American Foreign Policy*, 101.

This revolution has been seen most frequently through the eyes of crisis history, and this crisis history has failed the free world of the West in notable ways. It did not tell us what Asia was thinking about itself or about us. It did not lead us to ask whether the resources— material, intellectual, and spiritual—which we carried to Asia would be welcomed, accepted, and used as we thought they should be used. I am reminded that three years ago Rupert Emerson told us that "in the mid-thirties it would have occurred to virtually no one that we had responsibilities in Southeast Asia."[4]

The Example from Japan

The case of Japan provides some useful examples. Our historical manner of looking at Japan bears directly on the matter of crisis history. The Western world has been in intimate relations with Japan for a full century. Japan was the first great Asian state to affirm the goal of modernization in response to the Western impact. During this century of contact the West has produced an impressive and a varied historical literature on the meeting of East and West in Japan. It is, in many respects, a basic literature, but it has its limitations both in its substance and in what we learned from it. Its substantial contributions are many; but the notable thing is that our historical interpretations of Japan, especially in the United States, have been marked by a naive pattern of simplicity almost devoid of finer shadings. There have been two such patterns in our historical interpretation of Japan which, although they have not been exclusive, have tended to dominate American thought. In the first pattern, which prevailed for fifty years after Perry brought home his epochal treaty, Japan was the embodiment of virtue. She was everything that a Theodore Roosevelt could admire. She was young, energetic, progressive. She was determined to be Western, and she even told the truth, so Roosevelt said. She was our student, and we liked her because she seemed to learn so well what we taught her. This was the first pattern. It might be called the kimono and cherry blossom interpretation.

Then something happened. By progressive and rapid degrees after 1905, good Japan became bad Japan. She was still young and ener-

[4] Rupert Emerson, "Our Responsibilities in Southeast Asia," in *Southeast Asia in the Coming World,* edited by Philip W. Thayer (Baltimore: The Johns Hopkins Press, 1953), 62.

getic but she was no longer virtuous. She became first a juvenile delinquent and then a full-grown master criminal. White had become black in the history of the specious present, yet there was very little disposition to question the validity of these definitive and contrasting interpretations.[5] Moreover, the Japanese themselves, in time, outdid us in their adeptness with crisis history, and one may add, if events since 1931 have any meaning, that their capacity to anticipate the future was even less impressive than our own. The historian finds himself confronted with what looks like a very immature performance, namely, that from the beginning of our formal relations with Japan, we and they believed what each wanted to believe. For instance, Americans clung to the idea that Perry was the cause, not the occasion, for the opening of Japan. This idea was rather necessary to the cherry blossom interpretation. It enabled us to mark Japan's progress with the simple stamp of Westernization by which, in the main, we meant Americanization. The distinction between a Japan or an Asia western-ized as against an Asia moving into an era of its own distinct moderni-zation was not prominent in our historical thought. Indeed, it may be said that it was not until 1940 that E. Herbert Norman gave us the basic motivations behind Japan's emergence as a modern state and thereby enabled us to override some of our crisis history.[6] As late as 1946, Ruth Benedict in the first sentence of *The Chrysanthemum and the Sword* reminded us that in 1941 "the Japanese were the most *alien* enemy the United States had ever fought . . . ."[7] Moreover, her entire study, executed in the midst of war fever, again reminds us that we had not anticipated the future. A war which was on the way for nearly half a century was almost won before we had raised the ques-tion: how will our enemy act in defeat? Or again, it was not until 1950 that our insights into the nature of free Asia began to discover that accepted facts of Westernization in Asia were not as valid as

[5] See Arthur H. Dean, "Japan at the Crossroads," *Atlantic Monthly*, 194 (No-vember 1954), 30–35. "We conscientiously and rightfully opposed her desires and attempts to expand her empire by armed conquest. But we did not search for an alternative which would alleviate the problem of a growing population con-fined within a national territory possessed of relatively few economic blessings."

[6] E. Herbert Norman, *Japan's Emergence as a Modern State* (New York: Inter-national Secretariat, Institute of Pacific Relations, 1940).

[7] Ruth Benedict, *The Chrysanthemum and the Sword* (Boston: Houghton Mif-flin Company, 1946), 1. The italics are mine.

we had supposed them to be; indeed, that the things which we had
thought to be facts might not be facts at all. Again a basic illustration
comes from Japan. We had taken the first evidence at hand and from
it we had drawn the conclusion that the German model shaped the
Meiji constitution. The idea still has currency. Yet we now have the
challenging Sansom thesis, full of meaning for the whole theory of
modernization in Asia, that Japan even without German experience
to draw upon would have produced a political system almost precisely
like the one adopted.[8]

Some Chinese Cases

The bearing of crisis history upon the present relationship between
free Asia and our own world is perhaps even more arresting in the
case of China. It is proper here to acknowledge our debt to the small
but tireless band of scholars who sought to give us an historical understanding of both Japan and China. Yet the hard fact would seem to
be that our general ignorance of what China is like, and of what has
been going on in the mind of China during the past century did not
condition us to anticipate what happened in 1949, or permit our
influence to have its maximum effect. To practically all of us in this
country news of the Communist conquest was simply unbelievable.[9]
Neither our history nor the meanings we had seen fit to draw from it
equipped us for meeting the China or the Asia that emerged from
World War II. We were thereby dependent again on crisis history.
As a result there has been of late a commonly accepted assumption that
what happened in China in 1949 can be explained almost exclusively
by what had taken place since 1941, or, to put the matter in other
words, that our failure to anticipate the future is a malady to which
we have only recently been subject. Now it may well be that we have
been infected by some recent and newly discovered virus with which
our forefathers did not have to contend, but the evidence also suggests

[8] G. B. Sansom, *The Western World and Japan* (New York: Alfred A. Knopf,
1950), 358–63; Nobutaka Ike, *The Beginnings of Political Democracy in Japan*
(Baltimore: The Johns Hopkins Press, 1950), 171–80; and "Democracy *vs.* Ab-
solutism in Meiji Japan," a paper read before the American Historical Association, Chicago, 1950.

[9] See H. Arthur Steiner, "The United States and China: the Prospect before
Us," *The Yale Review*, XLIV (December 1954), 161–79.

that our recent and present troubles in Asia arise not only from events of yesterday but also from old and deep-seated conditions of mind that reach far back into the nineteenth century, and which we have not yet overcome.

One who attempts to see in historical perspective in the nineteenth century the mutual response between China and the United States on the Western impact is apt to be impressed by the conviction which prevailed at that time in this country to the effect that the Chinese admired us, were well-disposed toward us, and desired our help to the end that they might become like us. After the fall of the old Confucian bureaucracy in 1912, this pleasant conviction took on even greater vigor because most of the Chinese who came to us from republican China said it was so. When, therefore, the Chinese Communists turned the full blast of their fury against America with notable success, we were aghast. How should we understand and reconcile this reversal in Chinese thought and action by which a century of intimate friendship appeared to become overnight a nightmare of vituperation with America on the receiving end?

It would be fantastic to suggest that there was nothing real in "the long-standing sentimental, religious, and intellectual connections between the United States and China."[10] These connections have been important realities. The point is we were content to accept them as the entire reality.

This type of historical interpretation resting on what we have conceived to be absolute realities is not new with us. When in 1868 Anson Burlingame told us that China, the oldest civilization, was determined to learn from America, the youngest of civilizations, we believed him. When in the same year his successor at Peking, J. Ross Browne, told us this was not so, we not only refused to believe, we told Mr. Browne to stop talking and to come home. What had happened was that Browne had given us some ideas on free Asia in world affairs that we were not willing to face. Browne's words written eighty-seven years ago bear repeating.

An impression seems to have obtained in the United States that the Government of China is peculiarly friendly to our country, and that great advantages to our commerce are about to accrue from this

[10] Paul M. A. Linebarger, Djang Chu, Ardath W. Burks, *Far Eastern Governments and Politics* (New York: D. Van Nostrand, 1954), 239.

preference . . . I need scarcely say these anticipations are without foundation. The Government of China may have preferences; but it has no special regard for any foreign power. The dominant feeling is antipathy and distrust towards all who have come in to disturb the administration of its domestic affairs.[11]

J. Ross Browne, a minor and all but forgotten figure, may yet claim his place in history. He perceived, perhaps dimly, what we for so long failed to perceive at all, that the new Asia was developing minds of its own which we might influence but which we were not likely to control. We are now quite familiar with some of the results deriving from this lack of perception into the mind of either old or young Asia. Yet the fascinations of crisis history still have their appeal. How many times in the twentieth century have we been willing to accept as unchallengeable axioms: that the Chinese have a distinct preference for our political and economic system; that the Chinese "who reject the Western concept of a personal God" are nevertheless moved "by our moralistic strictures against 'atheistic' Communism?"[12] To how many Americans has the idea ever occurred that the Chinese might be willing to have democracy "if they do not have to have freedom as the price of it?"[13] Happily there is evidence today of an attempt to avoid the pitfalls of the historical specious present; evidence of a disposition to see that our capacity to understand and to influence China might well have been far greater had our minds been open to the complex intellectual response of China, old and new, to the Western impact; evidence that there is still time to do something about it.[14]

Since 1949 even the most thoughtful Americans stand baffled by the spectacle that faces them in China. Those who seek explanations from history have been asking whether the mind of the American

---

[11] U. S. Dept. of State, Archive section, *China Despatches*, XXV, No. 7, Browne to the Sec. of State, Peking, November 25, 1868, quoted in Paul H. Clyde, ed., *United States Policy toward China* (Durham: Duke University Press, 1940), 93.

[12] Steiner, "The United States and China," 168–69.

[13] Linebarger, Chu, and Burks, *Far Eastern Governments and Politics*, 235.

[14] The pioneer sources in this field for the nineteenth century are: Earl Swisher, *China's Management of the American Barbarians: A Study in Sino-American Relations 1841–1861, with Documents* (New Haven: Far Eastern Publications, Yale University, 1953); and Ssu-yü Teng and John K. Fairbank, *China's Response to the West: A Documentary Survey 1839–1923* (Cambridge: Harvard University Press, 1954).

people or the official mind of its government was ever historically sensitive and responsive to the mind and aspirations of this convulsive China of the twentieth century. Certainly American traditional policy, as seen by Americans, was generous; a policy of giving rather than taking, of building rather than destroying. Why did it fail? Why is it that after a century of American humanitarian endeavor, China turned to Russia not to America, to Marxism not to Christianity, to dictatorship and not to democracy? In our search for answers we are again confronted by the ways in which we have used history.

At the close of World War I there was in China "a general awakening of national consciousness and a popular demand for political and social reform."[15] The appearance of this demand was a natural and a predictable result of the Western impact, yet Sun Yat-sen's appeal to the free Western powers "fell on deaf ears." Sun and his great party, the Kuomintang, were rebuffed. Then between 1925 and the early 1940's the Kuomintang party line became both "official and sterile." This is to say that between two world wars both the free West and the Kuomintang were content to navigate in the history of the specious present. As a result, what happened was that under "the Kuomintang, the organizational aspect of the revolution developed much more rapidly than the ideological."[16] Yet as historians neither we in the free West nor the Kuomintang in China recognized this fact nor anticipated the tragic outcome most likely to follow in a Chinese civilization which provided one of the best examples of a society that operated by ideological control rather than by organized governmental direction.[17]

One could of course multiply the examples where free Asia and the free West have not anticipated the future. Enough, however, has been said to illustrate the thesis of these remarks. It is not contended that history predicts the future. It is suggested that free Asia and the free world in the years ahead will need sorely all the resources of real as opposed to crisis history. Even so late as the year 1955 an able American historian describing the rise of America to world power records that as unsought involvements increased the United States was assum-

[15] Linebarger, Chu, and Burks, *Far Eastern Governments and Politics*, 206.

[16] Linebarger, Chu, and Burks, *Far Eastern Governments and Politics*, 151.

[17] P. M. A. Linebarger, "Ideological Dynamics of the Postwar Far East," in F. M. Marx, ed., *Foreign Governments* (New York: Prentice-Hall, Inc., 1949), 549.

ing "far-flung responsibilities whose real significance the American people again sought to ignore by denying their existence."[18] Certainly if history is to serve us in the days ahead as it should have served us in Asia during the past one hundred years, it will require a revolutionary expansion of the timid beginnings that have been made here and in Asia. The task, if undertaken, will never be easy. The history of reality is rarely popular. Crisis history and the history of the specious present will give ground only as they are forced by free societies to do so.

[18] Foster Rhea Dulles, *America's Rise to World Power* (New York: Harper and Brothers, 1955), 60. The author is describing the American movement into world affairs in the first decade of this century.

commentary

PAUL M. A. LINEBARGER

School of Advanced International Studies

In a world designed by philosophers and administered by angels, it might be true that only the democracies could develop ultradestructive weapons, and that tyranny, as a consequence of its own nature, would possess only backward and ineffectual implements of war. In real life, unfortunately, this is not the case. The Hitlerite dictatorship, certainly one of the worst governments to afflict mankind for many decades, was able to summon to evil tasks the talents of many engineers and scientists. Only now are the Western powers overtaking the brilliant lead in the field of jet engines and rocket design established in Nazi Germany. Only now do the automobile turnpikes of the advanced democracies surpass the *Autobahne* established by the Führer's commands.

I cite this unhappy example. Is it necessary to point out that Soviet science and technology have flourished amid political conditions which most democratic-minded people would abhor?

How does science affect Southeast Asia? Unhappily, science begets tools which can be used for great effect. The position of each of the nations of the world for the last several centuries has depended as much on its productive capacity (for economic power) and its inventive capacity (for further development) and on its military strength as on its moral stature. Surely no one will today argue that it was moral deficiency which led the peoples of Java and Sumatra to fall to Dutch power or purely spiritual weakness which caused the defeat of India by the creeping British conquests of centuries past. The dramatic change in our own half-century has been the partial economic and military equalization of the Asian nations with the Western nations, an equalization which makes it impractical as well as immoral for those nations to be held by outsiders as colonial territories.[1]

The science which has marched thus far marches further. The health, education, and economic developments of our time are manifestations of technological development which came one hundred years ago or fifty years ago. The science being worked out right now may be laying the technical military conditions for the re-subjugation of the Asian states, or it may not.

On the one hand, the available evidence suggests that currently the Anglo-American and Russian lead over the non-atomic powers is being increased, and not being diminished. In other words, Bolivia, Ceylon, and Ireland are further behind the major atomic powers than they were ten years ago. On the other hand, there are signs that the Anglo-American and Russian nuclear weapons developments may go into a period of sustained stalemate, in which neither group dares to use the bulk of its power because retaliation from the other would have the effect of canceling out both sets of powers. No matter how fanatical any group of Soviet or anti-Soviet leaders may be, one can seriously doubt that any of them desire to make Brazil or Argentina the leading power

[1] In a very real sense, this comment is a sequel to the statement made by the present contributor in the predecessor to this volume, Philip W. Thayer, ed., *Southeast Asia in the Coming World* (Baltimore: The Johns Hopkins Press, 1953), pp. 180–88. Three years ago the writer suggested that the "chronic war" between Communism and traditionalist democracies was indeed a struggle between civilizations, a struggle which could not and should not end until a new and better civilization had engulfed them both. The chief development in the last three years has been the apparent realization that the two systems can coexist with long armistices which may, under fortunate conditions, pass for peace.

of the whole world by ruining or crippling all the powers of the northern hemisphere. Stalemate might even have some beneficent by-products. If the two major groups of powers begin to constitute fami-lies of nations, we shall have found a corrective to some of the frenzy and irresponsibility of nationalism. A sustained balance between a group of free powers and a group of Communist powers could conceiv-ably provide an area of maximum economic and political freedom for the neutrals in between.

Is this development likely? May the neutrals profit by cold war? It can be said at this time that the prospects for sustained struggle *with a diminished risk of global war* are very good. The danger of an American-Russian war has been much on the minds of sensitive Europeans and Asians. Should the Washington-Moscow antagonisms be brought to a moratorium, it is possible that the same sensitive Asians and Europeans would be terrified by the contingencies which they might expect to see presented by a Coalition of Two. There are not many countries of the world which could stand up very long against an American and Russian combination.

The strategic element underneath history, it can be argued, is being emphasized. Communism and anti-Communism do not depend on military elements alone. This is true, but not the whole truth. Most of past history has shown war to be a frequent although not unique *ultima ratio*. Anyone who questions whether an idea can be suppressed by force should ask the Aztec emperors, the Persian Zoroastrians, or the Polish Jews for their comments. Dead men have no ideas; wars still kill. Where are the hopeful liberals of the China mainland? Where are the Jugoslav constitutionalists?

Not all the picture is black. The near future may hold some very pleasant developments. The good developments of the near future need not be of the early twentieth century variety. They may be rela-tively new.

Economic progress will take place, but economic development will not of itself make democracy secure or make Communism weak. The most developed Asian state of 1941 was Japan, and militarist Japan marched off to suicide through the mistake of Pearl Harbor. The most developed state of mainland Europe was Weimar Germany, and Ger-many went into the tortured lunacy of Hitlerism. Economic progress is good; it is agreeable; I submit that it is not necessarily relevant

to political outlook, merely because the Communists and some liberals
have said that it is. Their case is not proved; neither is mine; but I
submit that in major enterprises we might distinguish between restoration and new development.[2]

Nor need it be argued that understanding itself will produce happiness or tranquility. The two Asian peoples who understood America
best were China and Japan. Each had a history of close association
with America. The Japanese fought the Americans in 1941 and the
mainland Chinese fought the Americans in 1950; international understanding, apart from promoting more efficient espionage systems, seems
to have had the effect of making it possible for those people to hate
us in detail, instead of hating us in general. Were the Chinese phi-
losopher Lao Tzu living, I am sure—if I may be permitted the
irreverence—that he would feel understanding oneself to be much
more conducive to peace than the understanding of foreigners.

What does this mean in international relations? It means, I expect,
that the future history of South and Southeast Asia will depend upon
the separate fortunes, good or bad, of each of the peoples of that area.
Some of those states will have foolish leaders; most of them, let us
hope, will have wise and brave leaders. India has already given
mankind one of the great figures of this century in the person of
Mohandas K. Gandhi. Burma lost much when Burma lost Aung San.
The total history of these countries will necessarily be a composite of
their individual histories. American aid may help hither and yon,
American friendship may prove cheering or pleasant to many persons,

[2] The old arguments on aid as an obligation are brilliantly but controversially
brought down to date in Tibor Mendes, *Southeast Asia between Two Worlds*, New
York, 1955. From the present writer's point of view, the work gives the best current statement of the "aid without strings" viewpoint, but Mendes' fundamental
weakness is revealed in his assumption that the Soviet standard of living may well
rise so rapidly as to surpass west Europe's in the 1960's. In the first place, the
Soviet military burden could not permit this to happen. Second, west Europe
has more vitality than the left-liberals think; the German economy is proof of this.
Third, even if the Soviet consumers' rate did rise, it would make no real difference in the political position of Soviet propaganda: those who believe the
propaganda for personal reasons will believe in Soviet wealth, whether it exists
or not, and those who do not believe in it will remain skeptics, facts or no facts.
In an age of mass communications, the "truth" is that which people live by, not
a scientific measurement in a remote place.

but the history of each country will be determined—short of military intervention on a colossal scale—by the peoples and leaders of those countries.

May I suggest that although all the future is unknowable, the general future of all Asia is especially unknowable?

The complex group of nations around the Indian Ocean and the South China Sea have one thing in common: they know each other very little at present, and they are bound to affect one another somewhat more in the future than they have in the past. Each of these nations will have its elections, its changes of leadership (for even Communist leaders sometimes die), and its internal events. Each of these will make its own kind of history. Out of what *does* happen, country by country, new international patterns will arise. Most of these particular patterns cannot be foreseen by any man living.

Take an example from another area. Twice the United States has given aid to Russia in very massive quantities, aid so large as to contribute to the survival of the Soviet state. The first was the period of the American Relief Administration, immediately after the Bolshevik Revolution, when American food kept Russia from starving. The second aid period was the time of Lend-Lease, followed by UNRRA, when American help to Russia was equally vital. I do not think that the American aid hurt America, but neither do I think it can be shown to have helped America. The aid is a past event, nothing more.

From this I draw a conclusion. The world is in a condition of ferment, ideological confusion, and struggle; the present is a cloudy period in the minds and destinies of mankind. The Asians should not try to solve their problems all at once, and now; and neither should the Americans try to solve all problems. Neither foreign aid, nor international friendship, nor intercultural understanding will determine the main course of human history. The destinies of men will be settled, as long as nations last, by the events within the territory of each nation.

The newly freed peoples of South and Southeast Asia have the delightful experience ahead of them of getting to know each other and their neighbors. Consider an example. From a technical point of view, the three most modern nations of Asia are Japan, Turkey and Israel. How many men in Rangoon, Djakarta, or Manila know all three? May I express the hope that if the Asians get to know each other better, they will find great happiness and will have less occasion to worry about America or Russia or other faraway places?

Another possibility unfolds itself. The direct economic and political influence of tropical America upon Asia is apt to remain slight—except for competition in matters such as the world markets for coffee, for sugar, for tin—but the musical, literary, architectural and other influences have a world of promise. I wish I could be present when the Indians really begin to appreciate the tremendous social and cultural accomplishments of Mexico, or when the Brazilians have a national craze of copying everything Indonesian. In all departments of peaceful living, the tropics-to-tropics pattern of world communications is one of the weakest and one of the most promising. Is it not a pity that the Bandung Conference did not include representatives from Peru, from Haiti, from Jamaica? These people speak Spanish or French or English, but their memories of colonialism and their reaction to tropical life are as rich as any in the world.

For myself, may I conclude by saying I think America should take the advice which Americans give to others. Many Americans approve of Indonesian nationalism; let us ourselves, *sinn fein* in the flaming Irish phrase, hammer out our own destiny. If we Americans go somewhere *at home*, the rest of the world will support us and follow us because of what we have done, and not because of what we say.

Consider a possibility. The entire Marxist-Leninist theory depends on the actual existence of a working class. Communist economics become more out of date every year; they still apply brilliantly to the economics of 1848 but only grotesquely to the cultures of 1955 or 1957. One more accomplishment is needed on the anti-Communist side. Suppose that an abundance of nuclear power and the increase of automation leads to the complete disappearance of an old-fashioned European-style proletariat from American soil. What happens to the Marxist theory of capitalism when the only exploited workers are machines? What the Americans do here will determine the history of the world far more than what the Americans may do in Asia.

This book is a happy sign that we watch each other. Let us continue to watch one another, calmly, serenely, confidently. The cold war and the hot peace can be surmounted by time itself. Perhaps we can all win our various and respective fights best by the ancient and very human process of living through them and beyond them.

The United Nations
and South and Southeast Asia

SUDJARWO TJONDRONEGORO

Chief Indonesian Delegate to the United Nations

The United Nations came into being through the desire of mankind to create a better world; a world in which it would be saved from the terrible calamities of war. The destruction and untold sorrow brought about by World War II prompted the major allied leaders to think of an organization, which would function as a common, international instrument for the preservation of the peace. It was then perfectly clear to all that peace would not be preserved without co-operation and mutual understanding among nations. In particular, the co-operation of the great Allied powers was considered imperative; but it was also recognized that the collaboration of all nations—all peace-loving nations, as it was to be phrased in the Charter—was necessary for the effective working of a truly international organization for peace.

Naturally, the major Allied powers thought primarily of those nations which had actively participated on their side in the war against the Axis powers, and when the United Nations met at San Francisco in 1945, on the eve of the victorious conclusion of the war, only these nations were invited to send representatives. Later, however, four more states, Argentina, the Byelorussian S.S.R., newly liberated Denmark, and the Ukrainian S.S.R., were admitted to the Conference; so that, in all, fifty states became the drafters of the Charter of the United Nations, the guide to building co-operatively a better world in peace.

Now, what was the state of South and Southeast Asia during this historic period? Did this important part of the world play any role

270

or exert any influence on the deliberations and ideas which gave birth to the United Nations? Did the promoters of the United Nations seriously consider this area and its future for a peaceful world?

Excepting Thailand, the countries of South and Southeast Asia, at that time, were legally still colonies of the Western Allied powers. They were at war with Japan and, what is more, the greater part of them were still occupied by Japanese forces. Obviously, the Western colonial powers were primarily interested in attaining the liberation of their colonies from Japanese hands. However, in view of the known aspirations of colonial peoples for freedom and independence, it was inevitable that the future of colonies, in general, would be discussed at San Francisco. Chapter XI of the Charter, concerning so-called non-self-governing territories, emerged from these deliberations. It provided for the development of self-government, "recognizing the principle that the interests of the inhabitants of the territories are paramount," but with the reservation that this policy be conducted with "due account being taken of the interests and well-being of the rest of the world, in social, economic and commercial matters." Thus, the colonial powers, as far as colonies were concerned, heeded timidly—one may even suggest, reluctantly—the surge of freedom rising from the struggle against fascism. Both the words "freedom" and "independence" were carefully avoided.

The cry of freedom from Asia itself was, in fact, hardly heard in San Francisco. India and the Philippines were represented there, but India was then still British India. It, therefore, fell upon the representative of the Philippines, General Carlos Romulo, to remind the assembled conferees that, in their efforts to secure the peace, the eyes of Asia were turned on them for recognition of their human rights and with "the plea that such a peace may not be appropriated for the purpose of freezing the political, economic and social order of that part of the world."

Indeed, all Asia was in ferment—in revolutionary ferment—with the desire to gain freedom, independence, human dignity and self-respect; to gain for itself—at long last—those very objectives which the Allied powers had officially proclaimed as their aim in prosecuting the war. The peoples of the colonial territories not only longed for the end of the war, but they were determined that its conclusion should also mean the end of colonialism and the rebirth of their freedom and independence. Already, when the Atlantic Charter was proclaimed in 1941, they looked to it with high expectations and, in particular, they looked to the promise it contained, to seek to restore "sovereign rights and self-government to those peoples deprived of them, and respect for the right of *all* peoples to choose their own forms of government."

Yet, when they confronted the colonial powers with this specific provision, their enthusiasm for the Charter's noble proclamation of democracy and freedom was met with coldness and silence. It was Mr. Churchill, one of the writers of the Atlantic Charter, who then provided the explanation. The colonial peoples were told, in effect, that the Charter rights were reserved for white people only and were not applicable to the colonies, and that, furthermore, the Atlantic Charter itself should be taken as "a guide and not a rule." Naturally, it became increasingly difficult for the peoples of Asia to take for granted that they, too, would enjoy freedom and self-government as a logical consequence of the fruits of victory in the war. It was really not easy to believe in the sincerity of the professed war aims of the Allied powers, at least as far as they concerned the peoples of our regions. Instead of confidence, there was in this part of the world scepticism and honest doubt as to the real aims and purposes of the Western Allied powers. In the territories occupied by Japanese forces, this feeling was, of course, fertile grist for the propaganda mills of the Japanese. It is, therefore, from a psychological standpoint, not surprising that some national leaders in Asia collaborated with the Japanese for the sake of their own national cause and to prevent the possible reimposition of Western colonialism.

In countries not occupied by the Japanese, such as India, the colonial powers sought to enlist the support of the people, but their efforts did not meet with enthusiastic response. On the contrary, they met with scepticism and even bitterness or, in some cases, outright hostility. For the people of these countries the war was not their war. In a report made to the late President Roosevelt, in September 1944, by the then United States Ambassador to India, Mr. William Phillips, these feelings were illuminatingly set down. Mr. Phillips said:

At present, the Indian people are at war only in a legal sense, as for various reasons the British Government declared India in the conflict without the formality of consulting Indian leaders or even the Indian Legislature. Indians feel they have no voice in the

Government and therefore no responsibility in the conduct of the
war. They feel that they have nothing to fight for, as they are
convinced that the professed war aims of the United Nations do not
apply to them.

The British Prime Minister, in fact, has stated that the provisions
of the Atlantic Charter are not applicable to India, and it is not
unnatural therefore that Indian leaders are beginning to wonder
whether the charter is only for the benefit of white races.

Mr. Phillips further said:

> The attitude of the general public toward the war is even worse.
> Lassitude and indifference and bitterness have increased as a result
> of the famine conditions, the growing high cost of living and con-
> tinued political deadlock.
>
> While India is broken politically into various parties and groups,
> all have one object in common—eventual freedom and independence
> from British domination.

And finally he observed:

> The peoples of Asia—and I am supported in the opinion by other
> diplomatic and military observers—cynically regard this war as
> one between fascist and imperialist powers.

Mr. Phillips suggested to the President of the United States that the
British should make a generous gesture to India in an effort to "improve
conditions and re-establish confidence among the Indian people that
their future independence is to be granted." Such a gesture, he said,
must consist not of mere words, but of acts, in order to assure the
people that the Allied powers "are in truth fighting for a better world."
Mr. Phillips added that the colonial people conquered by the Japanese then "might hopefully feel that they have something better to
look forward to than simply a return to their old masters."[1]

This testimony certainly represented a clear and intelligent appraisal
of the political psychology of Asia at that crucial time. But, despite
these regrettable facts and some unanswered questions for the future,
the UN Conference in San Francisco and the birth of its lofty Charter
in 1945, did kindle a new hope for the future in the dependent territories of Asia, and certainly in my country, Indonesia. At the same

---

[1] *Voices of History 1944–1945*, Nathan Ausubel, ed., "Report to President
Roosevelt by William Phillips, United States Ambassador to India," p. 400.

time, we were also ready to fight, if necessary, for the ideals of the Charter, which reflected our own long-cherished ideals of freedom, equality and peace.

When we of Indonesia proclaimed our independence and sovereignty on August 17, 1945, we looked indeed with high expectations to the Charter of the United Nations for support and sustenance. We had found, as I have already noted, our own ideals mirrored in those of the Charter. In our first political manifesto after the establishment of the republican government, we referred to these ideals. We stressed our determination to secure for the Indonesian people the inalienable rights proclaimed by the United Nations—the enjoyment of freedom of speech and of religion and freedom from want and from fear, as well as the enjoyment of healthy bodies and minds through the benefits of modern education and training. In the spirit of the Charter, we pledged to promote for mutual benefit closer social, economic, and cultural relations with all the nations of the world, while making our own fullest spiritual and material contributions. Finally, we announced our firm intention to seek a place in the Council of the United Nations to further and to implement the ideals contained in the San Francisco Charter. In our political ideals, nationalism and internationalism were not considered contradictory values. As President Sukarno has always taught us, if nationalism is a flower, internationalism is the garden in which this flower can best prosper, in harmony with others.

Indonesia was, of course, not alone in experiencing this resurgence of national consciousness; this reawakening was not limited to national boundaries, but gladly acknowledged the obligations it owed to the international community. The newly emerging nations of Asia were as one in their willingness—their eagerness—to enter the family of nations and to contribute their share in the great venture to secure peace and prosperity for mankind. The cry of freedom and equality was everywhere in the air, sweeping over this part of the world and carrying the teeming millions of Asia to new heights of endeavor and idealism. The time had certainly come to realize the noble objectives for which all peoples of the world had professed to fight.

In many cases the colonial powers eventually heeded these yearnings, redeeming—not without pressure—the solemn pledges they had made in the heat of war. I must say in this respect that the United States was an enlightened example. The Philippines, encouraged by

the liberal policy of the United States and by the mutual understanding
that had grown up between the American and the Philippine peoples,
very soon gained their full independence. In the British colonial territories, with the advent of a Labour government in Britain, we saw the
peaceful birth of the sovereign and independent states of India,
Pakistan, Burma and Ceylon.

Unfortunately, however, this enlightened path was not always followed. In Indochina, Malaya and Indonesia, the path to freedom and
independence was to lead through bloodshed, suffering, and mutual
bitterness. For my country, it was a matter of deep regret that the
Dutch government did not meet the proclamation of independence and
the subsequent establishment of the government of the Republic of
Indonesia with the same understanding and sympathy as did the
British Labour government the independence of India, Pakistan, Burma
and Ceylon. Instead of agreement, there was thus political conflict between our two countries, developing inevitably into armed conflict. Instead of peace we had war, a colonial war.

As you may recall, the United Nations intervened in this dangerous
conflict, on the request of our neighbors, India and Australia. Indonesia
wholeheartedly welcomed that intervention, believing as we do in the
just principles and purposes of the United Nations. And, though the
Dutch opposed intervention in what they termed a "domestic affair,"
the United Nations fortunately stood firm in its action. Backed by the
pressure of freedom-loving world public opinion—which had been
aroused by the heroic struggle of the Indonesian people and which was
later encouraged by the Asian Conference convened by India in 1949
to consider the Indonesian question—the negotiations between the
Netherlands and Indonesia, under the auspices of the United Nations,
eventually came to a successful conclusion in 1949. The sovereign Republic of Indonesia was formally recognized by the Dutch and the
world at large, and, in September 1950, was admitted as the sixtieth
member of the United Nations.

Thus, the United Nations successfully intervened in a colonial war,
contributing much to the establishment of freedom and independence
in an important area of Southeast Asia. By 1950, it had opened its
doors to five newly sovereign nations—Burma, India, Pakistan, the
Philippines and Indonesia—who, along with Thailand, represent the

voices of South and Southeast Asia in that international forum. But, since then, its doors have unfortunately remained shut.

It is our earnest hope, today, that the doors of the United Nations may soon be reopened, admitting our neighbors Ceylon, Nepal, Cambodia, Laos and we hope, a unified Viet-Nam, followed by an independent and sovereign Malaya. The exclusion from our ranks of these freedom-loving nations, as well as that of the many others of Asia, Africa and the European continent, is indeed a source of deep concern to us. Certainly, the United Nations and the world as a whole stand to gain much from their participation in our common quest for a lasting, universal peace. General Carlos Romulo, in his recent speech to the United Nations commemoration meeting in San Francisco, pointed out that "Asia (and Africa) takes the United Nations very seriously." I think that the United Nations should also show that it takes Asia (and Africa) very seriously by having their free voices more fully heard in the Council of the United Nations and by dealing with issues concerning the fight of democracy against colonialism—issues of such vital and immediate concern to the peoples of Asia (and Africa)— with greater sincerity.

Now, what does the United Nations—with our participation—mean in practical terms to the peoples of South and Southeast Asia?

It means, in the first place, that there is an international body to which all nations—large and small alike—can come to seek justice, peaceful solutions of their international problems, and assistance for social and economic advancement. When a question such as Kashmir has arisen, the United Nations has been able to prevent the worsening of the situation, while striving for a peaceful and just settlement. When Burma was beset by foreign forces on its soil, ravaging and desecrating its countryside and its people, Burma came to the United Nations for attention and a possible solution. It could find in the world organization needed moral strength and some assistance toward alleviating this intolerable situation. With regard to Indonesia, we of course still recognize with much gratitude the assistance rendered by the United Nations in the establishment of the independent and sovereign Republic of Indonesia.

Of great importance to us—to the people of Asia—is the role of the United Nations as an agency for the advancement of still-dependent peoples to self-government and to enjoyment of fundamental human rights without resort to violence. The Asian member states of the United Nations, together with their Arab and African brother countries, have annually brought to the attention of the General Assembly the urgent need for speedy solutions to colonial questions, such as the questions of Morocco and Tunisia, as well as the question of race conflict in the Union of South Africa. It has always been a hard fight. But we consider it as a fundamental function of the United Nations to tackle these problems seriously, in the interest of peace and justice for all peoples, in the interest of earnestly fulfilling the noble principles and purposes of the Charter.

Yet, there is unfortunately a discernible tendency among some rather powerful members of the United Nations to minimize or even ignore this very function. Indonesia itself brought before the ninth General Assembly session last fall the question of West Irian (West New Guinea), the easternmost portion of our country, still held under the colonial rule of the Dutch. We sought only the moral support to continue our efforts to find a peaceful solution to this burning dispute, as in fact called for in the agreements on the formal transfer of sovereignty, of 1949. Our resolution requested the Assembly merely to express its hope that negotiations between the governments of Indonesia and the Netherlands—between two member states—be resumed on this matter. This very modest request, however, was denied to us, although to insure that disputes of this kind are settled, not by armed force but by negotiations and other such peaceful means is unquestionably one of the primary aims of the United Nations. The peoples of South and Southeast Asia, it is true, have a large fund of faith in the United Nations, but it cannot be sustained by noble words enshrined in the Charter alone. It needs something more than that, if it is to endure. And it is our collective duty and responsibility to provide that something more, to see to it that the United Nations, by its actions, strengthens and secures the faith of Asians in the world body.

But if in the political field the intrusion of power politics has given us some reason for concern, there is, happily, one field in which the United Nations has been able to translate vividly its ideals into promising deeds. This is the field of technical assistance. The United Nations Technical Assistance Administration (UNTAA) is, indeed, a highly appreciated body in our region. The organs of the United Nations, such as UNICEF, WHO, FAO, and UNESCO, as well as the many others participating in the technical assistance program, have by their unstinting and dedicated work made the world organization a meaning-ful reality in the lives of hundreds of millions of peoples in Asia. They have, in co-operation with the governments concerned, made effective contributions to combatting such dreaded diseases as yaws and tubercu-losis, and have helped, in general, to raise the health and hygienic standards of the people. They have given immeasurable aid in training skilled personnel, in setting up pilot projects, in establishing and equipping research, technical, and education centers, and in encour-aging wider cultural exchange through books, pamphlets, and films. They have, in short, opened up new opportunities and infused with meaning the hope of a happier and healthier future for mankind. It is a selfless work that goes on day by day, and which in its own quiet way is spectacular and inspiring.

It is, moreover, a co-operative enterprise, in which the countries of South and Southeast Asia are at the same time both recipients and donors. Not only have they benefited greatly from this humanitarian venture, but they have given to it their maximum support and co-operation. Aside from the annual financial contribution to the United Nations Technical Assistance Administration, the South and Southeast Asian countries also contribute, to the greatest extent possible, in pro-viding training facilities and skilled experts in the field. For example, the excellent results yielded by the Indonesian methods of fish culture are being studied, under the auspices of FAO, by experts from Thai-land, Israel and other nations. In 1954, experts engaged on technical assistance projects included nationals from Ceylon (a non-UN member nation, by the way) and the Philippines, as well as fifty experts from India. In Bangkok, Thailand, are located the headquarters of the Economic Commission for Asia and the Far East (ECAFE). This regional body of the United Nations, in collaboration with other coun-tries from both the East and the West, has shown its increasing impor-tance for achieving economic co-operation and improvements in the area of South and Southeast Asia. On many occasions, the countries of South and Southeast Asia have played host to regional conferences of various UN economic and social bodies.

This sharing of skills in the field of technical assistance, this two-way street of giving and receiving help is indeed an essential meaning of the United Nations and one which is held dear by the peoples of

South and Southeast Asia. They welcome assistance, but they also wish
to contribute creatively in all the many peaceful and constructive
activities of the United Nations. This holds equally true as regards
the political endeavors of the United Nations for peace.

Some of the South and Southeast Asian countries are considered
neutrals in the cold war. But even this rather controversial policy has
proved to be useful in furthering the aims of the United Nations.
India played an important role in ending the fighting in Korea. The
Colombo powers, that is, Burma, Ceylon, India, Pakistan and Indonesia
which met in Colombo in April 1954 at the same time as the famous
conference on Indochina was held in Geneva certainly rendered their
contribution toward finding the best solution to ending the war in
Indochina. And indeed, it is by virtue of the existence of nonaligned
Southeast Asian powers that the supervision of the armistices in Korea
and in Indochina was made possible, with India shouldering the difficult task of chairmanship.

We earnestly hope that soon all fighting may cease and that peace
will be completely restored. Certainly, peace for Asia means a great
deal for peace of the world. We venture even to suggest that without
peace in Asia, an area containing almost half of the world's population,
there can be no peace in the rest of the world.

Recently, at the Asian-African Conference in Bandung, Indonesia,
the countries of Asia (and Africa) rededicated themselves to the common task of fostering good will and understanding among nations.
The Conference was convened outside the United Nations and included among its participants many who are still excluded from that
organization, but the spirit of the United Nations was, nevertheless,
within the Conference. In its final communiqué, the assembled dele-
gates laid down ten principles for promoting international peace and
security. Heading this list, as the very first principle, is "respect
for fundamental human rights and for the purposes and principles of
the Charter of the United Nations."

Free Asia is indeed not merely looking inwards. With independence, with self-realization, there has arisen in free Asia a new spirit,
a world spirit seeking fulfillment in promoting peace and harmony
among nations, and the well-being of the whole of humanity. It is in
this spirit that free Asia approaches the United Nations. And to the
extent that this spirit is the genuine spirit of the United Nations, the

United Nations to South and Southeast Asia means a great deal. It
means a partnership for realizing the principles and purposes of the
Charter for the common good. The countries of South and Southeast
Asia will continue to strive to realize these principles and purposes.

commentary

FRANCIS O. WILCOX

*Assistant Secretary of State
for International Organization Affairs*

I like very much the essay of our distinguished friend, the Ambassador
from Indonesia and I like the spirit in which he has presented it. As
a result, I do not have much of a quarrel to pick with him. If every
member nation would underline, as he has done, the role of the United
Nations as a partnership for realizing the purpose and principles of
the charter for the common good, we could be sure that we would never
have to face the dangers of an atomic war.

My remarks will be very brief and very much to the point, particularly directed to three or four comments in the distinguished Ambassador's paper which I would like to underline.

At the outset, I would like to remind my readers that we have made
a tremendous amount of progress in achieving the objectives which the
Ambassador has stressed—those objectives which were so very important to us many years ago when we struggled for our independence in
this country—the objectives of freedom, independence, and equality.
Anybody who has travelled in the East with his eyes open knows how
deeply those sentiments stir the people of that area. But I submit we
have made a great deal of progress in the last ten years in working
toward those objectives.

The list of states that have gained independence in the Middle East
and the Far East is an impressive one. There is Libya, the Philippines,
Ceylon, Israel, Laos, Cambodia, Jordan, Nepal, Viet-Nam, Burma,

India, Pakistan, Indonesia, Korea, and shortly before that, Syria and Lebanon. That is an astonishing list which will go down in history as perhaps indicative of the most significant bit of progress that has been made in this field in many centuries. There is no comparable period, it seems to me, that will begin to compare with this decade in bringing freedom and independence to the people of the world.

Some credit for this development—perhaps not all of it, but a great deal of it—should go to the United Nations. Some of these countries would have secured their independence had the United Nations not been in existence. That is entirely possible. But it seems to me that the objectives which were so clearly outlined in the United Nations Charter gave great stimulus to that movement, and the United Nations should have a rather considerable amount of credit for this progress.

Also, and this is something that many students of the Charter often forget, the United Nations not only established a trusteeship system and provided a very adequate framework for the discharge of its functions and its responsibilities in that area, but it also approved the very broad principles that are outlined in Chapter 11 of the Charter. Under this article the members of the United Nations which are responsible for the administration of a non-self-governing territory recognize that the interests of the territory are paramount, and they accept as a sacred trust the well-being of the people of the area. Also, we should not overlook their promise to develop self-government. That promise is contained in Chapter 11 of the Charter.

Now, it is true that during this period there has been some retrogression in our quest for freedom, because the progress that has been recorded on one side of the balance sheet has been somewhat offset by the developments that have taken place behind the Iron Curtain. When you consider the fact that, while many countries gained their independence, a number of other countries, totaling perhaps 800 millions of people, have fallen behind the Iron Curtain, you realize that all that has happened since 1945 certainly has not been in the direction of progress. And as a result of this latter development, the world is faced with another type of colonialism far more threatening, in my judgment, and far more dangerous for the peace of the world than the so-called Western colonialism. This is the colonialism of international Communism which has threatened, not only the peace and security of Asia, but the peace and security of the entire world.

When one goes to Asia, he gets the impression that Communists by a curious twist of fate appear to many there to be on the side of the angels. They wave the flag of nationalism. They denounce imperialism. They condemn colonialism. As a result, and this is one of the greatest ironies of history, they are not seen for what they really are. Sometimes one gets the impression that the people of Asia have been so absorbed with and so concerned about Western colonialism that they have overlooked this more immediate and more vital danger to their independence and security.

One further comment which the distinguished Ambassador made impressed me very much, and that relates to the problem of membership in the United Nations. I am convinced that one of the most important problems the United Nations faces in the future—and it is a question which is very closely tied in with the problem of Charter revision—is the problem of membership.

Too many peace-loving people in South and Southeast Asia and in the world, generally, find themselves outside the framework of the United Nations. There are some fourteen countries who have been approved by the General Assembly as meeting the Charter requirements for membership, and there are others who have not yet applied, perhaps who might apply if they felt there was an opportunity to secure admission to the organization.

My own conviction is that the United Nations cannot continue to function effectively for a long period of time without the assistance and the collaboration of Laos, Cambodia, Ceylon, Nepal, Libya, Jordan, Japan, Germany, Italy, Portugal, Ireland, and Finland,—important countries in the family of nations who do not now belong.

And here I might underline particularly the countries that attended the Bandung Conference. You will recall the Conference in its communiqué referred to those states that had not yet secured entry; Libya, Ceylon, Japan, Nepal, Jordan, Laos, and Cambodia, a long list of non-members who ought to be included in the membership of the United Nations, if that organization is to fulfill its destiny and to achieve its fullest effectiveness.

And I want to assure the distinguished Ambassador that one thing I hope to do, and I realize this is beyond the capacity of any one person, is to lend my energy toward the solution of this very difficult problem of membership. It seems to me that the membership deadlock has to be broken within the foreseeable future if the organization is to achieve its greatest measure of accomplishment.

In that connection, I think it is also important to assure Asia more adequate representation on the Security Council. The states of Asia, apart from the permanent members of the Security Council, who have been represented on that organ, have represented the British Commonwealth and not the countries of Asia generally. I refer to India, Pakistan, New Zealand, and Australia. I have not gone back to check history accurately on this point, but I think it is a fact that there have been no occasions when Asia generally has been represented by a non-permanent member of the Security Council, as have the countries of Latin America, western Europe, and the Middle East. One of the things that we ought to work toward in connection with this problem of membership is the reconstitution of the Security Council membership in such a way that Asia has what we might consider an adequate representation.

Reference has also been made to the matter of technical assistance, and I like the way the Ambassador raised this problem, when he pointed out that technical assistance is a two-way street. The people of the West have been inclined to look upon technical aid and economic development as being a kind of one-way thoroughfare in which we hand out our resources and we do not get very much back in return. Now that is a fallacious assumption. There is a great deal we can get back.

In the first place, from a hard-headed business point of view, it makes good sense economically, because we know from history that when countries are developed economically they fit into the structure of international business in such a way that the flow of goods brings additional profits to our merchants and our industries.

In the second place, we have a lot to learn from Asia from a cultural point of view. One thing we ought to do is to explore further the ways and means by which the people of Asia can make a greater contribution to this co-operative venture that we know of as technical assistance.

Now, I am pleased to say that in the legislation which Congress considered during 1954 we put a very considerable amount of emphasis upon economic assistance for the underdeveloped areas of Asia. In the bill Congress finally passed there was a special provision for the President to utilize large sums of money in helping the regional programs of Asia—and Congress put considerable emphasis on this regional aspect of the matter. Many members of Congress believe it would be desirable to stress that our assistance should go perhaps not to individual countries as such but to countries that are engaged in co-operative ventures in helping to develop the collective economic stability of Asia. There is a considerable amount of money available for that purpose. It is my strong hope, and I know it is the hope of the administration, and the Congress, that ways and means will be found to spend that money effectively.

In this connection, I would like to say that at long last we have worked out our contribution to the technical assistance program in such a way that we will be able to pay our share of that program at a time when it can be most effectively used by the United Nations. One of the big problems that we have had with the United Nations, budget-wise, stemmed from the fact that our fiscal year does not correspond to the fiscal year of the United Nations. As a result our representatives in New York have been confronted with an embarrassing situation each time they go before the Assembly's special committee dealing with this problem for they are not in a position to indicate with any degree of certainty how much money can be contributed by the United States.

In 1954, for example, the technical assistance program entered into its fiscal year without actually knowing whether over half of the money they hoped would be available would eventually be forth-coming. I would like to ask whether an industry or a university or other important institution could be expected to function satisfactorily not knowing after the fiscal year had started where half of its money was coming from, or whether it was going to be available at all.

My hope is that this recent development will amount to a rather sizable contribution to the success of the technical assistance program in the future.

I also want to join with the distinguished Ambassador in under-lining the importance of the work of the specialized agencies. That activity is not spectacular but through it the people of the world are working together to help themselves to a better standard of living and a better way of life.

I would like to close with just one thought, and that is this: one of the big tasks, it seems to me, that the people of Asia face in the future is that of canalizing the vitality and the vigor and the enthusiasm of the new-found nationalism of the Asian countries, which is a tremendous force, into productive and fruitful directions. And I am confident that the people of Asia will not let the Communists do this for them.

Backgrounds of Communism in Asia

HAROLD H. FISHER

Stanford University

I

There are many Asians but they face the same dilemmas. Most Asians wish to raise their levels of life, to attain or preserve their national independence and to retain the values of their ancient civilizations and as equals make their contribution to the developing world culture. But in order to preserve national independence and the values of Asian civilizations, it is necessary to assimilate many of those elements of Western civilizations that for the last four centuries have been undermining the culture of Asian countries.

Communism confronts the Asians with another set of dilemmas. The Communists promise to emancipate all the Asians from Western imperialism, present and future, but in order to be freed from taking orders from London, Paris, The Hague or Washington, Asians must be willing to take orders from Moscow or Peking. The Communists promise to raise the levels of life, increase production by industrialization and modernization, but only if the Asians are willing to replace ancient oriental despotisms with an up to date totalitarian dictatorship that decrees which economic methods, scientific facts, philosophical views, literary and artistic forms, the Asian communities are to be allowed to use and enjoy.

The backgrounds of the revolution in these ancient lands contain elements which affect the course of the Communist movement everywhere in Asia.

286

1. Most Asians are opposed to any system of world relationships that assigns to the Asian peoples a status inferior to that of Europeans, such as characterized imperialism and the colonial system. Since the greatest colonial powers in Asia have been Western parliamentary democracies, Asians naturally do not hold democracy in such high esteem as it is held in the West.

2. In many Asian countries religion is both a mystical faith and a way of life. Whenever Communism has tried to uproot or ignore Islam, Buddhism, Hinduism, or Christianity, it has encountered resistance which has been lessened only when Communism has represented its goals as the same as those of religion.

3. To many Asians, especially intellectuals, a co-operative or collectivist form of enterprise is more acceptable than a system based on individualism and regulated competition. In Asia, therefore, socialism is more popular than capitalism. But unlike the Communists, the Asian socialists make a clear distinction between socialism and communism.

4. Communist world policies were determined largely if not entirely by the ruling circles of the Russian Communist party, especially after the establishment of Stalin's dictatorship and the adoption of the doctrine of "socialism in one country." A corollary of that doctrine was that no sacrifice was too great for any national Communist party to make if it would serve the interests of the Soviet state, "the first land of socialism." A corollary of the doctrine of "the first land of socialism" was that the Russian way was the only way to revolutionary success. The Russian way, it turned out, was not always applicable to Asian conditions. Furthermore, the art of falsifying party history was practiced to such an extent in the Stalin epoch that it became increasingly difficult for subordinate Communists to know what the Russian way really was. The lessons of party history depended on what Stalin decided had happened.

5. The Soviet Communists, however, made great contributions to the Asian revolution. Among these contributions are: (a) Lenin's theory of imperialism as the final stage of capitalism; (b) the repudiation of unequal treaties and the championship of national self-determination and social justice; (c) the organizational principle of democratic centralism that proved to be an effective basis of political action for politically inexperienced peasants and workers; (d) the training

in the Soviet Union and elsewhere of party cadres in Marxism-Leninism and methods of organization, propaganda and indoctrination, conspiracy and guerilla warfare; (e) the example of effective development programs in the economically underdeveloped areas in Asiatic Russia and the Caucasus; and (f) funds which enabled the new parties to carry on their activities and kept these parties under Russian control.

6. In China, under conditions of social ferment, revolutionary strife and foreign invasion, the Chinese Communists have demonstrated that a party professing the ideology and using the organizational methods of the Russian Communists can carry out a revolutionary seizure of power on the basis of support of the peasants, a class theoretically opposed to the revolution, and without the support of the proletariat, the only class that theoretically can make such a revolution. This successful heresy has great significance for the future of revolution in the peasant lands of Asia, for Communist revolutionary theory and tactics, and for "proletarian internationalism," particularly the relations between the ruling circles of the Soviet Union and the People's Republic of China.

II

The Indian historian Sardar K. M. Panikkar divides the history of European relations with Asia into these periods: the Age of Expansion, 1498–1750; the Age of Conquest, 1750–1858; the Age of Empire, 1858–1914; the Civil War in Europe, 1914–1918; and Europe in Retreat, 1918–1939. Down to the Age of Empire the incentives of European expansion in the Asias were not colonization but political aggrandizement, trade in luxury goods and Christian zeal to convert and save the heathen. Unlike the Americas, the civilizations of the Asias were not under the pressure of Europeanization until the "new imperialisms" of the nineteenth and twentieth centuries began to undermine the foundations and change the character of the Asian ways of life. This new economic imperialism increased enormously the means and occasions by which the Asians were exposed to the ideas, institutions, and usages of the West.

The growth of interdependence and intercommunication between the Asias and the West created a great many overlapping discontents.

The Communists have used these discontents in their proselyting among the Asians.

Intellectual discontent developed when Western contacts produced a new class of intellectuals, differing from the mandarins, the Brahmins, the priests and scholar-officials of the past. These new intellectuals, like Western intellectuals, were stirred by the ideas of the Enlightenment, of the American revolt against imperialism, of the French Revolution, and of humanitarianism, Marxism, and social reform. The Reverend Dr. Dwight Whitney Learned of Doshisha University, Kyoto, is said to have been the first man to lecture on socialism in Japan. Like so many Europeans, Asians were shocked by the abuses of early industrialism, and the vulgarities and materialism of primitive capitalist individualism. Many decided that their ancient traditions were irrelevant to the new world and that Western learning must be acquired if the values of their culture were not to be entirely lost. Many new intellectuals were frustrated by the discovery that in their society at home there were no opportunities to use the knowledge and skills acquired abroad. Some accepted Marxism,—the theories of surplus value, the class struggle, the class nature of the state, and the social democratic ideal of a classless world society based on collectivism and democracy—as an explanation of this new world of industrialism. Leaders in the revolutionary movements in the first decade of the twentieth century in Russia, Turkey, China, India, and Japan were inspired by their intellectual discontent with things as they were. Most of those who began to call themselves Communists after the Bolshevik revolution had been students of Marxism or Social Democrats. Many Asians, particularly in India, Burma, Ceylon, Japan, Indonesia, who did not join the Communist movement, remained Marxists—not "Moscow Marxists" but Marxists who believed that there are other ways to reach Marxist goals than that followed by the Russians and who hoped that the Chinese had discovered and would follow another way.

National discontent has been most forcefully reflected in anti-imperialism; and this expresses itself in a sophisticated way as nationalism and in a cruder way as antiforeignism. Nearly everywhere Asians resent the past indignities of Western imperialism and are suspicious of present Western intentions. The idea of nationalism was imported into Asia where it has already raised some new problems in intra-Asian relations. It will undoubtedly raise more. In the meantime the sentiment of nationalism has been used to promote such unnational movements as Asia for the Asians, Pan-Turkism, Pan-Arabism, Pan-Islam and, of course, Communism, which takes the ambivalent position of, on the one hand, supporting the preservation of national cultures and the right of self-determination including the right of secession and, on the other hand, taking the antinationalist position that none but the Communists shall be allowed to exercise these rights and that no Communist is a true Communist who would exercise these rights contrary to the wishes of the oligarchy that dictates to the world Communist movement.

Agrarian discontent exists everywhere in Asia but in different forms. In certain places such as China, Japan, India, Java and in Egypt in the Middle East, the problem is first of all the pressure of population on the available land. This problem is complicated in some places by low productivity and by forms of land tenure and usury. Asia has some very large cities but it is a continent of villages, and throughout the continent, as was the case in the Balkans and Tsarist Russia, there is the immemorial conflict between village and town, the conflict, as Hugh Seton-Watson puts it, between the sixteenth and twentieth centuries. The peasant, in whom Marx took so little interest, has been forced to spend so much of his strength and energy in the elementary problem of living from day to day that revolutionary leaders have been driven to devise new methods of arousing him to political action. The peasant, once awakened, has been, as Marx feared, somewhat difficult to convince of the virtues of a totalitarian collectivism.

Finally there is social discontent. Under this I should include the great desire of Asian leaders to industrialize, to modernize, to catch up with the West in technology, to reduce poverty and illiteracy, and to improve public health and to lengthen life expectancy. The socially discontented are in a great hurry for fear that the gap between the developed and the underdeveloped countries will widen still further. They are not at all convinced that private enterprise is the best method for Asians to use. They have been impressed by Communist accomplishments in the matter of industrialization, and increase in production and employment; they have noted the Communists were able to avoid being drawn into the Great Depression and they have been struck by the fact that economic development is possible without imperialism. They have seen how quickly peasants and nomads could be trained to drive tractors, operate machines, and become proletarians. The cost of these transformations, if the Asians have computed it, has not diminished their eagerness "to learn from the Soviet example."

III

Contacts with the West and the resulting interlocking discontents have created the revolution that has ended colonialism and European dominance in Asia. Whether it has created a new colonialism remains to be seen. Asians used three general methods to make this revolution in the name of national self-determination and equality.

The first method was that used by Japan, a revolution from above aiming at modernization and self-determination without upsetting the social order. The Japanese were the first to take effective action against the Western threat to their institutions. They restored the emperor to the center of power and made of him the symbol of national unity, learned Western military and industrial techniques, adopted parliamentary and administrative institutions, and in fact westernized Japan without eliminating many of the most characteristic features of Japanese culture. The Meiji restoration industrialized Japan without introducing democracy. It accomplished what Japanese writers have called "the harmonization of eastern and western civilizations." Japan remained and remains Asian, but the most westernized of Asian countries and the pioneer that made the epochal demonstration that an Asian nation can learn to use those weapons of power that for centuries had been the basis of European rule over Asia. When the Japanese defeated the Russians in 1904–05, they proved that on occasion Asians could use Western weapons even better than Westerners. This victory and Japan's recognition as a great power are events of the greatest significance in the Asian revolution. The Asian revolutionaries of the twentieth century owe a great debt to the samurai who led a royal revolution in the interests of conservatism.

The second type of Asian revolution is that led by a single party against the existing ruling class and also against foreign intervention and domination. The nationalist movement in Turkey, the movement for liberation and reform in the Indian subcontinent led by the Indian

National Congress, and the nationalist movement in China led by Dr. Sun Yat-sen and later by Chiang Kai-shek are examples of this type of revolution. These movements differ in many particulars but they are all nationalistic aiming at independence or the restoration of status in the society of nations. They aim at reforming the social order, abolishing illiteracy, and modernizing economic life by modern science and technology. They intend to set up or maintain a parliamentary form of government based on political democracy and civil liberties. They have achieved or have tried to achieve these aims through the leadership of a single party, exercising governmental authority during a period of tutelage until such time as the people have acquired the interest and experience to exercise their rights and duties as free citizens.

The third type of Asian revolution is of course the Communist which developed in the Eurasian environment of Russia and has had its most spectacular Asian triumph in China. Like the two other types, the Communist revolution aims at radical reformation of the social order and the modernization of economic life by science and technology. It has given ardent support to national self-determination under the leadership of a party which acknowledges its subservience to a foreign party. This party promises a period of tutelage of indefinite length during which the ruling circles of the party exercise absolute power through the totalitarian institutions of a police state.

The events which most profoundly influenced the course of these three types of the Asian revolution are the two world wars. Sardar Panikkar writes that the first World War from the Asian point of view was "a civil war within the European community of nations." There were, of course, several earlier civil wars in the European community, but this one was notable for the fact that the Western allies felt obliged to call on the Asians to help them, for the effects on the Asians who served in Europe, and for the effects of President Wilson's eloquent advocacy of the right of nations to self-determination.

Finally the strains of the first World War diverted and in the end destroyed the Russian liberal movement for self-determination and social justice that had erupted in the revolution of 1905. Instead of a democracy based on the indigenous Russian socialism which, it appeared, a great majority of the Russian people favored, there emerged a new, ruthlessly efficient dictatorship based on dogmas originated in western Europe and implemented by methods that had been used with haphazard inefficiency by the Tsarist system.

IV

Russia's relations with the Asias stand out in the background of Asian Communism. These relations have been inspired or explained in different ways. One is the affinity of peasant Russia of Tsarist times for peasant Asia. This sentiment which many Russians of the "Eastern" schools shared is expressed in a famous quotation from Prince Ukhtomsky who wrote: "In the eternal conflict between Europe and Asia, Russia will decide in favor of Asia. No other judgment is possible where the judge is the brother of the complainant."

Russia has several times attempted to intervene in Asia as a means of frustrating her imperialist rivals, particularly Great Britain. The Emperor Paul once ordered the Don Cossacks to invade India without taking the trouble to provide them with maps or stores or equipment. A half a century later, during the Crimean War, Nicholas I ordered an invasion of India, where, it was believed, millions of oppressed Indians would rise to welcome 10,000 Russian liberators.

The Communists, like their Tsarist predecessors, found intervention in Asia the most feasible way to attack Britain which in the early years was the number one Soviet enemy as it had been the number one Tsarist enemy. Lenin's pupil and admirer, Bukharin, then an influential leader, put this very clearly to the Eighth Congress of the Russian Communist party in 1919:

> If we propound the solution of the right of self-determination for the colonies, the Hottentots, the Negroes, the Indians, etc., we lose nothing by it. On the contrary, we gain; for the national gain as a whole will damage foreign imperialism . . . . The most outright nationalist movement, for example, that of the Hindus, is only water for our mill, since it contributes to the destruction of English imperialism.

Finally the Russian Communists considered Asia a place where the struggle to overthrow world capitalism could be effectively waged by encouraging every kind of social, economic, and national discontent. Imperialism, Lenin explained, was monopoly capitalism in its highest and final phase of development. Capitalism had survived and prospered by the heartless exploitation not only of the proletariat of the economically advanced countries but also of the peasants of the colonies and other underdeveloped countries. The peasants of Asia were, therefore, the natural allies of the European proletariat. The emancipation of the colonies would be both an act of justice and an attack on capitalism at its weakest point. "The socialist revolution," said Lenin, "will not be only or chiefly a struggle of the revolutionary proletarians in each country against its bourgeoisie—no, it will be a struggle of all colonies and countries oppressed by imperialism, of all dependent countries, against international imperialism."

In applying Lenin's theory the Soviet government did four things that are part of the background of Communism in Asia: (1) Through the government or the party machinery the Communists called upon the oppressed Asians to rise against their oppressors both local and foreign; (2) Outside of Russia, the Soviets backed up these battle cries by declaring null and void the unequal treaties imposed by Tsarist Russia on Turkey, Persia, Afghanistan and China, and they repudiated the secret treaties drawn up during World War I, for partitioning the Ottoman Empire; (3) But inside Russia, where the Moslems of the Crimea, the Caucasus and Russian Central Asia responded to these summons, liberated themselves and declared their independence of Soviet Russia, their new governments were overthrown by the Communists and replaced by governments that would exercise the right of self-determination by staying in the Soviet federation; (4) The Soviet government gave moral support, advice and as much of such material aid as it could afford to the nationalist movements of other countries notably Turkey, Persia, Afghanistan and later China.

In all these cases, the nationalists of other countries first accepted the aid and then took measures to protect themselves from their Communist collaborators. The astute, able and ruthless Turkish leader, Mustapha Kemal, after taking the precaution to liquidate or incarcerate all authentic Communists, created a sham Communist party of his own. When it had served his purpose, Mustapha Kemal liquidated his ersatz party. The real Turkish Communists were never given a chance to make trouble. In Iran the Russians attempted to establish Communist beachheads in the shape of a Persian "Soviet Republic of Ghilan," but when they tried to expand the area of this puppet Soviet they encountered nationalist resistance. The nationalist leader, Reza Khan, seized control of the Iranian government (February 1921), defeated the pro-Soviet forces and then signed a treaty with the Soviets cancelling all Russian claims, concessions and extraterritorial privileges.

V

The Russian Communists, through the Comintern, shifted their revolutionary tactics from left to right, from hard to soft, from encouragement of the class struggle and guerilla warfare to peaceful coexistence, from advocacy of the "united front from below" to the "united front from above." These tactical decisions were sometimes made on the basis of dogmas or theories which turned out to be unsound. More often they were made on the basis of the existing international position of the Soviet Union and its foreign policy objectives, and without much regard to the existing situation or for the effects on Communist parties in the Asian countries. The national parties were told, in effect, that whatever was good for the Communist party of the Soviet Union, the "first land of Socialism" must necessarily be good for them.

VI

In China, in spite of the Russian attempts to make the Chinese follow the Russian pattern, a Communist party was developed along different lines by the adaptation of Soviet strategy and tactics to Chinese conditions. These developments took place during the 1930's and the second World War. They created a revolutionary movement that is Chinese and Asian and not a transplanted Russian or Eurasian movement.

First of all, China is China, not the oldest nation that ever was, but older, the Chinese believe, than any national community now in existence. China is a vast country and it contains one fifth of humanity. Along with the myth of antiquity is the myth of the Middle Kingdom, of China the center of civilization surrounded by the four kinds of barbarians, in the four corners of the world. As late as the middle of the eighteenth century, when the American colonies were making their successful revolt against imperialism, the dependencies of China included Tibet, Formosa, Outer Mongolia, Korea, Burma, Thailand,

Viet-Minh, Viet-Nam, Laos, Cambodia, Nepal, the Indian protectorates
of Sikkim and Bhutan, Russian Central Asia and what is now called
the Russian Far East, that is most of Siberia east of Lake Baikal including the maritime province in which Vladivostok is located. To
what extent the Chinese Communists have or will take over the old
Chinese ideology of world organization remains to be seen. The
existence of this ideology is one of the facts of international affairs
that gives the reunification of China under the Communists a special
significance to Asia and the rest of the world. It inspires both admiration and fear.

As has been suggested, the Comintern-guided strategy of collaborat-
ing with the Nationalists in order to gain the strength and seize control
of that movement ended in a disastrous defeat for the Chinese Communists. Whether the Stalinists or the Trotskyites were more at fault
is an interesting problem but irrelevant to this discussion. Most scholars who have studied the available documents agree that the Russians,
their experts in China and the Moscow-trained Chinese gave bad
leadership and that after 1930 the party foundations of a different and
more lasting character were laid by Mao Tse-tung, Chu Teh and their
associates with precious little help from Russia except several ill-
conceived orders that Mao had the good sense to disregard.

The first achievement of the years after 1930 of significance to
this discussion is that in order to survive the extermination campaigns
of the Nationalists the Communists had to rely on the peasants, and
on leading, organizing, and intensifying a revolution that had been
smouldering and sporadically breaking into flames for almost a century. "Mao's great achievement" says Dr. Mary Wright, "was to
secure recognition of peasant movements as the moving force of the
Chinese revolution rather than as a phenomena of merely temporary
and tactical utility."

As Mrs. Wright notes, the Chinese Communists have continued to
insist that they are really a proletarian party and that the indisputable
peasant pre-eminence in the period from the early 1930's to 1950 was
in no sense a deviation from orthodox Marxism-Leninism but only an
application of that science to Chinese conditions. The Chinese Communists follow their Russian comrades not only in self-criticism but
also in self-deception by historical distortion. This particular self-
deception may be due to the realization that while the peasant will

join the revolution for agrarian reform, he will resist long and stubbornly collectivization and other measures for which the party must look to the proletarians for support.

A second significant achievement of Marxism-Leninism-Maoism is the identification of Communism with national patriotism. From the time of their declaration of war against Japan in 1932 the Communists have tried to make it appear that it was they and not the Nationalists who were the uncompromising defenders of the homeland, that while the militarily stronger Nationalists were willing to appease the Japanese in order to fight the Communists, the Communists with their poorly armed Red Armies were ready and eager to fight the foreign enemy.

A third accomplishment of Marxism-Leninism-Maoism was to bring over to their side an increasing number of the new intellectuals, some as party members and some as fellow travellers who in growing numbers became disillusioned or frustrated by the Nationalists' inability, especially after 1938 when the capital was removed to Chungking, to deal vigorously and successfully with the agrarian problem, the Japanese, and issues relating to the democratic right of dissent. By stressing the alliance of the four classes rather than the single proletarian class dictatorship, the Communists convinced many intellectuals that they would be more effective than the Nationalists in carrying out Dr. Sun's principles of democracy, as well as nationality.

The Communists used the areas they controlled, first in Kiangsi and later in the northwest to demonstrate policies that won the support or at least the acquiescence of the four classes. All were urged to take part in co-operative community enterprises such as land reclamation, labor exchange, transport, and small business, and the Communists wisely limited their representation to one third of the members of official bodies. In these areas the new Red Armies were built up, not separate from the peasants as in the past, but as a part of the community for the first time respected and indoctrinated. An old saying went: "The people are the water, the ruler is the boat; the water can support the boat but it can also sink it." This the Communists revised: "The soldiers are fish and the people the water."

In this fashion Mao Tse-tung and his associates developed what M. N. Roy called a "spurious and perverted brand of Communism" that conquered China. Not all the elements of Maoism have proved effective in other Asian countries but it is so much better suited to Asian conditions as to have justified the suggestion that Marxism-Leninism-Maoism may either cause the center of Communist ideology to shift from Moscow to Peking or make Peking the center of a rival orthodoxy.

VII

The second World War brought about a rejuvenation of the Communist movement in Asia. As a result of having followed Moscow's orders the Communist parties had been hard pressed and outlawed everywhere in Asia. Their leaders had been executed, jailed, or driven into exile where they quarrelled among themselves and sent conflicting orders to their dwindling cohorts. Only in China was the movement being slowly rebuilt as a Chinese renovation of the Russian original.

Fortunately for the Asian Communists, the Kremlin soon was forced to change the orders to wage a class struggle against the war efforts of the Western powers. When the Germans invaded Russia, Communists were told to stop opposing Western war efforts. In many countries the outlawed Communist parties were legalized. Communist guerillas and other party agencies were given weapons and supplies. In India they were encouraged to take control of the labor unions away from the Congress party. But most significant of all was the fact that the weak Communist parties were so well organized, disciplined and experienced in conspirative activities and made so much of their opportunities that they gained greater influence and prestige among the people than they had ever enjoyed. The Asian Communists had the makings of a new program in which nationalism was more emphasized than internationalism, agrarian reform more than nationalization of industry and the land, and a new democracy more than the dictatorship of the proletariat.

commentary

LUCIAN W. PYE

Princeton University

Before the second World War all the Communist parties in Southeast Asia were petty, marginal, and far from profound political movements. They had a life that hardly extended beyond the activities of a few professional revolutionaries. Periodically they could create disturbances, but they were incapable of performing any sustained political roles and they represented no particular elements in the social order. Then, after less than four years of war and Japanese occupation these parties emerged as energetic and significant organizations, commanding the support of people who previously had shown no apparent interest in political activities. The extreme character of this change suggests that it must have followed from dramatic and conspicuous developments. It is hence understandable that our first inclination in seeking to explain the new strength of Communism should be to focus on those events that have received the greatest world-wide attention. We are impressed by the fact that the Japanese conquerors in driving out the Western colonial powers set in motion the sequence of developments which, in combination with what was happening elsewhere, hastened the end of colonialism. In several of the countries the Japanese occupation also shattered the power bases of those indigenous political leaders who had been the spokesmen of the more gradual path to self-government. At the same time, under a Japanese rule that divided and confused many of the potential leaders, it was the Communists who organized and led the only large-scale resistance movements in some of the countries. After the Allied victory there came a period of political uncertainty and economic dislocation during which the Communists sought to consolidate and strengthen their position first by surface co-operation with the Western allies, and then by professing to be the champions of national independence.

These are some of the dramatic events that immediately command our attention when we consider the postwar rise of Communism in

Southeast Asia. Viewed in such a perspective the Communist successes seem to follow from their tactical and organizational ingenuity and from their ability to appeal to the sentiments of nationalism and anti-colonialism. However, the more we come to understand the character of Communism in Asia the more we are impressed with the inadequacies of these explanations. Increasingly we find it necessary to relate the fundamental strength of Communism in Asia to a less spectacular but far more profound process of social and cultural change. We are well aware that in this area of the world the hold of traditional cultures has been increasingly broken by the impact of Western ideas and techniques and that this process has generated new forms of social and political activity.

Although the complex nature of what has been taking place in these societies defies any easy scheme of explanation, I feel that it is helpful to view it as a process of urbanization. In some cases the pattern of social change has followed from the introduction of those activities customarily identified with greater industrialization. However, the process of change has far outstripped the rate at which these societies have become industrialized; and this, indeed, may be the source of much of the trouble. In the region we find entire generations of people seeking to identify with a way of life more related to modern urban societies than the ways of their ancestors. For various reasons the ties of the peasant world have been weakened and the traditional units of the village and family no longer command the full attention nor satisfy all the social needs of increasingly large numbers of people. It is not just that the urban centers have expanded greatly but that people who have not physically moved away from the countryside find themselves also rootless and restless. Alienated from their traditional ways, they can sense the rich potentialities of modern urban life without being able to realize them.

This process, of course, began long before the second World War. However, one of the harshest consequences of the war and the occupation was the elimination or the weakening of most of the institutions in these societies which had facilitated the process of breaking from the old order and finding a place in the emerging one. In particular, most of the quasi-traditional groups or associations which retained to some extent the atmosphere of the old cultures while performing functions basic to a more urbanized way of life found it peculiarly difficult to survive the shock of war and its immediate aftermaths. By quasi-traditional groups, I have in mind the labor contractors, the guilds, the "benevolent" associations, the secret societies, provincial clubs and even the clan and family organizations which were so common among both the indigenous peoples of Southeast Asia and the overseas Chinese in the area. The leaders of such groups were in some cases the direct victims of the Japanese and in others they lost their following because they could not provide it with a sense of security. There were also the informal associations which were weakened because the Japanese forced them to assume onerous political responsibilities. The sum effect was the weakening of the basis of community for particularly those people who already were alienated from the traditional social order based on essentially face-to-face relationships, but who still felt insecure in a world of impersonal relationships.

Also, of course, the war itself by making life more unpredictable further weakened the traditional cultures without providing any new basis of stability. People learned that they could not live out their lives without taking into account the implications of major political developments. They were abruptly introduced to the sphere of politics as a consequence of living in an unstable world, and they developed their ideas about political action while they were seeking personal security. Most of them turned to political action without benefit of civics courses or calm and unimpassioned discussions of the relative merits of different political philosophies. If we are to use the common metaphor and call these reactions a political "awakening" it might be well to add that in many cases it was an awakening that followed a nightmare.

What is the relationship between these developments and the rise of Communism? To find the answer it may be helpful to turn our attention away from Asia for a moment and consider the situation in Europe at the time when Communism was first formulating its notions about the character and the qualifications of the good party member, the "proletarian revolutionary." In the nineteenth century Europe also was experiencing a new development in urban life that was, however, more directly related to a rise in industrial activities. The Communist leaders, and particularly Lenin, observed the rootless character of the lower class who were lost in the impersonal life of the cities. Lenin singled out this sense of rootlessness as being the essential characteristic of the ideal party worker, the good "proletarian revolutionary." Such people could find themselves by identifying with the party; and lacking any strong attachment to values that stood outside of the party, they could readily accept the orientation of the power tactician, the man dedicated to maximizing the strength of the party.

The subsequent history of urban life in the West has refuted the Communist contention that this rootless characteristic is related to the status of the industrial wage earner under capitalism. Then, as in Southeast Asia now, the sense of rootlessness seems to have been more closely related to a process of acculturation in which people were rejecting the earlier definitions of their social roles at a faster rate than the developing urban society could give them new social relationships which they felt were meaningful and satisfying. However, the history of the Communist movement has shown that Communist parties still need the type of person who is adrift but anxious to identify with those who can satisfy his need for security. This is what makes me wonder whether at present it is not precisely in those countries of Asia that lack a proletarian class that the Communists have their greatest reservoirs of potential "proletarian revolutionaries." For people who find themselves alienated from their traditional cultures and are desperately groping for a place in the modern world, Communism can appear to be a haven. The structure of the party, its total ideology, and possibly most important of all the very way of life of the party members can provide such people with at least a temporary solution to their personal problems. With the movement they may find a clearer relationship between individual effort and reward, between group purpose and action, than they had previously known in their confused world.

It seems that in societies which are experiencing fundamental forms of social and cultural change it is peculiarly difficult to differentiate between the sphere of politics and the other spheres of social life. In particular, large numbers of people may be drawn into political participation for reasons quite unrelated to the articulated political issues of the society. Indeed, much of the political discourse may hardly touch upon the problems that disturb these people. This is due, in part, to the fact that there are truly difficult problems of com-

munication in such societies since some of the people are still close
to the old traditional orders while others have adopted an extremely
modern outlook on life. The problem is further complicated when the
slogans and the very language of political life are mainly alien imports
with little modification to meet local conditions. Under these circumstances the political vocabulary commonly used at the level of national
issues may take on a stereotyped quality and not reflect accurately
the political orientations of either the leaders who use it or those
who support them. At the present time many considerations dictate
that the vocabulary of the political elites in Southeast Asia be effective
in communicating with a world audience, with the result that more
subtle means have to be used in the domestic scene to indicate the
various orientations of the competing political groups.

The foreign observer may note that the various non-Communist political groups in some of the countries of Southeast Asia seem to be
speaking as though they supported practically identical objectives and
thus be puzzled as to what separates those who are so actively opposing
each other. He may even arrive at the conclusion that it is personal
and quite private considerations that divide the participants. But in
doing so he may still fail to appreciate that, in societies in a state of
unpredictable change, the real political and social issues may in fact
be at precisely the level of personal relations. This is the case because
it is the area of personal relationships which is most directly under
attack when the traditional bonds of a society are being drastically
weakened.

An important implication which follows from this is that it would
be dangerous to assume that the appeal of Communism in Southeast
Asia is to be found solely in the slogans and the open political propaganda of the various Communist parties. Indeed, if we examine the
propaganda themes most commonly employed by the Communists we
find that they do not stand in sharp contrast with those advanced by
other groups. No group has a monopoly on the appeals of economic
improvement, national independence, anti-imperialism and the like.
In such a situation it is quite likely that large numbers of people
decide to identify with a particular political group not because of the
objectives stated in its propaganda but because of considerations
about the personal implications of becoming a supporter of one
group rather than another. In short, I suspect that the support Com-

munism has received in Southeast Asia follows from complex motivations among which basic questions of personal security are likely to have a very important place.

This leads me to the more general conclusion that the West has been extraordinarily successful in inspiring and directly causing the revolutionary changes in Southeast Asia, but it has been far less successful in providing these societies with new bases for stable social relationships. The Western impact has come as a frontal assault upon the traditional, and almost face-to-face forms of social intercourse around which these societies were once organized. At the same time the West has also provided the model for the formal institutions of the new societies, including those of representative government. However, in the vast area of the informal social and political relationships that compose the life of these societies and that will determine the future form and significance of the formal institutions, the West has made far less direct contribution. In contrast, the Communists, largely because of the peculiar character of life within their party organizations, have been one of the more effective groups in providing guidance and a sense of stability for those who are unsure of how they should react to their unpredictably changing world. Starting from their assumption that few phases of life are without political implications, the Communists have sought to make explicit to their supporters a code of conduct that meets the needs of many Southeast Asians for a way of life that appears to be related to modern standards and yet has the personal intimacy common to the more traditional relationships. In doing this the Communists have been performing an essentially conservative role by trying to give stability and predictability to human relationships and thus a sense of order to people confused by a world of erratic changes.

I would not want to give the impression that the appeals of Communism in Southeast Asia do not operate at the level of more conventional national political issues. The point is that the Communist appeal extends from such issues down to the extremely private motivations of people who lack a sense of belonging. It is this characteristic of the Communist movement which, in part, makes the Communists appear to have more "grass roots" support than most other groups that are active in matters of national politics. The fact that people are attracted to Communism for reasons that seem remote from politics

can mean that as they assimilate the Communist framework for viewing life they will arrive at an understanding of the major political
issues of the day that is more emotionally intense and more personally
meaningful than is likely to be the case for those who are only
introduced to these issues by the jargon of political slogans.

Finally, it may be desirable to point out that by identifying the
basic appeal of Communism in Southeast Asia with a process of
social and cultural change the suggestion is not being made that
all or even most of the people who are disturbed by this process will
turn to Communism. The rich diversity in the ways that men seek
to solve their problems insures that this will not be the case. The
more ominous implication is that the real struggle against Communism
may still lie in the future. Indeed, it is all too tempting to succumb
to wishful thinking and to believe that with the end of colonialism
Southeast Asia will experience only a brief period of readjustment
before healthy societies emerge in which Communism will have no
place. Actually it seems more likely that the example of the modern
world will continue to inspire people to a new way of life which they
cannot find in their societies. Thus, the attraction of Communism to
some of these rootless people will persist.

The essential question is whether or not the peoples of Southeast
Asia will develop a more coherent form of political life which will
better express the needs of those who are now confused by the uncertainties of a changing world. At present, most of the non-Communist
political groups in Southeast Asia tend to belong to one of two distinct types. There are, first, the highly westernized and secularized
leaders who in spite of controlling governments often do not seem to
be able to communicate effectively with the less urbanized masses.
The issues and problems which absorb their attention at the national
level are only partially comprehended and appreciated by the population at large. The other type of political group does have a basis of
popular support, but they tend to be more than just political parties.
In practice they often resemble protective associations that provide
their membership with a sense of community and a way of looking
at life in general. Some of these are based on traditional or even
syncretic religions, as with the sects in south Viet-Nam; others represent
racial, ethnic or geographic communities. These groups may be able
to satisfy many of the needs of their membership, but usually they

find it difficult to gain a more universal appeal. (It might be added that in some respects the secularized national leadership in a few of the Southeast Asian countries is not too different from these groups since they find a sense of community in their spirit of nationalism, but they have as yet not been able to translate this spirit into terms that are meaningful in the daily lives of the common people.)

It is difficult to see how a political process composed mainly of these two rather extreme types of groups can give a country stability and strong defense against subversion. If, on the one hand, the current nationalist leadership in Southeast Asia can introduce a more programatic form of politics in which action and aspiration are brought into closer relationship, and if, on the other hand, more informal associations with limited political objectives can take care of the diffuse social and personal needs of the people, then there will be in the region far stronger alternatives to Communism than now exist. Given such alternatives that can better answer the social needs of the people and the political problems of their governments we can be confident that there will be far fewer people ready to turn to Communism. Should such a basic form of political development not take place then all the efforts to strengthen the economies and the formal administration of government in Southeast Asia may not be adequate for the task. The struggle against Communism in these countries is, then, essentially a matter of very fundamental political organization: How best can these countries organize their political life so as to cope with the diverse problems of both their individual citizens and their total societies?

Techniques of Communist aggression and the Moscow-Peking axis

RODGER SWEARINGEN

University of Southern California

It is characteristic that the immediate and ultimate objectives of international Communism often appear diametrically opposed. A further confusing contrast becomes evident when Communist propaganda of a given period is examined in the light of Communist actions. The existence of these two apparent contradictions makes it necessary to consider current techniques of Communist aggression in South and Southeast Asia within the framework of postwar Moscow-Peking strategy and within the context of the present Communist policy of "coexistence" and "collective peace."

The Western view of the need for collective security is based squarely upon a study of Soviet policies and upon the record of Soviet and Chinese Communist behavior to date. United States foreign policy, as we know, contrasts sharply with that of a number of South and Southeast Asian nations, notably India, Burma and Indonesia. Prime Minister Nehru recently pointed up this difference when, in Peking, he characterized the SATO Conference as an obstacle to peace "based like other such organizations on fear and military sanctions," which he said "adds to the element of apprehension and tension."[1]

---

[1] *People's China*, No. 16, 1954, p. 11. A characteristic editorial in *United Asia* (Bombay, Feb. 1955) says that while not questioning the honesty of Western intentions, since the Communists object so strenuously to SATO and to other Western military pacts, such pacts clearly augment fear and increase tension.

The difference in approach between the Western nations and several of the new nations of South and Southeast Asia may be attributed in part to a fundamental difference in assumptions regarding the nature of Soviet and Chinese Communist aims and policies. It would therefore seem useful at the outset to state the assumptions concerning Soviet and Chinese Communist theory and behavior which underlie this paper, assumptions which I dare say are shared by the majority of serious students of Soviet and Chinese Communist affairs:[2]

1. The Soviet and Chinese Communist leaders operate from identical fundamental Marxist-Leninist premises and rules of party organization and behavior. The Maoist strategy has been accepted by Moscow as valid for all of Asia, and Peking has assumed tactical control of the Asian Communist parties.

2. While the Peking regime thus occupies a strong political and tactical position in Asia, Communist China at present lacks the strategic underpinnings for major power status and is accordingly dependent in the military, economic and technological spheres on the Soviet Union.

3. Explosive tensions could very well develop between Moscow and Peking five or ten years from now, but the substantial evidence to date supports the assumption of a current close mutually advantageous working relationship between the two regimes.

4. Both the Soviets and the Chinese Communists remain convinced that sooner or later their system should and will triumph everywhere. Consequently, all of the present and any future non-Communist governments in South and Southeast Asia are regarded by Moscow and Peking as both nonpermanent and, in the long run, unacceptable.

5. The immediate tactical objectives of Communism in Asia, (a) removal of United States influence and power, (b) neutralization of the region and (c) destruction of the Western alliance, are related to the long-range goal which is control of the area, and in turn, of the world.

6. Neither the current Communist policy of "collective peace" nor

---

[2] Perhaps the best two single sources for documenting these assumptions are: Robert North, *Moscow and the Chinese Communists* (Stanford University Press, 1953), p. 306, and W. W. Rostow, *The Prospects for Communist China* (Cambridge-New York: Technology Press, MIT and John Wiley and Sons, Inc., 1954), p. 379.

the "five principles of co-existence" articulated last year represent essentially new concepts.

The techniques of Communist aggression in South and Southeast Asia have varied in direction and emphasis according to the strategy of the particular period. While the character of Communist propaganda and activity has differed from area to area in response to particular problems, three basic strategies—of Moscow-Peking origin— are identifiable during the postwar decade, 1945–1955:[3]

The "right" strategy, united front from above (up to 1947): In the absence of any degree of Soviet initiative, Communist policy in the immediate postwar years continued to reflect the wartime pattern of co-operation, essentially the old Comintern 1935 united front line. This strategy regarded imperialism and feudalism (or in Western countries, fascism) as the Communists' main enemies. Accordingly, a two-stage revolution was prescribed which called first for a bourgeois-democratic revolution to prepare the ground for the subsequent proletarian-social revolution. Throughout South and Southeast Asia for the first two postwar years independent Communist activity was played down. Communists co-operated with nationalist movements and sought to maneuver themselves into key positions in the new governments, national parties, labor unions and student groups. In India, the Communists followed the "right" strategy of attempting to unify the Congress party and Moslem League. In Indochina, a broad united front—the Lien Viet Front, or Viet-Nam League of National Union—was formed, with Ho Chi-Minh's Viet-Minh as only one, although the leading one, of many component parties and groups. The Indonesian Communists (PKI) adopted a policy of co-operation with "all organizations here and abroad whose principles are not against the PKI."[4]

This policy which persisted until near the end of 1947 was abandoned probably for four reasons: In the first place, all the colonial powers, except France, were making progress towards negotiated settle-

---

[3] For background, perspective, and additional bibliography see Max Beloff, *Soviet Policy in the Far East, 1944–1951* (London: Oxford Univ. Press, 1953), and John F. Cady, "Southeast Asia" in Huszar and Associates, *Soviet Power and Policy* (New York: Thomas Y. Crowell Company, 1955), pp. 498–535.

[4] Quoted in Shen Yu-Dai, *Peking, Moscow and the Communist Parties of Colonial Asia* (Center for International Studies, MIT, July 1954), pp. 167.

ments covering the nationalist demands, hence reducing the effectiveness of the united front appeal. Secondly, the projected United States Marshall Plan promised to bring stability to Europe, where economic chaos seemed more in the Communist interests. Thirdly, a change to a more militant, disruptive policy could serve both to deny strategic raw materials to the West and to slow down the economic and political stabilization of the Far Eastern area, particularly as Japan, with rice and foreign trade needs, re-emerged as a factor in the situation. Fourthly, as World War II faded more into the background, confronted by increasing firmness in Europe, the Soviet government perhaps found it possible and desirable to cast about for new soft spots, potential areas of advance. South and Southeast Asia offered increasingly attractive possibilities.

The "left" strategy, united front from below, armed insurrection (1948–1949): More active Soviet interest in South and Southeast Asia was first evidenced toward the end of 1947 in a speech by Zhdanov at the opening conference of the Cominform, in which he called for Communist support for the national liberation movements.[5] This was followed by an article by Zhukov in *Bolshevik* emphasizing the same theme.[6] Mao Tse-tung, after praising the purposes and power of the Soviet bloc, asserting that "the superiority is already with us," and noting the significance of developments in Europe, told the Central Committee of the Communist party of China, December 25, 1947: "All anti-imperialist forces of the various eastern countries should also unite to oppose the oppression of imperialism and the reactionaries within each country, taking as the objective of their struggle the liberation of the more than a billion oppressed peoples of the East."[7] This new policy was discussed at the Calcutta Youth Congress in February 1948, and the following month the new "left" line was confirmed by the Second Congress of the Communist party of India.[8]

[5] *For a Lasting Peace, For a People's Democracy,* Nov. 10, 1947.

[6] *Bolshevik,* December 15, 1947.

[7] Mao Tse-tung on "The Present Situation and Our Tasks" to the Central Committee of the Communist Party of China, December 25, 1947, published in English under the title *Turning Point in China* (New York, New Century Publishers, 1948), p. 23.

[8] John H. Kautsky, *Moscow and the Communist Party of India: A Study in the Postwar Evolution of Communist Strategy* (Center for International Studies, MIT, October, 1954).

The Moscow "left" strategy considers capitalism and the native bourgeoisie enemies at least as important as imperialism and feudalism. Accordingly, the concept of the need for a bourgeois-democratic revolution was dropped in favor of an early socialist revolution, a "united front from below," and direct action.

Throughout South and Southeast Asia, Communists abandoned their earlier practice of co-operation with the non-Communist left; leaders of the nationalist parties were denounced as traitors to their followers and within six months of the announced change, terrorism and insurrections began or were intensified in India, Burma, Malaya, Indonesia, Indochina and the Philippines.[9]

It appears, however, that in the call for the abandonment of the "right" strategy, the Moscow planning staff was in fact undecided whether the old "left" strategy of the Comintern period or a version of Maoism should be authorized. This issue remained in doubt until 1949.[10] What was clear and significant, however, was Moscow's call for a switch away from the moderate, united front from above and the subsequent response of the Asian Communist parties to this call.

The Maoist strategy, 1950–1955: Moscow was clearly impressed and possibly even surprised by the swiftness of the Communist victory in China. After several hints had appeared in the Soviet press that Maoism would be authorized for all of Asia,[11] the Peking WFTU Conference of November 1949 proclaimed that the use of the Maoist strategy was now obligatory for all Asian Communist parties, defining it as inclusion of sections of the bourgeoisie in the united front, while authorizing the use of armed force only "wherever and whenever possible."[12]

Like the Moscow "right" strategy, Maoist strategy considers imperialism and feudalism its main enemies and prescribes a two-stage revolution, but like the Moscow "left" strategy, it seeks a united front from

[9] The implications of the new line were noted early by Milton Sacks in "The Strategy of Communism in Southeast Asia," *Pacific Affairs,* Sept. 1950. More detail and documentation by area is given in Shen-Yu-Dai, *op. cit.*

[10] Discussed in Kautsky, *op cit.*

[11] *Pravda* in June 1949, for example, published the Liu Shao-chi statement that all Asian parties must co-operate with sections of the bourgeoisie.

[12] The Conference is discussed and a number of quotations appear in Sacks, *op. cit.* See also article in *New Times* (Moscow) Nov. 30, 1949.

below. Its principal innovations are the four-class appeal and its military doctrine, both of which are employed with considerable flexibility. The Communists in this formulation are represented as the champions of not only the proletariat and the peasantry, but of the petty-bourgeoisie and the small and middle capitalist as well, although the latter two groups are assigned an inferior and frankly temporary role. Further, in cases where a non-Communist party is regarded as sufficiently anti-American and pro-Soviet, temporary cooperation with it may be encouraged as useful to the cause. Maoism's other aspect, the formula for armed struggle, prescribed creation of a guerrilla force drawn mainly from the peasantry with a geographical base in the countryside from which it can operate and expand until strong enough to confront and defeat the enemy's main force.

Adherence to the four-class formula, or peaceful Maoism, was prescribed in April 1951 in a statement by the Indian Communist party (CPI) which specifically rejected the Chinese model of peasant guerrilla warfare for the CPI (though not the principle of violence itself). The new policy was underlined by an appropriate change in party leadership and by a CPI directive ending fighting in Telengana. At a session of the Soviet Academy of Science, in November 1951, Zhukov stated explicitly that India could not now follow the Chinese model of armed struggle but should adhere instead to the four-class strategy.[13] A similar shift to peaceful Maoism occurred in Indonesia, Pakistan and Ceylon between 1951 and 1953.[14] The program of the Burmese Communists and their front groups since 1950 has shown increased emphasis on "peace" and co-operation, a strategy which has been characterized by one competent observer as "100 percent Maoist."[15] The Communist party of Thailand is comprised mostly of Chinese, who have remained relatively quiet, but clearly look to Communist China for guidance.

In Indochina, Malaya and the Philippines, the Maoist armed struggle strategy has been employed since 1950 although in the cases of

---

[13] Documentation and detail may be found in Kautsky, *op. cit.*, pp. 240–350.

[14] See, for example, Ruth Thomas McVey, *The Development of the Indonesian Communist Party and its Relations with the Soviet Union and with the Chinese People's Republic* (Cambridge, Center for International Studies, Massachusetts Institute of Technology, July 16, 1954).

[15] Shen Yu-Dai, *op. cit.*, p. 29.

both Malaya and the Philippines observers have noted decreasing militant activity since 1952 probably due to a combination of the Communist united front, coexistence, peace line and the increasing effectiveness of Malayan and Philippine government measures.[16]

It may be significant that the "liberation army" strategy has proved most successful in Indochina—a colonial area where French policy has not been particularly enlightened, a region with strong historical and cultural ties and a common frontier with China. The same strategy has been less successful in Malaya—also a colonial area, but one where British policy has been somewhat more flexible and enlightened, where a fundamental antagonism has existed between the Malays and the local Chinese, and an area which is a considerable distance from either of the main centers of international Communism. Communist strategy of armed struggle has been least effective, one might even say has been a failure, in the Philippines—an independent nation with a less painful colonial background and an enlightened government of its own which fully understands both the Communist threat and its appeal, and accordingly has dealt firmly with Communist terrorism and espionage and wisely with some of the Philippines' basic social and economic problems. The Philippine archipelago has, of course, the added strategic advantage of being isolated from Communist China by an expanse of the ocean.

When this formula is applied to the political and propaganda scene, one important exception must be noted. While an unhappy colonial background, lack of enlightened social and economic policy and the absence of a realistic appraisal of Communist intentions and tactics may have a direct relationship to the degree of Communist support in a given area, proximity to Communist China is not necessarily an advantage. The degree of enthusiasm and support for Communist China among the Chinese in Hong Kong, with close and regular contacts across the border, appears for example, considerably less than in more distant Indonesia or India, with controlled or limited contacts

---

[16] Documented and illustrated in Bernard B. Fall, *The Viet-Minh Regime* (Ithaca: Cornell University, issued jointly with the Institute of Pacific Relations, April 1954) ; Harry Miller, *The Communist Menace in Malaya* (New York: Frederick A. Praeger, 1954) ; Gene Z. Hanrahan, *The Communist Struggle in Malaya* (New York, Institute of Pacific Relations, 1954) ; and Carlos P. Romulo, *Crusade in Asia* (New York, The John Day Company, 1955).

with mainland China. Most observers agree that this can be explained, in large part, by the greater availability in Hong Kong of factual information on Communist China.

Communist propaganda may be expected to reach maximum effectiveness in Asia during the current phase of "coexistence" and "collective peace." Compared with the Western concept of "collective security," the Communist's policy of "collective peace" is the more dynamic and appealing formulation. Last year Communist China buttressed this policy with five principles of coexistence, which were first enunciated in the Indian-Chinese agreement on Tibet and have found wide approval in Burma, Indonesia and elsewhere in Asia. They are: (1) mutual respect for each other's territorial integrity and sovereignty, (2) nonaggression, (3) noninterference in each other's internal affairs, (4) equality and mutual benefits and (5) peaceful coexistence.

Again, history lends a certain perspective to such a development and gives one the uneasy feeling that he has been through this, perhaps in a slightly different version, at least once before. On the eve of one of the earlier Soviet shifts to a policy of coexistence in the nineteen thirties, a similar international Communist policy was articulated. At that time, it will be recalled, the Soviet leaders most of all desired peace, coexistence, mutual assistance and allies. The Litvinov note to President Roosevelt on the establishment of relations between the USSR and the United States, dated November 16, 1933, affords a model for the five principles of 1954–55.

The main lines of the current Chinese Communist "collective peace" campaign were laid down by Chou En-lai in his report on the Geneva Conference and Chinese Communist foreign policy to the Thirty-third Session of the Central Committee of the Chinese Communist Party. The significant points may be summarized as follows: (1) It is necessary to shatter the design of United States aggressive circles if peace and security in Asia are to be safeguarded; (2) If any of the nations concerned (in the Geneva Conference) should join the United States in (its) divisive activities (SATO, etc.) then the peace in Indochina would be endangered, for it is only possible to achieve the progressive relaxation of international tension provided all countries and peoples stand firmly against war and against the formation of antagonistic military blocs; (3) The Geneva Conference demonstrated that international disputes can be settled by the peaceful means of negotiation;

(4) The conciliatory spirit displayed by France and the United Kingdom at the Geneva Conference and the efforts made by the Colombo powers, notably India, in promoting the conclusion of an armistice in Indochina also contributed to its achievements. During the Conference an improvement was brought about in relations between the People's Republic of China and the United Kingdom. Such an improvement will help to increase the possibilities of establishing normal relations between China and the countries of the West; and (5) The part played by the People's Republic of China in the Geneva Conference has been universally recognized and can by no means be brushed aside by the United States aggressive circles.[17]

The manner in which these themes are elaborated in Soviet propaganda may be illustrated by two current, characteristic formulations. An *Izvestia* item of January 29, 1955 entitled "Malicious Violators of Geneva Agreements" is notable for managing to pack many of the principal themes and most of the Far East into a few lines, which charge that the United States intends to disrupt the Geneva agreements and points out that the reason for this is well known: "the U. S. A.," it charges, "wants to turn Ngo Dinh Diem into a Vietnamese Chiang Kai-shek, and Saigon into a new Formosa . . . with the hope of setting up in Indochina a sort of South Korea." In other words, the article concludes, "aggressive U. S. circles, with the obvious help of French ruling circles, are seeking to turn the Indochinese states into a springboard for preparing a war against the peace-loving peoples of Asia." The same approach has a positive, economic counterpart. An article in *Pravda* of March 14, 1955 entitled "Cooperation on Basis of Equality and Mutual Benefit" begins by pointing out that "Trade with the Chinese People's Republic is of great importance in the foreign trade development of underdeveloped countries. Despite obstacles raised by U. S. ruling circles, China is trading extensively on the basis of equality and mutual benefit with other countries, including India, Indonesia, Burma, Ceylon and Pakistan . . . . The U.S.S.R. and People's democracies, while giving underdeveloped countries technical aid are not interfering in their domestic affairs . . . ." This is then followed by an attack on the Colombo plan which is characterized as designed

---

[17] *People's China,* supplement, Sept. 1, 1954.

to "preserve the colonial nature of the countries" and concluded with the usual charges against United States aid.

In a word, peace and prosperity in South and Southeast Asia can be assured, we are told, only by the removal of the United States from the scene and by co-operation of all the peoples of South and Southeast Asia with the Soviet Union and Communist China, or at the very least, a kind of Southern Asian benevolent neutrality. Except for the difficulty one may encounter in dismissing as suddenly inapplicable the whole vast literature of Marxist-Leninist-Maoist theory and strategy, the impressive record of past actions and similar tactical lines, or certain contradictory, current Communist activities, Communist offers of collective peace and coexistence sound acceptable enough—indeed, they sound quite attractive.

We cannot, of course, rule out the possibility that fear of nuclear war and the evident military strength of the free world may be producing a genuine change in Soviet and Chinese Communist attitudes, approaches and long-range policy. In view of the past record and until present Communist actions conform on all levels more closely to current Communist talk, however, the presumption of a change in tactics rather than a change in attitude or objectives is still the more compelling logic.

Among current techniques of Communist aggression in Asian regions the following may be mentioned: (1) open political activity; (2) penetration and mobilization of groups and organizations; (3) cultural offensive; (4) diplomatic maneuvers; and (5) use of armed aggression and subversion.

(1) *Open Political Activity*. Since the world-wide switch to peaceful coexistence and the united front line, open political activity has been an increasingly important Communist technique in areas where the party enjoys legal status. The aims and tactics of this political strategy are not new to students of French politics and of the eastern European scene nor to anyone familiar with Mao Tse-tung's work *On Coalition Government*.[18] In South and Southeast Asia, the Communists are concentrating their propaganda and political activity on India, Indonesia

---

[18] A good brief summary of the latter is contained in Brandt, Schwartz and Fairbank, *A Documentary History of Chinese Communism* (London: Allen and Unwin, 1953).

and Indochina. The Communist party does not enjoy legal status in Thailand, the Philippines, Malaya or Burma, and it was recently outlawed in Pakistan. Ceylon is small and of somewhat less long-range strategic significance. Indochina represents a special case as a consequence of the Geneva Conference agreements. The Communists hope to be able to display the election results of 1956 as convincing evidence of popular support in Asia for their cause. It is regrettable that the West should have been forced into a critical test at this time in perhaps the only area in the free world where Communism stands a chance of considerable support in a free election.

In India, the importance the Communists have come to attach to the political weapon is reflected in the original policy statement of the Indian Communist party which, in 1950, after the switch to peaceful Maoism, laid down the new line. It instructed the party to throw all its resources into "parliamentary elections and elections in every sphere where the broad strata of people can be mobilized and their interests defended." We must, the directive emphasized "be whatever the masses are and (whatever they) would like us to be."[19] That this policy is still employed despite recent Communist setbacks in India is apparent from a statement issued by the Central Committee of the party on March 30, 1955 in which the Communist defeat in the Andhra elections is described as "a political defeat for the Party" attributable in part to a failure to emphasize sufficiently "the important part India was playing in recent times in the international arena in favor of world peace and against warmongers."[20] Prime Minister Nehru, it needs to be emphasized, has dealt firmly and with increasing effectiveness with the Indian Communists. Perhaps, in part, for sound political reasons, however, he has seen fit to maintain a certain distinction between domestic and international communism, between the Soviet Union and China. In his speech on January 15, 1955 in Vijayawada before the Andhra elections he said that "we cooperate with . . . and have no grievance against . . . the great countries in the world which are following the Communist doctrine." Then he added, "But how can our

[19] *Statement of policy*, May 1951 quoted in Madhu Limaye, "Indian Communism: The New Phase," *Pacific Affairs*, September 1954.

[20] *New York Times*, March 31, 1955. Details of Congress and Communist party policies and campaigns as well as the election results may be found in Marshall Windmiller, "The Andhra Election," *Far Eastern Survey*, April 1955.

country progress if our people (i.e., the Communists) continually curse this country and always praise other countries?"[21] At the same time, Nehru permitted U. N. Dhebar, his hand-picked President of the National Congress party, to say at Callapalli within the month: "The Communists have two sets of programs . . . . Their real motive is to establish Russian sovereignty in this country . . . . Everyone knows now that their loyalties are extra-territorial . . . . Once you vote the Communists to power," he concluded, "that will be the last election you will be called upon to participate in. A totalitarian state will be established and individual liberty will have come to an end."[22] Two intriguing points emerge here: the exclusion of any reference to the possibility of an attempt to establish Chinese Communist sovereignty in India, when Nehru and the Congress party are, of course, aware of the switch by the Indian Communists to Maoism; and Nehru's specific characterization of Communist China as following the Communist doctrine followed by Dhebar's characterization of such a nation as a totalitarian state where individual liberty has come to an end. One suspects that Nehru may be playing a more sophisticated game than is suggested by the remarks of his Western critics. It may also be a more dangerous game than he and his supporters realize.

The use and effectiveness of Communist political activity in Pakistan can be illustrated by the 1954 elections in East Bengal where a united front (including the Communist party and two "Communist fronts") defeated the Muslim League, Pakistan's ruling party since 1947. It has been estimated that between 50 and 60 of the Muslim seats alone (from a total of 237) are held by Communist or pro-Communist members. Ten seats reserved for minorities went to Communists.[23] Such a pro-Communist bloc, while a minority in the Parliament and not decisive, is in a strategic propaganda position and further is not likely to be ignored by a coalition leadership in constant need of support.

It is in Indonesia, however, that the Communist united front strategy has been the most successful. Since its collapse following the abortive Madiun rebellion of 1948 and its subsequent relapse when the govern-

[21] Quoted in Windmiller, *op. cit.*

[22] *Ibid.*

[23] Richard L. Park, "East Bengal: Pakistan's Troubled Province," *The Far Eastern Survey*, May 1954.

ment moved against the Communists in 1951, the Communist party has grown from less than 10,000 members to several hundred thousand (the party claims half a million members). Communists hold a strategic position in the Indonesian Parliament, in which the balance of forces is precarious and where Communist opposition might, almost at any time, bring about the downfall of the government. Current Indonesian foreign policy generally follows the Indian pattern.

(2) *Penetration and Mobilization of Groups and Organizations.* Closely related to open political activity, is the more devious, often underground, attempt to penetrate, influence and control critical groups and organizations. As this Communist technique is well known, it may suffice here to record one or two comments or illustrations of such activity with respect to the overseas Chinese, labor organizations, and educational institutions and student groups.

South and Southeast Asian Chinese form five-sixths of the near twelve and one-half million Chinese living abroad. They comprise a substantial share of the population in many of the countries of Southeast Asia. Normally they maintain dual citizenship. They dominate the commercial activity of many of these countries and have traditional cultural and political ties with China. It is not surprising, therefore, that Peking has devoted considerable effort and expense to secure their co-operation and loyalty. Bureaus for overseas Chinese are maintained at Peking, and in Hainan and in several South China provinces. Chinese Communist organizational and propaganda organs for the overseas Chinese are larger and more efficient than any comparable Kuomintang machinery. In addition to the standard organizational and propaganda techniques, methods include appeals to Chinese pride and nationalism, offers of educational opportunities and business futures in China, the championing of their cause against the "discrimination" of the local government, indoctrination of the students in Chinese schools, pressure on the overseas Chinese business enterprises, "squeeze" in the form of the celebrated "letters from home" and outright threats and intimidation.[24] Any attempt to evaluate Peking's success to date on the basis of currently available data may be mis-

[24] Two very useful, recent summaries of Peking policy toward the overseas Chinese may be found in Virginia Thompson and Richard Adloff, *Minority Problems in Southeast Asia* (Stanford, California: Stanford University Press, 1955), and John F. Cady, "Southeast Asia" in Huzar and Associates, *op. cit.*

leading. In general, however, the overseas Chinese appear to have swung back somewhat away from the active interest in the "New China" that characterized the months following the establishment of the Chinese People's Republic and subsequent Burmese, Indian, Indonesian and British recognition of the Peking government. This may be attributed to some of the Communist methods noted above, several of which backfired, and to a degree of disillusionment resulting from the increasing number of unfavorable reports reaching Southeast Asia from friends and relatives in, or recently out of, Communist China. It seems certain that one of the objectives of the new collective peace, co-existence line is to reverse this trend.

Current Communist strategy in the labor field in South and Southeast Asia works simultaneously on four groups: the labor leadership, the rank and file industrial worker, selected leaders of political parties (particularly the socialist parties) and the government. It has not been entirely successful. In most of the areas the labor movement is split down the middle with the main force in the non-Communist camp. Combination tactics of infiltration, skillful propaganda, the use of the socialists and pressure on the government have been devised in an attempt to redress that balance. The All-India Trade Union Congress (AITUC), for example, claims a membership of 758,314, is run by the Communists, but is only the third largest of Indian's union confederations. The importance of the labor union as a political weapon may be suggested by the fact that the AITUC is strongest in Bengal and very strong in Madras, the two areas where the Communist party has shown the greatest popular support.[25] On the other hand, it is certain that Communist influence on labor increases to the degree that the political environment is favorable, that the opposition is weak, that party tactics are adapted to the local scene and that the scope and urgency of basic socio-economic problems as well as the political consciousness (to borrow the Communist term) of the people exceeds the ability of the government and of private enterprises to meet their demands. Thus, in Indonesia, Communist influence on labor appears to be considerably stronger than in Malaya, Thailand or the Philippines.

[25] Oscar Ornati, "Indian Trade Unions Since Independence," *Far Eastern Survey*, August 1954.

Perhaps some special comment is in order regarding Communist work in the farm and fishing villages. Village penetration, including appeals to the daily needs of the peasants and support for their grievances, has proved a formidable weapon in the hands of the Communists and one which the West has found most difficult to deal with.

That the Communists are active in the schools and wherever intellectuals gather, that the penetration tactics extend to other groups, other areas and other peoples of South and Southeast Asia can scarcely be doubted by anyone familiar with Communist methods or with the Southeast Asian scene.[26]

(3) *Cultural Offensive.* Standing between domestic political activity and diplomatic maneuvers, helpful in producing a favorable reception for both, is an extensive cultural relations program directed from Moscow and Peking. Although the attention of the Communists has so far been focused primarily on the so-called neutralist bloc it may be significant that Chou En-lai, at Bandung, extended an invitation to the representatives of all the nations present to visit Communist China. Cultural activity has included propaganda, missions to and from Moscow and Peking, industrial exhibitions, cultural fairs, film shows and lectures, all designed to impress the South and Southeast Asians with the cultural depth, industrial progress, and peaceful intentions of the Soviet Union and Communist China.

Perhaps two hundred Indians have visited Communist China—diplomats, editors, journalists, university professors, outstanding Indian women and trade union leaders. The influence of their reports, generally favorable and widely read is out of all proportion to their relatively small numbers. Professor C. Martin Wilbur who recently studied the problem writes: "I have read every account I could lay hands on and talked with nearly a score of Indians who have taken this grand tour of China during the last few years. One thing is clear: The Chinese know how to be good hosts."[27] The number of Burmese visitors *People's China* tells us "has grown with each passing year. They come," it adds "from all walks of life—workers, young people, women,

[26] For a personalized account which contains a good deal of material on this topic see Walter C. Eells, *Communism in Education in Asia, Africa and the Far Pacific* (Washington, D. C.: American Council on Education, 1954).

[27] C. Martin Wilbur, "Mao's Paradise" as seen from India, *The Reporter*, May 19, 1955.

Buddhist priests and peace-loving people."[28] A few years ago pro-Communist groups in Burma organized a delegation to the Moscow International Trade Conference, returning with accounts of Russia's great industrial progress. Emphasis more recently has been on China.

Cultural activity is institutionalized by the standard technique of friendship associations. The character of these organizations is reflected in the membership of the Indonesian-China Friendship Association which was established in January, 1955. Among those who were present at the organizational meeting were Professor Prijono, International Stalin Peace Prize Winner and vice-chairman of the Indonesian Peace Committee and Tjan Tjoesom, Dean of the School of Sinology, University of Indonesia, who returned recently from a trip to Peking as a "guest of the Chinese people."

China also employs cultural delegations to carry its story into South and Southeast Asia: a group of Chinese scholars attended the Baroda Science Conference at New Year's; a troupe of performers toured India last winter; exhibits of arts and crafts from Communist China have been shown around India and Burma, while a similar exhibition held recently in Djakarta and subsequently in Jogjakarta, Surabaya and Medan, Indonesia, is reported to have attracted thousands. In a visit of an Indonesian art group to Communist China in August of 1954, on the other hand, the Chinese audience—we are told—saw "not only the richness and color of Indonesian art but the spirit of the Indonesian people—the spirit in which they waged their dogged fight against all oppressors and their struggle for freedom and peace."[29] Cultural propaganda of this kind fills the pages of *People's China* and the local Communist and Communist front publications in articles bearing such titles as "An Old Friendship Renewed—A Review of Sino-Burmese Relations"[30] or simply "Chinese-Indonesian Friendship."[31]

What the Indians, the Burmese and the Indonesians know about Communist China has come almost exclusively through these two channels: Communist propaganda machinery and reports brought back from visitors who have been taken on guided tours through China as guests of "the Chinese people." News coverage of Communist China in the

28 *People's China*, May 16, 1955.
29 *People's China*, March 16, 1955.
30 *People's China*, January 1, 1955.
31 *People's China*, March 16, 1955.

Indian, Indonesian and Burmese press is sketchy and one-sided. Newspapers of the region generally rely on the Communist press services
for news from mainland China. No systematic use is made of the
Hong Kong listening post and there is a tendency to regard Western
accounts, when they are unfavorable to Communist China or to the
Soviet Union, as mere propaganda.

(4) *Diplomatic Maneuvers*

(a) *Conference Diplomacy:* Apart from constant Soviet pressure
at the United Nations for the admittance of Communist China and
the use of that body for the general promotion of Communist interests
in South and Southeast Asia, the high point in the effectiveness of
conference diplomacy as a technique of Communist aggression was
reached at the recent Geneva and Bandung Conferences.

Undersecretary of State Walter Bedell Smith observed wisely that
when we analyze and discuss the results of the Geneva Conference it
is well to remember that "diplomacy has rarely gained at the conference
table what cannot be gained or held on the battlefield."[32] The Communists, aware of French weakness and apparently counting on British
and United States inability or unwillingness to meet the challenge
with collective action, applied maximum military force to coincide
with their diplomatic offensive. Reduced to strategic components, the
resulting Geneva agreements afford the Communists an opportunity to
(1) consolidate their power north of the 17th parallel, (2) effectively
block the Three Associated States from organizing a system of collective
security, (3) provide a three-nation neutral commission which favors
the Communist position since besides Canada the other two members
are Poland, a Soviet-controlled government, and India, which is on
record as against the concept of collective security, against United
States policy in Asia and anxious to keep on good terms with Communist China, (4) impress the Asians by the demonstrated ability of
Communist China to deal with the West on its own terms, (5) exploit
the theme that all questions should and can be settled, as at the
Geneva Conference, by peaceful negotiations, and (6) test the formidable proposition that resentment against the French, the popular appeal
of Ho Chi-minh's regime, growing prestige of Communist China, weakness and difficulty of the Diem regime, and intensive campaigning by

[32] *The New York Times,* July 24, 1954.

infiltration and propaganda will be sufficient to give the Communists a victory at the polls in 1956.[33]

After the more fanciful interpretations of Communist China's objectives and strategy at the Bandung Conference have been examined, it is difficult to escape returning to the simple conclusion that Chou En-lai's principal mission there was, in fact, revealed when he said that his delegation had come to Bandung "to seek unity and not to quarrel." Chou's charming manner and moderation throughout the conference lent credence to his portrayal of Communist China as peace-loving, entirely reasonable, and anxious to develop its relations with all nations on the basis of the five principles of collective peace. Chou struck a quiet blow at collective security and at United States policy in Asia when he said that Communist China would not "by one inch transgress on the territory of any other country," and then plunged the conference into an excited state of optimism on the final day by stating, "Communist China is willing to sit down with the United States Government to discuss the question of relaxing tensions in the Formosa area."[34]

Bandung, which Mr. Nehru called the "temporary capital of Africa and Asia," offered an ideal setting for further excursions into the realm of personal diplomacy. Chet Huntley, who was there as one of the few accredited correspondents from the United States, described Mr. Nehru as hosting Mr. Chou about at the conference and saying to his fellow Asians in effect, "Look here, this is a fellow we can get along with if only we try."[35] The *Nippon Times* pictured Chou as "courting Japan's chief delegate Tatsunosuke Takasaki," meeting with him for private talks, and "to the apparent dismay of his bodyguards marching across the street or room to approach Takasaki personally."[36]

(b) *Personal Diplomacy:* One does not have to be cynical to suggest that Chou En-lai's interest in promoting closer personal relations with Prime Minister Nehru and Mr. Krishna Menon of India or Premier U Nu of Burma or Mr. Takasaki of Japan is politically motivated. Four important points immediately come to mind with respect to

---

[33] "Geneva Conference on Indochina Concluded—Text of Final Declaration," *Department of State Bulletin*, 31:162, August 2, 1954.

[34] *New York Times*, April 24, 1955.

[35] Speech to the World Affairs Council, Biltmore Hotel, Los Angeles, May 31, 1955.

[36] *Nippon Times*, April 24, 1955.

India's special significance in Communist strategy: first, India is regularly a member of various neutral commissions; secondly, India is an important voice at international conferences and throughout South and Southeast Asia; thirdly, India's influence on British policy appears considerable; and fourthly, India has at times been outspokenly anti-Western and critical of the United States.

A careful reading of the "Communiqué on Talks Between the Chinese and Burmese Premiers in Peking," dated December 12, 1954, suggests the manner in which personal diplomacy relates to other aspects of Communist policy in the area, especially economic penetration, which might well be given separate treatment. Reaffirming the five principles of peaceful coexistence and pledging friendly co-operation between their two countries, the two premiers agreed that consulates-general should be mutually established in appropriate cities and hoped that this would be realized in the near future. Economic and cultural intercourse between the two countries, they said, would be increased and nationality and boundary questions could be amicably settled through normal diplomatic channels. Finally, after expressing their profound interest in the consolidation and enlargement of the area of peace, the two premiers held that "all countries were entitled to national independence and prosperity, free from foreign interference and aggression."[37]

It is a curious thing that amid the shattered dreams and demonstrated hypocrisy of the twentieth century, great men of faith and good will can still find it possible to say, as Premier U Nu said in Peking on December 2, 1954, "As our countries have agreed to the 'five principles' I have no doubt that peaceful coexistence is assured."[38] It is possible—and I have long suspected it to be the case—that the West underestimates the degree of sophistication of many of the Asian leaders.

(5) *Use of Open Armed Aggression and Subversion.* Three times before since the adoption of the Maoist strategy and despite assurances of peaceful intentions, the Communists have resorted to large-scale armed aggression in Asia: first, in Korea where they were repulsed by United Nations' collective military action; secondly, in Tibet, where they were met by the strongest possible protests from the Indian

[37] "Communique on Talks Between Chinese and Burmese Premiers and Other Documents," Supplement to *People's China*, January 1, 1955, p. 3.
[38] *Ibid.*, p. 8.

government, but were unopposed on the ground and hence occupied
the area; thirdly, in Indochina, where the Communist-led Viet-Minh
forces with organizational and logistic support from the Chinese Communists fought and maneuvered the French into an untenable position
resulting in the Geneva agreements.

What are the possibilities of a fourth resort to the technique of
aggression by armed force or insurrection on the part of the Communist bloc in Asia? In areas which do not have a common border
with Communist China or Viet-Nam a switch back to the militant
policy of the 1948–49 period seems immediately unlikely for several
reasons. In the cases of India, Pakistan, Ceylon and Indonesia the
military policy proved largely unproductive and damaging to the party.
What is perhaps more important is the fact that in all of these areas
the situation may be characterized as developing relatively satisfactorily from the perspective of Moscow or Peking, either in terms of
the influence and potential of the local Communist party and its front
organizations (Pakistan and Ceylon) or the foreign policy orientation
of the national government (India), or both, as in the case of Indonesia. In Malaya and the Philippines, as noted, the situations have
now been stabilized and Communist policy has shifted so that further
successful Communist insurrection does not appear an immediate
threat. This leaves the Indochina-Thailand-Burma region where two
developing situations must be noted.

Ho Chi-minh's forces have already taken over North Viet-Nam without in fact relinquishing much of the effective control they had over
large pockets of territory south of the 17th parallel. The Diem regime
faces critical political, economic and security problems, including
armed insurrection on the part of several religious groups with their
own armies. Long pacified provinces in South Viet-Nam are again
subject to strong Viet-Minh infiltration and in some districts the
population is reported openly to have recourse to Viet-Minh tribunals
or administrative officials, whose chances of enforcing a decision are
far better than those of local South Vietnamese government authorities.
Contrary to expectations, even the mass evacuation of anti-Communist
refugees from north to south has proved a doubtful propaganda weapon
for the West. Many Viet-Minh agents are believed to have accompanied
the refugees and appear to have instigated riots in the refugee camps.
The relocation of the refugees has severely taxed the already weak and
chaotic Vietnamese administration. The Diem government's own in-

formation bulletin *Viet-Nam*, published in France, acknowledges the seriousness of the situation by reprinting excerpts of French newspaper articles showing that the southern administration is being undermined by what the bulletin terms the "fifth column."[39] Persistent reports suggest that the French may have already worked out a secret deal with North Viet-Nam which would permit the Communists to take over the whole area.[40] In short, the Viet-Minh regime, with Chinese Communist assistance, appears to be maneuvering into a position where, should the elections fail to come off, or prove unsatisfactory, a locally inspired insurrection plus Viet-Minh assistance, could bring the country under Communist control. If such military action should occur, the Communists might adopt the Soviet Korean war strategy of standing clear, supplying the Communists with weapons and technical advice, while professing a benevolent neutrality based this time on the five principles.

Mention must also be made of the autonomous units of the south Chinese border region. A "Liberation Government of Laos" was set up in 1950 and its successor, the Pathetlao, was established in the northeast corner of the country in March 1951. The Chinese Communists have sponsored the creation of other so-called autonomous units such as the "Tai Nationality Autonomous People's Government" and the "Free Kachin State," in 1953, and the "Free Karen State," in 1954, along the southern border region to serve both as propaganda and cadre training centers and as bases from which, quite conceivably, attacks could be launched into Burma, Laos, Cambodia and Thailand in the name of liberation. In July 1954 Peking Radio broadcast an article allegedly written in the Chinese Communist capital by a former premier of Thailand, Pridi Banomyong, calling upon the Thai people to "wage a struggle against their rulers" whom he specified to be the American capitalists and their puppets, the government of Thailand.[41] Intensive and extensive railway construction in China's south and southwest border regions as well as the fact that on the official

---

[39] Developed in more detail in Bernard B. Fall, "Indochina Since Geneva," *Pacific Affairs*, March 1955.

[40] For the most substantial of several such reports see Gordon Walker, "Paris, Vietnam Reds Form Secret Pact," *The Christian Science Monitor*, May 5, 1955.

[41] These and related developments in the areas on Communist China's southern frontier are discussed in detail and documented in the excellent new work by Thompson and Adloff, *op. cit.*

map of the Chinese People's Republic published in November, 1954, China's southwestern border is shown as still "in dispute" or "unsettled" adds a further disquieting note. It will be recalled that Viet-Minh forces did, in fact, invade Laos in the spring of 1953 and again in 1954, only to withdraw both times under somewhat mysterious and as yet unexplained circumstances. By skillful propaganda and the work of agents who remained behind, the Communists were able to build up "Viet-Minhized" zones, which by early 1954 were reported to have covered probably one-third of the whole country. The Pathetlao were permitted by the Geneva agreements to keep the two northern provinces, contiguous to Viet-Minh territory.

Upon one of his recent returns from Asia, on March 8, 1955, Secretary of State Dulles stated that subversion was the greatest danger to the area. To illustrate the connection between direct and indirect aggression he, then, noted the situation in Laos. "The Laos Government," he said, "is seeking to reestablish control over its own territory. But it is worried lest, if it suppresses the Communists within, it will be struck by the Communists from without.[42]

The fact that the current Communist approach emphasizes coexistence and collective peace does not, in and of itself, eliminate the possibility of direct or indirect aggression, since all armed hostilities in which the Communists participate are characterized as either "defensive wars of resistance" or "liberation struggles." Nevertheless, a return to militant tactics or use of further armed aggression in the immediate future seems unlikely for two reasons: one, the relative effectiveness of the Communists' current foreign and domestic policies in several key areas in Asia and; two, the significance to the Communists of a possible victory at the polls in Viet-Nam in 1956. In suggesting this conclusion I am aware, of course, that a well-known Far Eastern correspondent wrote, two weeks before the North Korean attack: "Fears of an invasion have subsided . . . . There now is little apprehension about open war between the two halves of the dismembered country."[43]

[42] John Foster Dulles "Report from Asia," Department of State Press Release No. 131, March 8, 1955. See also John Kerry King, "Thailand's Bureaucracy and the Threat of Communist Subversion, *Far Eastern Survey*, Nov. 1954.

[43] *Nippon Times*, June 10, 1950.

Western influence and Asian opinion

CHARLES A. H. THOMSON

The Brookings Institution

I

During the past fifteen years, there has been increasing recognition among students of public opinion as well as key figures in the articulation and execution of government policies and actions, that the world of opinion-manipulation or measurement is but a sub-world of a larger field of action; yet the beliefs and practices of government officials still tend to divide action into spheres of deeds and of words. Those preoccupied with deeds arrogate most influence and prestige to their part of the total; the wordmongers play lesser roles. Yet the doers are far from insensitive to what is said about what they do, being even more concerned with their image in the opinions of others, domestic or foreign, than with the image which governmentally oriented wordmongers attempt to form and circulate about them and their actions. These interrelations are often cloaked and complex; they nevertheless play important roles in the development of government policy and functions. They seem easier to deal with when the main lines of the context are European, since so much of the heritage of the United States stems from Europe. The problems involving Asian politics and public opinion are more difficult for Americans to manage.

The purpose of this essay is to contribute to the clarification of these reciprocal interrelationships between Western efforts to exercise influence in Asia, and the responses expressed in overt Asian opinion. The Asia dealt with here is the arc bounded by India and Japan, including China in its curve; the interaction of opinion and influence in the Middle East and in Russian Asia is not considered.

There is no effort to sketch a working model of those deep-reaching historical roots of Western influence on Asia, whether castigated as imperialism (Communist or other), justified as the white man's burden, or described, in current fashion, as a struggle for power, loyalty and affection waged by means of military, economic, and technical assistance.

There is an effort to sketch how Asian responses to the Western impact condition Western policies and actions. In general, these Western responses seem to occur largely in an atmosphere of uncritical misconception of the nature of Asian opinion, its relation to politics in Asian countries, and the assumed or asserted requirements for adjusting Asian opinion to the tastes if not the necessities of Western policy makers. In estimating Asian influence, the West necessarily includes Communist Russia. For purposes of estimating the reflection of Asian opinion on Western action, the West refers to the free world, and in most contexts, to the United States.

In concluding, some suggestions are offered for a changed outlook on problems and expressions of Asian opinion and on the general relations between East and West, which may provide some comfort to our people or to our policy-makers, if these suggestions do not point the way to increased efficiency of our efforts to modify either the relations or the expressions of opinion about them emerging from the Far East.

Influence is commonly categorized today under four heads: political, military, economic, and informational. The political effects of the West on Asia include the heritage of colonialism, the unloosing of special forms of Asian nationalism, the pressures and temptations of Communism, and the tradition of Western-conceived notions of individualism and democracy. All of these forms, with the exception of the Communist impact, have long histories, which include much concrete experience as well as theoretical formulations, criticisms and justifications. The first great moves toward colonialism sprang from economic rather than political objects. The transition to political expression came on the heels of, and as a necessary means to, economic exploitation. But the justifications of colonialism, and its major criticisms, did not appear until much later in the day, as increased awareness in the Western metropoles of the acts of their countrymen in foreign parts loosed a wave of moralistic indignation at home which did not fail to lap Eastern shores too. At the same time, however, the British in particular carried the ideas and practices of the rule of law, of liberal institutions, of public administration and of social welfare to their Asian possessions. Other colonial powers restricted their political influence to the top layers, leaving the great mass of Asian village life politically untouched. Educated middle classes appeared which were frustrated by having little independent to do with the political development of their countries. Severed by language, status, and ambition from their native cultures, these native professionals were not accepted either into the colonial ruling elite.

Western military influence for many years was wielded by extremely small forces committed to tip the balance of fighting between Eastern potentates, in patterns shaped also by the shifting conflicts and alliances of the Western powers. West met West in the Asian theater too, as fleets and forces of the Portuguese, the Spanish, the French, the Dutch, and the English battled for local supremacy. Through agreements and alliances with local rulers, sanctioned by military power, the colonial powers laid increasing tribute on the economic wealth of the area, gaining and losing monopolies and control over trade and shipping, and fastening demands on the Eastern societies which appeared mysterious, onerous, uncontrollable, and inescapable to the great mass of village society below.

Only in the past century have really large military forces been committed to the East by Western powers. In this period the great victories were won and defeats inflicted which created the myth of Western invincibility. Shaken by the Japanese victory at Tsushima and shattered by the Japanese conquest of former colonial areas in the 1940's, the myth was only partly re-established by the defeat of Japan. It was further crippled by the spectacle of French and Dutch weakness in 1945. And the dominance of Western arms was dealt a near-fatal blow by events in Korea and Indochina, as the West failed to bring its most advanced military technology into play, and proved unable to outmaneuver and outfight the native forces with the technology chosen.

Main elements of economic influence are shaped by, but not confined to, the colonial experience. That influence altered markedly and widely

the pattern of the self-sufficient subsistence village economy. The shift
to a plantation economy in many areas, with its consequences of economic insecurity and disruption of stable life patterns penetrated
into the lower orders of society far more than other aspects of Western
influence. At the same time, the Western economic example loosed
among the literate, the vocal, and the influential cadres of Eastern
leaders demands for economic improvement—chiefly taking the form
of industrialization as opposed to the role of producers of raw materials. Eastern leaders clamored for the creation of national economies,
without too much regard for the requirements of immediate balance
or a healthy relation with the world economy, chiefly because of the
elements of apparent independence, heightened prestige, and economic
maturity. Economics thus blended with politics into the curious
amalgam of nationalism and social democracy which characterizes
much of the current politics of the area.

The informational sector is the least explored, the least demonstrated, the least matured. Forms of exchange of persons and cultural
exchange have of course been in effect for centuries. Missionary movements and the training of Eastern scholars in Western institutions were
not commenced yesterday. But systematic programs for information
and educational exchange, particularly as articulated elements in programs of power and influence, are recent. Their growth has been
restricted both by the nature of communications in the Far East, and
by the temper of those intellectuals who occupy critical positions in
the communications of Asian nations.

II

Can there be such a thing as Asian opinion? There is little for the
critical Western scholar to go on in answering this question, or in
making an estimate of the nature of public opinion from India to
Japan. There does seem to be fairly general agreement that there is
no such thing as public opinion in the Eastern countries, if by that one
means something which plays a political role comparable to that
played by public opinion in Great Britain or the United States today.
There appear to be two sharply distinct levels of public opinion in
Asia today. The first is the highly localized, parochial opinion of
the village, expressed verbally and directly through the village council

or by the village elders, and concerned both with the evocation of old memories and the day-to-day governance of the people and goods of the village. It is an opinion oblivious to national politics, let alone world issues. The second level is the opinion of an educated elite, which in appearance if not function more closely approximates public opinion in the West. There is an enormous gap between these two levels. The latter is confined to no more than ten per cent of the population of each country, and is probably less than that. The answer is not merely one of literacy. China, and probably Viet-Minh, offer strong temptation to conclude that mass opinion is being created and manipulated much as in Soviet Russia. While the functions of literacy and of political involvement are being intensively broadened, this is within the framework of a totalitarian order. So the task of interpreting Chinese opinion is very similar to that of dealing with Russian opinion, turning on success in the task of discerning what popular opinion might be if it were not moulded and masked by the propaganda machinery of the state.

But in appraisals of opinion in the emerging non-totalitarian states, requirements of propaganda and the biases of democratic preference in the West combine to increase the amount of democracy and freedom and efficacy of public opinion imputed to the common man of the East. Furthermore, Western assumptions concerning the role of mass media both as disseminators and as indices of public opinion obscure the other ways in which information is spread and opinions are formed. The role of Western armies during World War II, and later, is of great significance; many rural dwellers living beyond the reach of Eastern press and radio have gained through contact with our soldiers some sort of personal knowledge of the West. The person-to-person contacts are ever so slowly being increased as representatives of Western military, economic and technical assistance programs themselves penetrate into the core beyond the reach of mass media.

For various reasons, the top layer of the articulate East is overtly, violently, and often irrationally anti-Western. These opinions are held by people educated in the West, or in the Western tradition. They have had opportunities not only to experience the good in the truth about the West; they have known something of its shortcomings—including the experience of a race prejudice neither comprehended nor forgiven by Eastern practitioners of racialism and caste division. Based on

such experience, these Asian detractors are not to be wooed and won
by Western efforts at mass communications based on tactics and techniques of advertising—efforts to "sell" the Western way by slogan and
eye-catching phrases. The etiology of these opinions raises a serious
question whether they can be changed by more subtle, more powerful,
and more intellectually inclusive methods. And even if Western efforts
to change Asian opinion—whether by the diplomacy of argument or
by other verbal means—were successful, Eastern leaders would still
be tempted to express anti-Western attitudes for reasons of local politics. Difficulties for the Western end of the relationship are caused
when such anti-Western opinions are reported there, causing flurries
among legislators, executives, and publicists.

The concentrated and pyramidal structure of Asian opinion seems
to compare closely to what was considered to be public opinion in
the West of a century or a century and a half ago, before the
democratizing and populist movements in Western politics broadened
the franchise and widened the politically significant public. Public
opinion in the old Western sense consisted of the opinions of those
who counted politically; a restricted group both in England and the
United States prior to 1832. Now if elite opinion in the West grew
into the wider significant public opinion of today, cannot a similar
development be expected in Asia? The prospect of it is by no means
certain. Broaden the group will, in terms of the percentage of the
populace that is literate and politically involved; but the mere spread
of education and political involvement may only increase channels
for totalitarian practices, and the ultimate development and role of
mass opinion may take quite other directions than those it has followed
in the West.

A further complication in assessing Asian opinion is its unscientific
and incomplete description. Some of the difficulties come from attempts
to speak as if there were an identifiable and analyzable entity called
Asian public opinion at all. It is probably nearer the mark to say
that there is public opinion in Asia, but there is no meaningful way
in which the relatively specialized and restricted expressions of opinion
in each Asian country can be combined to constitute a politically
significant entity which could rightly be called Asian opinion. When
the effort is made today, suspect the speaker either of an effort at
intellectual simplification, or worse, of some ulterior motive: he

wants so to characterize an expression by relating it to an enormous and amorphous geographical and political expression as to achieve a propagandist result.

Another difficulty is the infrequency or absence of any of the more formal methods of assessing public opinion and relating it to social and political structure which are becoming more common and useful in the West. Progress toward careful assessment of Eastern public opinion is hampered by the simple absence of census data and other sociological information necessary to describe a population accurately enough to permit respectable sampling or reliable interpretation of the results of observation. The study of public opinion and related forms of market research is encountering continuing obstacles in the West; *a fortiori*, progress in the East seems even more remote. So we are left to work with generalized and insufficient methods of personal observation, press analysis, and occasional anecdote-telling which have characterized opinion estimates in Asia—and elsewhere—down through recorded history.

A further and less prominent difficulty arises from the interest of government information agencies in survival, and their consequent interest in reporting startling evidence of failure or success; failures are needed to shock appropriating authorities into a mood to make funds available to combat circulation of anti-Western statements; successes are needed to validate current efforts, and to demonstrate feasibility of further ones. The middle-of-the-road balanced appraisal is deemed useful for neither of these ends, and tends to be suppressed despite any representative quality.

Citation of dramatic successes or failures is not confined to the process of determining information policies, however; the same reasons are valid when basic policies are brought in question, or when the forms of action are criticized. Indices of Asian dislike may well include reports of Asian opinion that are no more than rumors or allegations put about by opposing propagandists, and may or may not be supported by adequate observation of the results of Western policies or actions. A recent case is furnished by the charges and countercharges arising over United States use of surplus rice to alleviate shortages in the Orient. Reports of the intention immediately called forth charges that we were threatening the interests of our friends in the East, notably Thailand. The demand was made that we stop exporting rice under these terms, and reinforced by reference to Asian expressions of alarm over the interference with government revenues and other economic arrangements. There was, of course, no reference to the domestic problems faced by the United States, or the relation of surplus disposals to United States politics. The whole affair was interpreted as stupidity in using goods to alienate friends.

The alliance of opinion measurement with policy interests puts great pressure on interpretations of expressions of opinion in Asia and elsewhere; it serves to complicate achievement of a balanced and objective appraisal of opinion trends. These biases are further reinforced by psychological predispositions to attribute excessive competence and skill to others. American bungling is bracketed with reports of increase in British prestige. Communist propaganda is overestimated in its appeal to the Asian masses, and the difficulties and parochialisms of Communist agitation are often understated.

III

No matter what the difficulties and dangers of talking about opinion in Asia, it is nevertheless clear that what the West says and does has an undoubted impact on Asian public opinion, if only to provide the choice of stimuli which call forth expressions of favor or disfavor which are rooted in the predispositions and interests of the Asian publicist. It is worth discussing the probable impact of recent United States moves in the field of foreign policy, on opinion in Asia. The policy of massive retaliation is currently prominent. Seen from the standpoint of the United States, this policy can be understood as an effort on the part of our government to free itself from the commitments and shortcomings of a policy of containment; an effort to recapture freedom of action and the diplomatic and military initiative at the same time that military expenditures and forces are being reduced; an effort to interpret our policies and commitments as a reasonable and reliable function of our military and diplomatic capabilities; and, at bottom, an effort to use to the maximum the threat inherent in our military capabilities. It is not argued in this paper whether any of these objectives are reasonable or likely to succeed. The point is that they are comprehensible in terms of the demands and developments of politics in the United States, a field of interest that includes both domestic and foreign aspects which must be reconciled somehow, abolishing in fact if not in speech the false dichotomy between foreign and domestic policy. At the same time, the development, assertion and congruence of the massive retaliation policy with events in the Far East have had an enormous if imponderable impact on Asian opinion.

Estimates of that impact are distorted by the biases just noted. Friends of the policy deflate evidence of Asian fears and apprehensions over its statement and application. Critics cry that we have thus identified ourselves as trigger-happy materialists at worst, and, hardly better, have proved ourselves no more than a paper tiger. What is hard to discern is how far, if at all, we have been successful in interpreting to Asian elites the way in which our massive retaliation policy works to their interest. Conceivably its reliance on threat operates as a deterrent against forms of expansion that are not in the interest of the democratic Asian states, but how far have we given comfort to those whose interests we are trying to protect, and whose freedom we mean to guarantee? The apparent balance of talk seems to favor the detractors rather than the supporters of our policy. Does this mean anything more than a tribute to the effectiveness of opposing propagandists? Such detractors are not confined to the Far East; many of the British left-wing and European neutralists seize on this policy as further evidence of our inhumanity and reliance on brute force. At the same time, the picture of dwindling United States military power in the Far East is assiduously circulated by the Communists and by many neutralists, based on our alleged defeat in Korea and our involvement in the Indochina debacle—a picture which cannot today be offset by reference to any resounding recent military victories. This propaganda disability has been all the more easy for opposing propagandists to exploit because of our signal failure to define our political and military aims in advance, both in Korea and in Indochina, and to show how these have been furthered by our actions.

It is not surprising, moreover, that opposing propagandists characteristically fail to mention, in structuring the world situation in which a policy of massive retaliation is justified and its exercise is understandable, the one main point which makes such a policy viable: the element of threat that called the policy into being, and the provocation that would trigger it into action. Yet the very concept of retaliation implies a prior blow. In our policy, this has always been assumed or specified to be a military move of such power and threat that our freedom and safety are in mortal peril. But before the actual precipitation of aggression, which carries in itself the justification of our reply, the opposing propagandist can effectively play down or ignore this element, and concentrate on the horrors which we casually plan to loose on a world we do not like.

In general, the question of the moral effects of the launching of a nuclear blow will vary with what the launcher says and does at the time; whether warning is given; whether provocation is clear and sufficient; whether the target is appropriate to the situation and to the weapons chosen; whether the prospect of all-out nuclear war on a world scale is enhanced or reduced. This latter point is worth a moment's speculation. Much of the strategic speculation of recent years has taken almost for granted the view that the launching of atomic attack by anyone anywhere is sure to be the commencement of all-out atomic war. Much of this speculation was born at a time when the family of atomic weapons was far less numerous, and its capabilities less flexible, than is true today. Development of tactical nuclear weapons has proceeded apace, and it is far easier to fit weapon to target than even a few years ago. It thus becomes possible to wage a relatively controlled and restricted nuclear engagement, and the leap from initial bang to world conflict is no longer necessary from the strategic standpoint of the opposing coalition. The problems of radiological fall-out present enormous threat, but also can be controlled. A strategy of nice balance of blow and counterblow is now feasible; a Communist attack on a Western military target could be repaid in kind—as for example, one Western ship for one Red Chinese airfield. The difficulty for opinion manipulation today lies chiefly in the fact that there has been no concrete demonstration of the capabilities of the West for restrained use of atomic weapons; the argument proceeds within the uncertainties and the distortions born of anxiety, fear, and hate uncorrected by empirical example.

A main liability of our massive retaliation policy has been the fact that it has drawn onto the United States the expectation that if anyone looses nuclear warfare, we will do it. This may not be the case. Nuclear capabilities are being spread more widely in the world. The Russians seem to be moving rapidly toward nuclear parity, and seem more willing to make the investment in human and material resources to reduce the gap, than the United States does to retain its leadership. Today it is quite possible that the Russians could put a limited nuclear capability at the disposal of the Chinese Communists, and it is by no means certain that either power need always refrain from launching nuclear attack. Considerations of sheer expediency counsel them against it, so long as they estimate that they will be hurt worse than we; but the Russians are already revaluing their military appraisal of the role of surprise in war, conceiving, as Stalin did not, that under modern conditions surprise may bring genuine victory. Despite the possibility that the opponents will be the ones to commence nuclear warfare, the facts that our military position today depends so strongly on our nuclear superiority and our policy is clearly related to it, put upon us the burden of proof of the moral and expedient value of our intentions. One comforting reflection emerging from the structure of Asian opinion is the point that a great many Asians are largely unaware of the game or the threat, just as they remain unaware of the political and economic tensions and struggles among their own elites, and between those elites and the Western powers. It has recently been estimated that neither the Chinese leaders or people are at all aware of the nature of nuclear power, regarding it as a vastly overrated firecracker. If this is the case, an invitation to the next Russian test explosions might have salutary and sobering effects on Red Chinese leadership.

IV

One frequently recurring theme in the great debate on American foreign policy over whether to favor West or East, is the claim that our deliberate choice of the West alienates the vocal East and opens the road to Communist victory by leaving a vital flank unprotected. Asia resents second-cousin treatment, it is asserted, when economic aid and military assistance are being handed out. And Asia also resents being cast in the role of recipient of technical assistance, a form of aid not nearly so publicized when offered to developed Europe. Asia resents the conscious and unconscious devaluation of Eastern culture implicit in our proffers of aid and in other forms of contact. These resentments are founded deeply not only in the emotionalism of the vocal East, but also in many of the practices of colonialism. These

practices have characteristically restricted technical training for East-
erners and have further reserved the best technical posts for Europeans
and have created proportionately small but intensely frustrated classes
of technicians and professionals, both divorced from their own cultures
and unable to find appropriate positions in the governing groups.
With the emergence of at least eight nations into independence in
South and Southeast Asia since 1945, the position of these persons
vis-à-vis the metropolitan powers has been improved, but it now presents certain strains and stresses within the new polity. Achievement
of independence is not yet the achievement of internal unity; the
defense of independence is more important than the acceptance of economic partnership which would go far toward the creation of economic
strength and balance.

Given this structure, it is easy to see that these sources of disaffection,
which eventuate in anti-Western statements, are going to be with us
for some time to come. For Western policy, notably United States
policy, is formulated not alone with the requirements of smooth relations or of opinion in a small sector of a foreign country in mind. Those
prescriptions for foreign policy which demand that policy shall always
express the interest of other powers remain historically utopian, even
though the practices of diplomacy and of information policy may do
something to present foreign policy as an expression of joint rather
than unilateral interest. The case for a Europe-first policy seems to
be strong enough to warrant its continuance for some time to come.
The task for United States leaders and publicists is to live with the
benefits of that policy, to explain it in terms of world interests to
Asian powers, and to be grateful not to have to deal with the expressions of dismay or worse which would come if we left the most
important power complex in our coalition in a secondary position.

Another recurring comment on Western influence is the oft-repeated
theme that Asia wants something of our material tactics and technique, but needs nothing of our culture or of our philosophy. This
is taken as a signal by some to demonstrate to Asian elites our respect
for and competence in the fields of culture and philosophy, and to play
down or reduce our economic, and particularly our military aid. It
appears that the proposed changes in tactics and philosophy will be
ineffective. The Asian assertion of cultural and philosophical superiority is rooted in something other than a rational appraisal of the

comparative contributions of each to world culture. It is based on a need to assert areas of superiority, to keep something of a balance in the relationships, and to celebrate aspects of life in which the beliefs in superiority can be protected. And these assertions are also based on the assumed requirements of local politics, in which local prestige, personal and national, can be increased by attacks on the large and the powerful in the West.

Now the appearance of inferiority feelings, immaturity, and consequent irrational attacks on the position and the prestige of other countries are not confined to the new nations of the Far East. My suggestion is that the so-called problems raised by such expressions are problems chiefly because of the way that the West, and in particular Americans, react to them. I suggest that our basic position and prospects in the world are strong, and are far stronger than would be suggested by the sometimes frantic demands for reassurance expressed by some American politicians and group leaders when confronted with unfavorable opinions from abroad.

We Americans have a tremendous need to be loved and praised, and become agitated when shown that other countries do not take us at our own appraisal. The demands of Congress, expressed in our mutual security legislation, that other countries which receive our aid must publicize it locally, are but one among a host of illustrations of this demand. A major justification for our information program, at its inception and today, has been the need to rectify misconceptions about us, and to publicize the American way of life abroad.[1] Sometimes this task is justified as a step in the cold war, but a reading of Congressional investigations and debates relating to our information programs suggests that the major requirement may be for more purely narcissistic purposes.

Americans also demonstrate characteristic impatience, demanding immediate solutions to international problems and seeking immediate palliatives, when dealing with international issues. We overestimate our strength and influence; our China debate has turned on the

---

[1] See, for example, Edward Barrett, *Truth is our Weapon* (New York, 1953); Wallace Carroll, *Persuade or Perish* (Boston, 1948); Paul M. A. Linebarger, *Psychological Warfare* (2d edition, Washington, 1955); and Charles A. H. Thomson, *The Overseas Information Service of the U. S. Government* (Washington, 1948).

assumption that our power in China was sufficient to have stemmed the tide of revolution, and has lent credence to the charges that only deliberate conspiracy in Washington made it possible for a country so strong to have failed so signally to achieve its goals. We may even overestimate our strategic, diplomatic, and informational requirements, looking for appearances rather than fundamental interests at the same time we think our safety and prosperity depend on amelioration of unfavorable foreign opinion about us. Agreements based on concepts of interest solidly held by foreign leaders are more valuable to us than favorable attitudes expressed by persons of little or no political influence. And fortunately or unfortunately, many expressions of public opinion in the mass communications of Asian countries do not bear closely on the consolidation and retention of strength by the free world in its struggle with totalitarian expansion.

v

Much talk has been devoted to America's posture in the world, ever since a certain American general introduced that curious description of our country's attitudes and capabilities into the language of our foreign affairs. I have a suggestion for the improvement of our posture, which, without flippancy, is immediately relevant to the treatment of the problems or pseudo-problems just mentioned. It is for us to stand up straight. Vulnerability to kicks is somewhat less in a vertical position than in others of which the human frame is capable. And the emotional and psychological connotations make for increased self-respect, a greater sense of maturity and security—feelings we need to cultivate if we are to pursue a steady course in the world politics of the future. We need more genuine faith in our policies, our institutions, our ideals, and our strength. We need less reassurance concerning our position by the flattery of praise or of adoption of our institutions abroad. We need more tolerance of the shortcomings and the special problems of the politicians and publicists of foreign countries. Even more than these emotional redefinitions, we need policies that allow for broader ranges of political forms and activities among allies and neutrals than those we tend to insist on as criteria of full participation in cold war.

This latter requirement is worth a little expansion. Much of the political pressure in the United States for conformity among allies turns on the judgment that he who is not with us is against us. This Leninist prescription has been applied by many of the most vocal anti-Communists among us. It has been used as the touchstone of political appraisals and policy judgments concerning the value of foreign countries to us in our mortal struggle. It is suggested that this criterion, sharply applied, alienates friends and drives neutrals toward the enemy. This becomes a form of Western influence which not only affects Asian opinion, but the political future of Asian states in directions redounding to our harm. Based at bottom on a lack of faith and respect for the political leaders abroad who have more to consider than the interests of United States foreign policy and the preferences of sectors of United States opinion, insistence on this criterion may reduce the likelihood that those leaders will in fact serve our interests.

Another homily addressed to our government is advice to foster better balanced expectations about the future of Asia. The massive retaliation policy was developed and publicized in a way which highlighted confusing if not conflicting predictions about the consequences for Southeast Asia of a Communist victory at Dien Bien Phu. The reports of expectations and policy emendations from Washington gave grounds for the impression that the government did not know its mind or its policy, was unduly threatening and prematurely alarmed, and possibly was engaged in trial ballooning American public opinion without just regard for the consequences abroad. The forms of Western action and the themes of Asian opinion need not be complicated by overoptimistic or overpessimistic or overcertain predictions associated with changes in policy. A further danger in expressing unbalanced or ill-founded expectations is that we become captive to our estimates of the worst; we may insure an unhappy result simply because we treat it as so likely in our planning that we cannot avoid it. By reminding ourselves that time is running out in Asia, we turn legitimate demands for sound and prompt action into precipitate and desperate action which turns our fear into reality.

In both policies and practices we need to share more widely both power and respect. Beneficial effects on our influence and our position in Asian opinion will follow.

Our long-term objective could well be the achievement of security in the world by an appropriate diversification of power. Even further Communist conquests may increase opportunities for such diversification. As the area of nominally monolithic control extends, prospects and possibilities increase for internal stress if not disruption. National Communism, although not likely, is not impossible, and we should make every attempt to foster trends toward reduction of Communist cohesiveness. Communism in Asia is based on Asian nationalism, and it is by no means certain that the political demands of the Communist international conspiracy coincided with those of the emerging Asian nationalisms. Communist strategy has played down divisive elements in the early phases of struggle, but will not be able much longer to postpone the inevitable choices of trend and loyalty.

In sharing power with our allies in the Far East, and in working softly to build favorable actions among neutrals, we can reduce somewhat the danger of incurring the disabilities of the former colonial powers, which the Communists are trying so hard to pin on us. We cannot relax our efforts to demonstrate military strength in the area; and to convince South and Southeast Asian leaders that we mean business in the area; but at the same time we must build military strength on the interests and capabilities of the governments on the ground. We cannot avoid hostility; we must bear the charge that such arrangements as SATO are not really in Asian interests but in Western interests. But we can temper its force and draw its venom if our actions serve Eastern interests as well as our own. There are inviting possibilities, as the growth of Indian power and the return of Japan to a status of great power make it possible to leave the tasks of balancing forces more and more to the Asian countries.

The sharing of respect goes hand in hand with the sharing of power, and if anything, is the more vital. We need to demonstrate respect for the position and the political requirements of Asian nationalist leaders by allying ourselves with them in such a way that we do not discredit them, and by tolerance of the practices—which may include anti-Western statements—of local leaders in gaining and maintaining power. We need to be able to live with economic and political institutions which are viable in the area, however different they may be from the legal, the political, and the economic institutions of the United States. It should be enough for us that these institutions are responsive to the needs and demands of the local population; that they are compatible with growing commercial and cultural intercourse; and that they do not threaten the foundations of free institutions and our practice of freedom in the world.

The consolidation of balanced power, and the sharing of respect will go far to solve the pseudo-problems of unfavorable expressions of Asian opinion. We need to keep main interests clearly in view. If we preserve them persistently and skilfully, taking account of the interests and the sensitivities of our companions in the venture, the informational problems will take care of themselves.

commentary

WILLIAM C. JOHNSTONE, JR.

School of Advanced International Studies

Dr. Thomson has attempted to throw some light on a subject which, by its very nature, defies analysis. Yet it is a subject about which there is real concern, if one listens to the commentators and reads the newspapers. It is a sensitive subject, since expressions of opinion and estimates of the attitudes of different peoples have a way of exerting their own influence on affairs of state, sometimes out of all proportion to their intrinsic value. What I have to say will be in the nature less of comments on Dr. Thomson's paper than of additional thoughts and comments on the subject itself.

There is no doubt of the very profound impact of the West on the peoples of Asian countries. Their opinions, their ways of thinking, their social habits, their customs, their political behavior and their economic, social and political institutions have been substantially changed by the impact of what we call Western civilization. The depth of this impact has been well illustrated by Professor Rupert Emerson in his recent book, *Representative Government in Southeast Asia*, in which he says, "It is a striking fact that all the countries of Southeast Asia which have had the opportunity to shape their destinies freely have adopted constitutions which are basically modeled on well-established

Western patterns, rather than seeking inspiration from their own remoter past or that of other Asian peoples. Under the guidance of the largely westernized elites which have been the spearheads of the nationalist movements everywhere, the constitution makers have turned to Western Europe and the United States to furnish the experience on which they might draw."[1]

Furthermore, there is no doubt that the opinions of people in Asian countries have been, and are being influenced by the West as well as by the Communist bloc. But how do we assess these vague things called "Western influence" and "Asian opinion." Colonel Thomson has outlined the difficulties very clearly. In spite of these difficulties, writers, journalists, politicians and just ordinary travelers are attempting the impossible almost daily. There are few people who travel in Asia, no matter what their competence, who, on their return to America, England, France or any Western country, escape being asked, "What do they think of us?" "What do they feel about this, or that?" Few travelers seem to show enough modesty to refrain from a reply. It is equally true that it is the common experience of almost all Asians when they come to the United States to be asked what they think of America, of our people, our cities, and our institutions—even what they think of Coca-Cola. I suspect it is true in England and in western Europe as well, except for the Coca-Cola. From the record, the Russian and Chinese Communists are even more eager, if possible, to know what their visitors from Asia think about their own systems. And of course, this is no one-sided affair. Our eagerness to know the opinions of people in Asia is surely matched by the eagerness of Asian peoples to learn our opinions about their own countries, as any traveler to Asia can testify.

But does all of this concern accomplish anything? Do we really have a better basis for an analysis of the attitudes and opinions of people in our respective countries? I think not. In fact, this constant attempt of so many people to state what Asian opinion is on any subject reminds me of the old story of the blind men and the elephant. I recently saw a modern version of this on television. Three women were introduced to the audience and of course each was presented with a package of the sponsor's product. They were told that they would

---

[1] Rupert Emerson, *op. cit.*, pp. 5–6.

be blindfolded and asked to touch an object. If they guessed it correctly, they might win the usual fabulous array of household appliances and a TV set. When the blindfolds were in place, a live elephant was brought on stage and the master of ceremonies led each woman in turn up to touch the object and guess its identity. The first guessed it was a rug. The second woman guessed it was a tree trunk and the third guessed it was her husband.

Now I do not intend to engage in this guessing game, even without a blindfold. But I would like to suggest some things which I believe to be pertinent to our consideration of this broad and admittedly somewhat vague subject. First of all, why are we (in the United States, in particular) really concerned about this matter? We are concerned because we are engaged in a struggle for survival—survival of the values of Western civilization which we highly prize—survival of civilization itself from the horrors of unprecedented mass destruction. The core of this concern, moreover, is Communist imperialism which we believe to be more destructive of the values of Western civilization than any system of the past.

We have seen the nations of eastern Europe become enslaved to the Kremlin. We have seen the expansion of Chinese Communist power to North Korea and North Viet-Nam and we see the evidence of serious intent at further expansion day after day. It is our view of this threat represented in the policies and actions of the Moscow-Peking axis, that has erected the obvious present barrier to understanding of each other's opinions and attitudes by the peoples of Asia and the peoples of the free Western nations. We know that the Asian attitude toward the central problem of Communist expansion is different from our own. It has been very well summed up by an Indian writer M. R. Masani in an article called, "The Mind of Asia" when he says, "In the view of the most of us in Asia, the world is divided into two power-blocs, with a few peace-loving nations in between. We see the efforts made by this Third Force as the major influence restraining the two armed giants from World War III. This 'two-power bloc' thesis is at the root of much of our thinking and it makes it possible for us to equate the total suppression of liberty in Russia and China with the continuing practice of colonialism by some of the Western Powers and of racial discrimination in Africa and the United States." Masani goes on to say that, "Having judged both sides equally guilty, we do not find it difficult to move on to an acceptance of the theory of equidistance preached by the Indian Socialist leader, Dr. Rammanohar Lohia, who urges, 'an attitude of mind that keeps away as sharply from the Atlantic camp as from the Soviet camp, from capitalism as well as Communism. To prefer one is to weaken our capacity to combat the other and to build our own way.' "[2]

How then, are we to reduce the barriers to understanding and appreciation of each other which are created by this fundamental difference in viewing the problems of world Communism as the free nations of the West see it and as the free nations of Asia see it?

I would like to suggest that barriers to better understanding are more formidable than they need be because people here and in Asia have not yet divested themselves of stereotyped concepts and ideas fed by propaganda and not yet replaced by knowledge of each other's history and culture.

The study of English history in the universities of India is no substitute for thorough study of the development of the nations of western Europe and the history of the United States. Likewise, the study of Chinese history in England or the United States is no substitute for a study of the history and culture of the nations of South and Southeast Asia. Lacking knowledge, we fall back on fiction, clichés and stereotypes. Let me illustrate with just a few examples from the many that I am sure each one of you could offer.

In the United States, we have formed the very bad habit, in my view, of constantly using the term "Asia" or "Asian." This has now largely replaced the term "Far East" in our vocabulary. But it is dangerous usage. For there is no entity "Asia." Nor, I would assert, is there any such thing as "Asian economy," "Asian politics," or even "Asian opinion," in spite of its use in the topic we are discussing. The danger in this use of "Asia" and of "Asian" leads us to accept the idea that there is something big called "Asia" but too big to really understand, so we tend to avoid learning more about the diversity of the peoples of the Asian nations and the problems of their individual countries which are as varied as are their efforts to deal with them. Since we have too easily accepted the term "Asia" as an entity, we are equally misled by the scare stories put out by journalists and others

[2] *Foreign Affairs*, July 1955, pp. 51–55.

who delight in adding up the resources and the population of the free countries of Asia and implying that unless we take drastic and immediate action, this vast territory with its vast population may be captured by the Communists overnight. This naturally leads us to the conclusion that since the free nations of Asia have not formed themselves into a tight anti-Communist alliance ready to resist at a moment's notice, they must be supinely awaiting the status of satellites of the Communist bloc. The facts are different. I believe also that lack of knowledge leads us to estimate improperly the nature of the Communist challenge for each separate country of Asia. We have been told that Communism feeds on empty stomachs and there is the implication that all the people of Asia are on a near starvation diet. In the countries of Southeast Asia, the facts indicate there are far fewer people on the edge of starvation or with totally inadequate diets than in many areas of Communist China.

We have many other misconceptions about the peoples of Asia, some of which are slowly passing, but the lack of knowledge and the stereotypes are by no means all on our side.

I would be bold enough to make the assertion that to a very large extent the educated people of the different Asian countries still have pretty much a nineteenth- or early twentieth-century view of the United States and of western Europe. An example is that of the editor of a prominent Asian newspaper on a recent visit to this country whose knowledge of American capitalism ended with the period of the so-called robber-barons in American business of the late nineteenth century. I think it is not far from the truth to say that the economics taught in the universities of South and Southeast Asia before World War II, were largely theoretical and fitted neatly into the avid interest accorded to the theories of Marx and Lenin by the students of these universities. The history of economic change in Western nations was not studied and is still not well known. Again, the history of the westward expansion of the United States and its vital bearing on the development of our economy, our culture and social habits and on our political behavior is a subject almost unknown among most educated people in Asian countries. In this they share their ignorance with many educated people in England and western Europe.

What follows then, is the conclusion that what people in the free Western nations think and feel about the different countries of Asia and the attitudes and opinions of the peoples of these countries can only be understood when knowledge replaces ignorance of each other and past stereotypes and clichés are forgotten. It is easy to reach this conclusion. It is far harder to solve the problems of ignorance. Yet these problems must be solved between the free Western nations and free nations of Asia, for the Communists are making large scale efforts day after day to fill the minds of people there with their own dogmas, efforts which dwarf almost into insignificance the effects of the increasing flow of peoples between the countries of South and Southeast Asia and western Europe, Britain and the United States. Communist books and pamphlets are to be found everywhere. Printed material from the United States, Britain and western Europe is scarce.

Yet it would be unfair to say that the barriers to understanding have not been breached in the decade since 1945, for much has been done. People learn and acquire knowledge slowly, but in ten years many have learned and many have replaced shibboleths with facts, and stereotypes with hard information. This has been true both in the Asian nations and in the West.

Just one illustration of progress. We in America are accused, not without reason, of attempting to influence people of Asian countries only in favor of things American and of being intolerant of deviations from the American way of doing things or from the American form of government. I would like to quote from the conclusions of a study mission to Asia, consisting of members of the House of Representatives Foreign Affairs Committee. The group was composed of four members, three Republicans and one Democrat, led by Congressman Walter Judd. Its report was published in January, 1954. All members of the subcommittee participated in drafting the report which states in its conclusions:

> "The Asian nations must work out their own political pattern in the light of their own background and experience. The western concept of democracy will be modified by local innovations, adaptations, and circumstances. Part of our responsibility will be an understanding of this diversity rather than its castigation, and a willingness to work with it toward the solution of common problems."[3]

[3] "Report of Special Study Mission to Southeast Asia and the Pacific," House Foreign Affairs Committee, 83rd Congress, 2nd session, January 29, 1954, Washington, p. 105.

If we in the West and if people in the different free Asian nations can act on the premise that it is far better to expend our energy on finding the interests we have in common and trying to solve our common problems than in jumping from our chairs at every expression of a difference of opinion, there is yet time to achieve that understanding and respect for each other on which sound and secure relations among our nations can be built.

Policy choices of South and Southeast Asia

SUJONO SURJOTJONDRO[1]

Counselor, Embassy of the Republic of Indonesia

A fair and comprehensive treatment of policy choices of South and Southeast Asia would require a much broader canvas than the scope of this chapter will permit. Consequently my presentation of the subject will have to be made in an impressionistic vein. This, however, does not necessarily give us a distorted view. I hope to be able to bring out all the essentials required for a substantial analysis upon which reasonable conclusions can be based.

General Historical Background

In the not too distant past the countries that now comprise South and Southeast Asia, bounded in the western extremity by Pakistan and in the east by the Philippines were countries in which the achievements of man were very great. Although the progress among all inhabitants was largely uneven, projected against the scale of the development of human culture, the record was impressive indeed.

There was a time when the Indian subcontinent became the cradle of great new civilizations that had a lasting influence far beyond the borders of their original homeland. The impact of the vast systems of thought, newly conceived cultural values, and the entirely new cos-

---

[1] The views expressed in this paper are the author's own and do not necessarily reflect policies of the Indonesian government.

mology contained in Indian Hinduism and Buddhism left traces throughout Southeast Asia which in many cases are still very much alive up to the present day. Even Islam came to such countries as Malaya and Indonesia by way of the western part of the Indian subcontinent, propagated by merchant seafarers many centuries after its original revelation in Arabia.

A general decline of the power of the rulers in the area began to set in with the arrival of Western conquerors. The feudalistic Asian society, racked by internal stresses and strains, was not able to withstand successfully the aggressive concepts of commerce and the superior technology and organization embodied in the leadership of the Western merchant-adventurers. Gradually the ultimate consummation of Western control of South and Southeast Asia coincided with the emergence of the national state in Europe. The fissiparous tendencies of feudalistic Asian societies had been checked and alien systems of government were superimposed upon the indigenous base.

The emergence of the next phase of Western imperialism generated by the industrial revolution in western Europe found the ground prepared for the achievement of its multifarious objectives. In this process, which took centuries to complete, by and large the institutional structure of feudalism had been left intact. By such devices as protectorate, dyarchy, paramountcy and indirect rule sufficient control could be exercised, especially at the initial stages of the colonial administration.

Throughout this entire period of colonial history the great majority of the population remained an illiterate and amorphous mass. Roughly toward the end of the nineteenth century new important groupings were added to the ancient society, such as industrial labor and a new type of intellectual.

Geographical Position

South and Southeast Asia constitute part of the so-called Rimland of the greatest land mass of the globe. However, material obstacles in the form of formidable mountain ranges and impenetrable rain forests have not facilitated intercourse with the inner land mass. The great rivers that are navigable all flow in the direction of the southern seas. Part of the region consists of a string of islands separated from the mainland by ocean and seas. As a consequence, since time immemorial the seas have been the main artery of communication. Chinese Buddhists sailed them in search of knowledge; Arab traders in search of commerce; Japanese conquerors crossed them in search of glory; and by means of them Western navigators "stumbled" upon empires.

A large portion of the region has a tropical climate capable of producing the agricultural raw materials for the factories of the industrialized countries, in the East as well as in the West. It also produces the agricultural consumer goods to which Western nations have become accustomed, such as tea, coffee, and spices. Many parts of the region have a surplus yield of rice, the staple diet for large numbers of Asians. The region has a wealth of minerals in current demand in world markets.

The strategic importance of the region—because of its geographical location and its strategic raw materials as well as its vast population—has grown ever since conflicts among the major powers in the world have assumed global ramifications. This strategic importance is not likely to diminish as long as no foolproof safeguard can be found for the peaceful settlement of great international issues.

Politico-Cultural Factors

Up to the present time ancient traditions play an important role in the every day life of the peoples of South and Southeast Asia. In pre-independence days only a minor degree of social mobility could be observed.

The impact of Western political doctrines and cultural values on the Asian body of ideas was most prominent in those areas where direct colonial rule had been most effective. This had come about either by the active choice of Asians or by osmosis.

During the gestation period of the nationalist independence movements an extensive re-examination of values was taking place. The nationalist leaders saw that many aspects of the old indigenous order had become completely obsolete. Concepts of political and economic democracy began to take root firmly in the minds not only of the leaders but in those of the rank and file as well.

Secular ideas about the rights of man, the dignity of the individual, the construction of society, the identity of destiny among large sections of humanity, material welfare and new concepts of service to society and their fellow men provided the underlying rationale for the actions of the nationalist leaders. Bias against the colonial rulers was entertained in so far as they were the exponents of forces hindering the realization of those ideas.

The leaders of the nationalist movements became the new elite of the South and Southeast Asian societies in addition to and sometimes in competition with the existing ones. These new leaders were in most cases drawn from the middle class. They were a new generation of educated people who had absorbed various elements of Western culture. They were conversant with a mode of thinking which was different in many respects from that which prevailed in the minds of the traditional leadership. This was partly due to the new type of organized knowledge which the leaders had acquired.

A new social awareness was also responsible for the intellectual attitude that became increasingly preoccupied with the elevation of the lot of the broad masses of the population.

The independence movements were based on voluntary action by large masses of the population and this provided the pattern of relationship between leadership and rank and file. Persuasion had been the instrument used by the leadership in the conversion of the supporters of the movements and in this way the foundations of modern democracy were laid.

The new relationship also involved a greater degree of social mobility. The political parties as components of the independence movements as a rule had an open membership. The trend toward secularization of public life was conducive to the minimization of the influence of religious hierarchies wherever they existed.

Economic Problems

The independence movements in South and Southeast Asia regarded national liberation as an objective which should be viewed in the light of the general desire to work for better standards of living for the common people. The leaders in their appeal for support of the population committed themselves to putting economic development programs in the forefront of their actions. Moreover, there has always been a sense of identification on the part of the leaders with the lot of the common man, a psychological frame of reference which made it easier for them to give topmost priority to the interests of the populations at large.

A number of countries in the region are very sensitive to the course of economic cycles. This is partly due to the heritage of the colonial period which has as a result the overdependence of the economy on a few export commodities.

Prior to independence no comprehensive projects of diversification existed. Consequently the task of balanced reconstruction is tremendous even if the damages caused by war and revolution are not taken into account.

The task of reconstruction can best be undertaken in an atmosphere of peace, internal as well as external. Internal peace is a prerequisite because a nation torn by strife is not in a favorable position to do constructive work. External or international peace is necessary because it is conducive to the international exchange of goods, capital, services and ideas. Underdeveloped countries are sorely in need of international exchange because they have to catch up for so much in so little time. It makes sense that the generation which has made independence a reality should be given the chance to taste its first fruits.

Major International Political Phenomena

The Cold War. The new South and Southeast Asian nations found upon their birth a large segment of the world involved in a so-called cold war which was in reality neither cold nor war. They found themselves in an atmosphere of mounting international tensions. The haunting specter of atomic and thermonuclear warfare filled the days as one test explosion followed the other. In the meantime the conflict between the two contending blocs erupted in violent fashion on several occasions, as in the Balkans and in Korea.

In such a situation one was entitled to ask, "Is this to be the dress rehearsal for the holocaust?" One recalls the lessons from the interwar period that violence breeds violence. And yet all parties concerned seem to agree that an atomic war will benefit nobody, nobody at all.

From other fields of human endeavor we know that there seem to be no final solutions to human problems. The human race has a propensity to create its own problems. We may take as an illustration the realm of public health. The experts have told us that even in countries where an optimum situation of public health prevails, other types of diseases may be on the increase. Where contagious diseases like malaria, plague and the like may be kept under control, the incidence of other types of diseases like mental disorders, heart ailments and other old-age diseases may be on the increase.

Of all the sciences the science of human relations has demonstrated fewer spectacular results, superficially speaking at least. Perhaps this is due to the fact that no laboratory experiment could be conducted of social conditions. Perhaps it is because we have come to the point whereby experimentation with human lives has become unthinkable and revolting. However, we have come at least so far in our quest for insight in the complex world of human behavior that there is the possibility of pushing the boundaries of our ignorance farther and farther back. What we need is patience, perseverance and time.

This apparent digression into the realm of the abstract has much to do with our subject in so far as it may provide a frame of reference for the relevant questions we have to ask. Moreover, I think we do not need a public avowal of the practice of the Golden Rule in order to extend even toward our temporary adversaries that measure of understanding which makes hope something worth living for.

What alternative courses of action are there to choose from for the countries of South and Southeast Asia, confronted as they are with the problem of the cold war? Which course of action is likely to be in their best interests? Which course of action is likely to promote the interests of the region and the world at large? How are the chances for a durable peace to be maximized?

The countries involved may join the issue and resolve to fortify either one of the two blocs. However the old prescriptions for a balance of power have undergone a radical change with the advent of the absolute weapon capable of producing radioactive clouds which threaten all humanity with extinction. Moreover, the experience of two world wars demonstrated that the unindustrialized countries in our part of the world will just become another battlefield. Another danger in this kind of approach is that as soon as the line-up is complete it will generate a feeling that the game is all set to begin. In this instance, the game involves the survival of the human race.

An alternative approach is not to join the issue but to try to find ways to resolve it by means of exploring new avenues for the peaceful settlement of disputes. A first step in that direction seems to be to minimize existing international tensions and to prevent tensions from cropping up. If one wants to start nearer home, an effort should be made within the South and Southeast Asian region with the expectation that the benevolent atmosphere may eventually spread elsewhere. This approach may also serve as kind of drag that will help break the headlong momentum which may result from a precipitous armaments race.

The People's Republic of China. The emergence of the People's Republic of China on the Asian scene necessitated the determination of what policy South and Southeast Asian countries should adopt toward it.

In the first place there was the problem of recognition of a new government. Some countries like Pakistan, India, Burma, Ceylon and Indonesia at an early stage understood that recognition of the new government was inevitable and took steps accordingly. Recognition of course did not imply moral judgment one way or the other. It was only the recognition of the established fact that the new government was effectively functioning and its authority recognized by its own people. Recognition by itself does not necessarily involve exchange of representatives but most of the nations that recognized the new government of China have fully accredited representatives at the capital. A curious development ensued when the General Assembly by majority vote termed the government of China an aggressor while at the same time many of the voting members did not recognize the existence of that government.

Hostilities had broken out in the China area and countries adjacent to that area naturally were very much concerned. One way to meet such a situation is to band together in order to be prepared for all eventualities; another is to try to get to the heart of the matter and to locate the causes of friction.

We should avoid the development of a situation whereby the peoples of the Communist bloc would be strengthened in their doctrinal belief that the outside world is all hostile. That "war begins in the minds of men" may not be an exact proposition, but the minds of men have a potentiality to deflect the course of history and as long as men of different persuasions can reach each other's mind the chances of a peaceful settlement of all disputes will be enhanced.

Conclusions

The young nations in South and Southeast Asia which have recently emerged from colonial status to become independent must give close attention to their internal problems of reconstruction. The job of building our own house for the first time generates a sense of exhilaration perhaps long forgotten by older nations which have become settled in their ways. We know that most of the world is sympathetic to our endeavor and has put its resources at our disposal whenever our needs would require their employment. On the other hand, in our own small way, we attempt to do our part in contributing to the solution of the world's problems. The recent Bandung Conference which amounted to an attempt to do the impossible, has shown unequivocally that common ground can be found when common ground is sought.

commentary

SYED AMJAD ALI

Ambassador from Pakistan to the United States

I should like to say a few words on the very lucid exposition of the policy choices in Southeast Asia which my colleague from Indonesia, Mr. Surjotjondro, has presented.

First I should like to emphasize one fact which I think needs a little emphasis. My colleague very rightly mentioned the influences of Islam on Southeast Asia. I think this requires a little more to be said because Islam originating in Arabia moved to the west and reached Spain and to the east and reached Indonesia and China. This expansion of Islam not only embraced a very large number of people who took Islam as their religion but also influenced their thinking, their culture, and some of the older religions of their countries. So Islam has played a very important part in Southeast Asia on the cultural side as well as on the political side. The conversion, for instance, of the descendants of Genghis Khan was a great epic in the Middle Ages and the results of it were felt in the subcontinent of India for the next five or six centuries.

My second remark concerns the political policy choices in Southeast Asia. Now, Southeast Asia comprises a number of countries; some have natural barriers like the ocean, as my colleague from Indonesia is fortunate to have; some, as we in Pakistan, have not. Above all, we in Pakistan are divided into parts a thousand miles apart, into West Pakistan and East Pakistan, one bordering Iran, Afghanistan, the Soviet Union, and China, the other bordering our very friendly neighbors, the Burmese, who in their turn border Communist China.

Also in the subcontinent of India, we have had thirty centuries of aggression, and invasion. For all these reasons our position is somewhat different from that of my colleague from Indonesia, and therefore, our thinking is not the same as his in relationship to the cold war.

Our interpretation of the last two wars also is a little different. It is not the choice by a country of neutralism which keeps it from being overrun when an aggressor is on the move. The last war proved that; instances I could cite would be all too familiar.

Our effort is, as my colleague has said, to see that this world remains at peace, and we in our very humble way are trying to contribute toward that effort together with almost all other nations in the world. But at the same time we feel that small countries, like Pakistan, which are in a vulnerable position and which cannot afford to spend the amount of money required to make their defenses adequate, must join hands with friends who can give them security in case there comes into the mind of some country the idea of expanding territorially. And therefore, while we stand for peace, we also believe in systems of collective security. Such systems we think are efforts toward peace, for weakness offers temptation which might invite aggression.

To my mind, the crucial problem of Asia is poverty. The poverty of Asia I think is the greatest menace to the world, because the very large populations of Asia, if they remain poor, are bound to be restless. If they are restless, they are bound to be misguided, and their decisions would be very disadvantageous to the democracy-loving people of the world. So, if we are to have and maintain democracy in Asia, we should make every attempt to help Asia fight the great menace of poverty.

If we look back, study figures, we will see that progressively Asia has become poorer, in the first instance, through colonial rule and, in the second, through the adverse terms of trade.

Some very interesting figures show that if in 1871 one hundred units of raw material could purchase one hundred units of manufactured goods, in 1945 one hundred units of raw material could purchase only sixty-one units of manufactured goods. And since 1945, in view of the wage increases which are constantly taking place in Europe and in the United States, the terms of trade have further moved against Asia. Thus, Asia to buy the same quantity of capital goods or manufactured goods from Europe or the United States, has to give more, or sell more, of her raw material. In the course of time this is making Asia poorer.

I could cite another figure. In 1951 the gold and dollar reserves of the arc of Asia, that is from Japan to Pakistan, were I believe $4 billion, but in 1953 they dropped to $3 billion, a reduction of $1 billion. That again confirms and proves what I said earlier that Asia is getting poorer.

The Western governments which once ruled parts of Asia have given to them the great lesson of democracy, and this great lesson has created an urge in the Asians to improve their lot, to improve their standards of living. Go to the smallest village, anywhere in Pakistan, and you will find people wanting things. This urge to improve is translating itself into demands which the governments cannot meet on account of their limited budgets and their unexplored resources. So, there again, unless capital moves large quantities of goods quickly, the acceleration of development cannot take place and, therefore, the standard of living of the people will not improve on account of the very high birth rate of the peoples of Southeast Asia.

Lastly, poverty poses another problem for democracy. Democracy no doubt is the best form of government, but it is also the most difficult because people can only rule themselves if they are enlightened and if they are educated, and they can only be enlightened and educated if their standard of living is high. That is why some of us who have as our objective a democratic way of life run into trouble now and then because our electorate is still very poor and still very illiterate.

Policy choices before the
Western world

PATRICK GORDON WALKER

Privy Councillor, Member of Parliament

The aim of the West in South and Southeast Asia must be to pass from the defensive and to seize the political initiative. If we are to do this, we must first realize why we are at present so much on the defensive—and we must distinguish between the immediate and the ultimate causes.

The immediate cause is the catastrophe of the loss of China to Communism—a colossal reverse that has dramatically shifted the balance of power in Asia against us. We have been left scraping and scratching around in the attempt to retain precarious footholds on a cliff that is crumbling under our weight—in Malaya and Indochina, in Formosa and Hong Kong. If we slip much further, a landslide may start that will carry us away with it.

We have therefore a simple short-run aim—to avoid sliding any further. This is in the first instance a question of force—both military and economic. We must draw a line somewhere and make clear to any potential aggressor that transgression of this line would be met by force. We have to draw this line where we can, not where we would like. The line drawn by SATO is probably about the best we can do.

Even in the short-run it is necessary to observe the limits of force. First, we must use it defensively; it must be genuinely held in reserve to resist aggression. We would lose all moral support in Asia if we gave even a hint of an impression that we would resort to force in our own interests. It is quite irrelevant to argue, as do some military men,

363

that the aggressive use of force might be militarily successful. For reasons that I shall discuss in a moment, even a victorious war would be a defeat for the West. We might win the war: we would indubitably lose Asia.

Secondly, we must not bluff. The defensive use of force is by its nature exposed to the test of probing actions by those with aggressive aims: bluffs will always be called. If you won't shoot, you must shut up.

The long-term limits upon the use of force by the West in South and Southeast Asia are even graver. We must get out of our heads the idea that the West has permanent superiority of force in Asia, regardless of the views of Asian peoples. It can never be easy for us to bring forces to bear at such great distances from home. We cannot do more than our public opinion will allow. British soldiers, too, have mothers. Even our superiority in weapons may be an illusion. In Asian warfare manpower might be more potent than nuclear weapons. An H-bomb might not be so effective against a swarm of human locusts; and it would take quite a few H-bombs to wreak the damage that is yearly brought by flood and famine to China.

In any case it would be extremely difficult to strike with nuclear weapons at critical danger points. To use them to repel a Communist invasion of other Asian nations would be the *reductio ad absurdum* of liberation. Moreover one's friends might go in fear of retaliation from a China that has Russian nuclear weapons at its disposal. Even Chiang Kai-shek might regard the annihilation of Formosa as a high price to pay for the destruction of Shanghai or Canton.

We cannot, as some people easily suggest, substitute economic for military power; for these are not alternatives. Indeed, effective economic aid presupposes the defense of the independence of the recipients. It would do precious little good either to them or to us if they were nonetheless to fall into Communist hands.

The West must certainly give South and Southeast Asia all the economic aid it can afford—perhaps more than it can afford. Poverty and misery lie at the root of the instability of the area. But let us have no illusions about the speed or effectiveness of economic aid. You have to run even to keep standing still; for the first effect of economic aid is an increase in the population that keeps the per capita income where it was before. And if you try to move too fast you outrun the capacity of the people to use the aid, and a great deal of it goes to waste in inefficiency and corruption. The rate at which aid can be used is set by the time it takes to train people in new and unfamiliar skills. You can't short-circuit this; for if you go into other peoples' countries and apply your economic aid for them, this appears as a new form of imperialism and the whole purpose of the operation is undone. As Mr. Lester Pearson recently said, a conscious flaunting of superior know-how is only a modern version of the old holier-than-thou attitude.

Economic aid, which seems to us in the West a generous and unselfish act, can easily appear to Asians in a more sinister light. Generosity is often harder to bear than blows.

We should for this reason be very careful not to disturb the admirable working of the Colombo Plan which has largely disarmed Asian suspicions and which includes every single non-Communist state of Asia. It is a matter for rejoicing that the United States is now a full partner in the Colombo Plan: I devoutly hope that the flow of American aid will be stepped up and that it will be channeled through the Colombo Plan and not through SATO, which excludes India.

Despite the limits to the effectiveness of Western power, whether military or economic, nonetheless the immediate short-run choice before us in South and Southeast Asia is whether we are to draw a line somewhere against aggression and stick to it in the double sense that we will not ourselves transgress it and that we will resist to the utmost anyone else who does. It was for this reason that I defended SATO when it came up for debate in the House of Commons.

If we don't make this first choice there will be no other choices for the West to make in Asia, for we shan't be there to make them. The landslide will have carried us away.

But if we make this first short-run choice, as we have done, we are at once faced with an incredibly difficult and complex long-term problem. The loss of China to Communism, which has caused our immediate difficulties, is only a symptom of the sickness of the West in Asia, not its fundamental cause. It is not just a diplomatic revolution or military reverse that has brought embarrassment—it is part of a tidal change that will overwhelm any Western Canutes that try to stem it by setting up their dollar or sterling thrones in front of it. In the last resort it is men's minds that are the battlefield; and we must realize that, as things are, the mental and emotional terrain favors Communism.

It was, I believe, Disraeli, who made the profound remark that Russia always turns its Asiatic face to Europe and its European face to Asia. To us Russia seems barbaric; but in Asia Russia appears the model of modernity.

Communism appeals to Asians as a short-cut that can alone cope with abject poverty and shorten the galling lead enjoyed by the industrial powers of the West. It appears as the social system that is free of the color bar. It also offers the human satisfaction of participation in a proud and powerful community. Rooting for a nation to which one belongs and which enlarges one's self-esteem by winning victories—particularly over the West—can be a greater attraction than a hungry and ineffective choice between equally rapacious candidates in a free but corrupt election—which is often all that democracy can mean at the moment in some Asian countries.

In the last resort China went Communist for the same reasons that earlier led Japan into authoritarian capitalism. Russia in the twentieth century is a better model than was Prussia in the nineteenth, of the material advantages you can, at any rate in the short-run, derive from a monstrous deformation of Western civilization.

I do not mean that Asians are incapable of the desire for individual liberty. Many have shown that they regard true democracy as a high good. What I mean is that we must not be guilty of the liberal illusion that democracy as we know it is an absolute good to all men in all circumstances: that it needs only to be dangled before their eyes to be at once embraced by them. It is a subtle manifestation of an imperialist state of mind blandly to assume that everyone in a Communist Asian state is a slave longing to throw off his chains and run into the arms of the West. Before you can lose your chains you have first to acquire them—and they can be quite a handy weapon for banging Westerners in the face.

Communism starts in Asia with the advantage that the very word "imperialism" has an anti-Western connotation. You may intellectually persuade an Asian that Communism is the latter-day version of Western imperialism, but he will still think of the Western democratic powers as imperialist because they seem to be the immediate obstacles in the way of full independence. Worse the devil you know than the devil you know not. Moreover it is Western nations—whether Portuguese, Dutch, French, British, German or American—who have for centuries one after the other insulted Asians by coolly taking for granted their superiority over them. Westerners have regarded as God-given the advantages that they owed to history.

It is not necessary today for a country to possess colonies for it to be regarded as imperialist in Asia; it is enough for it to be Western and to deploy its power in Asia. As America has discovered, it is the extent of its power rather than the number of its colonies that stamps it as imperialist. Every time an Asian country—even a Communist one—worsts a Western nation, it strikes a chord in the Asian heart. Few among even the most anti-Communist Asians—whatever their feelings about the need to resist aggression—could resist a certain guilty feeling of pride when Asians killed Europeans in Korea.

The white man's burden has shifted on his back. Today it is a load of suspicion that he finds it hard to cast off his shoulders.

The problem for the West in Asia is made none the easier by the fact that the two Western powers primarily concerned, the United States and the United Kingdom, tend to make different instinctive choices in South and Southeast Asia. This is partly the result of history, partly of geography, partly of psychology.

For the United States, the Far East is really the Far West—the opposite shore of a vast but shrinking ocean that seems to lie uncomfortably close to its own western front door. For Britain, the Far East is very much the Far East—the terminus of a long and precarious but vital line of communications that runs eastwards from our shores. America tends to make a peripheral approach to the problems of strategy in Asia: it thinks of any move by Communist China as endangering a defense-chain. British strategy is far more concerned with the realities of power and politics in and around the Indian Ocean than with minor shifts of power on the China coast. Britain's interest is to keep its lines open to India, Australia and New Zealand and of course to maintain its bastion in Malaya. While America wants to keep Communism out of the Pacific, Britain wants to keep it out of the Indian Ocean.

Emotion reinforces strategic considerations. G. F. Hudson once said that Americans yearn to be loved by China and Britons yearn to be loved by India. America's rigid strategy and stern refusal to recognize Peking is colored by the psychological need for a substitute China in

Formosa. Britain's approach to China is conditioned by the psychological need to pay high regard to the views of India, Pakistan, and Ceylon; that this is a persistent and paramount British interest is shown by the fact that both a Labour and a Conservative government have adopted the same policy about recognition of China, although other Commonwealth countries like Australia, New Zealand, Canada and South Africa have so far taken the other view. For like reasons Britain tends to overrate the chance of splitting Russia and China, while America underrates the consequences of a policy that positively drives them into one another's arms.

One of the prime tasks of the West in South and Southeast Asia must be to find an accommodation between British and American views. So long as these differ, this adds to the fundamental and structural weakness of the West. What we must do is to work toward agreement in terms of the long-term choices before the West in South and Southeast Asia.

It follows, I hope logically, from what I have said that the long-term choices before us are extremely limited. The West only has a permanent role to play in Asia if we realize that we must choose between real and not imaginary alternatives—between alternatives that we cannot impose but which are imposed upon us.

The only way by which we can move from the defensive is by gaining a moral basis for ourselves in Asia. Even to see how to set about this we must to the best of our ability enter into the Asian mind: that is to say, we must construct our policies in Asia on Asia's logic not on ours.

This applies particularly to ideas of democracy. If we proceed on the simple idea that Western democracy is manifestly good, that Communism is evil, and that everyone but a rascal or a poltroon must be on our side—well, this sort of political logic may work in regions of the world where Western democracy is part of the texture of social life; but in Asia it will be looking-glass logic. It will mean that we must regard the vast majority of Asians as rascals or poltroons— which will not give us a very large moral base to rest on.

The attempt to divide the whole world into two camps and to force everyone to choose between them will produce the very opposite of the result we want in Asia. If we insist on treating everyone as a goat who is not a sheep, we may find a disconcertingly rapid increase in the Asian goat population. Even the attempt to create a single un-differentiated democratic bloc in Asia is short-sighted. Such an Asian bloc can only subsist on the doctrine of "Asia for the Asians"—a notion that must in its nature be anti-Western. The very idea of Asia as a distinct political and sociological entity is a Western creation; it has come into existence as an integral part of native movements that only felt themselves akin because they were united in the common aim of getting free from Western thraldom.

What we want in Asia is not a unified bloc, whether democratic or not, but national differentiation. We want all sorts of Asian nations, each going its own way, each proud of its own national distinction. The only sure way to save Asia from Communism is by turning against Communism the even more potent force of nationalism. As long as there are nationalist forces in Asia that feel that it is Western power, either military or economic, that stands in their way—so long will Communism be a danger. Frustrated nationalists will ally with the devil to achieve their aims; and, as I have said, they will find the wiles of the devil seductive. Nehru openly flirted with Communism in his struggle for independence against Britain; now, as a national leader, he is a bitter opponent of Communism in India.

The West must return to an earlier and more primitive version of liberal democracy. We must go back to the idea that national self-determination is the essential precondition and expression of individual liberty. In the nineteenth and early twentieth century neither America nor Britain worried overmuch about what free nations would do with their freedom; we made the easy though often false assumption that they would adopt democracy. But we did firmly associate Western democracy with the force of nationalism, the most potent political emotion in the world.

We must do the same again in Asia. We must, of course, do our best to help Asian nations to be democratic; we need not be quite so simple-minded as we were in the nineteenth century. But, in order to do this, we must accept that democracy may mean different things, when seen through Western or through Asian eyes. We are thinking in terms of Western not Asian political logic if we get hot under the collar at the mere thought that some Asian nation may refuse to identify democracy with a militant, whole-hog anti-Communist foreign policy.

You can certainly in Asia be a good democrat without being pro-West; indeed, during this present epoch, it may well be that you cannot be a good Asian democrat if you are simply pro-West. A democrat must stand up for himself; and in Asia that means telling the Westerners from time to time where they get off.

An example of the way in which the West, through insistence upon its own logical categories, forfeits influence and effect in Asia is the tendency which exists in Britain but is a good deal stronger in America to decry and underrate Nehru. His policies or at least his speeches are sometimes irritating and erratic, but he is a great moral force in Asia. Hundreds of millions listen to him, model themselves on him, who turn a deaf ear to the siren-calls of the West—however high-pressure the salesmanship behind them. And Nehru is a genuine democrat who detests the practice of Communism and who, incidentally, understands admirably the British type of parliamentary democracy.

If we are to distinguish between different versions of genuine democracy, we must go further and make the difficult admission that there are different types of neutralism and that not all are equally bad.

Indian neutralism, for instance, is motivated neither by fear nor by secret sympathy with Communism. It may appear shortsighted to us, it may even be shortsighted; but we must accept as a fact that it can appear as a logical and positive policy to intelligent and moral men. It should not really be so difficult for us to understand this, when we recall the neutralism of Britain at the time of Munich or America's neutralism for a good while longer at a time when Western democracy was faced not as today by potential but by actual military menace.

If we accept the policy of setting the force of nationalism against Communism in Asia, this may involve us in a number of awkward situations and decisions. We may have to yield up, or at least expose to risk, strategic bastions. But strategy is the handmaid of politics, both in war and peace. We cannot divorce the two, as military men are often tempted to. Even great military power is ineffective without the moral adherence of the people on the spot to your cause—and that we still lack in Asia. When we consider the defense lines drawn up by strategists who know everything about logistics we must remember that no strategic line in Asia—or for that matter anywhere else—has any long-term strength unless it is buttressed by the will of the peoples.

The West will not be strong in Asia until we have found a line where further Communist aggression appals the moral conscience of Asia. We have perhaps got something like this in Indochina; but we have not yet got it in the Formosa Straits. Until we have it everywhere in Asia, we will lack the moral basis without which military strength is a temporary and wasting asset. Once we can find moral readiness to ally at need with the tremendous power of the West, we will be able, should in fact Communist aggression continue, to transform SATO into a NATO type alliance. But we cannot do that until there are true nations in Asia that are more scared of losing their independence to Communist aggression or infiltration than of never quite gaining it at all owing to the suffocating nature of Western support.

We have the difficult task of conducting simultaneously a withdrawal and a holding operation. As I have said, we must for the time being use military strength to draw a line somewhere. A precipitate withdrawal would leave a fatal and inchoate vacuum, and dictators like nature abhor a vacuum.

The real choices before us relate to the co-ordination of the filling up of this vacuum with a retraction of our immediate power. Communism will only be revealed to Asian minds as the real and immediate imperialist menace if we withdraw what Asians regard as Western imperialism. We must prepare for our withdrawal by building up the new nations of Asia by military and economic aid and training. But we must find the way to do this that will create confidence in our honest respect for national independence. We must leave not puppets behind us but real Asian patriots—and they will show their patriotism by having their own ideas about democracy and neutralism.

Asia will express its ideas in symbols of its own choice not of ours and it will follow men who personalize and embody these symbols.

This whole operation will be difficult for all of us and particularly for America. It involves in the end the abandonment of Formosa and the recognition of the Peking government. Britain has also had and will have difficult decisions to make. It has firmly identified itself with Asian nationalism in India, Pakistan, Ceylon and Burma. We were at that time encouraged in this course by the pressure of public opinion in America. We will, as quickly as the military situation and the development of self-government allow, follow the same policy in Malaya. It is because we are trusted in this that our present position in Malaya has not been denounced as imperialist by Nehru and other democratic Asian leaders.

To sum up in two phrases the policy choices before the Western world in South and Southeast Asia, as I see them: *First, it is on balance better to run military than political risks in Asia.* Military risks can be covered and reinsured; political risks may be fatal. Secondly, *we have the choice between Nehru and Mao Tse-tung.* Or rather, that is the choice before Asia that is imposed upon us. Asians will adhere to one or the other as the personalization of the two ways to independence that lie before them.

We too must choose between Nehru and Mao Tse-tung—unless we want to be left with no choices at all in Asia.

commentary

JOHN J. MCCLOY

Chairman of the Board, The Chase Manhattan Bank

It is apparent that Mr. Walker is wise, knowledgeable and imaginative in respect of a policy for Southeast Asia. I know the area only from rapid wartime visits and the detached reading and conversations in which one deeply interested in foreign policy and international affairs might be expected to indulge. But perhaps detachment is a good base from which to test a policy.

I go along fully with Mr. Walker's analysis of the great forces and the great stir of emotions which have taken place in South and Southeast Asia. Certainly, I also agree with him as to the mighty consequences of the Chinese defection. I am impressed by the paucity of alternatives and by our own lack of initiative in respect of them, but I do not know that I would agree either with his list of alternatives or his choice between them. I think both his list and his choice may be too narrow.

Perhaps nationalism is the answer as Mr. Walker suggests, and it may be that democracy only in the sense of nationalism is our cure. However, I am impressed by the paradox of finding nationalism in the West an insufficient barrier to Communism and at the same time pressing it as an answer to Communism in the East. What makes one believe that the undeveloped nationalities of this area, as compared with the highly developed ones of Europe, can better stand up against the Communist forces of Moscow and China? I understand that nationalism in the area is working just as heavily against the West as with it. In Singapore the Chinese, I am told, who represent so large a portion of the population are most nationalistic in their alignment with Red China, and the likelihood is they will take over control of Singapore when existing regulations regarding voting are removed. While paradoxes seem inevitable, with every new development in communication, with every action in one part of the world promptly reflected in another far-off part of it, paradoxes become of more doubtful validity and subject to closer scrutiny. In short, I am not certain that the new nations in the area are strong enough in themselves to present a national stand which would amount to very much against a heavy Communist attack.

Mr. Walker has pointed out the fatuity of our belief that democracy and free elections will make friends and win the world. Yet I have the feeling we should not accept too readily the thought that the Asian may not be interested in developing his individual freedoms. Do we not abandon too much to Communism if we cease stressing the simple doctrine of freedom from the oppression of the secret police and the concentration camp? The Asian may be far less sensitive than a Briton to his rights as an individual, but he understands them, or, let us say, recognizes them. Certainly he would appreciate it if he were no longer subject to arbitrary arrest or decapitation. There is something more fundamental here than an electoral system, and given a fair increase in the Asian standard of living, the idea may as readily catch fire in Asia as it did in an earlier day in Europe.

What the political form will be in this part of the world is hard to say—it may be a welfare state presided over by an oligarchy— it may well be something far less than parliamentary democracy, as we know it. But constant emphasis on freedom from the police call and slave labor is appealing even if the individual or his whole country never heard of the Bill of Rights. This is a true asset of the West and it is no illusion to continue to feel that *all* men are attracted to it and better off for it.

If, in Mr. Walker's mind, our concept of democracy in this area can be pared down to narrow nationalism I would suggest it is at least equally possible to pare it down to personal freedom, let us say, from arbitrary arrests. Even the Romans enjoyed and recognized this freedom after free elections were no longer customary in Rome.

Economic rehabilitation is another doubtful field to Mr. Walker and I can sympathize with his reasoning and his experience. These prompt him to state it is not the total solution. But it still remains, as I gather he would not deny, one of the few alternatives we do possess. It seems he would route continued United States aid—indeed in so far as United States aid is concerned, I gather he would step it up—through the Colombo Plan rather than through SATO. But, if economic conditions are the basic cause of the Asian peoples' urge to experiment with the short cut via Communism to industrial rehabilitation, why is not economic aid the answer? From such experience as we have had thus far, certainly partially frustrating, though in Europe brilliantly successful, it is clear that great administrative skills and imagination are needed to make it effective. In South and Southeast Asia as he says, you have to run to keep standing still. Yet standing still in Asia in these days is something and if the effect of economic aid would only be to check the slow but heavy approach of Communism, there would be real accomplishment. If a way can be pointed out which reaches the objective without the incidents of statism, to which I have already referred, we may here have the counter to the short cut to industrial power with which the Soviet Union blandishes the depressed peoples of the area.

There is another thing which does not satisfy me about Mr. Walker's paper and I suppose it does not entirely satisfy him either. That is the thought that we must at all costs cling to a somewhat ragged outer line beyond which Communism must not advance and which we, ourselves, must scrupulously respect. Where does that line lie? I assume from what he says that, at least presently, it includes Hong Kong, Malaya, and Singapore, but I rather doubt that, as he draws it, it would so clearly include Formosa. I wonder whether anti-imperialism in Asia is apt to be any better countered by holding to such a line.

Today it seems that the opprobrium of imperialism, which such a short time ago was cast at the European powers, attaches more now to the United States, which only a short time ago pressed for the independence so many now enjoy. But will the retention of these outposts in any way diminish the surge of feeling against the Western imperialist powers? I doubt it, but still I would not advocate abandoning Singapore or Malaya, or, indeed, Formosa. I somewhat single out Formosa because I feel that Formosa strikes far less of an imperial note in Asian minds than does Malaya, or even Hong Kong. Formosa is a strategic accident so far as American foreign policy goes. It certainly is not a colonial outpost as such.

Mr. Walker has pointed up the differing strategic philosophies of Britain and the United States—the British emphasis on the Indian Ocean versus the United States' emphasis on the Pacific. He has stressed the importance of a united policy in Asia as we have had a united policy in Europe. I do not think anyone who is sensitive to the play of forces throughout the world would differ with him on this, but I wonder whether there is not something more substantial operating in this area which Mr. Walker, and perhaps others, overlook.

I refer to the independent attitudes, and at the same time clearly expressed disposition, to side with the West and with its ideas which were, for example, expressed at the Bandung Conference. General Romulo spoke for the Philippines but he seems to have mustered support from a very substantial number of nations, the color of whose people is shaded and whose experience has all been more or less associated with colonial memories. This was a substantial expression of pro-democratic support:

> Does the road to greater freedom really lie through an indefinite period of less freedom? Is it for this that we have in this generation raised our heads and taken up the struggle against foreign tyrannies?
>
> Has all the sacrifice, struggle and devotion, all been, then, for the purpose of *replacing foreign tyranny by domestic tyranny?* Do we fight to regain our manhood from Western colonial rulers only to surrender it to rulers among ourselves who seize the power to keep us enslaved?

General Romulo also said in a debate with Premier Nehru at that Conference:

> Let me say to Premier Nehru in conclusion, the empires of yesterday on which it used to be said "the sun never set" are departing one by one from Asia. What we fear now are the new empires on which we know, the sun never rises.

This episode made me wonder whether Asians were so insensitive to democratic liberties in the rush to achieve a higher standard of living, as so many observers suggest.

Now Mr. Walker has spoken of Nehru and here I venture on a very delicate subject for I repeat I do not know India well and Mr. Nehru not at all. I do not know at first hand the influence which Mr. Nehru carries throughout the East, but I recognize him as a powerful force not only in his country but in the entire area. I do not quarrel with his neutralism, but I cannot escape the conclusion that his so-called neutralism apparently takes him to Moscow's bosom and Moscow to his, in most respects, except within India itself. On international affairs wherein does his policy differ from the expressed objectives of Moscow? On China, on Germany, on disarmament, it seems to be in parallel. This looks like alignment, except domestically. I admit he displays a very active policy against Communism at home. If we compare his visit to Moscow with his visit to the United States, it is rather interesting. In this country Mr. Nehru had a rather prosaic, taken-for-granted, sort of visit, and only generalities were issued by him by way of a statement upon his departure. From reports, we rather failed to impress him, except unfavorably, whereas his Moscow visit, on the other hand, was something in the nature of a Roman triumph with people packing the streets and cheering, and it was followed with a pronouncement of rather concrete endorsement of Soviet policy. Moreover, according to Marshal Tito and to others who saw him shortly after his visit, he was most animatedly impressed by it all.

The importance of India, the need for adequate development of the country and its living conditions, *a fortiori* because of the defection of China, can be wholeheartedly accepted, but it is something less than a demand for whole-hog anti-Communist foreign policy which makes us gag a bit at the thought of attaching our interests wholly to one who seems whole-hog pro-Communist in the foreign field. I do not question Mr. Nehru's sincerity—he is evidently a very remarkable man. I would certainly keep on friendly and communicating terms with him, but I would not concede him the role of either the great mediator or the director of our Eastern policy, or grant that our only alternatives are between him and Mao Tse-tung. I think that Asia will certainly develop many leaders and from them will come real contributions to the peace and progress of the world.

These are my inadequate comments on a most penetrating and fair-minded paper—primarily they are skeptical and unaffirmative, but Mr. Walker's own approach is also negative and limited: a graceful retreat emphasizing an alignment with a particular country, India, is about what it comes to. SATO is viewed, I gather as inadequate. What better can we evolve?

Index

Acheh: 42
Adat law: 58
Adloff, Richard: 144, 145
Adyar: 18
Afghanistan: 79, 294, 360
Africa: 5, 42, 56, 347
Agriculture:
agrarian patterns, reforms of,
205–206;
industrialization of, 211–12, 221–23;
land, cultivation of, 219;
raw materials of, 354;
rural income from, 208;
surveys of labor conditions in,
204–205;
underemployment in, 186, 189–90,
195–96, 206–207;
see also economic development; labor
AITUC: *see* All-India Trade Union
Congress
Alaungpaya, King (Burma): 39, 41, 84
Albania: 5
Albuquerque, Affonso de: 37
All-India Trade Union Congress
(AITUC): 320
Ambonese, the: 148–49, 151, 235, 236
American Relief Administration: 268
American Revolution: 4, 9, 102, 165, 168
Amsterdam: 62
Anawrahta, King (Burma): 84, 85
Andhra: 108, 317
Angkhor Wat, the: 48
Anglo-Burmese wars: 49, 84
Anglo-Dutch Treaty (1824): 40
Anglo-Dutch War (1780–84): 40
Animal Farm: 95
Annam: 43
Annamese, the: 67, 115

Anti-Fascist People's Freedom League
(Burma): 103, 164
Antigua: 202
Arabia: 353, 359
Arakan: 38, 41, 49, 149, 151
Arakanese, the: 148, 235
Arakan mountains: 158
Argenlieu, Admiral d': 120–21
Argentina: 265
Aristotle: 152
Art, Eastern: 52
Asia, Free:
balanced power in, 344–45;
birth of, as free world, 253–55;
and Communism, attitude toward,
21–25;
development of new international
patterns in, 268–69;
diversity in, 7–8;
dollar reserves of, 361;
economic problems of, 355–56;
effect of science on, 265–66;
geographical position of, 353–54;
historical foundation of, 254–55,
352–53;
history of European relations with,
288–91;
isolation of countries of, 13;
main preoccupations common to
countries of, 30–32;
major international political phenomena in, 356–58, 360;
misconceptions about United States
in, 349;
policy choices of the West in, 363–72;
politico-cultural factors of, 354–55;
poverty of, 360–62;
respect of, for Western nations,
348–51;

379